THE POLISH ECONOMIC CRISIS

How did the recession of the early 1980s influence events in Poland in 1989?

In order to understand the dramatic events of 1989 it is necessary to examine the circumstances leading up to them. As is often the case in revolutions, the fundamental factors can be traced some way back and are of an economic nature.

In analysing the economic crisis of the late 1970s and early 1980s *The Polish Economic Crisis* examines one of the key factors in the events of 1989 and places it in its wider political-economic context. Batara Simatupang identifies the issues involved in this recession. He finds these to be a combination of governmental economic incompetence, a lumbering bureaucracy and the tenuous legitimacy of the ruling Communist Party – all set within the international economic environment in which Poland then existed. The book also analyses the aftermath of this crisis and the steady process from recession to slump. The apparent initial success of the regime in overcoming the crisis of 1979–82 proved to be temporary. Its poor economic performance, the failed attempt to reform the economic and political systems in 1988–9, the loss of geopolitical support and the disintegration of the state socialism, all culminated in a new and much more serious crisis. Unlike previous ones, this could not be resolved by 'regulation through crisis' but resulted in the collapse of the regime. This event made possible the combination of a deflationary shock and a rapid transition to a market economy in 1990. *The Polish Economic Crisis* traces the path to political breakthrough in Poland in 1989 and relates it to the collapse of 'really existing socialism' in the rest of Eastern Europe and the former Soviet Union.

Batara Simatupang is Research Fellow in the Faculty of Economics at the University of Amsterdam. He is the author of a number of articles published in professional journals. These include 'Polish agriculture in the 1970s and the prospects for early 1980' (1982), 'The Polish economic crisis' (1983) and 'Economic crisis and full employment: the Polish case' (1988).

THE POLISH ECONOMIC CRISIS

Background, causes and aftermath

Batara Simatupang

ROUTLEDGE

London and New York

First published 1994
by Routledge
11 New Fetter Lane, London EC4P 4EE

Simultaneously published in the USA and Canada
by Routledge
29 West 35th Street, New York, NY 10001

Typeset in Scantext September by Solidus (Bristol) Ltd
Printed and bound in Great Britain by
TJ Press (Padstow) Ltd, Padstow, Cornwall

British Library Cataloguing in Publication Data
A catalogue record for this book is available from the British Library
ISBN 0-415-08824-0

Library of Congress Cataloging in Publication Data
Simatupang, Batara, 1932–
The Polish economic crisis : background, causes and aftermath /
Batara Simatupang.
p. cm.
Includes bibliographical references and index.
ISBN 0-415-08824-0
1. Poland—Economic conditions—1980– 2. Poland—Economic conditions—1945–1980. 3. Poland—Politics and government—1980–1989. I. Title.
HC340.3.S56 1994
330.9438′05–dc20 92-45850
CIP

CONTENTS

LIST OF FIGURE AND TABLES

FIGURE

TABLES

FOREWORD

In the long struggle against communism, Poland played a leading role. Its defeat of the Red Army in 1920 protected Central Europe from Bolshevization. Its firm support for Gomulka in 1956 led to the creation of a regime which tolerated the Church and private agriculture and which was accordingly, although state socialist, not totalitarian. The repeated struggles of its workers, in 1970, 1976 and 1980–1, severely constrained the freedom of manoeuvre of the ruling elite. Its Round Table conference of 1989 and the outcome of the resulting elections played an important role in the collapse of state socialism in Europe.

A major role in this collapse was played by the economic failures of the regime. A regime which had come to power after the Second World War with the ambition to rebuild Poland and transform it into a modern industrial state turned out to be quite incapable of matching the achievements of Western Europe. This failure became increasingly visible from the 1960s onwards.

The economic failures of the regime were shown up particularly vividly by the great crisis of 1979–82. The very sharp fall in output and consumption in 1979–82, the rapid inflation, acute shortages, and external bankruptcy; these formed a crisis unprecedented in the history of Europe since the Second World War. It was a foretaste of the Soviet/Commonwealth of Independent States (CIS) economic crisis of 1988 onwards and a sign that the economic system in which it took place was lurching to its doom. The Polish crisis had an effect analogous to that of the great depression of the 1930s in the West – it undermined the legitimacy of the socio-economic system and transformed criticism of it from a minority intellectual activity to a daily activity of a large part of the population. It was in the crisis of 1979–82 that the leadership and the organization arose which were to come to power in 1989–90.

In this book Batara Simatupang explains how this crisis developed, how it related to the apparent success of the regime in the early 1970s, and the roles of particular economic sectors such as investment, agriculture and foreign trade. Although communists used to think that state control of investment was a characteristic advantage of socialism, Batara Simatupang shows that it gave rise to investment cycles and led to an inefficient allocation of investment resources. Costs rose, resources were wasted on uncompleted investment projects and there was a failure to invest in agriculture, consumer goods production and export-oriented sectors. He devotes attention to inflation and labour, two very important sources of the crisis. The widespread shortages combined with rising prices played a key role in undermining the regime. The failure of the employment system to meet the aspirations and expectations of the labour force played an important role in the formation of Solidarność in 1980. There is also a chapter surveying the views of Polish economists on the crisis. This gives a good picture of the varying interpretations offered in Poland of such a deep crisis. A particularly important feature of the book is that it does not concern itself with purely economic factors, but also devotes a chapter to the (il)legitimacy of the regime and the implications of this for economic policy. Since the crisis, and the subsequent failure of the regime to place the country on a stable growth path, were very important factors explaining the final collapse of the regime in 1989, there is also a chapter on developments between 1982 and 1989.

The book combines deep knowledge of Polish economic developments in the 1970s and 1980s with a determination to place them in their wider political-economic context and a consciousness of the complex interaction between economic and political processes in the specific Polish context. The author has a very good knowledge of both the Polish and the Western literature on this theme. This book can be thoroughly recommended to anyone interested in Polish economic and political history since 1971, the collapse of state socialism, or economic crises in general.

Michael Ellman

PREFACE

Parts of this book have been previously published in journals such as the *European Review of Agricultural Economics*, *The Journal of Communist Studies*, *Soviet Studies* and *Economisch Statistische Berichten*, as a chapter in a book and in various *Research Memoranda* of the Faculty of Economics, University of Amsterdam. These papers have been revised as a result of new information and insights after their publication, and they have also been modified to suit the structure of the book. The last four chapters are new and have not been previously published in any form.

I would like to use this opportunity to express, first of all, my thanks to Professor M. Ellman for his continuous encouragement and guidance, which made the writing of this book possible. Pat Ellman corrected the English text. P. Visser-van Dielen and L. Lotze did the typing. M. Kirejczyk checked the Polish. My thanks also to Dr I. Wahab. Furthermore, I am grateful to the Faculty of Economics and the Department of Microeconomics, University of Amsterdam, for supporting the research. Last but not least, my thanks to Sekartini Markiahtoen for her patience and companionship during the writing of the book.

Batara Simatupang
University of Amsterdam

INTRODUCTION

This book analyses the deep Polish economic crisis of 1979–82 and its aftermath. To understand the economic crisis of 1979–82, it is necessary to consider the basic features of Gierek's 'new economic strategy' (high growth of investment, consumption and indebtedness to the West, etc.), its implementation and the result; the systemic shortcomings of the centrally planned economies (CPEs); and the specific socio-political environment facing the regime. The study attempts to focus attention on the interaction of economic policy, the economic system and specific features of the Polish political scene, which together caused such a dramatic economic crisis in 1979–82.

The study also gives an account of the aftermath of the crisis of 1979–82. At the end of 1981 the regime declared martial law which lasted until 21 July 1983. The initial partial success of the regime's attempt to 'normalize' the political situation and to revive the economy after the crisis of 1979–82 did not last long. The poor economic performance, the regime's long standing lack of political legitimacy, the failed economic reform in 1987–8, the decomposition of state socialism, and the defeat of the communists at the June 1989 election following the Round Table agreement, led to a new economic crisis in 1988–9. Unlike previous crises, however, the crisis of 1988–9, was not resolved by 'regulation through crisis' but by the collapse of the regime.

Table In.1 shows basic indicators of Polish economic development in the period 1971–82. This period can be roughly divided into three sub-periods, each with its own specific features.

The first sub-period (1971–5) was the time of great optimism, of Gierek's 'new economic strategy', characterized by high rates of growth of net material product, investment, employment, Western imports and debt, accompanied by rapid growth in real wages, incomes and consumption. Efficiency of investment, utilization of industrial productive capacity and growth in labour productivity improved noticeably. However, during the last years of the first half of the 1970s, investment tensions, shortages and market disequilibrium began to accumulate.

The second sub-period (1976–8), known under the slogan of 'economic manoeuvre', was a time of growing discouragement and pessimism, characterized by a significant slow-down in the rates of growth of net material product,

Table In.1 Basic indicators of economic development, 1971–82 (percentage growth with respect to previous year in constant prices)

	1971	1972	1973	1974	1975	1976	1977	1978	1979	1980	1981	1982	1982 as per cent of 1980	1982 as per cent of 1978
Domestic net material product[a]	8.1	10.6	10.8	10.4	9.0	6.8	5.0	3.0	−2.3	−6.0	−12.1	−5.5	83.2	76.5
National net material product[a]	9.8	12.7	14.3	12.1	10.9	7.0	2.7	0.5	−3.7	−6.0	−12.3	−11.5	80.2	72.5
Gross industrial production	7.9	10.7	11.2	11.4	10.9	9.3	6.9	4.9	2.7	0	−10.8	−2.1	87.2	89.6
Gross agricultural product	3.6	8.4	7.3	1.6	−2.1	−1.1	1.4	4.1	−1.5	−10.7	5.3	−2.8	101.0	88.9
Imports of which:	13.8	22.1	22.6	14.2	5.0	10.3	0.4	1.5	−1.2	−1.9	−16.9	−13.7	71.7	69.5
socialist countries	10.3	10.1	12.7	11.	−2.1	7.8	12.3	4.0	1.7	2.4	−6.3	−5.6	88.5	92.1
capitalist countries	20.7	46.6	37.8	19.2	12.2	11.4	−10.9	−2.0	−4.5	−7.2	−31.5	−24.2	51.9	46.0
Exports of which:	6.5	5.2	11.0	12.8	8.3	5.4	8.8	5.7	6.8	−4.2	−19.0	8.7	88.0	90.1
socialist countries	6.9	15.9	12.0	16.0	9.6	−0.3	10.6	7.5	9.6	−9.5	−17.0	16.6	96.8	96.0
capitalist countries	4.9	14.8	10.9	5.9	5.8	12.3	4.0	2.9	2.1	5.0	−22.1	0.9	78.6	84.3
Gross investment	7.4	23.0	25.4	22.3	10.7	1.0	3.1	2.1	−7.9	−12.3	−22.3	−12.1	68.2	55.1
Average employment in soc. sector	3.1	4.4	3.9	3.5	2.3	1.0	1.4	0.6	0.1	0.	0.2	−4.2	95.3	95.7
Monthly nominal wages in soc. sector[b]	5.5	6.4	11.5	13.8	11.8	8.8	7.3	5.8	8.8	13.5	27.4	51.3	191.6	236.9
Cost of living	−0.2	0	2.6	6.8	3.0	4.7	4.9	8.7	6.7	9.1[c]	24.4[c]	101.5	243.4	284.9

Average real wages in soc. sector	5.7	6.4	8.7	6.6	8.5	3.9	2.3	−2.7	2.0	4.0	2.4	−24.9	76.7	81.5
Personal real income per head	8.4	11.4	9.3	6.0	8.9	5.7	5.3	0.4	2.4	1.0	3.3	−18.0	84.6	87.5
Economic effectiveness[d]														
Productivity of fixed capital[e]	1.8	3.8	3.0	1.0	−1.1	−2.6	−4.3	−5.6	−9.6	−11.0	−15.1	−7.2	–	–
Labour productivity[f]	6.9	8.6	9.0	8.2	8.3	7.7	5.0	3.3	−1.5	−4.0	−11.7	−2.4	–	–
Fixed capital per person	4.9	4.6	5.9	7.1	9.4	10.6	9.7	9.5	8.9	8.0	3.7	5.2	–	–
Structure of income in per cent[d]														
Total	100	100	100	100	100	100	100	100	100	100	100	100	–	–
Consumption	72.5	70.4	67.0	64.4	64.8	65.9	68.5	69.2	73.8	79.8	79.3	78.4	–	–
Accumulation	27.5	29.6	33.0	35.6	35.2	34.1	31.5	30.8	26.2	20.2	20.7	21.6	–	–

Source: *Rządowy raport o stanie gospodarki*, Warsawa, 1981, p. 120; *Rocznik Statystyczny* of various years.

Notes: [a]Domestic net material product – 'produced income' in Marxian terminology; national net material product = 'national income for distribution' = domestic net material product ± balance in current account of the balance of payment;

[b]since 1981, price compensation is included;

[c]price increase of alcohol is not included;

[d]up to 1980, in constant prices of 1977, and the rest in constant prices, 1982;

[e]income produced per unit of fixed capital;

[f]labour productivity in the sphere of material production.

investment, real wages and incomes, and a stagnation in Western imports. The efficiency of investment, rate of utilization of industrial productive capacity and growth of labour productivity were falling, accompanied by a growing burden of Western debt servicing which reached a critical level, growing shortages and market disequilibrium.

The third sub-period (1979–82) was a time of deepening socio-political and economic crises, which led to a collapse of the economy and the declaration of martial law at the end of 1981. Net material product, real wages and income, consumption, investment and Western imports fell drastically. This was accompanied by large external and internal imbalances, which forced the regime to request Western debt rescheduling, introduce rationing of basic consumer goods and raise prices sharply.

The book consists of ten chapters. Each of the first nine chapters deals with one particular topic and related issues in detail. All the chapters taken together provide a comprehensive analysis of Polish economic development during the period 1971–89, dealing with Gierek's economic policy of the 1970s, the economic crisis of 1979–82 and the aftermath of the crisis covering the period till the establishment in 1989 of the non-communist government, headed by T. Mazowiecki from Solidarność.

Chapter 1 describes and analyses the background and major factors influencing Gierek's decision to pursue the strategy of high economic growth and industrial modernization with the help of a massive import of Western capital and technology, highlighting the repercussions and impact of the investment leap. The chapter starts with a discussion of post-war investment cycles in Poland, followed by a description and analysis of the rush for rapid economic growth, investment leap and tension, inefficiency of investment and distortions in the structure of investment.

Chapter 2 deals with Poland's external economic relationships. It examines Gierek's import-led growth strategy, the causes of the lack of correlation between the import of Western technology (and capital) and hard currency export growth, rising hard currency import intensity of production, and shortcomings in foreign trade planning and regulation. As a result the debt trap became tight and the balance of payment crisis was inevitable.

Chapter 3 considers various aspects of inflation, confining the description and analysis to inflation in the consumer goods market. The chapter begins with the description of (official) open inflation, followed by a discussion of certain aspects of hidden and repressed inflation, the relationship between inflation and the economic collapse of 1980–2, and a brief analysis of the causes (sources) of inflation.

Chapter 4 is an analysis of the role of Gierek's agricultural policies in the generation of the economic crisis. It examines the variation in Gierek's agricultural policies and its repercussions, the growing hard currency deficits in agriculture-related foreign trade and the basic features of food demand. Furthermore, the chapter discusses the discrimination against private agriculture, efficiency comparison between socialized and private farming and certain structural aspects of Polish agriculture.

Chapter 5 examines a number of important factors determining the supply of labour (in particular during the period 1971–82) such as post-war demographic development in Poland, participation rates, average working time and labour turnover. The chapter also describes and analyses certain aspects of labour quality (growth in skill and education levels, labour discipline, etc.), age composition of the labour force, professional aspirations, job misassignment of skilled personnel and job (dis)satisfaction.

Chapter 6 discusses a number of important factors influencing the demand for labour, describing and analysing the post-war drive towards full employment, employment policies and labour regulations. The drive towards full employment led to permanent labour shortages, occurring simultanously with widespread labour hoarding and underutilization of labour in enterprises and state non-profit organizations. This chapter also discusses problems concerning the relationship between full employment and rationalization of employment and the resolution of the economic crisis.

Chapter 7 is a brief analytical survey of the writings of Polish dissident economists before August 1980 on the approaching socio-economic crises, followed by a survey of Polish economists' writing during the 'odnowa' (renewal) period of 1980–1. The discussion covers a wide range of Polish economists' views about the nature and major causes (etiologies) of the economic crisis of 1979–82.

Chapter 8 analyses briefly several factors (history, ideology, politics and institutional processes, etc.) underlying the tenuous legitimation of communist rule in Poland. The chapter describes briefly Gierek's strategy of legitimation through economic success and consumer satisfaction, the uncertainty and vulnerability of the strategy, and the systemically built-in legitimation strains in state socialism.

Chapter 9 analyses the aftermath of the economic crisis of 1979–82. It describes and analyses the regime's efforts to 'normalize' the political situation, to revive the economy from the deep crisis and to reform the political and economic systems. Because of the poor economic performance, the failed reforms of the economic and political systems, the decomposition of state socialism, the exhaustion of the extensive economic growth factors and the collapse of the 'geopolitical' legitimation, the economic crisis of 1988–9, unlike previous crises, could not be resolved by the traditional 'regulation through crisis' and was only resolved by the collapse of the regime in 1989.

The book ends with a conclusion, outlining the background, circumstances and factors influencing Gierek's decision to pursue the 'new economic strategy', and briefly summarizes the major systemic, policy and political constraints that contributed to the Polish economic crisis of 1979–82. This outline is followed by a brief account of the regime's efforts to overcome the crisis and to revive the economy, to reform the economic and political systems, the limited succes and failure of these policies, the emergence of the new economic crisis of 1988–9, the political breakthrough and the collapse of the regime in 1989.

The Polish economic crisis of 1979–82, its aftermath and the political breakthrough in 1988–9 are particularly interesting in view of their roles in both Polish and East European history. In Poland they contributed to the revival of civil society, undermined 'really existing socialism' and led ultimately to the collapse of the regime, which made possible the combination of a deflationary shock and a rapid transition to a market economy in 1990. In Eastern Europe as a whole the Polish economic crisis of 1979–82 contributed to the liquidity crisis of 1982 and exhibited in an extreme form economic, social and politial problems which existed throughout the region in the 1980s. The political breakthrough in Poland in 1989 contributed to the collapse of 'really existing socialism' in Central Europe and the Balkans in 1989 and in the former USSR in 1991.

1

INVESTMENT

INTRODUCTION

The excessively rapid growth of productive investment in the first half of the 1970s, accompanied by a rapid growth of real wages, incomes and consumption, both made possible by large Western credits, led to serious investment tension, shortages, inflation and external imbalances. The economy was overheated when investment growth in the first half of the 1970s exceeded the absorptive capacity of the economy, leading to a fast deterioration in the efficiency of resource use, low returns on investment and ineffective implementation of investment projects. Due to growing investment tension, strong pressure of the population demanding sustained growth of consumption and the mounting burden of servicing the Western debt, the government was forced to reduce the growth of productive investment and Western imports from 1976, aiming at the same time to redirect investment outlays according to new production priorities. The eagerly hoped for boost to hard currency exports, which should have resulted from the large import of Western technology, capital and large investment outlays ('investment harvest'), did not take place. The situation deteriorated rapidly when the government failed to curb consumption growth. The drastic cut in both Western imports and investment generated a 'negative multiplier', and contributed to the large drop in the net material product in 1979–82. The failure of the government to redirect investment outlays in the second half of the 1970s aggravated the distortions in the structure of investment.

This chapter will describe and analyse a number of important factors influencing Gierek's drive towards overinvestment and its consequences. It will discuss certain problems of investment cycles in Poland's post-war economy, the background underlying the rush for high economic growth and industrial modernization, the investment leap and investment tension, inefficiency and distortions in the structure of investment, disinvestment and the legacy of the investment crisis.

PROBLEMS OF INVESTMENT CYCLES

Statistical studies and writings of the Polish economists have concluded unanimously that post-war 'planned' Polish economic and investment growth proceeded in a recurrent cyclical movement. They differ, however, in their interpretation of the nature and causes of the fluctuation. Early writings on post-war economic development tended to interpret the fluctuation in the rates of economic and investment growth as being specific to a certain 'stage' ('etapowosc') of economic development and being related to a certain strategy of economic growth pursued in a particular period. It was argued that the central planner pursued a sequence of economic tasks, such as a phase of high investment growth during the economic upswing followed by a phase of high consumption growth combined with a low investment growth, i.e. a two-phase cycle (R. Chelinski 1964: 1043–5; J. Pajestka 1965); or, for instance, a sequence like post-war economic recovery, forced industrialization, development of a raw material base and export promotion (A. Karpinski 1968). This approach was in line with the official economic doctrine of a harmonious socialist planned economy and it tends, moreover, to be apologetic in its evaluation of post-war Polish economic development.

Later writings on post-war economic growth made a distinction between 'growth by stages' ('etapowosc wzrostu') and 'cyclical development' ('cykliczność rozwoju'); and it was argued that the latter might appear independent of the former. For 'cyclical development' to appear, two conditions are necessary: (a) a periodic occurrence of the growth cycle and; (b) an endogenous feature, i.e. an upswing phase of a cycle must contain the seed for a downswing phase and vice versa (M. Gruszczynski and G. Kołodko 1975: 428–9; P. Dziewulski and A. Maciejewski 1980; J. Winiecki 1982).

Views and hypotheses concerning the nature, duration, probable causes and controllability of the cycles expressed in Polish economic literature varied widely. Those who denied the inherent existence of (endogenous) cycles in state socialist economies tended to attribute the oscillations in economic activities to imperfect planning methods, errors in economic policy, initial underdevelopment of the economy and technical factors like indivisibility of investment, the time gap between investment outlays and expected increase in output, the 'echo effect' of reinvestment cycles, etc. They believed that intense fluctuations in economic and investment growth would vanish with improvements in planning methods and/or a higher level of economic development. Moreover a number of economists considered cyclical growth not only to be controllable but also advantageous, since the economy could gain from a hypothetical trade-off between more intensified current investment efforts with a higher rise in future income (consumption) per capita (unbalanced growth) and less intensified current investment with a lower rise in future income (balanced growth) during a certain planning period.[1] Both expectations turned out to be illusory.

It is highly doubtful whether the alleged gain to be accrued from the intensified investment efforts (unbalanced growth) could have offset the huge losses caused by investment tension, shortages and the rapid deterioration in the efficiency of investment and resource use.[2] It is also misleading to propose an abstract calculus on the losses and gains associated with an unbalanced economic growth programme, independent of the built-in systemic shortcomings of the CPEs, absorptive capacity of the economy (the ability to organize and to carry out an investment programme in a reasonably efficient way) and social acceptance.

Discussion about the likely causes of investment cycles remained controversial. For instance, P. von der Lippe listed twenty conceivable causes of investment cycles cited by Polish economists, including defects in planning coordination, misjudgement in economic policy, an expansive management system, the 'echo effect' of reinvestment cycles, etc. (P. von der Lippe 1980: 6–7). A close look at the list of conceivable causes of investment cycles shows, however, that they can be classified into two broad groups consisting of economic policy variables and systemic factors.

Economic policy variables

The central planner (i.e. the top decision-making units) tended to opt for a rapid rate of economic growth, either rightly or wrongly, for such reasons as the fulfilment of an ambition of the regime to put an end to economic backwardness or the 'development mission' of the state (J. Pajestka 1983), to achieve full employment (L. Podkaminer 1985), the strengthening of the defence potential and the need to raise the prestige of the ruling elite, etc. The impatient drive 'from above' for an ambitious economic growth programme, requiring high growth of productive investment, tended to overestimate the extent of growth potentialities (reserves) of the economy and the capability of the planner to mobilize reserves and use resources effectively. Investment plan targets, initially fixed at reasonable levels, but being adjusted upwards in the course of plan realization, tended to be taut. This led to economic disproportions and increasing shortages in construction and building capacity. The trade balance and the balance of payments situation became worrying, whilst productive investment projects competed with non-productive investment and household consumption for resources.

With the approaching of the 'tolerance limits' (J. Kornai 1980) or 'growth barriers' (M. Kalecki 1963) of the economy, the government begain to pull the brake on investment growth by means of measures such as a reduction in the 'approval coefficient' of new investments (T. Bauer 1978: 250), a decline in the annual limits of investment outlays and suspension of low priority investment projects. Investment growth was reduced. Slowly, after a certain time, the shock effects of overinvestment began to disappear and the regime regained its optimism and determination to renew the drive towards higher investment. The upward phase of a new investment cycle was then initiated.

Systemic factors

The drive towards overinvestment was also conditioned by the built-in features of the CPEs and the plan construction process in particular. Lower planning organs tended to bargain for greater investment allocation, higher than the amount of investment considered feasible by higher planning organs to carry out the planned targets. Due to the complexity and extent of the information concerning the investment planning process, higher planning organs were not actually in a position to control and to verify investment claims effectively.

In general, enterprises and industrial associations ('zjednoczenia') considered (new) investment outlays (plus employment growth) the easiest way to carry out production plan targets; and plan fulfilment was the main criterion in the evaluation of plan performance and the size of the bonus for managers. Enterprises and industrial associations were therefore extremely interested in obtaining higher investment allocations. One of the significant control instruments of the central planner was the annual investment allocation limits. A number of well-known methods adopted by enterprises and associations to obtain higher investment allocations – such as ensuring a foothold in the national investment plan or 'hooking on to the plan' ('zaczepianie się o plan'), systematic underestimation of the real investment costs of projects (hence making them more attractive to the superiors), hiding necessary supplementary investment, etc. – contributed towards overinvestment. It is interesting to note, on the basis of Hungarian experiences with economic reform in the 1970s, that the pressure for overinvestment 'from below' did still operate even if the drive 'from above' for rapid economic growth did not play a major role (K. Attila Soos 1975; T. Bauer 1978). It was argued that as long as the enterprise's budget constraint was 'soft' (J. Kornai 1980), restraint on overinvestment must came from 'outside' (central planner).

Polish economists (with a few exceptions) had analysed economic cycles in terms of changes in the rates of growth of the economy and investment.[3] Figure 1.1 shows the actual rates of growth of the economy (net material product) and investments for 1950–82. The growth of net material product runs parallel to investment growth with a small time lag. Investment growth fluctuated more than the growth in net material product.

With slight variations, the outcome of dating economic and investment growth cycles by various Polish economists is pretty close (G. Kołodko 1979; L. Zienkowski 1979; P. Dziewulski and A. Maciejewski 1980; A. Jezierski 1981). The duration of individual economic and investment growth cycles was not identical to the official Five Year Plans. Table 1.1 shows four investment growth cycles for the period 1950–81, the average annual rate of growth of investment in the upward (Phase A) and downward (Phase B) stage of an individual cycle. One can note that the duration and amplitude of the investment cycle for the period 1972–81 were longer and greater than for the cycles of the preceding years. Moreover, in 1976–81, unlike in the previous cycles, there was a decline

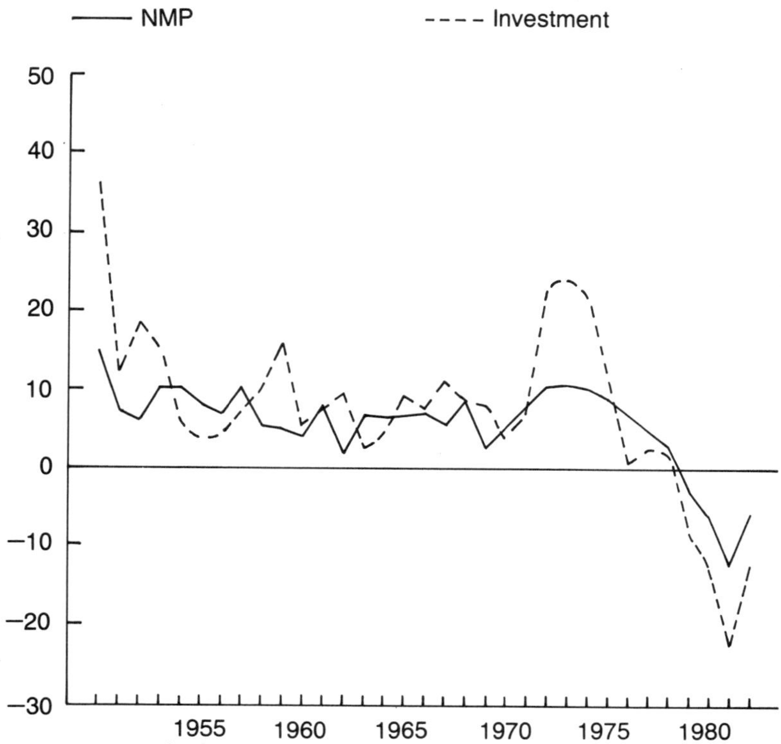

Figure 1.1 Annual growth of net material product (NMP) and investment in fixed assets in per cent and constant prices, 1950–82

not just in the rate of growth of investment but also in the level of investment. In addition, the downward phase of the cycle for 1972–81 was longer than the downward phase of preceding cycles. These facts indicate the depth and seriousness of the economic crisis of 1979–82 in comparison to previous crises.

In the Polish People's Republic, an approaching economic crisis, as has been empirically confirmed, was commonly characterized by a number of recurrent phenomena: 1) a deterioration in the efficiency of investment; 2) a fall in the average rate of utilization of productive capacity; 3) a fall in the rate of growth of productivity of fixed capital; 4) a decline in the rate of economic growth; 5) growing inflation accompanied by stagnation or a fall in average real wages (J. Staniszkis 1979: 248–77). The ruling elite reacted typically by introducing more control in enterprises, higher turnover of managerial and political cadres, intensified propaganda against ideological 'revisionism', suspension of certain investment projects in progress, reallocation of investment favouring the consumption goods sector and services, etc. The closing stage of an economic crisis may turn into a political crisis, caused by violent protests of the workers

(1956, 1970, 1980), precipitated by the increase in prices of consumer goods, an increase in work norms and a deterioration in working conditions. The political leadership was replaced by a new one which offered an increase in wages to pacify the rebellious workers. Generally speaking an economic crisis was essentially a regulating mechanism of Poland's post-war economic system, albeit a very costly one, which aimed to straighten out the growing economic disproportions.

Table 1.1 Average annual rate of growth of investment in the individual cycles and phases of development (in per cent constant prices)

	Development cycles (years)							
	1950–7		*1958–64*		*1965–71*		*1972–81*	
	Phase A	*Phase B*	*Phase A*	*Phase B*	*Phase A*	*Phase B*	*Phase A*	*Phase B*
	Years							
	1950–3	*1954–7*	*1958–62*	*1963–4*	*1965–9*	*1970–1*	*1972–5*	*1976–81*
Total investment	20.4	5.5	9.9	3.7	9.2	5.8	21.3	−5.6
of which in:								
productive sphere	23.8	3.5	10.8	4.4	10.3	6.2	22.9	−6.7
industry	34.4	1.3	10.8	3.7	9.0	5.6	25.0	−8.3

Source: U. Wojciechowska (ed.) *Inwestycje i budownietwo w PRL*, Warsaw, 1982, p. 39; Statistical Yearbook of various years.
Notes: Phase A = accelerated rates of growth
Phase B = decelerated rates of growth

GIEREK'S RUSH FOR RAPID ECONOMIC GROWTH, AND ECONOMIC SLUMP

The economic guide-line for the period 1971–5 designed under Gomulka at the Vth Party Congress held in 1968, was intended to retain the slow growth in consumption and real wages of the 1960s which would be accompanied by an increase in the rate of growth of productive investment. The latter was thought to be necessary for the modernization of industry (fuel, chemicals, electronics and mechanical engineering). The so-called 'selective development' strategy had the aim of boosting the falling rates of growth of labour and capital productivity and national product ('V Zjazd PZPR', *Nowe Drogi*, 2, 1968). The new 'incentive system', planned to be implemented at the end of 1971, would strive for a closer relationship between the growth of labour productivity and growth of wages, which in practice meant higher work norms for the workers. The policy of further restriction of consumption growth and rationalization of the consumption pattern, which expressed itself in the announcement of a large price increase of the highly subsidized basic consumer goods in December 1970, met with violent opposition from the workers in the Baltic coast towns, resulting in the fall of Gomulka and his replacement by Gierek.

Gomulka's economic growth strategy was rather conservative and cautious. His intention was to avoid extensive domestic and external disequilibrium and he was reluctant to take large amounts of foreign credit, following the old Polish proverb that 'one must cut one's coat according to one's cloth' ('tak krawiec kraje jak mu materii staje'). Gomulka was convinced that he could rely on the workers' tolerance for his austerity policy which included a temporary fall or stagnation in real wages, an increase in work norms, unemployment and price increases. Under strong pressure from the workers, however, the new leadership under Gierek was forced to rescind the announced price increase and the unpopular new 'incentive system'. A new style of political leadership which professed to seek close consultation with the masses was cultivated. Gierek promised tangible growth in the standard of living, a modernization of the obsolete machinery park and the restructuring of production in order to be able to meet the envisaged rapid growth in consumption.

From the economic point of view, Gierek's leadership faced the same basic dilemma as Gomulka, namely a choice between high economic growth with massive capital accumulation and modernization of production structure on the one hand and a visibly higher standard of living which was necessary to pacify the rebellious workers and to stimulate growth in labour productivity on the other. The adoption of an 'import led growth' strategy (S. Gomulka 1978), i.e. a policy of large-scale import of modern machinery, equipment, industrial inputs and grain from the West, largely financed by Western credits, had temporarily suspended the basic dilemma of choosing between a high growth of capital accumulation and consumption. Poland could have both of them simultaneously. In fact the Western credits helped to fund Gierek's policy of 'consumerism', i.e. a policy which aimed to seek political support and legitimacy in exchange for a visible increase in the standard of living, as a substitute for the overdue political and economic reform.[4]

Gierek's almost 'unlimited hunger for investment' in the first half of the 1970s was conditioned by both systemic factors and the specific circumstances facing the leadership. The latter included the following factors:

1 the urgent requirement to modernize the capital stock and to overhaul the production structure in order to raise the falling growth trend in output and labour productivity, especially during the second half of the 1960s;
2 the social pressure for full employment and job security in a situation where the supply of labour was growing rapidly;
3 the need to meet the demand of certain bureaucratic factions (for instance of heavy industry) for more allocation of investment funds, a reaction against Gomulka's strategy of 'selective industrial development' (W. Kuczyński 1981: 83–4; A. Karpinski 1986: 149–50);

4 the excess liquidity of the Western banking system caused by 'petro-dollars' and limited investment opportunities due to economic recession in the West, the banks' eagerness to seek investment outlets, and the favourable influence of political détente in Europe;
5 the misinterpretation of the exceptionally good economic results in the early 1970s as a confirmation of Gierek's 'new economic strategy', thereby encouraging high investment growth.

The VIth Party Congress held in December 1971 fixed higher growth targets for net material product, consumption, wages, employment and investment for the period 1971–5 than the preliminary targets set in Gomulka's economic guide-line. The planned rates of growth of average real wages and consumption for 1971–5 were nearly twice the actual growth achieved in the preceding five-year period. In the course of implementing the Five Year Plan (1971–5), the initial targets were raised on a number of occasions in an arbitrary and haphazard way, euphemistically known as 'open-ended' planning. As a result the quality of planning deteriorated considerably and the resulting situation was ironically described as 'planned chaos' (W. Brus 1979a: 43–6). Table 1.2 briefly sets out the unrestrained modifications in plan targets and the actual economic results at the end of the plan period.[5]

The IVth Central Committee Plenary meeting in March 1972 increased the growth targets for investment and output of industrial consumer goods (*Nowe Drogi*, 1972: 26), and subsequently these changes were incorporated in the Five Year Plan (1971–5) which was passed by the Sejm (parliament) in June 1972. However, these figures were soon overtaken by reality. The exceptionally favourable economic results in 1971–2 surpassed the regime's most optimistic expectations, particularly when bearing in mind the gloomy economic situation of the years 1969–70.

Both consumption and investment grew rapidly, giving the impression that the dilemma of having to choose between the two had been eliminated. The regime interpreted these favourable economic results as being due to Gierek's new economic policy and as having a durable character. Following the euphoria of the high economic growth and relative stability of the years 1971–2, the then prime minister P. Jaroszewicz told a meeting of Party activists in January 1973 that the planned targets for the remaining years of the Five Year Plan (1971–5) should be corrected upwards (*Nowe Drogi*, 1973: 22). Subsequently the First National Conference of the Party held in October 1973 fixed higher plan targets for industrial investment and real wages for the residual years (1974–5) of the Five Year Plan. The actual growth of net material product, consumption, real wages, imports and investment, however, exceeded even the revised planned targets. On the other hand, the actual growth of exports fell below the target.

The euphoria of the economic boom in the early 1970s was also evident in the theoretical discussions on economic growth in Poland. Kalecki, a prominent Polish economist, analysed the factors determining the rate of economic growth

Table 1.2 Selected plan targets, 1971–5, and their realization (constant prices)

	Resolutions of the VIth Party Congress (Dec. 1971)	*Five Year Plan passed by Sejm (June 1972)*	*Resolutions of the 1st National Conference of the Party (October 1973)*	*Realization*
Net material product, 1970 = 100	138–9	139	155	159.4
Consumption, 1970 = 100	138–9	139	149–50	151.5
Average real wages, 1970 = 100	117–18	118	138	141.5
Gross industrial output, 1970 = 100	148–50	150	166	165.1
Gross agricultural output, 1970 = 100	118–21	119–21	122.5	120
Exports, 1970 = 100	–	155	202	166.4
Imports, 1970 = 100	–	159	–	204.3
Total investment in billion zloty	1430	1454	1900	1919
Total investment, 1966–70 = 100	142	145	179	190
Industrial investment in billion zloty	–	627	777	841
Agricultural investment in billion zloty	–	204	217	263
Value of consumer goods, 1970 = 100	141	143	163	–

Source: *VII Zjazd PZPR*, Stenogram, Warsaw, 1976, p. 76; *Rocznik Statystyczny 1976*, Warsaw 1977.

in state socialist economies, stressing the economic, social and technical 'barriers' (slow growth in consumption, market disequilibrium, shortages of construction and building materials, shortages of labour, etc.) which are associated with the policy of an accelerated rate of economic growth (M. Kalecki 1963). His growth theory significantly influenced economic writing and thinking in Poland for many years. Under the influence of the euphoria of the economic boom, however, Kalecki's growth theory was attacked in the Party's theoretical journal for being 'obsolete', a 'mechanical transplantation' of the saving–investment theory of bourgeois economics into socialist economies. The rapid growth of both consumption and investment in the early 1970s, with relatively stable markets, had supposedly corrected the allegedly false theory of economic growth of Kalecki (A. Kraczewska 1972; W. Dudzinski 1972). On this count, his growth theory was criticized for not taking into account 'the social aspects of production' by neglecting the favourable impact of improved consumption on output growth, enabling the economy to increase the rates of growth of consumption and investment simultaneously (W. Iskra 1972: 83).

Caution and moderation were not in demand, the general mood was for higher economic growth. An example is a fantastic growth model forecast that it would be feasible to achieve an annual economic growth of 10 per cent with a 40 per cent average rate of capital accumulation for the coming eighteen years, in a paper published in the Party's theoretical monthly (Z. Rurarz 1972: 136–8). When a 9.5 per cent growth in the economy was achieved in 1973, the same author demanded that the growth plans should be rounded up to 10 per cent per annum for the period until 1990 (Z. Rurarz 1974). A contemporary critic pointed out how absurd and unrealistic this ambitious growth variant was (M. Nasiłowski 1974b).

The rapid economic growth which was accompanied by a rapid growth of both consumption and investment in the first years of the 1970s proceeded relatively smoothly, thanks to good harvests and a deal with the peasantry, 'the reserve of past mistakes', favourable terms of trade, putting past investment on stream and large imports, etc. In 1973–4, however, domestic disequilibrium, shortages and investment tension built up rapidly. Instead of putting an immediate brake on the rapid growth of investment and consumption, the regime maintained a high growth of both during 1974–5. This policy led to greater investment tensions and disproportions, making it more difficult for the regime to relieve the disproportions in the future.

Gierek mistakenly believed that a continuation of a high growth of investment through large imports of capital and technology from the West would help to ease the disproportions within a relatively short time. At the National Conference of the Party in October 1973 he stated:

> The essence of the question lies in the choice of the way to master the [economic] tensions. It should be achieved by maintaining the high tempo of economic growth ... and we will follow this path ... the more so ... because by the end of next year the large investment expansion will already yield fruit.
>
> (cited in Kuczyński 1981: 98)

Needless to say, the regime overestimated the investment absorption capacity of the economy to utilize the resources efficiently. Moreover the initial decision of the central authority to expand investment generated additional heavy pressure from 'below' for more investment (J. Kotowicz-Jawor 1979) and thereby contributing to greater investment tensions and disproportions.

At the end of 1974, the gross debts (short, medium and long term) in hard currency were US$5.2 billion. This increased in the following year to US$8.4 billion whilst the debt-service ratios were 20.2 per cent and 27.2 per cent respectively, having already reached a critical level (see Table 2.11). The regime seemed to be conscious of the constraint when the growth of imports from the capitalist countries fell from 53.4 per cent in 1974 to 16.6 per cent in 1975 (in current prices).

The government had initially the intention mainly to curb import items which were directly or indirectly serving consumption purposes, whilst imports for investment purposes and supplies of inputs (raw materials, semi-finished goods, fuel, etc.), which were necessary for running industrial production capacity would be less affected by the import curb (W. Kuczyński 1981: 134–5). A substantial increase in the price of basic consumer goods was planned and formally announced in the summer of 1976. The main aim was to cut the growth of consumption, particularly meat consumption, thereby reducing food grain and animal feed imports. Assuming that the price increase for the basic consumer goods would be successful, the regime believed that sufficient imports of industrial supplies and investment goods, which were necessary both to sustain a high utilization of the newly established industrial productive capacity and to complete the unfinished investment projects, would be available with a manageable high debt-service ratio. According to this scenario, maintaining high rates of growth of both investment (although less than in previous years) and of the economy would be feasible at the cost of consumption growth, bearing in mind the rapid growth of consumption in the first half of the 1970s.

The plan of the government was unacceptable and within twenty-four hours the regime was forced to withdraw the announced price increase under pressure of workers' violent protest. By the end of 1976 the government decided to launch a new economic programme, the so-called economic manoeuvre, whose main aims were to reduce investment growth and to restructure investments in accordance with the new production priorities (exports, agriculture and production for domestic market). Due to bad harvests in 1975–6 and partly because of the dangerous political consequences of a large drop in consumption for the regime, the government stepped up the annual import of food grain and fodder. The tightening of the balance of payment constraint forced the regime to reduce imports of industrial supplies and capital goods as well, leading to a fall in the rate of utilization of installed productive capacity and an increase in the volume of frozen and committed investments.

A Polish dissident economist writing in 1978 correctly evaluated the harmful effects of the abrupt changes in economic policy in the 1970s and the so-called economic manoeuvre.

> The whole programme boils down to the slogan of economic manoeuvre which confines itself to investment and imports. Economic manoeuvre is presented as a wonder medicine, while its painful consequences are hidden. The drastic reduction in the course of one year of the growth of investment from an annual average of 18.4 per cent over 1971–5 to 2.5 per cent in 1976 and the reduction in the rate of growth of imports from capitalist countries from an annual average of 37.8 per cent to 8.5 per cent must

produce huge losses. Vast amounts of resources become frozen and production and supply are disrupted.

(Uwagi 1979: 24)

The paper adds that the losses could have been avoided if the reductions in investment growth had been gradual and spread out over many years.

In 1977–8 the annual average growth of investment at constant prices was maintained at the low level of 2.1 per cent, accompanied by a decline in imports from capitalist countries at constant prices of 6.4 per cent annually. The economic situation deteriorated rapidly at a time of a deepening political crisis. Investment and imports from capitalist countries in constant prices dropped by 10.6 per cent and 5.8 per cent annually in 1979–80; and the situation worsened dramatically when investment and imports from capitalist countries (at constant prices) dropped by 20.8 per cent and 27.8 per cent annually in 1981–2.[6] The dramatic fall in both investments and imports contributed substantially to the large decline in net material product and growing shortages in the economy.

THE DRIVE TOWARDS OVERINVESTMENT, TENSION AND INEFFICIENCY

State socialist economies were *inter alia* characterized by a strong tendency towards overinvestment. The propensity to overinvestment seemed to prevail in economic and administrative units at all levels of the planning hierarchy (J. Kotowicz-Jawor 1979), and was conditioned by both socio-economic policy variables and the systemic factors. Investment had been considered as the main stimulus to economic growth, a basic instrument for technical modernization and for changes in the structure of production. Job creation through high investment was thought to be indispensable for achieving the goal of full employment. A deeply rooted idea held by political and economic decision makers was that investment was indispensable for the growth of output, an attitude which was institutionally sanctioned and rewarded by the system of management.[7] The prestige and strength of an individual economic ministry, industrial association ('zjednoczenie'), region and enterprise were enhanced by the amount of investment at its disposal.

The drive towards economic expansion, which was rooted deeply in the thinking and praxis of the decision makers at all levels, was the basic motivation for the permanent 'insatiable investment hunger' in a resource constrained economic system. Given the 'soft budget constraint' on industrial associations or firms, demand for investment was not limited by the fear of losses or bankruptcy. Since investment came as a gift to the claimant, no one would ever renounce investment voluntarily. Investment self-restraint did not operate in the medium or high level decision-making units, and the basic dilemma of 'investment versus consumption', well-known in economic growth theories, operated in principle only at the very peak of the decision-making hierarchy (J. Kornai 1980: 191–5).

Therefore the existence and reproduction of investment tension[8] was basic to CPEs and it generated a state of permanent shortage. Investment tension became more intense when the government decided to force up the rate of economic growth, to step up the rate of productive investment, favouring investment for the expansion of producer goods at the expense of agriculture and so on.

The CPEs encouraged a distortion of information flow in the construction of an investment plan. As a rule, investment proposals submitted to higher planning organs were presented in the most favourable light possible by underestimating expected costs,[9] overestimating the expected results, and withholding information about the required complementary investment, imports, etc.

The reasoning behind the strategy of ensuring a foothold in the national economic plan ('zaczepianie się o plan') was the expectation (which was often confirmed by the events) that the superior would approve the additional investment costs in the future, since suspension of unfinished or incomplete investment projects would bring greater economic losses. From the point of view of the investment claimants, their bargaining position *vis-à-vis* their superior in the struggle for a higher annual investment quota (investment limit) would improve, the greater the number of unfinished projects in their portfolio. This praxis led to an excessively broad investment front (i.e. too large a number of investment projects being started more or less simultaneously), a dispersion of resources and a prolongation of the investment construction period. Ensuring a foothold in the national investment plan by illegal methods, i.e. starting construction without waiting for the consent of the superior, thereby creating a *fait accompli*, was widely practised in Poland in the 1970s by economic ministries, industrial associations, regions and enterprises. They were officially condemned but in most cases, however, they were tolerated by the central authority (*Raport* 1981: 34–5).

From the point of view of investment claimants, the practically free investment resources encouraged them to secure (oversecure) and guarantee the conditions needed for the implementation of their task. The central planning organs did not have much insight into the individual investment and production processes, particularly information on new investments. Because of the lack of a clear-cut selection criteria, every investment application seemed to be 'justified in itself'. The central planning organs tried to control the investment pressure 'from below' without great success by a system of annual investment limits, material balances for important producer goods, balances in construction and building activities and procurement plans, allocating goods and capacities according to certain priority, and investment criteria.

The notion of overinvestment is of course relative and it expresses a certain relationship between capital accumulation or investment and other relevant socio-economic magnitudes. Most Polish economists considered that a 30 per cent rate of capital accumulation (or 21 per cent rate of investment) was the upper limit of a socially tolerable level of capital accumulation. In 1973–8, however, the rate of capital accumulation exceeded the 30 per cent limit.

Overinvestment basically expresses the tension in the economy, the taut relationship between supply and demand for producer goods, labour, consumer goods and foreign exchange, as well as the options adopted to solve the disproportions. With reference to the situation in Poland in the 1970s, one can speak of an excessive capital accumulation or investment with respect to a number of factors:

1 The unwillingness of the population to accept an open inflation solution (price increases) to the rising costs of production of goods and market disequilibrium in 1970 and 1976, which constrained the regime's effort to rationalize and to curb consumption.
2 Insufficient development of the consumption sector compared to the growth of the producer goods sector, thereby strengthening the inflationary pressure, shortages, long queues in retail trade, black market, etc.
3 Actual investment exceeded by far the absorptive capacity of the economy. The capacity of the construction industry was short of the demand for construction. This led to a significant prolongation of the average construction period of investment projects, a dispersion and excessive volume of frozen and committed investment.
4 The failure of the large investment outlays to generate sufficient hard currency exports to meet the burden of servicing the Western debts.
5 A persistent excess of investment outlays over planned costs, the inability of the central planner to control and coordinate activities properly, resulting in a disorganization of the economy.

There seemed to be a significant improvement in the efficiency of resource use in the early years of the 1970s. The share of the so-called intensive growth factors increased compared to the share during the second half of the 1960s (S. Albinowski 1982: 17; M. Nasiłowski 1974a: 164). The productivity growth of fixed capital (income produced per unit of fixed capital) was significant. This improvement in the efficiency of fixed capital utilization was, however, attributed largely to greater supply of industrial inputs thanks to the rapid growth of import of industrial supplies and favourable harvests. Official statistics also noted an initial improvement in the implementation of investment projects. For instance, the average construction period of investment projects in the socialized sector decreased from 48.8 months in 1971 to 40.0 in 1973 and to 30.3 in 1975 (*Inwestycje 1979*, 1979: 192).

The regime was very optimistic, but a closer look indicates however that the optimism was ill-founded. The decline in the average construction period of investment projects was not the result of an improvement in economic planning and management as the regime maintained. The mild winters in 1971–3 enabled on average a longer period of activity in construction. Moreover, a high growth of investment in the construction industry, a larger supply of inputs, forcing the construction of priority investment projects at the cost of non-priority investment, a large expenditure on over-time payments and quality deterioration, etc., had all contributed to the pseudo-improvement in the implementation of investment projects (W. Kuczyński 1981: 90–1; U. Wojciechowska 1982: 113–14).

The investment leap in the first half of the 1970s led to an excessively wide investment front, bottle-necks in the construction and building industries, labour shortages and dispersion of investment funds. Efficiency in the implementation of investment projects declined rapidly in the second half of the 1970s and early 1980s. The gap between planned investment tasks and the means available to carry out the tasks was growing rapidly. For instance, the so-called balance gap between the production capacity in the construction industry and the demand, which amounted to only 4.4 billion zloty in 1975, went up to around 50 billion zloty in 1978 and to almost 90 billion zloty in 1979 (U. Wojciechowska 1982: 62). As a result the average construction period of investment projects increased sharply from an average of 30.3 months in 1975 to 41.9 months in 1978 (*Inwestycje 1979*: 129). If in 1975 around 37 per cent of the implemented investment projects had an average construction period above the 'standard', in 1980 it was around 61 per cent (*Raport* 1981: 91). The values of frozen and committed investment were growing rapidly whilst the value of commissioned (completed) investment was declining.

THE STRUCTURAL ALLOCATION OF INVESTMENT

Decisions on investment structure (distribution of investment between economic sectors, branches of production, types of investment, etc.) are just as important as decisions on the volume and rate of growth of investment. These decisions affect the efficiency of investment resources and the degree of satisfaction of demand. To a significant extent under state socialist conditions the investment structure expressed the configuration of the bargaining positions of various social and political groups ('lobbies') participating in the process of investment decision-making. The deep economic crisis in the late 1970s and early 1980s was not only attributed to excessive growth of productive investment in the years 1971–5, but also to serious distortions in the structure of investment.

Traditionally, state socialist economies had a preference for the expansion of production in the 'material sphere', relative to the expansion of output or services in the 'non-material sphere', such as residential construction, health services, education and culture, etc. In general, during the upswing phase of the investment cycle, which was normally accompanied by investment tensions and growing shortages, the central planner tended in the first place to cut non-productive investment. A cut in non-productive investment fulfilled the function of a first line cushion against investment tensions and shortages (K. Leowski 1980: 370). Subsequently, the cumulated backlog in the social sphere (severe housing shortages, deterioration in health services, etc.), was bound to generate social pressure for greater non-productive investment to compensate for the arrears, which occurred normally during the slow-down phase of the investment cycle (K. Leowski 1980: 365–9).

Table 1.3 shows the growth and distribution of total productive and non-productive investment for the period 1961–82. On average, the annual growth of productive investment was greater than non-productive investment and the percentage of investment allocated to the productive sphere grew during 1961–75. The many years of neglect of non-productive investment in the 1960s helped to trigger off the violent demand by the workers in December 1970 for a better social infrastructure and housing.

The investment boom in 1971–5 raised the rate of growth of non-productive investment considerably in comparison with the 1960s, but its share in total investment was falling. The long-term relative decline of non-productive investment led to underinvestment in certain fields such as the health service. Extremely old and poorly equipped hospitals, clinics and psychiatric institutions (*Raport* 1981: 115–16), shortage of housing, etc. helped to generate the feeling of being socially deprived. The shift in the distribution of the rapidly falling volume of total investment favouring non-productive investment in 1976–82 failed to reduce the cumulative backlog in social services.

Intersectoral distribution of investment in the 1970s, particularly during the first half of the decade, was biased towards the development of the industry and construction sector. On the other hand the proportion of investment allocated to agriculture, trade, housing and public services in 1971–5 was falling in comparison to the preceding five-year period (see Table 1.4). This led amongst other things to a relative neglect of agriculture and social services and an inability of the trading sector to cope with the growing trade turnover. The 'corrections' in intersectoral allocation of investment in 1976–82 had a limited impact on the structure of investment and output due to the rigidity and distortions in the structure of committed investment.

Traditionally investment policy accorded a high priority to the development of the producer goods sector (the so-called 'A' group industries) in comparison to the consumer goods sector (the so-called 'B' group industries) and agriculture. In 1972–4, industrial investment favoured the development of industrial branches producing consumer goods. Approximately 30.4 per cent of the total industrial investment in 1971–5 was allocated to branches producing consumer goods (the so-called 'B' sector) compared to 25.8 per cent in 1966–70 (A. Müller 1985: 166). This was made possible by the rapid growth of imports of machinery and equipment from the West, financed largely by credits. Despite the reallocation of industrial investment favouring the development of consumer goods industries in 1972–4, the share of the so-called 'B' industries in total industrial output by 1975 was less than in 1970 (A. Müller 1985: 165–7). From 1974 industrial investment policy was reversed, with investment being allocated increasingly to the expansion of industrial branches producing producer goods (*Raport* 1981: 82).

In 1971–5, there was a shift in the interbranch allocation of industrial investment favouring the development of metallurgy, electro-machinery and the food processing industry. More than 40 per cent of the total industrial

Table 1.3 Annual average growth and structure of investment (productive and non-productive) in constant prices

	Annual average growth in per cent				*Structure in per cent*				
	1961–70	*1971–5*	*1976–80*	*1981–2*	*1961–5*	*1966–70*	*1971–5*	*1976–80*	*1981–2*
Total investment	7.4	17.5	−3.0	−17.9	100	100	100	100	100
Productive investment	8.6	19.2	−4.7	−22.0	69.4	73.3	77.8	75.5	68.9
Non-productive investment	4.4	12.2	2.4	16.1	30.6	26.7	22.2	24.5	31.1

Sources: *Rocznik Statystyczny 1981*, Warsaw 1981, p. 182; *Rocznik Statystyczny 1982*, Warsaw 1982, p. 143; *Mały Rocznik Statystyczny 1983*, Warsaw 1983, p. 109.

Table 1.4 Sectoral structure of investment, 1961–82 (in constant prices and in per cent)

	1961–5	*1966–70*	*1971–5*	*1976–80*	*1982*
Total investment	100	100	100	100	100
Sectoral distribution:					
industry	38.3	37.6	42.0	38.9	31.0
construction	3.8	3.6	4.6	5.0	3.2
agriculture	15.0	17.4	15.2	16.3	18.4
transport and communication	9.5	10.0	10.3	9.2	6.7
trade	2.8	3.2	2.6	2.0	2.2
housing and public utilities	–	17.7	14.4	17.0	22.8

Sources: *Rocznik Statystyczny 1981*, Warsaw 1981, p. 182; *Mały Rocznik Statystyczny 1983*, Warsaw 1983, p. 109.

investment was allocated for the development of metallurgy and electro-machinery industry in 1975, i.e. an increase of around 7 percentage points in comparison to 1970 (see Table 1.5). Many of the large industrial investment projects were inadequately prepared, the expected costs were grossly under-estimated and they were economically unsound.

The percentage of investment allocated for the development of fuel and energy and the chemicals industry fell during the first half of the 1970s. The neglect of investment in fuel and energy contributed to the growing disturbances in the supply of electricity and production stoppages in the second half of the 1970s. The fall in the output of a number of chemical products like fertilizers and pesticides in the second half of the 1970s was partly attributed to under-investment. On the whole, Polish industrial development was less favourable towards agriculture. In 1966–70, investment in industrial branches producing agricultural inputs dropped by 5.1 per cent annually, while investment in the economy as a whole increased by 8.4 per cent annually. In 1971–5, although the rate of growth of investment in industrial branches producing agricultural inputs increased relatively quickly, it was still below the rate of growth of investment for the whole economy (E. Gorzelak 1980: 185–91).

Agricultural investment in the 1970s fluctuated much less sharply than industrial investment. During Gierek's pro-peasantry agricultural policy in 1971–4, the rate of growth of investment in private agriculture was high but it stagnated in 1975–7 when the policy was reversed. This slowed down the progress of mechanization of private farms (A. Szemberg 1980: 163–4), and adversely affected the growth of crop production.

The private production sector was practically excluded from the advantages of the investment leap of the first half of the 1970s, which was largely financed by Western credits. The investment leap even helped to strengthen the traditional, dogmatic economic and investment policy favouring the development of the

Table 1.5 Annual average growth of investment and its distribution, socialized industry, 1961–80, in constant prices

	1961–5	*1966–70*	*1971–5*	*1976–80*	*1970*	*1975*	*1980*
	annual average growth in per cent					*per cent*	
Total investment in socialized industry	8.0	7.7	21.0	−7.1	100	100	100
of which in:							
fuel and energy	9.4	3.3	13.6	5.1	26.4	19.2	35.7
metallurgy	6.6	11.0	27.3	−14.5	13.1	16.8	11.1
electro-machinery industry	12.2	11.5	25.5	−8.3	20.5	24.7	23.1
chemicals	11.4	6.5	14.4	−6.3	12.7	9.6	10.1
mining	−1.0	11.9	17.6	−17.3	8.2	7.1	3.8
wood and paper	10.3	5.3	26.3	−11.5	3.7	4.6	3.6
light industry	−0.3	15.6	19.9	−16.4	6.4	6.1	3.6
food processing	4.7	5.9	27.1	−11.3	7.9	10.1	8.0
others	12.9	−1.3	32.3	−16.9	1.1	1.8	1.0

Sources: *Rocznik Statystyczny Przemysłu 1980*, Warsaw 1980, pp. 264–5; *Rocznik Statystyczny 1981*, Warsaw, pp. 253–4.

socialized (state) sector, which occurred at the cost of the private sector. In 1960 private investment constituted 17.4 per cent of total investment, falling to around 14 per cent in 1970, and in 1975 it was only 9 per cent (*Inwestycje 1979*: 1). Private handicrafts and private farmers were discriminated against in the allocation of machinery, equipment and raw materials in comparison with the socialized sector.

On the whole the investment programme in the 1970s was not oriented towards export markets and there was no close correlation between the use of Western credits for productive investment and the expansion of production capacity whose output could be used to boost hard currency exports and serve the rising burden of the credits. The newly created or modernized production capacity was largely oriented towards the production of products for the domestic market. With the falling rate of economic growth during the second half of the 1970s and the failure of the government to curb the growth in domestic consumption effectively, domestic markets absorbed a greater portion of the potentially exportable products. Moreover, a significant part of the Western medium-term credits was invested in projects with a long pay-back period (for example, in mining and raw materials production) so that servicing the credits could not be met by new export capacities in the medium term (R. Portes 1981: 13). The rigid and bureaucratic system of planning and management of industry and foreign trade made it unsuitable for the aim of hard currency export promotion of industrial products.

The Polish economy was highly material, fuel and energy intensive in comparison to industrialized Western countries and the gap was growing in the second half of the 1970s. A number of factors, such as the ageing machinery park, obsolete machinery design and construction, the slow rate of technical innovations, defects of the enterprises' system of incentives and low prices of raw materials, fuel and energy, etc., contributed to high material, fuel and energy intensiveness of production. The planners' preference for investment in new plants (high percentage of outlays for construction and buildings in total investment), instead of investment for modernization of existing plants, also contributed to the increase in material, fuel and energy intensiveness of production (J. Macieja 1978: 433–7). There was a strong bias against investment for the purpose of saving raw materials, fuel and energy.

Traditionally the planners preferred to invest in new industrial complexes or factories instead of investing for the purpose of modernization, expansion and replacement of the old machinery of existing plants, despite the fact that the latter offered greater economic advantages. According to an estimate made in 1968, only around 17 per cent of the total industrial investment was allocated for the modernization of existing plants (A. Płocica 1970: 12). Despite certain improvements being made in the field of the technical structure of investment in the 1970s,[10] the traditional pattern of investment allocation was maintained. On average only 20 per cent of the total gross industrial investment was earmarked for the modernization and replacement of fixed assets in 1971–5, compared to 50–70 per cent in the industrialized West (A. Płocica 1976: 65–7; *Raport* 1981: 18; P. Glikman 1982: 273).[11] The percentage of investment allocated for the construction of new and large plants increased significantly during the first half of the 1970s, accompanied by a corresponding decline in the percentage of investment allocated for the modernization and replacement of obsolete plants (J. Boguszewski 1979: 16–17; W. Walkowiak 1983: 38).

In general the bias towards new investment was partly attributed to systemic features of the CPEs. As a rule, the success and the size of the bonus received by enterprises depended to a large extent on how far production targets were fulfilled. Investment was the easiest way to achieve additional production targets. Normally investment for the purpose of modernization and renovation of the stock of machines at existing plants was bound to disturb the regular rhythm of production and thereby risk the loss of bonus. The main aim of the enterprise was to minimize the risk of non-fulfillment of the production targets. From this point of view, new investments provided the least risk for the enterprises (J. Winiecki 1982: 502). In addition to that, the central planning organs preferred new, large and prestigious investment projects in the distribution of scarce producer goods, construction and building capacity. Investment project offices and building and construction enterprises were in general less inclined to carry out assignments for modernization investments of existing plants (A. Płocica 1976: 68–9).

The Five Year Plan (1976–80) aimed to limit investment growth in new projects, and favoured quick-yielding investment outlays like, for instance, investment for modernization or replacement of obsolete machinery and equipment. Moreover, it intended that investment should be concentrated on the completion of the rapidly growing volume of unfinished investment projects. The government appealed without success for stricter observance of investment discipline, threatening severe sanctions against violation.[12]

The rate of growth of investment dropped considerably in 1976–9, although initially less than what was considered to be desirable. The drive for overinvestment was, however, still strong and investment in new projects could not be stopped. There was a great tendency to cut investment in small and medium-sized enterprises, whilst large and prestigious investment projects (e.g. the steel combine Huta Katowicza, the Warsaw automobile factory, etc.), backed by strong bureaucratic pressure groups or lobbies, suffered much less from the investment curb (M. Mieszczankowski 1980a: 149). The so-called economic manoeuvre programme failed to reanimate the flagging economy and to redirect investment resources in conformity with the new priority, perpetuating the distorted investment and production structure.

DISINVESTMENT AND THE LEGACY OF THE INVESTMENT CRISIS

The deep economic crisis of 1979–82 found its expression in, amongst other things, the faster decline in both capital accumulation and investment than the decline in both net material product and consumption. In 1979–82, both per capita capital accumulation and net investment fell by 63 per cent compared to a per capita decline in the net material product (for distribution) and consumption of 30 per cent and 14 per cent respectively (J. Kotowicz 1985: 339). The redistribution of national income during the deep economic crisis relatively favoured basic consumption at the expense of investment.

The uncontrolled investment leap during the first half of the 1970s was followed by a significant slow-down of investment growth in the second half of the decade, and from 1979 by a drastic cut in investment. As a result, both the cumulative costs of investment in progress and the estimated costs of completing investment projects already started were growing rapidly. Annual investment outlays lagged increasingly behind the rapidly growing estimated further investment outlays required for the completion of the unfinished investment projects (committed investment). This fact was reflected in the rising ratio of committed investment to annual investment in the socialized sector. It rose from 2.0 in 1975 to 3.6 in 1980 and to 5.1 in 1982 (see Table 1.6). In other words, if no new investment projects at all were started, and at the rate of investment implemented in 1982, it would have taken more than five years to complete all the ongoing investment programmes, compared to only two years in 1975 and nearly four years in 1980, at the rate of investment in the respective year. The planners' rule of thumb considered a ratio of 2–2.5 between committed investment and annual investment outlays for construction as reasonably good.

Table 1.6 Investment in construction, frozen, committed investments and investment outlays in the socialized sector, 1975–82 (current prices)

	1975	*1978*	*1979*	*1980*	*1981*	*1982*[d]
			in billion zlotys			
Total cost of investment in progress[a] of which:	1352.3	2053.1	2199.7	2346.3	2292.4	4833.2
newly started (during year)	393.8	438.1	378.2	221.1	142.7	679.8
Investment commissioned (during year)	276.9	350.6	348.3	256.5	240.3	380.5
Frozen investments[b]	360.7	620.9	664.8	797.5	835.5	1113.5
of which: machinery	27.2	47.5	45.3	53.2	67.2	83.0
Committed investments[c]	714.7	1081.6	1186.6	1292.3	1216.6	3339.2
Investment outlays (during year)	359.7	431.4	391.7	361.1	278.7	658.5
		coefficients				
Frozen investment ratio to:						
annual investment	1.0	1.44	1.70	2.21	3.0	1.78
net material product	0.25	0.32	0.3	0.39	0.38	–
Committed investment ratio to:						
annual investment	2.0	2.5	3.0	3.6	4.4	5.1
net material product	0.49	0.36	0.34	0.24	0.22	–

Source: *Rocznik Statystyczny 1981, 1982* and *1983*.
Notes: [a]Cumulated cost of investment in progress, current year's investment included, but investment commissioned is excluded;
[b]Cumulated outlays on investment projects started but unfinished;
[c]Estimated outlays necessary for the completion of investment projects already started (end year).
[d]In 1982 prices rose sharply.

The average gestation period of investment rose constantly from 1975 but it went up particularly fast in 1979–82, as the tendency to spread investment resources too thinly over too many projects remained strong. As a result, the rate of investment project completion was low and the volume of investment projects commissioned lagged considerably behind the targets. This led to a rising disinvestment in the stock of physical capital. A growing proportion of the stock of physical capital, particularly in industry (light industry, chemicals, construction and building industries, etc.) became obsolete, unreliable, high cost and worn-out (A. Płocica 1986: 12–15; J. Kotowicz 1986: 105–6). The sharp cut in imports of investment goods (machinery, equipment and spare parts, etc.) aggravated the process of disinvestment which constrained output growth and blocked a speedy economic recovery.

Due to misallocation of investment between economic sectors and industrial branches during the 1970s, the structure of unfinished investment projects in the late 1970s and early 1980s was distorted. The proportion of unfinished investment projects, which required a long period for their completion and were concentrated in the industrial producer goods sector (e.g. fuel and energy, coal mining industry in particular), was high in the total committed investment. The share of industrial branches, which could be instrumental for technical modernization, raw material and fuel saving innovations, was small (*Raport*, 1981: 89–90). The structure of the unfinished investment projects was incompatible with the newly declared investment priorities (agriculture and industries working for agriculture, exports, housing, economies in raw materials, fuel and energy, etc.). Moreover, many of the unfinished industrial investment projects were originally planned to have a relatively high hard currency import intensity, both for their completion (machinery, equipments etc.) and current operation (semi-finished products, spare parts etc.).

Because of the severe limitation of investment resources and the distortions in the structure of unfinished investment projects, it would have been unfeasible and economically unjustified to continue work on all investment projects in progress. The commission set up by the government in late 1980 to select investment projects for continuation accorded priorities to projects with a high ratio of sunk to total costs, and a high contribution to food production, exports and import substitution. By the end of 1982, work was suspended on around 1600 incompleted investment projects with an estimated cost of 495 billion zloty (at current prices), which was approximately 10 per cent of the total cost of the ongoing investment programme (*Mały Rocznik Statystyczny 1984* 1984: 119–20). A high percentage of annual investment outlays (85 per cent in 1982) was expended on a continuation of work on the unfinished investment projects.

However, the government's success in trimming and restructuring the investment programme in accordance with the new investment and production priorities was limited. The pressure for a resumption of the suspended investment projects (either by illegal or semi-illegal ways) was strong. In this context the bureaucratic pressure exerted by the heavy industry lobby (including the coal mining industry), demanding a great share in the total investment fund, was particularly strong. It succeeded in preventing investment restructuring in conformity with the new production priority and maintaining the 'investment arteriosclerosis' in the economy.

CONCLUSION

Post-war Polish economic and investment growth proceeded in a recurrent cyclical movement, which was caused largely by variation in economic policies and by systemic factors characteristic of CPEs. The duration and amplitude of the economic and investment growth cycles for the period 1971–82 were longer and greater than for the cycles of the preceding years. The large fall of net material product and investment in 1979–82 indicated the grave nature of the economic crisis.

Gierek's investment leap during the first half of the 1970s, accompanied by rapid consumption growth, both made possible by the large Western credits, led to great domestic and external imbalances. The overinvestment drive, which exceeded by far the absorptive capacity of the economy, led to rapidly rising costs of investment, investment tensions, the extension of the investment gestation period, an excessively broad investment front, and inefficiency and waste of investment resources. These shortcomings were aggravated by widespread distortions in the allocation of investment between economic sectors and industrial branches (neglect of infrastructure, agricultural and consumer goods sectors, lack of export orientation, discrimination against private production, etc.). The planners prefered costly investment in new projects to investment for modernization and renovation of obsolete plants.

Failure to enforce the curb in consumption growth announced in the summer of 1976, a critically rising burden of servicing the Western debt, and insufficient growth of hard currency exports forced the government to cut the growth of investment and Western imports. Both contributed to a considerable fall in economic growth. The so-called economic manoeuvre programme failed to reanimate the flagging economy and to redirect investments towards promoting Western exports, agricultural and consumer goods production, and housing. The drastic cuts in Western imports and investment in 1979–82 led to a fast growth in the volume of frozen and committed investment, a slow rate of completion of investment projects and a rising disinvestment in the stock of physical capital. Restructuring the investment programme was successfully blocked by strong vested interest groups.

2

EXTERNAL ECONOMIC RELATIONSHIPS

INTRODUCTION

This chapter deals with Poland's external economic relationships in the 1970s and the economic crisis of 1979–82. The communist regime emphasized the deterioration of the external economic environment (Western economic recession, price explosion of oil and raw materials since 1973, worsening terms of trade, growing protectionism in the industrialized West and rapid rise of interest rates on the international capital markets) as the main cause of the economic crisis of 1979–82. The imposition of Western economic sanctions after the declaration of martial law at the end of 1981, which affected the Polish economy unfavourably, seemed to confirm the regime's argument.

No doubt, some aspects of the external economic environment did affect Poland's economy unfavourably. None the less, in the 1970s Western behaviour made large borrowing and imports of Western technology feasible, initially stimulating the acceleration of economic growth, consumption and industrial modernization. Moreover, Poland's terms of trade were favourable up to 1978, whilst protectionism affected Poland's Western exports of manufactured goods only slightly. It was mainly supply constraints which inhibited the urgently needed hard currency export boost. The hypothesis adopted in this chapter is that internal factors such as basic errors in economic policies (overinvestment, misallocation of investment, wage drift, and the instability of agricultural policy), the systemic defects of the CPEs and the political weakness of the regime were primarily responsible for causing the balance of payment and economic crises of 1979–82.

This chapter will describe and analyse the complex factors determining the lack of correlation between the large imports of Western technology and hard currency export growth, the rising import intensity of production, the mounting debt trap and the balance of payment crisis. It consists of sections dealing with the problems of export growth and performance, import growth and import intensity of production, the structure of Poland's foreign trade, foreign trade planning and regulation, the debt trap, and a conclusion.

NATIONAL ECONOMY, EXPORT DYNAMICS AND EXPORT PERFORMANCE

The large imports of Western capital and technology in the 1970s contributed to the high rates of growth of net material product, investment and consumption, particularly during the first half of the decade. But Gierek's 'import-led growth' strategy did not lead, however, to a high growth of hard currency exports as was expected. This section of the chapter will analyse briefly the significance of exports in the economy, export growth and export performance, Polish export specialization and the causes of the failure of Gierek's 'import-led growth' strategy to produce sufficient growth of hard currency exports.

Exports and the national economy

The ratio of exports to gross national product can be considered as an aggregate indication of a country's participation in the international division of labour. Its computation in CPEs, however, raises great difficulties, due to domestic price distortions, arbitrary exchange rates and methodological problems of national income accounting. Table 2.1 shows a rough estimate of the ratio of exports to gross national product of Poland at current prices in 1966–82, calculated according to the Western method in terms of domestic prices and in US dollar prices. The ratio of exports to gross national product in terms of current domestic prices rose from around 16 per cent in 1966 to around 18 per cent in 1970, and to around 23 per cent in 1980. It dropped however to around 20 per cent in 1982. The estimate does not seem to vary significantly from estimates made by observers in the West. For instance, Kazmer estimates that the ratio of exports to gross national product in terms of domestic zloty in 1977 increased from around 17 per cent in 1970 to around 20 per cent in 1974 and to around 24 per cent in 1980; the ratio fell to around 20 per cent in 1981 (D. Kazmer 1986: 404).

In general, the ratio of exports to gross national product in domestic prices was higher than in US dollar prices, partly because of the policy of fixing low prices for basic consumer goods in Poland and a relatively low participation of services in Polish foreign trade (B. Wojciechowski 1977: 64–7). The ratio of exports to the gross national product of Poland had been low in comparison with other European CMEA countries (with the exception of the former Soviet Union). During the crisis years, for instance in 1982, the value of Poland's exports per capita was estimated at US$309, i.e. the lowest exports per capita amongst the European CMEA countries (*Rocznik Statystyczny 1983* 1983: 550). Poland's export ratios, varying between 9–13 per cent in 1966–82 in terms of US dollar prices, were low in comparison with export ratios of market economies of a comparable size and level of economic development.

Poland's ratio of exports to gross national product in terms of both domestic and international prices showed a rising trend through 1966–80, and only in 1982 did it fall (see Table 2.1). Because of the rigid mechanism of adaptation of

Table 2.1 Ratio of exports to gross national product, 1966–82 (current prices)

	In domestic prices			*In international prices*		
Year	*Gross nat. product[a] in bill. zloty*	*Exports[c] in bill. zloty*	*Ratio of exports to GNP per cent*	*Gross nat. product[b] in bill. US$*	*Exports[c] in bill. US$*	*Ratio of exports to GNP per cent*
1966	713	117	16.4	28.5	2.58	9.1
1970	948	172	18.1	39.0	4.0	10.3
1974	1492	302	20.2	73.0	9.3	12.7
1978	2365	515	21.8	128.3	15.5	12.1
1980	2316	570	22.8	139.8	18.7	13.4
1982	5667	1153	20.3	130.0[d]	12.5	9.6

Source: B. Wojciechowski in 'Problemy współpracy z zagranicą', *Studia Ekonomiczne*, Polska Akademia Nauk, 7, 1984, p. 74.
Notes: [a]gross national product, calculated according to United Nations accounting method, in terms of domestic prices;
[b]gross national product recalculated according to prices in industrialized west (international US$);
[c]goods and services at f.o.b. prices;
[d]provisional estimate.

the CPEs in response to rapidly changing external conditions, Poland may not have benefited fully from greater efficiency in resource use and economies of scale originating from foreign trade. There is ample evidence which suggests that the gain in Poland's export ratio in the 1970s, particularly during the second half of the decade, did not contribute towards economic growth (H. Gabrisch 1983: 86–97). The increase in the export ratio most probably signified a deterioration in the efficiency of export production, requiring a greater amount of allocated resources to obtain one value-unit of export product. There was a high and growing capital, materials and hard currency import intensity of export production (B. Wojciechowski 1984b: 75 and 81; Z. Piotrowski 1984b: 7–8). The deterioration in the efficiency of export production, particularly with regard to exports to non-socialist countries, was considerable during the second half of the 1970s (B. Wojciechowski 1984a: 48–9).

The dynamics of exports

The traditional pattern of economic development (autarchic bias) and the systemic features of the CPEs both attached a low priority to exports (F. Holzman 1974: 104–6). Exports were considered to be required activities only to the extent that they were necessary for financing imports to achieve planned economic growth. Table 2.2 sets out the dynamics of net material product and exports to both socialist and non-socialist countries for the period 1966–82 at constant 1977 prices. The yearly average growth of exports at constant prices

Table 2.2 Export growth and export elasticity with respect to net material product 1961–82 (in constant prices of 1977)

	Annual growth in per cent				*Export elasticity*		
		Exports					
Period	*Net material product*	*Total exports*	*Exports to socialist countries*	*Exports to non-socialist countries*	*Total exports*	*Exports to socialist countries*	*Exports to non-socialist countries*
1961–5	6.5	10.1	9.1	10.6	1.55	1.46	1.63
1966–70	6.1	9.1	11.0	8.2	1.57	1.80	1.34
1971–5	9.4	10.1	11.2	8.8	1.07	1.19	0.94
1976–80	1.5	3.2	3.7	2.6	2.13	2.47	1.73
1981–2	−8.1	−5.9	−1.5	−11.2	.72	.19	1.38

Sources: B. Wojciechowski, *Importochłonność produkeji w Polsce*, Warsaw, 1981 (mimeograph), pp. 11–12; H. Gabrisch, *Polens krise und aussenwirtschaftliche entwicklung*, Hamburg, 1983, p. 85; *Rocznik Statystyczny 1983*, Warsaw, 1983, p. 74; *Rocznik Statystyczny Handlu Zagranicznego 1983*, Warsaw, 1983, p. 5.

during the boom period of 1971–5 was only slightly higher than the growth of exports during the preceding five-year period; the yearly average growth of exports to non-socialist countries remained practically at the same level. As a result of the price rise of fuels and raw materials in international markets, Poland's terms of trade improved during 1971–7. Export elasticity with respect to net material product dropped, however, during the first half of the 1970s in comparison with the preceding five-year period. This was partly attributed to favourable terms of trade, ample Western credits and the rapidly growing domestic demand, but also indicated the economy's weak export orientation.

When economic growth slowed down significantly during the second half of the 1970s, export growth to both socialist and non-socialist countries declined considerably. Export elasticity with regard to net material product, however, was rising during the second half of the 1970s, probably reflecting the government's efforts to force the growth of unprofitable exports (Z. Piotrowski 1984a: 131). Despite repeated government statements on the absolute necessity of boosting Western exports, the annual average growth of export volume to the industrialized West dropped to a low level of 2.7 per cent in 1977–80. Poland's failure to expand Western export volume sufficiently in combination with the growing burden of servicing Western debts contributed to a fast decline in its credit rating on the international financial markets. The cut in Western imports from 1977 led to underutilization of industrial production capacity and a decline in the export growth of manufacturing.

The large decline in the output of two important export sectors (coal and agriculture) in 1981, aggravated by a strong political pressure to give greater priority to domestic markets during the legal period of Solidarność, contributed to a drastic fall in exports to non-socialist countries and a lesser decline in exports to socialist countries. A further drastic cut in Western imports in 1981–2 led to a large fall in output and aggravated the socio-economic and political crises.

The annual average growth of exports was higher to socialist countries than to non-socialist countries throughout 1966–80; and with the deepening of the economic crises, the fall in Western exports was more dramatic than the exports decline to socialist countries. The steep rise in Western imports of capital goods, industrial components and materials during the first half of the 1970s was coupled with a declining growth of imports from the CMEA countries. This process occurred simultaneously with a rising growth of the volume of exports to the CMEA and a slow-down in exports' growth volume to the industrialized West. This asymmetrical export growth trend during the first half of the 1970s reinforced the rising trade deficits in hard currency. The modernization of Poland's industrial machinery and equipment through large-scale imports of Western technology stimulated the exports of capital goods to the CMEA countries. Instead of penetrating the competitive manufacturing markets of the Western countries, Poland preferred the soft CMEA markets.

Investment and export performance

Gierek's 'new economic strategy' was marked by a simultaneous rapid growth of both productive investment and consumption, which was made possible by large Western credits. It was hoped that industrial modernization, after the consummation of the investment gestation period, would lead to a sufficiently rapid expansion of exports to service the debt; and that the fast consumption growth would stimulate a rapid increase in labour productivity. But the investment leap and the rapid consumption growth in the first half of the 1970s led to increasing shortages, inefficiency in resource use, wage drift and inflation. An increasing amount of potential export products was absorbed by the rapid growth of investment and domestic consumption, thereby reducing actual export growth (A. Budnikowski and J. Misala 1981: 21).

With the exception of 1972–4, the bulk of the investment fund was allocated to industry with a preference for the capital goods sector (the so-called 'A' sector industry), investment for import substitution and other investment oriented towards the satisfaction of domestic demand. The structure of the expanded and modernized industry was not oriented towards exports. Industrial branches producing machinery, equipment and means of transportation as well as the traditional branches of industry (steel, coal, electricity) which were supporting the rapid expansion of the capital goods sector, received the lion's share of the industrial investment (A. Müller, 1985: 163–73). Agriculture, transportation, communication and social service facilities received inadequate investment. Outdated and obsolete domestic transportation hampered exports (e.g. coal) and became a serious bottle-neck for the economy.

A significant amount of investment was allocated for the development of mining and Poland was an important producer and exporter of coal, copper, silver and sulphur. Relatively less investment was expended toward the development of plants for processing the raw materials into more valuable semi-finished or finished products. The decision of Poland to specialize in the export of raw materials and fuel (sulphur, coal and copper) to the West did not, however, take into account the rapid growth of domestic consumption resulting from the fast increase in raw material and fuel intensive production during the second half of the 1970s and the early 1980s (J. Dembowski 1983: 542; W. Gorzawski 1985: 206–8; K. Dubczynski and M. Dytman 1981: 12–18). A large proportion of the industries that were selected for specialization or to provide substitutes for imports had more than average material intensity. The main investment projects like iron and steel, non-ferrous metals, chemicals and building materials that were started in the first half of the 1970s were highly material intensive and therefore also import intensive. Demand for fuel and energy increased rapidly as a result of the fuel intensiveness of investment projects (Z. Fallenbuchl 1981: 39–41). The growing material and fuel intensiveness of production severely limited Poland's capacity to export primary products, encouraged their import and created thereby a built-in balance of payments disequilibrium.

Gierek's import-led growth strategy brought a rapid increase in the number and type of licences purchased from the industrialized West in the 1970s. A large number of the licences purchased involved the production of machinery, equipment, electronics and means of transportation. These sectors were under the administration of the powerful Ministry of Machinery and Heavy Industry. Licences were put into use slowly (Z. Fallenbuchl 1983: 48–9). For instance, only 55 per cent of the purchased licences were put into use according the planned time-schedule in the 1970s and, for about one-half of them, the targeted production capacity utilization was not achieved (J. Cieslik 1983: 228; *Raport* 1981: 94) due to poor planning, lack of investment funds and shortages of industrial supplies and components. In fact, industrial production with the aid of Western licences was not more export-oriented than industries using mainly domestic technologies if one takes into account the high import intensiveness of the first group of industries. Therefore, the former contributed significantly to the deficits in the hard currency balance of payment (J. Monkiewicz 1980: 36–7; W. Gorzawski 1985: 111–12). It was import substitutes and domestic demand which benefited most from the import of Western licences.

Table 2.3 illustrates the lack of correlation between the rates of growth of investment and exports in constant prices during the period of 1966–82. Assuming a reasonably realistic four-year gestation period of investment production for exports, the growth of exports is related to the growth of investment in the past. The elasticity of exports with regard to investment outlays dropped in the 1970s and it deteriorated drastically during the period 1978–82. The growth of exports lagged behind the rapid expansion of industrial

Table 2.3 Annual average growth of investment and exports (in constant prices)

Four-year period		*Annual average growth in per cent*		*Investment exports elasticity*
Investment	*Exports*	*Investment*	*Exports*	
1966–70	1970–4	8.0	11.3	1.41
1970–4	1974–8	14.0	7.2	0.51
1974–8	1978–82	4.2	−2.9	−0.69

Source: E. Krakowiak and B. Wojciechowski, 'Zdolność do eksportu gospodarki narodowej', *Studia Ekonomiczne*, 7, VII, 1984, p. 83.

production capacity in the 1970s. It is estimated that each 1 per cent increase of the industrial production capacity generated on average a 2 per cent growth of exports in the 1960s, but only 1.6 per cent and 0.8 per cent during the first and second half of the 1970s respectively (A. Czepurko 1982: 104–5; *Raport* 1981: 75). From the point of view of export promotion, the huge investment outlays and the rapid expansion of industrial production capacity in the 1970s did not lead to a corresponding increase in Poland's performance.

Export specialization

With the exception of a number of primary products such as coal, coke, sulphur, and industrial products such as ships, metal working machinery, rolling stock, etc., the degree of Poland's export specialization was low. The concentration of export production was low and the number of enterprises and plants which engaged in export production was small. Of the 3,600 or so industrial enterprises producing for export, around 369 enterprises exported more than 30 per cent of their production and for the rest exports played an insignificant role (*Raport* 1981: 75–6), and they contributed little to the total export revenue (M. Frouk and J. Wierzbolowski 1981: 20). Despite the large imports of Western technology, progress in export specialization was hardly noticeable in the 1970s (S. Gruzewski 1982: 5–6). At the end of 1970s and in the early 1980s, Poland's export specialization in machinery and equipments deteriorated significantly (P. Glinski 1980: 12; E. Böhm 1985: 162–4).

Poland's industry was marked by a relatively low level of inter-industry deliveries or sales in comparison with industrialized market economies. Moreover industry was engaged in the production of too many items. For instance, Poland's machinery industry was producing around 100,000 industrial components, comprising approximately 40 per cent of the total world assortment of components in the machinery industry (W. Gorzawski 1985: 236). As a result the proportion of large-scale production was small, contributing to a high cost of production, low quality and lack of competitiveness in the Western market.

The CMEA countries were facing growing competition from the newly industrializing countries (NICs) in the OECD market for export products like ships, machinery, equipment and products of light industry from the second half of the 1970s. They lost their lead, for example, in steel, ships, passenger cars and all major items of manufactured exports to the West (K. Poznanski 1986: 62). The dramatic loss in Poland's share in the OECD imports of machinery, equipment and other manufactured goods in 1979–83 was less a result of changes in the demand structure than of a deterioration in Poland's production and supply conditions (H. Gabrisch 1986: 35–47).

IMPORT DYNAMICS AND THE IMPORT INTENSIVENESS OF PRODUCTION

The significance of imports in the economy was growing through 1960–76. For instance the ratio of imports to total value of final products[1] at constant price increased from 15.4 per cent in 1960 to 19.8 per cent in 1970, and it rose further to 25.8 per cent in 1976. In the following years the ratio of imports to final products fell gradually to 22.2 per cent in 1981 (B. Wojciechowski 1982: 4). The increase in the ratio of imports to final products during the 1960s was mainly attributed to trade expansion with the CMEA countries. The adoption of the import-led growth strategy in the 1970s led to an increase in the ratio of Western imports to final products from 8.3 per cent in 1970 to 16 per cent in 1976. On the other hand the ratio of soft currency imports to final products fell slightly during this period (B. Wojciechowski 1982: 4). Western imports were cut at an increasing rate from 1977, whilst the growth of soft currency imports was sustained at a relatively high rate during the second half of the 1970s.

The rate of growth of total imports at constant prices fluctuated sharply in 1971–82, varying between an average peak growth of 16.6 per cent p.a in 1971–5 and 0.8 per cent in 1976–80; and it dropped further deeply to −14.2 per cent in 1981–2. Imports from the socialist countries were relatively stable, the annual average growth fell from 7.4 per cent in 1971–5 to 5.5 per cent in 1976–80. During the deep economic crisis, however, soft currency imports fell by −5.8 per cent annually in 1981–2. Western imports fluctuated sharply and erratically causing great economic losses. The peak Western imports growth at constant prices averaged 25.8 per cent p.a. in 1971–5, coinciding with Gierek's investment leap. Overindebtedness and poor hard currency export performance forced Poland to cut Western import volume by an average of 2.7 per cent annually in the second half of the 1970s. The outbreak of the hard currency balance of payments crisis in 1980 and credit sanctions after the declaration of martial law at the end of 1981, caused a 24.1 per cent annual drop in Western import volume during 1981–2 (see Table 2.4). The excessive and erratic fluctuation in Western imports contributed to the generation of the economic crisis in 1979–82.

The fluctuation in import volume was highly sensitive to the variation in the rates of growth of gross investment. The annual average growth of gross investment at constant prices in 1971–5 was more than twice the average growth of gross investment in the 1960s. The import of machinery and equipment ('embodied technology') from the industrialized West was the main vehicle of the import of modern technology, and its share in the total import of capital goods was growing (Z. Fallenbuchl 1983: 30–2). The annual average growth of Western imports of capital goods during 1971–5 was approximately 46 per cent, i.e. more than five times the average growth of the 1960s (see Table 2.4).

The share of machinery and equipment outlays in total investment increased significantly during the 1970s. By itself this was a favourable trend, an improvement in the traditional investment structure which was biased towards building and construction outlays. The share of imports in the investment outlays for machinery and equipment varied between 35–40 per cent in the 1960s and they originated largely from the CMEA countries (B. Wojciechowski 1977:198).

Table 2.4 Growth of imports, final production, gross investment and consumption, 1960–82 (in constant prices of 1977)

	1961–70	*1971–5*	*1976–80*	*1981–2*
Average growth per annum in per cent				
Total imports of which:	9.5	16.6	0.8	−14.2
imports from soc. countries	10.7	7.4	5.5	−5.8
imports from cap. countries	8.2	25.8	−2.7	−24.1
Imports of semi-finished prod. of which:				
imports from soc. countries	10.8	5.5	5.6	–
imports from cap. countries	8.1	21.8	0.2	–
Imports of capital goods of which:	9.5	28.4	7.0	−30.5[c]
imports from soc. countries	10.1	12.2	6.0	–
imports from cap. countries	8.4	45.8	−17.6	–
Imports of consumer goods of which:	9.8	13.5	5.8	2.5[b]
imports from soc. countries	10.3	10.9	4.5	–
imports from cap. countries	8.6	18.9	7.7	–
Total production of final goods	6.6	10.4	2.2	−8.8[d]
Gross investment	8.0	17.5	−3.0	−17.5
Consumption	4.9	8.5	4.3	−8.1
Final production[a] elasticity of imports of semi-finished prod. of which:	1.44	1.35	1.05	–
imports from soc. countries	1.64	0.53	2.55	–
imports from cap. countries	1.23	2.10	0.09	–

Sources: Z. Sosnowski and B. Wojciechowski, in 'Importochtonność gospodarki norodowej', *Studia Ekonomiczne*, 7, 1984, p. 107; *Rocznik Statystyczny* 1983, pp. 70, 74, 156 and 329;
B. Wojciechowski, 'Przemiany strukturalne a trudności importowe Polski', *Gospodarka Planowa*, 9, 1984, p. 370.
Notes: [a]final product in domestic prices;
[b]elasticity of imports of semi-finished products with regard to gross national product;
[c]average annual change in 1979–82 at transaction prices of 1982;
[d]net material product.

The share of imports in the investment outlays for machinery and equipment was growing considerably during the first half of the the 1970s, and this was attributed exclusively to the rapid growth of Western imports (see Table 2.5). With the exhaustion of the Western credit possibilities and the hard currency balance of payments crisis, the import pattern of machinery and equipment was restored to its traditional shape by the end of the 1970s.

The sharp growth of Western imports of machinery, production licences and know-how led to an increasing dependence of Poland's industrial production on hard currency imports (e.g. raw materials, intermediate goods, components, spare parts, etc.) during the first half of the 1970s. The hard currency imports intensity of industrial production stabilized during the second half of the decade (B. Wojciechowski 1984b: 100–1). Imports of industrial inputs consisted of three groups of commodities: a) basic raw materials and fuels; b) semi-finished products; c) industrial components and spare parts. Basic raw materials and fuels were dominant in the imports of supplies from the CMEA countries, particularly from the Soviet Union. Imports of industrial semi-finished products, components and spare parts dominated the hard currency imports of supplies in the 1970s.

The increase in the hard currency import intensity of production during the 1970s was also the result of specific economic policy and systemic factors:

- Investment allocation preferred the development of upstream industries producing final goods (cars, machinery, durable household equipment, etc.) and industrial branches with above average imports intensity (chemicals, electronics etc.), causing an increase in hard currency imports of industrial intermediate goods and components;
- The quality of home-produced industrial inputs was below the technical standard required by plants working with Western technology and licences, and incentives for technical innovations were weak;

Table 2.5 Import intensity of investment, 1970–80 (constant prices of 1977) in per cent

		Import share in total outlays for machinery and equipment		
Year	*Share of machinery and equipment in total investment*	*Total*	*Imports from socialist countries*	*Imports from capitalist countries*
1970	35.0	40.6	26.2	14.4
1975	42.0	52.2	17.1	35.1
1978	42.0	45.8	23.6	22.2
1979	41.0	43.2	25.7	17.5
1980	44.0	40.1	25.3	14.8

Source: Z. Sosnowski and B. Wojciechowski, in 'Problemy współpracy z zagranicą', *Studia Ekonomiczne*, 7, 1984, p. 107.

- The low prices of raw materials and fuels encouraged waste and inefficiency, and incentives for raw materials and fuel saving innovations were absent;
- Errors in agricultural policy, poor weather and a high level of meat consumption caused high imports of grain.

The rapid growth of Western imports of industrial inputs helped to eliminate the bottle-necks in inputs; and the rate of industrial productive capacity utilization did not fall below 97 per cent in 1971–6 (A. Stanczyk 1982: 129). For the first time in the 1970s, hard currency imports of supplies dropped by around 10 per cent in 1977 and the industrial supplies deteriorated during the following years. The deep cuts in the Western imports of industrial supplies and the limited possibility of their substitution by CMEA imports disrupted the supply of industrial input and output seriously, through the operation of the 'import bottle-neck multiplier' (F. Holzman 1974: 126).

THE STRUCTURE OF POLAND'S FOREIGN TRADE

The share of primary products in Poland's total foreign trade turnover in 1970–82 at current prices was significant. The export of primary products varied between 26–32 per cent of the total value of exports and the import of primary products ranged between 31–48 per cent of the total value of imports. The share of intermediate products and manufactured goods in the total value of exports varied between 68–74 per cent and their share in the total value of imports ranged between 52–70 per cent. An analysis of the structure of Poland's foreign trade with the CMEA and the Western industrialized countries will highlight its main structural problems.

The structure of trade with the CMEA countries

Intra-CMEA trade, production cooperation and specialization were coordinated and regulated in the Five Year Plans, annual plans and trade protocols. Trade in commodities was the main form of intra-CMEA economic relations. Other forms, such as bilateral and multilateral agreements over production specialization and cooperation, common investment projects, joint research and production developments, were only secondary to trade. The realization of the goal of socialist economic integration, specified in the Complex Programme adopted at Bucharest by the Council in 1971, was highly unsatisfactory. For instance, the share of intra-CMEA trade in the total foreign trade turnover of CMEA members fell from 60 per cent in 1970 to 50.7 per cent in 1980 (B. Wojciechowski 1984a: 23). Trade bilateralism, currency inconvertibility, price distortions and the rigidity of the foreign trade system (e.g. exchange of raw materials for raw materials or machinery for machinery) limited intra-CMEA trade expansion.

A high percentage (around 85 per cent) of the intra-CMEA agreements on production cooperation and specialization dealt with the production and trade of machinery, equipment and means of transportation. The impact of socialist economic integration on the formation of the industrial structure of a member country was small. Appropriate economic criteria and institutional frameworks stimulating rational CMEA production cooperation and specialization were absent (J. Ptaszek 1979: 21).

In comparison with other small European CMEA countries, Poland's participation in intra-CMEA trade based on production cooperation and specialization in machinery, equipment and means of transportation, was the lowest in 1977 (17.1 per cent), placing it next only to Romania (J. Kowalewski 1980: 17). Moreover, the degree of Poland's export specialization[2] in machinery and equipment (SITC: 7) to the CMEA countries was falling during 1965–75. When Gierek pursued the import-led growth strategy, the share of CMEA trade in Poland's foreign trade turnover fell from around 63 per cent in 1970 to around 50 per cent in 1975. Only when Western imports fell during 1977–82 did the share of CMEA trade in Poland's foreign trade rise.

The share of exports of primary products (SITC: 0–4), of which coal was the main item, was more or less stable in 1971–82 (1980 and 1981 were exceptions), varying between 16–20 per cent of the total value of exports to the CMEA at current prices. The share of imports of primary products (crude oil, natural gas, iron ore, cotton), largely from the Soviet Union, remained stable at a level of 30 per cent up to 1975. But, because of the large price rise of fuel (oil), the share of imports of primary products rose from around 30 per cent in 1975 to 36 per cent and 46 per cent in 1980 and 1982 respectively (see Tables 2.6 and 2.7). From 1978, Poland's terms of trade worsened, and it was estimated that around one-half of the 3 billion transferable rouble trade deficit with the Soviet Union in 1981–3 was attributed to the price increase of oil (B. Wojciechowski 1984a: 32–3). Trade in food and agricultural products was declining (see Tables 2.6 and 2.7).

Trade in intermediate industrial products and manufactured goods constituted a high proportion of Poland's total trade with the CMEA countries, resembling the trade pattern between industrial nations. The exchange consisted largely of industrial final products and it was much less oriented to trade in industrial components, parts and intermediates. The share of exports of machinery, equipment and means of transportation (SITC:7) was high, varying between 52–60 per cent of Poland's total exports to the CMEA countries (see Table 2.6). Poland's imports of Western technology in the 1970s stimulated exports of capital goods to the CMEA; but Poland's hard currency obligations could not be met by export expansion in the East. Despite the rapid growth of Western imports of capital goods in 1971–5, the CMEA countries remained an important supplier of machinery and equipment, whose share varied between 41–3 per cent of the total imports from the CMEA countries (see Table 2.7). Intra-CMEA trade in consumer goods was less developed.

Table 2.6 Commodity structure of total exports, exports to CMEA and industrialized West, 1971–82 (at current prices) in per cent

	Total exports					*Exports to CMEA*					*Exports to industrialized West*[a]				
SITC Commodity group	*1971*	*1975*	*1978*	*1980*	*1982*	*1971*	*1975*	*1978*	*1980*	*1982*	*1971*	*1975*	*1978*	*1980*	*1982*
0,1 Food, live animals beverages and tobacco	11.4	8.5	8.0	6.7	6.3	3.7	5.1	3.1	2.5	2.1	29.1	15.6	16.8	14.3	13.9
2,4 Raw materials (excluding materials for food production)	4.2	3.8	4.5	5.0	5.8	2.2	1.1	2.0	2.3	2.7	9.1	8.7	9.4	9.3	9.8
3 Mineral fuels	14.0	20.1	15.6	14.2	15.4	12.5	14.0	11.5	8.4	11.5	20.9	34.8	25.7	24.2	25.6
Total primary product	29.6	32.4	28.1	25.9	27.5	18.4	20.2	16.6	13.2	16.3	59.1	59.1	51.9	47.8	49.3
5 Chemicals	8.0	7.6	5.4	5.5	4.8	7.9	6.7	6.0	6.2	5.6	6.5	5.4	3.7	4.4	4.4
7 Machinery, equipment and means of transportation	38.8	38.2	41.8	43.1	44.0	51.9	51.3	53.9	59.7	58.2	10.5	15.0	18.8	16.6	19.4
6,8,9 Other intermediate products and manufactures	23.6	21.8	24.5	25.5	23.7	21.8	21.8	23.5	20.9	19.9	23.9	20.5	25.6	31.2	26.9
Total intermediate products and manufactures	70.4	67.6	71.9	74.1	72.5	81.6	79.8	83.4	86.8	83.7	40.9	40.9	48.1	52.2	50.7
TOTAL	100	100	100	100	100	100	100	100	100	100	100	100	100	100	100

Sources: *Rocznik Statystyczny Handlu Zagranicznego* from various years; B. Wojciechowski, 'Problemy współpracy z zagranicą', *Studia Ekonomiczne*, 7, 1984, p. 27 and p. 43; E. Böhm, *Die Krise des polnischen Aussenhandelssystems*, Hamburg, 1985, p. 231.
Note: [a]European industrialized market economics, Japan, Rep. of South Africa, United States of America, Canada, Australia and New Zealand.

Table 2.7 Commodity structure of total imports, imports from CMEA and industrialized West, 1971–82 (at current prices) in per cent

	Total imports					*Imports to CMEA*					*Imports to industrialized West*[a]				
SITC Commodity group	*1971*	*1975*	*1978*	*1980*	*1983*	*1971*	*1975*	*1978*	*1980*	*1982*	*1971*	*1975*	*1978*	*1980*	*1982*
0,1 Food, live animals and tobacco	12.5	9.3	11.7	13.1	14.1	9.5	5.5	4.0	3.6	3.9	13.9	10.8	17.3	23.1	25.1
2,4 Raw materials (excluding material for food production)	16.0	11.8	10.5	10.6	11.8	12.0	9.7	7.9	8.3	8.8	19.5	10.3	12.0	11.4	13.1
3 Mineral fuels	6.1	9.2	12.8	18.2	21.9	9.0	14.6	19.4	24.0	33.5	1.3	4.7	3.8	3.9	4.5
Total primary product	34.8	30.3	35.0	41.9	47.8	30.5	29.8	31.3	35.9	46.2	34.7	25.8	33.1	38.4	42.7
5 Chemicals	6.8	7.4	7.7	7.9	9.4	5.0	5.9	5.4	4.9	5.7	12.6	9.4	11.5	14.8	18.7
7 Machineryand transport equipment	34.5	37.7	37.2	32.4	24.4	40.5	41.3	44.4	42.7	30.0	28.0	38.3	32.9	25.3	19.0
6,8,9 Other intermediate products and manufactures	24.0	24.6	20.1	17.8	18.4	24.0	23.0	18.9	16.5	18.1	24.7	26.5	22.5	20.5	19.6
Total intermediate products and manufactures	65.2	69.7	65.0	58.1	52.2	69.5	70.2	68.7	64.1	53.8	65.3	74.2	66.9	61.6	57.3
TOTAL	100	100	100	100	100	100	100	100	100	100	100	100	100	100	100

Source: See Table 2.6.
Note: [a]See Table 2.6.

The structure of trade with the industrialized West

The share of primary products (SITC: 0–4) in the total value of exports to the industrialized West during 1970–82 was still high, although it fell from 60 per cent in 1971 to 50 per cent in 1978–82 (see Table 2.6). The share of food exports (particularly meat and meat products) dropped considerably in the 1970s, largely due to rising domestic consumption and the stagnation of agricultural output during the period 1975–81. The gain in the share of mineral fuel exports (coal) at current prices, which peaked in 1975, reflected mainly the high export prices of coal. Coal, coke and briquette, which accounted for around 18 per cent of the total export value to the West, were produced under conditions of rising costs, growing domestic demand for coal and environmental problems.

The share of Western exports of intermediate and industrial products having a low degree of processing like chemicals, iron and steel etc. (SITC: 5–6) remained stable at around 20 per cent (G. Teske 1981: 78). On the whole, around 70 per cent of Western exports consisted of primary products, intermediate and industrial products with a relatively low degree of processing. The gain in the Western exports of machinery, equipment and manufacturing (SITC: 7–8) in the 1970s could not compensate for the decline in traditional exports like food and agricultural products.

Poland's trade with the industrialized West was marked by a trade pattern similar to the economic relationship between developing and industrialized countries. Poland was exporting mainly primary products and low quality manufacturing on the one hand, and importing high quality machinery, equipment and industrial supplies and components on the other. About 74 per cent of the total value of Western imports in 1975 consisted of industrial products, of which more than one-half consisted of machinery and equipment. With the growing difficulties and crisis in the hard currency balance of payments and a drastic cut in investment, Western imports of capital goods were severely cut. The volume of imports of machinery and equipment in 1982 was only one-fifth of the level of 1975, and their share dropped from 38 per cent to only 19 per cent of the total Western imports during the period (see Table 2.7). The share of food and agricultural products in Western imports (food grain and animal feed), mainly from the USA, increased considerably during 1976–81; but it fell drastically in 1982 due to Western credit sanctions.

Nearly three-quarters of hard currency earnings from the export of finished manufactured goods in 1978 came from transport equipment (SITC: 73), power generating machinery (SITC: 72) and clothing (SITC: 84). Poland's shipyards were highly export oriented and expanded rapidly in the 1970s. Ship exports to the West in 1978 were a hard currency earner second to coal exports. The world economic recession, competition from the NICs and an excessively high hard currency import intensity, reaching 50 per cent of the total value of certain ships (P. Tarnowski 1982: 8), combined with severe hard currency shortages, caused the large drop in output and exports in the last years of the 1970s and the early 1980s.

Table 2.8 Geographical structure of Polish foreign trade, 1970–82 (at current prices)[a]

	1970	*1972*	*1974*	*1976*	*1978*	*1979*	*1980*	*1981*	*1982*
Exports	100	100	100	100	100	100	100	100	100
CMEA countries	60.6	60.6	53.0	57.0	58.0	57.8	53.3	45.7	50.0
Industrialized West	28.4	30.4	36.3	32.0	31.3	31.1	34.4	36.9	32.6
of which:									
EC	17.1	18.1	22.1	18.4	19.2	19.8	21.3	23.2	21.1
Developing countries	7.7	6.0	8.0	8.3	7.6	8.0	9.7	14.5	13.8
Rest	3.3	3.0	2.7	2.7	3.1	3.1	2.6	2.9	3.6
Imports	100	100	100	100	100	100	100	100	100
CMEA countries	65.9	58.2	42.3	44.9	51.9	51.7	53.3	51.8	59.2
Industrialized West	25.8	34.1	50.8	48.9	40.5	37.9	35.0	37.2	0.7
of which: EC	16.7	21.2	30.3	26.6	22.0	20.0	19.0	20.4	18.2
Developing countries	5.7	4.7	3.8	4.2	5.3	7.8	9.4	7.9	5.8
Rest	2.6	3.0	2.1	2.0	2.3	2.4	2.3	3.1	4.3

Sources: *Rocznik Statystyczny Handlu Zagranicznego*, 1975, p. 21; 1981, p. 4; *Mały Rocznik Statystyczny*, 1984, p. 224.
Note: [a]Because of valuation effects (price differences between intra-CMEA trade and world market prices, arbitrary exchange rates etc.) the figures can be misleading.

The government promoted the passenger car industry through large imports of Western machinery, equipment and components combined with the purchases of licences (Fiat) and Poland hoped for a rapid growth of car sales to the West. This turned out to be an illusion, mainly due to a sharp increase in car demand at home, a lack of competitiveness abroad and a high share of hard currency import components in the value of the car.

In general Poland's Western exports of machinery (non-electric machinery, working machine tools etc.) were facing a saturated, long declined market, combined with a lack of competitiveness (R. Teske 1981: 86–92; H. Gabrisch 1983: 130–41; A. Budnikowski and J. Misala 1981: 20–3). Moreover, Poland specialized in the export of bulky, heavy and material-intensive machinery and equipment (rolling stock, construction machinery etc.) having low unit values (per kilogram). For instance, Poland was exporting on average 2–6 tons of machinery and equipment in exchange for 1 ton of imports from the industrialized West in the 1970s (*Raport* 1981: 76). A comparison with the NICs indicated moreover Poland's low export-unit values of machinery. For instance, Poland obtained only US$1.98 per kilogram for its textile and leather machinery. This contrasted sharply with the US$6.25 per kilogram paid on the OECD-Europe market to Taiwan (K. Poznanski 1986: 70–1), indicating the low effectiveness of Poland's export of machinery.

Products of light industry like clothing, textiles and fabrics, and footwear occupied an important place in the total export of manufactured goods to the industrialized West. From the second half of the 1970s, Eastern European countries (including Poland) were losing their market share, under the pressure of growing competition from the NICs in the OECD countries. Because of delivery difficulties, many of the light industry export quotas to OECD markets were not utilized (H. Gabrisch 1983: 145). In certain cases the quota system benefited Poland. For example the textile quota system guaranteed Poland's export position in the OECD market, protecting its share against the aggressive competition of the Far Eastern NICs (B. Wojciechowski 1984a: 47).

FOREIGN TRADE PLANNING AND REGULATION

In 1966 the government made a timid attempt to relax the rigid and detailed plan targets in foreign trade, by setting for instance obligatory export targets expressed in 'currency zloty' ('złoty dewizowy'), classified into groups of products. The export bonus was made dependent on calculated export pay-off. The export and import tasks were allocated to individual industrial ministries which were responsible for carrying out export production and the purchase of imports (U. Płowiec 1979: 16). Because of the distortions in domestic prices and exchange rates, export prices had to be corrected by an 'accounting coefficient' ('przelicznik kalkulacyjny') in order to determine calculated profit and bonus for the producers and traders. Nevertheless obligatory targets for foreign trade in real terms for basic raw materials, intermediates and foods were maintained (L. Skibiński 1979: 25–6).

The reorganization of foreign trade in 1971 gave new powers to industrial ministries to direct foreign trade activities of the branches falling within the confines of an individual ministry, in cooperation with the Ministry of Foreign Trade. The reorganization strove for close cooperation between industrial producers and foreign trade enterprises selling the products abroad so that impulses and signals from international markets could be transmitted effectively to the producers. The most common form of transaction in industrial products between producers and foreign trade enterprises was trading on commission where the latter acted as an agent for the former, charging a certain fee for the services (T. Sobczuk 1979: 158). In such a situation, the interests of the trading partners were not always identical and friction between them was not uncommon. Long-term contracts were rare and the 'commodity competence' classification prevented competition among foreign trade enterprises (E. Böhm 1985: 39–40).

An important change in the system of foreign trade planning and regulation in 1971 was the introduction of exchange rates in trading, which were adapted to the purchasing power of foreign currencies and which were diversified according to payment areas. In principle, export producers and users of imported inputs should receive/pay for the goods at international prices, to be converted into domestic zloty prices by appropriate exchange rates. This was called the transaction price, i.e. the domestic zloty price of traded commodities abroad, priced in foreign currency which was converted first to 'currency zloty' ('złoty dewizowy') and then multiplied by a 'coefficient of relative currency value' ('wskaznik względnej wartosci walut'), diversified according to two (socialist and non-socialist) payment areas.[3] Theoretically the transaction price would provide the producers or users of imported inputs with appropriate information for desirable export specialization and import substitution. Furthermore, effective parametric regulation of foreign trade would be made feasible (U. Płowiec 1979: 17; J. Kafarski 1980: 12–13).

A consistent application of transaction pricing, particularly with regard to the import of basic raw materials, intermediate goods and fuels, etc., would have required flexible domestic pricing. This seemed to be incompatible with the cherished principles of price rigidity in the CPEs. Moreover, the bureaucracy was against price flexibility. When the government adopted transaction pricing and wholesale price reform in early 1971, the prices of imported basic raw materials, semi-finished products and fuels, as well as the prices of raw materials produced domestically but also sold partly abroad (copper, asbestos etc.), were excluded. Their prices remained fixed for more than three years. So, in practice, domestic prices were insulated from world price fluctuations by subsidies and equalization payments. In the early 1970s, around 80 per cent of the value of imported raw materials was sold domestically at fixed prices (E. Böhm 1985: 85). In general the sale price of domestically produced raw materials was determined by industrial average cost of production plus a certain profit margin. The domestic price of coal, a very important export item and source of fuel and energy, was set below the cost of production absorbing a large amount of price subsidies.

The introduction of the WOG reform in 1973 (a reorganization of industry into large organizations with more autonomy) offered greater opportunities for industrial associations ('zjednoczenie') to engage directly in foreign trade. The number of directives was reduced significantly and it was intended that the government would steer industrial associations towards achieving the targets set up by the central plan with the help of economic parameters (tax rates, prices, exchange rates, financial results, etc.). The scope of transaction pricing for exports became larger. About nine-tenths of the export transactions between industrial producers and foreign trade enterprises in 1975 were reckoned in transaction prices (E. Böhm 1985: 91–8). This favourable trend, however, was largely overshadowed by distortions in the structure of domestic costs of production and prices. Because of the rapid increase of world prices of raw materials and fuels since 1973 on the one hand and the insistence of the regime on maintaining price stability in the state sector on the other, domestic wholesale prices of raw materials and fuels increasingly diverged from transaction prices. Price subsidies for imported raw materials increased rapidly,[4] contributing to greater price and cost distortions. The low prices of raw materials, semi-finished products and fuels contributed significantly to a distortion of the export specialization of Poland and a rapid rise in the material and fuel intensity of production and exports, particularly during the second half of the 1970s (U. Wojciechowski 1978: 44–5). Economies in raw materials and fuels were unprofitable for enterprises and the incentive system tended to encourage waste.

With the growing domestic imbalances (excessive growth of investment and inflation) and increasing trade deficits with the West, the WOG reform was 'suspended' and later on 'modified' in the second half of the 1970s. This actually meant a recentralization of decision-making. The domestic cost of production was increasingly insulated from external economic conditions, combined with growing price distortions. Transaction price had less and less influence on production; foreign trade planning and management relied more and more on administrative regulation (W. Gorzawski 1985: 43–5).

Export plan targets (gross sales in domestic prices and later on also in hard currency) and bonuses were related to their (over)fulfilment and pressures by the superiors became the main instruments employed in planning and regulation of the foreign trade. The targets seemed to be provisional and they were changed through the course of the year, with bonuses paid on the basis of the final, not the initial, targets. Exporters were inclined to conceal their export capabilities mainly in order to gain from the soft targets but partly also because of the fear that targets in subsequent years would be set higher than the level of the past year's performances; and incentives to increase exports were weak (K. Crane 1986: 443–4). On the whole industrial associations and enterprises had no incentive to reduce imports voluntarily, so that import allocations had to be made at the centre. In the case of import plans, managers could bargain for change in import targets in the course of the year. It was common for managers to 'manufacture' above-plan hard currency export orders in order to argue for an increased import quota of hard currency imports (K. Crane 1986: 438–9; E. Böhm 1985: 77). On the whole, export targets and import allocations were determined in an *ad hoc* and arbitrary manner through bargaining between the central planner, industrial ministries, associations and enterprises.[5]

The so-called open-ended planning and external economic relationships

Frequent and *ad hoc* revisions of the initial targets of the Five Year Plan (1971–5) and annual plans were the origin of the so-called open-ended planning. Coordination between economic ministries and between industries was poor, and decisions to carry out investment projects were not sufficiently prepared, rendering central planning ineffective. The result of the actual decision-making process – concerning such questions as, What? How much? From where to import? and Who would obtain the hard currency allocation? – was significantly determined by the 'penetration power' ('siła przebicia') or bargaining strength of an individual ministry, industrial association or manager. This in turn depended largely on political and personal patronage or connections. In this context, it is important to note the role of the powerful bureaucratic group associated with the Ministry of Heavy Industry and Machinery which received the lion's share of industrial investment funds and Western credits in the 1970s (P. Bożyk 1983: 55–7).[6] The praxis of open-ended planning contributed considerably to the growing trade deficits in hard currency and the balance of payments crisis at the end of the 1970s (S. Jędrychowski 1982: 25–54).

The realized value of exports, imports and trade deficits with the non-socialist countries in 1971–2 did not differ significantly from the annual foreign trade plans. In this period, the terms of trade were favourable. In the course of 1973–5, the regime revised the initial targets in foreign trade upwards on a number of occasions (S. Jędrychowski 1982: 41 and 48–50). The trade deficits with the non-socialist countries (calculated at official exchange rates) increased from around US$250 million in 1972 to around US$1500 million in 1973, i.e. slightly less than two times the corrected trade deficit target (see Table 2.9). The Western import boom was reinforced by the decisions of the regime to continue the investment drive in 1974–5. In response to the rapidly growing hard currency trade deficits in 1973–4, the regime set an unrealistically high (39.5 per cent) exports growth target and a relatively low (16 per cent) imports growth target for 1975 (see Table 2.9; S. Jędrychowski 1982: 49–50). The outcome, however, was that the peak in hard currency trade deficit between 1972–81 was reached in 1975, caused by a considerable fall in the growth of hard currency exports and high imports growth.

The chronic underfulfilment of exports targets to non-socialist countries, combined with the frequent 'import plan corrections' (i.e. extra imports), led to growing trade deficits in hard currency and debts. The decision of the regime to proceed with additional 'above-plan imports' ('import pozaplanowy'), which were supposed to be covered by additional exports originating from the so-called 'self-financing in foreign exchange' ('system samospłaty dewizowej') investment projects,[7] was bound to reinforce the trade deficits (Z. Karcz 1980: 7–8).

The foreign trade targets set out in the Five Year Plan (1976–80) were unrealistic. The total volume of exports and imports were to grow by 75 per cent and 26 per cent respectively for the period 1976–80 (J. Swierkocki 1982: 10). The plan targeted a balancing of trade in hard currency during the second half of the 1970s, a cut in imports of grain (animal feed) and steel products by 50 per cent and 40 per cent respectively during the plan period and a 14 per cent annual growth of exports to non-socialist countries, with a substantial gain in the share of exports of machinery and equipment (T. Wrzaszczyk 1977: 8–9). Instead of the planned cut in imports of grain by one-half there was a doubling of grain imports in the planned period. Poland failed to close the hard currency trade deficits in 1976–80 as planned, and the obligations for principal and interest payments were rising fast. Poland was forced to take new credits with stringent conditions to finance the deficits on current account.

DEBT TRAP AND ECONOMIC CRISIS

The workers' riot in December 1970 was precipitated by an announcement of a price rise for basic consumer goods. The former prime minister, P. Jaroszewicz, told the VIth Party Congress at the end of 1971 during a discussion over the Five

Table 2.9 Plan and realized trade turnover and balances with non-socialist countries (in current prices), 1971–82

	Annual plan target			*Plan realization*					*Plan realization/Plan target in per cent*	
Year	*Exports in bil. zl. dew.*	*Imports in bil. zl. dew.*	*Balance in bil. zl. dew.*	*Exports in bil. zl. dew.*	*Imports in bil. zl. dew.*	*Balance in bil. zl. dew.*	*Ratio of exports to imports (5:6) in per cent*	*Difference (7–4) bil. zl. dew.*	*Exports*	*Imports*
1	*2*	*3*	*4*	*5*	*6*	*7*	*8*	*9*	*10*	*11*
1971	5.4	5.7	−0.3	5.8	5.4	+0.4	108	+0.7	107.4	94.7
1972	6.4	7.7	−1.3	6.5	7.4	−0.9	88	+0.4	101.5	91.1
1973	8.0	10.6	−2.6	8.4	13.3	−4.9	63	−2.3	105.0	125.5
1974	11.2	16.6	−5.4	12.9	20.1	−7.2	63	−1.8	115.2	121.1
1975	18.0	22.7	−4.7	14.5	24.5	−10.0	59	−5.3	80.5	107.9
1971–5	49.0	63.3	−14.4	48.1	70.7	−22.6	68	−8.3	98.2	111.7
1976	19.2	26.7	−7.5	15.0	24.8	−9.8	61	−2.3	78.1	92.9
1977	19.9	24.9	−5.0	16.9	23.6	−6.7	72	−1.7	84.9	94.8
1978	20.2	24.9	−4.7	18.1	24.1	−6.0	75	−1.3	89.6	96.8
1979	22.0	23.7	−2.7	20.3	27.1	−6.8	75	−4.1	96.7	114.3
1980				24.2	26.6	−2.4	89			
1976–80				94.5	126.2	−31.7	75			
1981	–	–	–	18.3	18.2	+0.1	101	–	–	–
1982[a]	–	–	–	441.6	319.2	122.4	138.3	–	–	–

Sources: Z. Karcz, 'Jeszcze o sprawie zadłuzenia', *Handel Zagraniczny*, 12, 1980, p. 8; B. Kosinski, 'O polityce płatniczej Polski w nowym dziesięcioleciu 1981–90', *Bank i Kredyt*, 3, 1981, p. 71; E. Böhm, *Die Krise des polnischen Aussenhandelssystems*, Hamburg, 1985, p. 70; *Rocznik Statystyczny Handlu Zagranicznego 1983*, p. 4.
Note: [a]Since 1982 the value for foreign trade turnover is expressed in zloty instead of zloty dewizowy.

Year Plan (1971–5), that the planned industrial modernization combined with a simultaneous increase in the standard of living would require a foreign capital injection.[8] It was hoped that the extra investment, financed by foreign credits, after the lapse of the investment gestation period, would generate sufficiently high growth of both labour productivity and exports to cover the rise in real wages and the burden of debt servicing.

The size of trade deficits and credits envisaged in the Five Year Plan (1971–5) was relatively small. According to the initial Five Year Plan (1971–5), credits were to be drawn from both CMEA and industrialized Western countries. About two-thirds of the total trade deficits forecasted during the first half of the 1970s would originate from the trade with the CMEA countries (S. Albinowski 1982: 320). The plan was revised many times in an arbitrary and obscure manner. Contrary to the initial plan target, the large trade deficits and the credits drawn during the plan period originated only from the industrialized West.

The international political and economic situation was favourable for large-scale borrowing in the world money and capital markets during the 1970s. This encouraged lending to Eastern Europe in general and to Poland in particular. Eastern European countries were prompt in meeting their financial obligations abroad. Moreover, the banking community wrongly assumed that a 'Soviet financial umbrella', i.e. that the USSR would bail out a CMEA member in financial difficulty, was operating.

The idea that the high inflation prevailing in the industrialized West during the 1970s would lead to low or even negative real interest rates in the long run, making the real cost of borrowing extremely cheap, gave additional encouragement for the regime to borrow abroad on a large scale (W. Rydygier 1985: 230–1). M. Jagielski, the former vice-premier and head of the Central Planning Commission, told reporters in December 1974 that Poland gained considerably from the Western borrowing because of the high inflation and depreciation of the value of money, making the real cost of servicing foreign debts low. This was emphasized in official propaganda, justifying the heavy borrowing in 1975 in order to continue the investment drive at a time when the growth of hard currency exports fell considerably (S. Jędrychowski 1982: 51–2). The reasoning underlying the assumption of a long run zero or negative real cost of borrowing under conditions of high inflation in the Western countries was misleading (W. Rydygier 1985: 230–43). The fallacy of the assumption became painfully obvious when international finance and creditors charged floating interest rates on international loans based on the short-term interest rate of dollar bank deposits in London (LIBOR), which rose sharply from around 5.5 per cent in 1976 to 18–20 per cent in 1980–2.

Poland's import-led growth strategy adopted a foreign borrowing variant which assumed a sharp increase in imports of capital goods and a rapid cumulation of foreign debts within a relatively short period. Then, a critical phase would follow when the rising debts must be stopped from growing through a rapid growth of hard currency exports to cover the rising costs of servicing the debts in order to prevent an unmanageable level of foreign debts. Hence a period of rapid debt reduction was assumed as a part of the rapid indebtedness variant (S. Gomulka 1978: 2; W. Rydygier 1980). This borrowing variant, however, carried a high risk that the economy might get caught into a mounting debt trap because of poor export performance, investment inefficiency, systemic defects of the CPEs, wage drift, errors in economic policy and an unfavourable political environment. Actually the regime rejected the alternative of a more cautious foreign borrowing variant which assumed a gradual increase in imports of capital goods, credits and investment, which was to be adjusted to the growth in export capability.

Poland did utilize Western credits supporting economic development to a limited extent during the 1960s. By the end of 1970 the long- and medium-term gross debt in hard currency was only US$1.2 billion and it stabilized at this level until the end of 1972. Gierek's ambitious industrial modernization received extra encouragement from the high growth of hard currency exports in 1972–4, stimulating an extraordinaryly high growth of Western imports. Hard currency trade deficits increased from US$0.25 billion in 1972 to an average of US$2.2 billion per annum in 1975–9. Thanks to great efforts to raise exports, the hard currency trade deficit in 1980 dropped to about one-third of the level of the preceding year (see Table 2.10). The bulk of the trade deficits were financed by loans. Both hard currency imports and exports fell considerably in 1981–2, and for the first time since 1971 Poland had a small hard currency trade surplus in 1982.

The gross debts in hard currency increased rapidly from US$1.2 billion at the end of 1972 to US$24.1 billion at the end of 1980, i.e. a twenty-fold increase over eight years. Gross debts in hard currency increased less than the cost of servicing foreign debts (principal and interest payments), which rose from only US$0.3 billion in 1972 to US$8.1 billion in 1980 (see Table 2.11), i.e. an almost thirty-fold increase over eight years. The debt service ratio was low and falling during 1972–3, partly because of the high growth of hard currency exports and good harvests. But by the end of 1975 a higher than internationally accepted level of a safe debt service ratio (27.2 per cent) had been reached. In view of the rapidly increasing burden of servicing the outstanding debts, it was estimated that a sustained average growth of hard currency exports of 25–30 per cent p.a (at current prices) was necessary for a certain period in order to prevent a mounting debt level which would be otherwise unmanageable (W. Rydygier 1985: 247–55). Such a high export growth was not feasible for the Polish economy. Hence, the rapid growth of hard currency debts during 1972–7 predisposed the Polish economy towards a balance of payments crisis.

An increasing proportion of the new borrowing during the second half of the 1970s was devoted to covering the rapid growth of the burden of servicing the debts. As long as the creditors were willing to provide roll-over credits under normal conditions then the day of reckoning could be deferred at low cost. Gradually a growing number of creditors came to the conclusion that Poland had

Table 2.10 Balance of payments in convertible currencies (million US$*), 1970–82

	1970	*1971*	*1972*	*1973*	*1974*	*1975*	*1976*	*1977*	*1978*	*1979*	*1980*	*1981*[a]	*1982*[a]
Current account													
Exports	1300	1460	1776	2514	3869	4354	4525	5072	5714	6579	7954	5487	4975
Imports	1200	1351	2021	3993	6025	7353	7477	7092	7597	8773	8745	6237	4617
Balance of trade	100	100	−245	−1479	−2156	−2999	−2952	−2020	−1883	−2194	−791	−750	358
Service receipts	175	203	234	350	506	567	625	635	702	857	953	650	490
Service payments	150	178	208	307	472	504	612	681	802	1027	1090	500	408
Service balance	25	25	26	43	34	63	13	−46	−100	−169	−137	150	82
Transfer receipts	75	86	145	204	203	259	326	411	613	781	1010[b]	1287[b]	316
Transfer payments	–	–	2	2	3	3	4	99	159	254	485	637	97
Transfers balance	75	86	143	202	200	256	322	312	454	527	525	650	319
Interest receipts	–	14	17	18	30	34	35	34	36	69	13	168	86
Interest payments	50	47	52	95	293	504	665	902	1208	1708	2467	3272[a]	3099[a]
Interest balance	−50	−33	−35	−77	−263	−470	−630	−868	−1171	−1639	−2331	−3104	−3013
Balance on current account	150	187	−111	−1300	−2186	−3149	−3248	−2622	−2700	−3475	−2734	−3054	−2254

Capital account													
Extended credits (medium- and long-term)	−50	−48	−31	−40	−50	−118	−188	−276	−106	−98	−165	−416	5
Received credits (medium and long-term)	–	23	194	1321	1712	2663	3295	2254	2369	908	3290	1755	−747
Short-term credits	−25	−81	−15	34	695	685	157	−5	478	92	−742	−833	−110
Bank accounts	−50	−52	−3	50	−90	26	−54	641	62	30	666	238	−56
Finance operation	−25	−21	−26	−45	−78	−96	53	24	−103	−466	−135	−476	−115
Refinance												2378	2050
Others	–	−8	−8	−8	−9	−11	−15	−16	–	+9	−20	409[a]	1237[a]
Balance on capital account	−150	−187	+111	+1311	+2186	+3349	+3248	+2622	+2700	+3471	+2734	+3845	+2254

Sources: Figures supplied by Ministry of Finance reproduced in *Finanse*, 6, 1982: 57–63; *Bank i Kredyt*, 3, 1982: 97; *Bank i Kredyt*, 6, 1983: 181; *Rocznik Statystyczny Handlu Zagranicznego 1983* 1983: 73; G. Fink 'Poland's Statistics on Current Account of the Balance of Payments in Convertible Currencies' mimeographed, *Forschungsberichte*, 91, 1983, Wiener Institut für Internationale Wirtschaftvergleiche, Vienna.

Notes: *converted at official rates: up to 1971, 1 US$=4.00 zl. dew., in 1972 = 3.68 zl. dew., from 1973 up to 1977=3.22 zl. dew., in 1978 = 3.166 zl. dew., in 1979 = 3.089, in 1980 = 3.054 zl. dew., in 1981 = 3.361 zl. dew., in 1982 = 82.823 zl. dew., in 1983 = 91.02 zl. dew.

[a]includes interest due but not paid, or formally not yet rescheduled by then;

[b]includes US$460 million grant given by the USSR in 1980 and 1981.

Table 2.11 Poland's debt in convertible currencies (in million US$), 1970–82

Year	*Cumulated current acc. balance*	*Gross debt (end year)*	*Long-term debt*	*Medium-term debt*	*Short-term debt*	*Total debt service*	*Capital repayment*	*Interest*	*Exports of goods, comm., serv. and transfer receipts*	*Debt service (per cent) 6.9*
	1	*2*	*3*	*4*	*5*	*6*	*7*	*8*	*9*	*10*
1970	−850	1025								
1971	−664	876	639	341	6	290	244	46	1751	16.5
1972	−774	1248	813	434	2	321	269	52	2157	14.9
1973	−2079	2625	1641	923	61	931	336	95	3051	14.1
1974	−4265	5224	2916	1485	823	927	633	294	4582	20.2
1975	−7414	8388	4716	2161	1510	1413	910	503	5183	27.2
1976	−10662	12149	6622	3549	1977	1876	1211	665	5476	34.2
1977	−13283	14927	7431	5519	1977	2792	1890	902	6119	45.6
1978	−15882	18990	8365	7946	2679	4327	3119	1207	7026	61.5
1979	−19454	23833	9833	11110	2890	6156	4451	1705	8212	74.9
1980	−22066	24128	9608	12516	2011	8080	5610	2470	9930	81.3
1981	−25125[a]	25480[a]	13080	10877	1100	9083[b]	5811[b]	3272[b]	7415	122.5
1982	−27378[a]	26286[a]	8286	10696	1100	9010[b]	5911[b]	3099[b]	5881	153.2

Source: see Table 2.10.
Notes: [a]Included rescheduled debt in 1981 and US$ 400 mill. unspecified interest or principal; in 1982 US$ 6200 mill. unspecified/unpaid interest or principal; [b]loan and interest obligations before debt relief.

reached the prudent credit limits and they were more concerned with their exposure. The creditors imposed more strict and costly conditions of borrowing which led, amongst other problems, to a considerable deterioration of the debt structure. For instance, at the end of 1973 around 63 per cent of the total Western debts consisted of long-term credit, but its share fell to 41 per cent at the end of 1979. On the other hand the share of medium- and short-term credits increased from 35 per cent and 2 per cent respectively to 47 per cent and 12 per cent during the same period ('Bilans płatniczy Polski w latach 1971–81', *Finanse*, 6, 1982: 59).

The percentage of loans guaranteed by Western governments was also falling in the 1970s (R. Portes 1981: 51). The bankers were more reluctant to supply Poland with long-term credits. It was forced to seek, to an increasing extent, expensive short- and medium-term loans in order to finance the growing import needs of industrial procurements and grain (*Raport* 1981: 80–1). As a result, the principal and interest obligations accumulated rapidly by the end of the 1970s and early 1980s, causing severe liquidity problems.

Interest payments rose rapidly from US$0.9 billion in 1977 to around US$2.5 billion in 1980 (see Table 2.11), caused by the rapid growth of both the size of outstanding debts and the rate of interest. The sharply rising rate of interest in the international money market at the end of the 1970s and the early 1980s coincided with the deterioration of Poland's credit rating. At first it was widely believed that the problem was one of short-run liquidity difficulties. This belief, however, ignored the long-term structural and systemic factors causing the financial crisis. The hard currency debt service ratio in 1977 was close to 50 per cent. Poland was forced to cut the volume of Western imports.

This caused dislocation in industrial procurements, and a slow-down in the growth of industrial output and hard currency exports. Western exports growth lagged behind the requirements to meet the financial obligations. The government's failure in the summer of 1976 to trim meat consumption through a price increase exacerbated the deficits on the hard currency current account. In 1979 the debt service ratio was 75 per cent and the economy deteriorated rapidly. Despite the hectic efforts to boost exports in 1980 the debt service ratio in 1980 was rising and it was obvious that either default or orderly debt rescheduling were inevitable.

Actually, Poland was already facing hard currency liquidity difficulties by the end of 1975, when the Polish central bank was unable to meet a US$100 million obligation to the West. It was thanks to Soviet help that a liquidity crisis was avoided. Despite this liquidity difficulty, the Gierek leadership did not heed the warning (P. Bożyk 1983: 86–7). An experts' report, prepared at the end of July 1977 but not released until 1980, advised the government to negotiate urgently debt rescheduling with the creditors, to freeze all new investment and to reapply for IMF membership. All these recommendations were ignored (*Polityka* 1980). According to Gierek's testimony before the so-called Grabski Commission, he was informed for the first time about the critical level of the hard currency debt in early 1978 and only then did he put the question on the agenda of the next Politbureau session (G. Pomian 1986: 65). The report of the Grabski Commission shows the incompetence and irresponsibility of Gierek and the highest leadership of both the Party and the state in the management of the hard currency debt, which contributed significantly to the balance of payments crisis in 1980.

The first clear sign of the financial crisis occurred when Western banks, net credit flows (new credits less repayments) to Poland declined from US$3.4 billion in 1979 to US$0.3 billion in 1980; this was followed by a new outflow of US$0.9 billion in 1981 (CIA 1986b: 153). Too late, Poland admitted that it could not meet its financial obligations any more, requested negotiations on debt rescheduling and in March 1981 declared a moratorium. The agreement with the Western governments assembled in the Paris Club in April 1981 stipulated a 90 per cent rescheduling of the debt service obligations due in 1981. A provisional agreement with the Western banks was reached at the end of 1981, stipulating a 95 per cent rescheduling of the principal obligations due for 1981. Both agreements covered a debt rescheduling of about US$4.9 billion, comprising less than one-half of Poland's hard currency financing to cover its projected trade deficit and debt service obligations (A. Clapp and H. Shapiro 1986: 245–6).

The international banks reacted nervously to the Polish balance of payments crisis by curtailing credits to other Eastern European countries and withdrawing deposits from them, causing liquidity crises, disruption of imports and supplies, and a slow-down of economic growth in those countries. When martial law was declared at the end of 1981 the Western governments suspended the negotiations on debt rescheduling for obligations due for 1982 and imposed credit and economic sanctions. Poland responded by suspending payments to government creditors. As in 1981, the banks agreed in August 1982 to reschedule 95 per cent of the principal due in that year and also agreed to relend one-half of the interest payments to Poland in the form of short-term trade credits to finance Western imports. Poland had arrears (including those to Western governments) of over US $7 billion in 1982 (CIA 1986b: 160). Despite the debt rescheduling agreements reached sooner or later with all its Western creditors (banks and governments), the debt burden was one of the basic obstacles to sustained economic recovery.

CONCLUSION

Poland's export capability was low in comparison both with the small European CMEA countries and with market economies at a comparable level of economic development. The rapid growth of investment, imports of Western capital and technology during the first half of the 1970s did not lead to an export boost. On the contrary, export performance in 1970–82, hard currency exports in particular, was relatively worse than the export achievement of the 1960s. The efficiency of export production was deteriorating. Poland's underperformance in hard currency exports was mainly a result of both basic errors in Gierek's new development strategy and systemic deficiencies of the CPEs.

The rapid growth of consumption and (real) wages, which was accompanied by an insufficient growth in labour productivity, contributed to the wage drift, domestic imbalances and inflation. A growing proportion of production of exportable goods was absorbed by domestic demand, hence reducing actual export growth. The correlation between the rates of growth of investment and exports was weak. A large proportion of investment was allocated to industry with a preference for the expansion of capital goods industries (machinery, equipment and means of transportation), oriented towards domestic demand and import substitution. A high proportion of the investment projects developed (iron and steel, chemicals, building materials) had high material, fuel and energy intensity of production and hence were import biased. With the exception of a small number of primary and industrial products (coal, coke, sulphur, metal working machinery), the degree of Poland's export specialization was low. The share of primary products, intermediate and industrial final products with a relatively low degree of processing was relatively high in total Western exports. Poland faced growing competition from the NICs and lost the battle in the OECD export market for major items of manufactured products.

The rapid growth of Western imports of machinery, production processes and licences contributed to an increasing dependence of Poland's current production on hard currency imports of industrial inputs. The excessive and erratic fluctuations in Western imports and their drastic cuts from 1977, due to weak export performance and the rising burden of debt servicing, led to grave economic dislocations and contributed significantly to the economic crisis of 1979–82.

The domestic price and incentive systems were increasingly distorted, and foreign trade planning and regulation relied more on administrative measures. Imports, exports and hard currency allocation were increasingly determined by *ad hoc* bargaining and lobbying between central planner, ministries, industrial associations and enterprises. The so-called open-ended planning contributed considerably to the unchecked growth of hard currency trade deficits and the debt trap. A growing proportion of the new loans, contracted under more stringent conditions, were devoted to covering the imports of industrial inputs for current production, grain and the costs of servicing the debts. The debt structure was deteriorating, aggravated by a rapid rise of interest rates in international money markets and a rapid decline in Poland's creditworthiness, making a financial crisis inevitable. The outbreak of the economic and political crises in the summer of 1980, combined with a large fall in the output of coal and agricultural production (two main hard currency export earners) and grave market imbalances, aggravated the balance of payments crisis and forced Poland to seek debt rescheduling.

3

INFLATION

INTRODUCTION

This chapter describes and analyses various aspects of inflation in Poland, focusing mainly on the period 1971–82. It is confined to inflation in the consumer goods market. Shortages and price rises in the producer goods market are also important, and have consequences for the consumer goods market, but will not be analysed here. As a starting point, the chapter begins with a description and analysis of open (official) inflation in Poland. It is well-known that in CPEs open price increases do not fully capture the complex nature of inflation. Hence a discussion of certain aspects of hidden and repressed inflation is necessary for a good understanding of the nature of inflation in CPEs in general and in Poland in particular. The chapter will further describe the relationship between inflation and the economic collapse of 1980–2, followed by a brief discussion of the causes of inflation, and a conclusion.

OPEN INFLATION

Inflation, 1945–70

The drastic monetary reform introduced in April 1945 initially succeeded in mopping up the large 'inflationary overhang' accumulated during the Second World War. This helped to achieve a relatively stable consumer market and prices until the fourth quarter of 1946. But in 1947 consumer prices increased by 30–5 per cent, followed by a lower price increase in 1948, thanks largely to a good harvest and the favourable results of the post-war economic recovery programme (A. Wernik 1984a: 25).

Starting with an acceleration of investment growth in 1949, which prepared the way for the 'forced industrialization' programme contained in the Six Year Plan (1950–5), excess money, inflation and shortages flared up again. Retail trade and distribution were additionally disrupted by the campaign against private trade and for nationalization of trade ('bitwa o handel') in 1947–9. The conversion of saving deposits at a rate of three new to 100 old zlotys and cash at one to 100 resulting from the monetary reform of October 1950, which meant that two-thirds of the people's cash holdings were confiscated (J. Montias 1962: 69–70), was unable to arrest the upward movement of prices in the following years.

By the end of 1953, the official cost of living index stood at 233 (1949=100). This high open inflation was accompanied by great market imbalances, extensive black market activity and shortages. The regime introduced rationing of basic consumer goods such as meat, edible fat, sugar and soap in 1951–2. Employment, money income and the wage fund rose rapidly, largely resulting from the fast growth of productive investment, allocated mainly to the producer goods sector and the armaments industry.[1] Agricultural production dropped substantially in 1951–3 as a result of the collectivization drive, the imposition of heavy (progressive) taxation and the obligatory delivery of agricultural products, and also the unfavourable weather conditions. It has been estimated that average real wages fell by 7–13 per cent in 1952–3 (J. Meller 1977: 55), but the fall was recovered during the last two years of the Six Year Plan (1950–5).

The price and wage reforms of 1953, in combination with the decline in the rates of growth of both investment and employment, plus a relative improvement in agricultural output, helped to stabilize the consumer market and prices in 1954–6. Disposable income increased considerably in 1956–7, generated by a rapid growth in wage rates following the workers' protests in 1956, an increase in pensions and a considerable growth of the income of the peasantry due to an increase in both production and procurement prices. With the exception of the years 1956–7, official price increases were low during the second half of the 1950s.

Whereas in the 1950s the officially registered average consumer price increase was 6.9 per cent annually, it dropped to only 1.8 per cent in the 1960s. Inflationary pressure and excess demand in the 1960s were relatively moderate. The government pursued a deflationary incomes policy by curbing wage growth and keeping procument prices of agricultural products low. The average annual growth of real wages – according to official data – was only 1.8 per cent in the 1960s, which was low compared both to the rate of growth of real wages in other CMEA countries[2] and to Poland's economic growth. A large portion of the growth in the net material product was allocated to productive investment so that the rate of investment grew from 16.1 per cent in 1960 to 20.5 per cent in 1970.

The moderate excess aggregate demand prevailing in the 1960s was accompanied, however, by individual market imbalances, an unattractive product mix and poor quality of the products. Meat production and supply were persistently short. The meat price rise of 1967 (after which the price of meat in the state shops remained stable until 1977) was unable to balance the meat market partly due to a relatively high income elasticity of demand. Housing and durable consumer goods (cars, electronics, households equipments and furniture) were in short supply. The outdated and unattractive product mix, low quality and obsolete designs of durable consumer goods offered to the buyers, led to growing unsaleable inventories (A. Wernik 1984a: 33) and magnified the perception of a near stagnation of consumption in the 1960s. Moreover, consumers' deprivation and frustration were aggravated by the poor and insufficient retail trade outlets, so that shopping for even basic necessities was troublesome (J. Turcan 1977).

The declining rate of economic growth and the increasing rate of capital investment, particularly during the second half of the 1960s, combined with a near stagnation (or fall) of real wages during 1968–70 and a deep political malaise after the 'March event' in 1968, all reflected the critical political and economic situation. Gomulka's 'selective development' strategy and the so-called 'new incentive' system, if they had been implemented, would have led to a real wage freeze or even a drop in real wages for certain groups of workers and employees. The aborted price increase for basic foodstuffs in December 1970 precipitated the crisis which brought a sharp turn in Poland's economic policy under Gierek's leadership.

Inflation, 1971–82

Under strong protests and pressure of the workers (strikes in Łodz and threats of strike elsewhere) the new leadership under Gierek was forced to freeze the planned price increase of December 1970. It decided formally on 1 March 1971 to freeze food prices initially until the end of 1972. Price cuts of certain industrial consumer goods, announced in December 1970, were retained. The new leadership abandoned the old deflationary incomes policy and introduced instead the so-called active wage policy making rapid growth of wages and consumption an engine of economic growth. Actually Gierek's new economic growth model opted implicitly for moderate inflation (presumably subject to regulation) of 2–4 per cent per annum, an idea influenced to some extent by Western economic growth doctrines of the 1960s (G. Kołodko 1987: 175). The implementation of Gierek's economic growth strategy showed that the assumption of moderate inflation was an illusion. Official inflation developed from being insignificant in the early 1970s to three-digits in 1982, accompanied by a deep economic crisis and shortages.

Personal money income (net of taxes) increased on average by 12.5 per cent yearly in 1971–3 which was matched by a yearly average increase of 11 per cent in retail sales of goods and services at current prices (see Table 3.6). Production of agricultural marketed products and industrial consumer goods increased on average by 6.4 and 10.1 per cent per annum respectively during 1971–3 (see Table 3.2). The rapid growth of imports of both consumer goods and producer goods for the production of consumer goods led to a considerable improvement in the situation in the consumer market. The official consumer price index fell slightly in 1971–2 and only in 1973 was a price rise of 3 per cent recorded, caused mainly by a price increase of food in the private market and non-food items (shoes, furniture) in the state retail shops.

Table 3.1 Annual price changes (in per cent and in comparison with preceding year) of goods and services bought by the population in Poland, 1961–82

	Goods and services bought by the population	*Consumption goods*	*Foodstuffs (excluding alcoholic beverages)*	*State and cooperative retail shops*	*Restaurants, cafeterias etc.*	*Private markets*	*Non-food consumption goods*	*Consumption services*	*Non-consumption goods*	*Non-consumption services*
1961	0.7	0.6	1.2	1.3	2.8	−0.7	−0.1	1.2	2.0	2.6
1962	2.5	2.6	4.5	2.8	4.6	13.6	0.2	0.8	3.4	1.8
1963	0.8	0.4	−1.6	−0.2	2.2	−1.3	3.1	5.2	0.5	2.5
1964	1.2	1.1	1.2	1.6	3.4	−2.6	1.1	1.7	0.4	1.7
1965	0.9	0.7	1.3	0.6	2.3	4.0	0	2.6	0.6	0.3
1966	1.2	0	−0.9	−0.3	0	−4.7	1.3	10.2	1.8	0.5
1967	1.5	1.4	1.3	0.5	1.6	4.8	1.4	2.9	0.5	2.7
1968	1.6	1.5	2.6	2.4	3.5	3.0	0	2.9	0.3	2.2
1969	1.4	1.5	2.7	1.7	2.4	7.6	0.1	0.1	0.1	1.1
1970	1.1	1.2	2.2	2.7	5.1	−2.4	−0.1	0.5	0.8	1.9
1971	−0.1	−0.2	1.9	1.2	0.9	7.6	−2.8	0.3	5.7	1.1
1972	0	−0.1	−0.1	−0.8	−1.9	4.0	−0.1	0.6	0.1	0.9
1973	2.8	3.0	1.1	1.0	0.1	2.1	5.8	1.9	1.0	3.2
1974	7.1	7.2	6.2	1.6	17.4	18.2	3.6	6.5	2.1	5.3
1975	3.0	3.2	0.5	0.2	1.2	1.4	6.3	1.7	1.0	5.2
1976	4.4	4.6	4.6	2.7	7.4	19.3	6.0	3.2	16.8	5.4
1977	4.9	5.0	7.4	6.0	12.9	10.6	4.7	4.8	15.6	12.0

Table 3.1 continued.

	Goods and services bought by the population	*Consumption goods*	*Foodstuffs (excluding alcoholic beverages)*	*State and cooperative retail shops*	*Restaurants, cafeterias etc.*	*Private markets*	*Non-food consumption goods*	*Consumption services*	*Non-consumption goods*	*Non-consumption services*
1978	8.1	8.8	7.4	6.3	9.3	13.2	7.3	3.9	1.8	5.8
1979	7.0	7.1	7.5	8.7	3.5	3.7	5.9	6.6	2.1	8.0
1980	9.4	9.6	12.8	10.0	10.1	32.3	8.5	8.2	3.9	8.4
1981	21.2	22.1	22.5	14.6	19.7	56.4	13.1	15.3	18.6	27.1
1982	110.8	106.8	136.3	162.8	117.0	76.6	85.4	62.9	136.1	102.1
1961–5[a]	1.3	1.1	1.3	1.2	3.1	3.4	0.9	2.3	1.4	1.8
1966–70[a]	1.3	1.1	1.6	1.5	2.5	2.6	0.5	3.3	0.7	1.7
1971–5[a]	2.5	2.7	2.0	0.7	3.7	6.7	3.1	2.2	2.0	3.1
1976–80[a]	6.8	7.0	7.9	6.7	8.6	15.8	6.5	5.3	8.0	7.9
1981–2[a]	61.0	64.5	79.4	88.7	66.5	66.5	49.3	39.1	77.3	64.5

Source: Statistical Yearbooks of various years.
Note: [a] Average per year.

The economic boom (high growth of the economy, investment, consumption and real wages) of 1971–3 and the prevailing general optimism were in sharp contrast with the near stagnation of real wages and political malaise of 1968–70. The successful mobilization of the so-called shallow economic growth reserves (higher supply of raw materials and industrial inputs, greater productive capacity utilization and a deal with the peasantry) and conditional cooperation of the workers contributed significantly to the economic boom.

Gierek's repeated requests to the workers for 'help' to solve Poland's economic difficulties by appealing directly to their self-interest in better work, which was to be compensated by higher income, initially yielded good results. The relaxation of part of the rigid administrative rules concerning wage fund regulation and the subsequent growth of wages helped to stimulate relatively high growth in the productivity of labour and fixed assets (P. Bożyk 1983: 37–9). Moreover, the new leadership exploited, initially with some success, its political bonus, utilizing economic growth reserves which originated from the 'errors' of the previous leadership (W. Kuczyński 1981: 87).

On the whole the consumer market could be described as satisfactory during the first years of the 1970s. Official price increases were insignificant. An important part of the potential excess demand was absorbed by a significant rise in the ratio of money (and savings) balances to household money income in the years 1971–4. A number of Polish economists interpreted this increase in the savings ratio as an expression by households of cautious optimism about the

Table 3.2 Changes in retail prices, output of marketed agricultural products and industrial consumer goods, 1971–82
(preceding year = 100)

Years	*Retail prices in state shops*		*Output (constant prices of 1970)*	
	Food	*Industrial cons. goods*	*Marketed agric. products*	*Industrial cons. goods*
1971	101.5	97.2	103.6	108.2
1972	99.2	99.9	108.4	111.0
1973	101.0	105.8	107.3	110.8
1974	101.6	103.6	101.6	110.6
1975	100.2	106.2	97.9	111.4
1976	102.7	105.8	98.9	108.8
1977	106.0	104.7	101.4	107.3
1978	106.3	107.3	104.1	105.3
1979	108.5	106.0	98.5	102.2
1980	110.1	108.5	89.3	100.0
1981	114.6	110.9	88.6	91.4
1982	262.8	185.6	104.2	96.4

Source: Z. Krasiński, H. Mruk and H. Szulce, *Ceny a rynek*, 1985: 170.

future and expectation for the future of a better and more varied supply of durable consumer goods, on which to spend their savings (A. Wernik 1984b: 30; M. Pohorille 1982: 193).

Despite the relatively satisfactory market situation in the early 1970s, it became clear that inflationary pressure and shortages were growing from the end of the first half of 1973. The supply of meat, durable consumer goods, housing and services was insufficient to meet the growing demand. Meat supply became increasingly short and people were queuing from 3 a.m. to buy it. The search for goods on which to spend the available money became more intense. For instance, when visas for travel to the German Democratic Republic were abolished, the number of Poles visiting this country increased from 142,000 in 1970 to almost 7 million in 1974. Many of them were in search of goods unavailable in Poland (R. Leslie 1980: 434).

According to official figures, the price of consumer goods increased by 7.2 per cent in 1974, the second highest official inflation level since 1957. On average, food prices rose by about 6.2 per cent in 1974, which consisted of a 17.4 per cent price rise of prepared food sold in restaurants, an 18.2 per cent price rise of food sold in private markets, but only a 1.6 per cent price rise of food sold in the state retail shops. Alcoholic drink rose on average by 25 per cent whilst prices of services went up on average by 10 per cent in 1974. The official consumer price increase in 1975 was less than the preceding year.

Polish economists complained that the government did not have a consistent price policy which strove for a rationalization of consumption and an orderly adjustment of demand to production. The main aim of the price policy was to siphon off excess purchasing power through price increases. The monopoly position of enterprises or sellers' market conditions encouraged uncontrolled price increases which aggravated the absence of a consistent price policy.

By the end of 1973 the Polish economy was overheated and prudent economic policy required that the leadership put an immediate brake on the rapid growth of investment, consumption and real wages. However, the regime decided instead to step up the growth targets for industrial investment, consumption and real wages for the last two years of the Five Year Plan (1971–5). The actual growth of investment, consumption and real wages was even higher than the planned targets (see Chapter 1, p. 14).

Overestimation of Poland's investment absorption capacity, false evaluation of the expected 'investment harvest' (i.e the result of investment in the form of growth of production) and easy access to Western credits encouraged the regime's decision to prolong the economic boom. The inflationary pressure generated by the rapid growth of both investment and disposable income could be alleviated initially by the fast growth of trade deficits with the West, financed largely by credits. But the overdose of both investment and Western credits led to a drastic fall in investment efficiency and hence contributed directly or indirectly to inflation.

The price freeze on basic food at state retail shops and certain other services was maintained longer than initially planned. Moreover, a high growth of consumption and a stable price of basic consumer goods and services had become a condition for an agreeable and seemingly harmonious relationship between the regime and society during the first half of the 1970s. For the regime, the so-called 'December event' of 1970, as the fall of Gomulka following the aborted price rise of basic consumer goods and the workers' riot became known, haunted the Gierek leadership and reminded it of its own possible fate.

As explained in previous chapters, by 1975 Gierek's growth strategy had begun to fail. This was partly due to factors which were beyond Poland's control (unfavourable weather, economic recession in the West). To a large extent, however, it was due to poor economic policy and inadequate control over the economy (excessive growth of industrial investment, investment tension, wage drift, inadequate hard currency export growth) and also to the systemic defects of the CPEs. Harvests were unfavourable in 1974–5 and there was a rapidly growing volume of Western debts and a critical debt service ratio.

The VIIth Congress of the Polish United Workers Party, held in December 1975, praising Gierek's economic achievement during the first half of the 1970s, recommended lower targets of economic growth, investment, consumption and real wages for the second half of the 1970s, combined with a faster growth of Western exports. The Congress was also convinced that a considerable price increase of consumer goods (food in particular) and services was inevitable in the near future. Price increases were planned for the near future, according to Gierek, after careful analysis and 'consultation with the working people'.[3] The leadership hoped that it would succeed in convincing the population of the economic necessity of a significant slow-down of consumption growth during the second half of the 1970s, following a five-year rapid rise in the standard of living. A price increase of consumer goods and a significant slow-down of consumption growth would enable the economy to maintain a high level of Western imports of producer goods, allowing a moderate growth of investment and a high rate of utilization of the newly installed industrial capacity.

Without real prior consultation with the population as promised by the leadership, an across-the-board price rise for basic foodstuffs was announced in June 1976. It was planned that on average the price of food would go up by 39 per cent, and the price of meat would increase by 69 per cent. As part of the government package to encourage the peasantry to produce more, state procurement prices for agricultural products were to be raised. Price compensation for the low income group was promised. It was estimated that the effect of the price increases would be an increase in the cost of living of 16 per cent (Z. Szeliga 1976).

Within twenty-four hours the regime withdrew the price hike, with great loss of prestige, under strong pressure from strikes in a number of plants in Warsaw and other towns. The relationship with the population deteriorated considerably and the conditionality of the workers' support for Gierek was clearly shown. This Pyrrhic victory for the workers made it more difficult to correct the economic imbalances and inflation in the future. Shortages of consumer goods became more intense partly because of a household shopping spree in anticipation of price increases. The households' saving ratio began to drop after 1974, reflecting partly a growing market shortage and partly a future expectation of higher inflation as well as the negative real interest rates.[4] A two-tier distribution of sugar, one with ration cards and the other being free purchase at a higher price, was introduced in August 1976. One month later the government introduced coal rationing for household consumption. The latter caused widespread discontent among the population, the more so since Poland was the world's fourth biggest producer and the second largest exporter of coal after the United States of America.

The so-called economic manoeuvre, a medium-run economic restructuring programme with new priorities, launched in early 1977, completely failed to achieve its main objectives of boosting Western exports and the output of agriculture and consumer goods. The production and supply of consumer goods deteriorated rapidly, particularly during the last two years of the 1970s.

The average growth of marketed agricultural products and industrial consumer goods fell from 3.8 and 10 per cent respectively per annum in 1971–5 to −1.5 per cent and 4.7 per cent in 1976–80 (see Table 3.2). In 1979–80 the volume of market supply of certain food items like sugar and edible fat fell by 2 per cent; the supply of vodka dropped by 12 per cent; and the supply of industrial consumer goods like clothing, passenger cars, refrigerators and deep freezes, washing machines and vacuum cleaners dropped by between 4.5 and 10 per cent (see Table 3.3). Despite a slow-down in the rate of growth of money income in the years from 1978 until mid 1980, the inflationary spiral and market disequilibrium could not be arrested because of a considerable drop in the rate of production and supply of consumer goods.

Inflation was considerably higher during the second half of the 1970s. According to official figures, the annual average price rise of consumer goods for the years 1976–80 was 7 per cent, compared to 2.7 per cent in the years 1971–5. Food prices in state retail shops increased on average by 6.7 per cent per annum in the years 1976–80, compared to only 0.7 per cent per annum in the years 1971–5. The average price rise of foodstuffs (including the average price rise of food in state retail shops) in the years 1976–80 was higher than the average price rise of non-food consumer goods (see Table 3.1). This trend of relatively higher prices of food products was accelerated and magnified in 1981–2.

The demand for 'consumption services' exceeded supply considerably and the excess demand was growing during the 1970s, particularly in the second half of the decade (M. Pohorille 1982: 163). It is interesting to observe that in the 1970s, on average, the growth of prices of consumer goods (59.7 per cent) was higher than the growth of prices of 'consumption services' (50.2 per cent). Within the category of 'consumption services', the official price index for central heating, warm water, and gas increased by only 7.1 per cent and 19.8 per cent respectively in the years 1970–80; electricity tariffs remained unchanged; rent for highly subsidized housing ('dom kwaterunkowy') rose by 19.7 per cent, public transport rose by 39 per cent; while the price index for education expenses (school requirements, creche, kindergarten) increased by 137 per cent (*Ceny Detaliczne 1971–1985* 1985: 2–3 and 22–3).

The government's attempt to reduce excess demand for meat through general sharp price rises in 1970 and 1976 failed. Instead of a 'shock' price rise, in 1977 the government introduced parallel state retail shops for meat and meat products by opening 'commercial shops' offering better (real or alleged) quality meat for much higher prices. The share of 'commercial' sales, particularly quality meat, was rising in the last years of the 1970s. The government's decision, in July 1980, to increase substantially the share of 'commercial' sales of meat in total sales, triggered a wave of workers' strikes at different plants and regions and the birth of Solidarność.

The economic and political situation deteriorated rapidly in 1981–2. The exceptionally bad harvests of 1979–80, combined with the drastic fall in Western imports and a substantial cut in average weekly working hours in 1981 led to a dramatic fall of output in general and consumer goods in particular. From the second half of 1980 the growth of money income of the population exploded, contributing to a complete dislocation and collapse of the consumer market in 1981. The official consumer goods price index jumped by 22.1 per cent, and was accompanied by large market imbalances and higher black market prices, panic buying, hoarding and a flight from the zloty. The black market rate for the US dollar increased rapidly, caused by a great demand for a hedge against rapidly growing inflation.

The consumer price increase, announced by the government in 1981, had a limited scope as it was confined largely to price rises for alcoholic drinks, bread and tobacco. This was followed in early 1982 by a drastic and comprehensive increase of both wholesale prices of basic raw materials, fuel and semi-finished products, and retail prices of basic consumer goods and services. This drastic price increase was introduced as an integral part of a package of economic reforms and a realistic incomes policy, which was carried out under martial law. According to official figures the consumer goods retail price index increased by 106.8 per cent (of which the food price increase was 163 per cent) in 1982, accompanied by a deep fall in output, shortages, rationing, the black market, queuing and repressed inflation, a situation described by Polish economists as 'barbaric inflation' (G. Kołodko 1987: 208–18). In 1982 food became relatively more expensive, particularly in the state retail shops, and increased much faster than the prices of non-food consumer goods and services.

Basic foodstuffs (meat, cereal products, edible fat, cooking oil) and a number of industrial consumer goods (shoes, cigarettes, vodka) were rationed in 1980. Moreover *de facto* rationing at the local level covering a wider range of products, alongside the official national list, was practised on a wide scale. According to Z. Krasiński, a former Minister of Price Regulation, around 75 per cent of the value of marketed supplies of food and 30 per cent of industrial consumer goods were

Table 3.3 Market delivery of selected consumer goods, 1975–82

	Units	1975	1976	1977	1978	1979	1980	1981	1982	$\frac{1975}{1970} \times 100$	$\frac{1980}{1975} \times 100$	$\frac{1980}{1978} \times 100$	$\frac{1982}{1980} \times 100$
Food, beverages and cigarettes													
Bread	1000 tons	2665	2804	2711	2771	2707	2799	3017	3001	109.3	105.0	101.0	107.2
Noodles	1000 tons	72	106	69	82	86	90	96	87	138.5	125.0	189.8	96.2
Groats	1000 tons	190	228	243	256	275	303	322	219	128.4	139.4	118.3	82.2
Meat, meat products and offal	1000 tons	1728	1792	1816	1889	2005	2034	1675	1426	172.1	117.7	107.6	69.7
Fish and fish products	1000 tons	226	251	246	241	252	271	240	202	117.1	119.9	112.4	74.2
Edible fat (trade weight)	1000 tons	519	551	562	583	600	618	617	530	123.3	119.0	106.0	86.7
Sugar	1000 tons	1163	1116	1060	1080	1112	1059	88	1094	120.9	91.0	98.0	103.3
Edible potatoes	1000 tons	1367	1594	1324	1340	1686	1336	1090	1274	170.9	97.7	99.7	95.3
Vegatables (fresh)	1000 tons	667	672	677	729	860	789	752	761	117.4	118.2	108.2	96.4
Fruits (domestic prod. and fresh)	1000 tons	263	310	262	213	313	264	271	303	132.2	100.0	123.4	115.2
Milk	mill. lit.	1651	1723	1842	2166	2312	2389	2667	2659	132.3	144.7	110.2	111.3
Coffee	1000 tons	27	27	22	26	32	29	28	15	260.2	107.4	111.5	51.7
Tea	1000 tons	15	16	15	19	22	25	25	27	185.1	166.6	131.5	108.0
Vodka (pure content)	mill. lit.	46	54	60	52	41	46	78	45	200.0	100.0	88.4	97.8
Beer	mill. lit	1259	1200	1175	1106	1088	1082	1026	1032	123.3	85.9	97.8	95.3
Cigarettes	bill. pcs.	84	89	91	91	92	94	90	91	123.5	111.9	103.2	96.8

Non-food consumer goods													
Clothing	mill. m.	538	549	550	529	509	399	322	224	117.9	74.7	76.3	56.1
Garments	bill. zl[a]	200	–	–	207	–	210	178	157	149.5	100.5	97.1	78.1
Shoes (leather, cloth and rubber)	mill. pairs	128	120	117	115	120	122	109	110	134.5	95.3	106.0	90.1
Furniture	bill. zl.[a]	83	–	–	101	–	94	87	77	180.5	113.2	93.0	81.9
Radio sets	1000 pcs.	1588	1820	2005	2154	2193	2135	2121	1508	154.2	134.4	99.1	70.6
Televisions	1000 pcs.	1071	1018	1044	1063	1023	923	813	630	195.9	86.1	86.8	68.2
Tape recorders	1000 pcs.	542	603	589	621	712	652	444	287	584.8	120.2	104.9	44.0
Washing machines and spin driers	1000 pcs.	702	771	791	871	795	822	746	759	162.5	117.0	94.3	92.3
of which: automatic washing machines	1000 pcs.	64	160	215	291	317	357	326	310	–	–	122.6	86.8
Sewing machines	1000 pcs.	161	162	183	184	250	220	238	203	132.0	136.6	119.5	92.2
Refrigerators and deepfreezes	1000 pcs.	926	1027	1035	979	943	708	648	590	248.3	76.4	72.3	83.3
Vacuum cleaners	1000 pcs.	862	761	753	785	668	711	639	637	215.0	82.4	90.5	89.5
Passenger cars	1000 pcs.	111	146	193	224	218	165	143	160	226.5	148.6	73.0	96.9
Motorcycles	1000 pcs.	100	93	92	102	103	108	90	96	101.0	108.0	105.8	88.8
Toilet soap	1000 tons	42	38	36	38	45	39	35	42	182.6	92.8	102.6	107.6
Washing powder	1000 tons	141	139	157	154	176	181	178	210	114.6	128.3	117.5	116.0
Coal and coal briquets	mill. tons	25	27	27	28	29	32	30	30	108.7	128.0	114.2	93.7

Sources: *Rocznik Statystyczny 1987*, 1987: 303; *Rocznik Statystyczny 1981* 1981: 433–4; *Rocznik Statystyczny 1984* 1984: 372–3.
Note: [a]at constant prices.

rationed by the summer of 1982 (Z. Krasiński 1984: 160). Rationing, which may be justified on socio-political grounds (protection of the lowest income group, state paternalism, prevention of riots) will, however, lead to misallocation of resources and a distortion of prices and incentives. For instance, the rationing of alcohol and cigarettes encouraged a rise in the consumption of both.[5] This was a sort of 'forced purchase and consumption' of the rationed items by ration card holders, while leaving other people, who were willing to purchase and to consume above the rationed amount, short of them. Swap operations were possible but inconvenient.

HIDDEN AND REPRESSED INFLATION

In a reasonably well-functioning market economy, a price change is an expression of an adjustment process, balancing market demand and the supply of inputs and outputs. In such a situation price increases can be identified to a high degree of approximation with inflation. It was commonly accepted by many observers of the CPEs that official consumer price indices understated the actual rate of inflation. In general, planners were inclined to prefer price rigidity for a considerable time, queuing, and quantity adjustment of demand and supply instead of flexible, market-clearing price adjustment or open inflation.

Inflationary pressures which do not take the form of official price increases can express itself in the form of hidden and/or repressed inflation. In this connection a number of economists are of the view that official consumer price indices were less relevant as an indication of inflation because of permanent shortages and imbalances, attributed to systemic-specific features of the CPEs (J. Mujżel 1975: 818; J. Kornai 1980), economic policy distortions and statistical manipulations. This part of the chapter will discuss briefly various aspects and problems of hidden and repressed inflation in Poland.

Hidden inflation

In general, unrecorded or hidden inflation can occur for at least three reasons:

1 price rises above the official level due to quality deterioration of products, bribery and reselling state goods at higher prices;
2 understatement of the relative weight of goods with a relatively faster price rise;
3 forced substitution of (unavailable) goods at low prices by goods with higher prices.

(D. Nuti 1986a: 45–6)

These factors appeared in various combinations in Poland at different times.

Hidden inflation can result from the pricing behaviour of firms and enterprises. Despite rigid state price control covering a wide range of products and services, in many cases firms and enterprises succeeded in pocketing extra profits by hidden price rises through the manipulation of the product mix, product quality and cost of production. Allegedly 'new products' (old products with new packaging, colour etc.) sold for higher prices and the withdrawal of low-priced items while keeping them in the statistical consumer's basket were well-known examples of hidden inflation. Monopoly power or sellers' market position of the firms and enterprises encouraged hidden price rises.

The economic reform of the system of 'large corporations' (WOG) of 1973–5, operating under new rules which gave them greater autonomy, reinforced industrial concentration and the monopoly position of the large corporations. In a number of industrial branches like clothing, confectionary and furniture industries, there were hardly any technological arguments favouring greater production concentration (D.M. Nuti 1977: 348–52). The WOG reform gave more discretion to corporations to fix prices of the so-called market novelties. In their efforts to maximize value added and profits, corporations made wide use of their monopoly power, raising prices through manipulation of the product mix, quality and pseudo-new products (P. Wanless 1980: 41–2; L. Miastkowski 1979: 534). So hidden inflation was frequently engineered by enterprises trying to improve the plan realization and bonuses (J. Winiecki 1985: 41).

It is most likely that hidden inflation was increasing when the divergence between real and official inflation was thought to be growing after 1975 (*Uwagi* 1979: 11). It is argued that the fall in households' savings ratio in 1975–7 was partly caused by a rise in both official and hidden inflation (J. Winiecki 1986: 213). In a discussion on statistical manipulations, organized by the economic weekly *Życie Gospodarcze* in late 1980, the Vice-Chairman of the Central Statistical Office admitted amongst other things that the bread price actually rose by 57 per cent in the years 1976–80, whilst according to official figures the bread price was unchanged (*Życie Gospodarcze*, no. 40: 1980)! Although the Polish Statistical Office made regular studies of inflation in the 1970s, so far there is no official estimate of hidden inflation.[6]

The quality of the products, which had been chronically unsatisfactory, deteriorated particularly rapidly during the deepening of the economic crisis in the early 1980s. Quality deterioration in the early 1980s was estimated to vary between 10–15 per cent of the value of industrial production (E. Kindlarski 1984). It also caused widespread dissatisfaction and frustration among consumers. The quality deterioration was partly due to drastic cuts in Western imports of industrial inputs, a substitution of Western industrial inputs by inferior domestic production and CMEA imports, and a growing disinvestment of installed machinery and equipments. Moreover, a continuation of the traditional striving to maximize output quantity in CPEs (M. Ellman 1989), which occurred at the expense of quality, contributed significantly to product quality deterioration and misallocation of resources.

Using different methods of computation and approaches, a number of Western economists, who doubted the accuracy of official inflation figures in the

European CMEA countries, arrived at various estimates of hidden inflation and/or divergence between official and alternative (or implicit) consumer price indices for individual countries at different periods.[7] Table 3.4 shows official inflation rates and various estimates of alternative or implicit indices of consumer prices in Poland. The divergence between official and implicit price indices varied between 2.1 and 4.3 percentage points per annum during 1960–78, differing according to the individual author's estimate and period of time. The official price deflator tends to overestimate the growth of real wages and consumption. For instance, according to official figures, average real wages and consumption per capita increased by 3.9 per cent and 2.2 per cent respectively in 1980, whilst actually the supply of consumer goods and services at constant prices fell by around 5 per cent.

Repressed inflation

In general, the sum of official and hidden inflation was inversely related to repressed inflation, i.e the higher the rate of price inflation the less would be repressed inflation (J. Pajestka 1983: 341). Shortages, queuing and frustration of consumption intentions, which occurred in parallel with increasing liquid assets (money and savings) relative to incomes and sales, could be considered as signs of excess demand and repressed inflation. By themselves queues and an increase in households' savings ratios were not conclusive evidence of the existence of

Table 3.4 Estimates of hidden inflation in Poland, 1960–78

	Price indices 1970 = 100		*Average annual change (per cent)*		
	1975	*1978*	*1971–5*	*1976–8*	*1978*
Official: retail prices	113.3	134.1	2.5	5.9	8.1
Alternative[a]	131.8	168.5	5.7	8.0	8.9
			Average annual rates of inflation (1960–70) (per cent)		
Officially reported			1.2		
Estimate[b]			5.5		
			Average annual rates of inflation (1964–78) (per cent)		
Officially reported			2.9		
Estimate[c]			5.2		

Notes: [a]T. Alton *et. al.*, 'Official and Alternative Consumer Price Indices in Eastern Europe, Selected Years, 1960–78', *Working Papers*, L.W.I.F.R., New York, 1979, cited in D.M. Nuti 1986a: 50; [b]W.P.Culbertson Jr and R.C. Amacher, 'Inflation in the Planned Economies: Some Estimates for Eastern Europe', *Southern Economic Journal*, 45, 2, 1978: 393; [c]B. Askanas and K. Laski, 'Consumer Prices and Private Consumption in Poland and Austria', *Journal of Comparative Economics*, 9, 2, 1985: 168–9.

repressed inflation.[8] This information should be supplemented by careful observations of the actual state of the markets in order to arrive at a meaningful conclusion. It would also be unreasonable to consider, as some observers did, the vexations and frustrations resulting from queuing, shortages, forced substitutions, bribery and privileges as merely 'anecdotes'.

In Poland, a combination of administrative rationing, queueing and (parallel) markets was functioning in the market for housing, cars and certain food items (e.g meat). Administrative rationing of scarce goods and services contributed directly and indirectly to the black market, corruption and privileges for the few. 'Parallel currency', i.e. the sale of quality consumer goods which were in short supply for hard currency (PEWEX shops, POLMOT sales of cars and the purchase of flats in hard currency with a short waiting period), had existed for a long time[9] and its share was expanding.

The private market was not unimportant in the total sale of certain items such as food, fashionable articles (hats, smart clothes) and certain kind of services (tailoring, car-repairs). In the 1960s, the growth of the price level of food in the private market ('artykułów rolno-spożywczych na targowisku') was only slightly higher than in the state retail shops, and in both markets price rises were relatively low. The discrepancy between the price of food in 1974–81 in state shops and in the private market widened rapidly (see Table 3.5). Bearing in mind certain reservations in comparing both markets (the private market covered only a relatively narrow segment of food products, produced by the peasantry and sold in local markets), the growing discrepancy between prices in state shops and at the private market was conceived as an indication of growing repressed inflation in the state sector (B. Simatupang 1980: 582–3; P.T. Wanless 1985: 406–7).

Besides the legal private market, one should add other markets, ranging from 'grey' up to 'black' market, 'moonlighting', 'informal sector' or 'second economy', which were tolerated by the authorities and probably even indispensable for the functioning of the economy. Market disequilibrium, shortages and rationing encouraged the so-called 'second economy' extensively. A significant part of the unsatisfied demand in the 'first economy' found its outlet in the 'second economy', whose extent was expanding with the growing shortages and imbalances. The volume of the 'second economy' was estimated to be approximately 11–13 per cent of the disposable income of the population in 1982–83 (M. Wisniewski 1984; M. Bednarski 1984).

During the economic crisis and the ensuing severe market disruption, households' own production and self-help services were encouraged and their volume was growing. For instance the average share of households' consumption of meat originating from 'own production' grew from 16 per cent in 1980 to 24 per cent in 1983 (*Warunki Życia Ludności w Latach 1980–1983* 1984: 51). The 'unregistered' consumption of alcohol was growing in 1980–2. It was estimated that between 30–50 per cent of the consumption of strong alcoholic drink in Poland in 1982 originated from 'illicit distillation' (cited in *Spożycie Napojów*

Table 3.5 Indices of retail prices for food in Poland, 1960–82 (1960 = 100)

	1965	*1970*	*1971*	*1972*	*1973*	*1974*	*1975*	*1976*	*1977*	*1978*	*1979*	*1980*	*1981*	*1982*
All food	102.7	109.2	111.9	111.8	112.2	119.1	120.7	126.1	135.5	145.5	156.4	176.3	207.9	510.4
State and cooperative shops	102.4	107.7	109.3	108.4	109.6	111.3	111.5	114.5	121.4	129.0	140.2	154.0	176.5	463.8
Restaurants	109.0	122.3	124.3	121.9	122.0	143.2	144.9	156.3	178.8	192.1	198.8	218.9	262.0	568.6
Private market[a]	101.4	109.6	117.9	122.6	125.3	148.0	150	179.6	198.0	224.1	232.4	307.5	481.1	849.7
Line 4 divided by line 2 in per cent	99	102	108	113	114	133	135	157	163	174	166	200	273	183

Source: Statistical Yearbook of various years.
Note: [a]food and agricultural products.

Alkoholowych w Latach 1970–1983 1984: 25–6).

Table 3.6 shows basic magnitudes illustrating the formation of market (dis)equilibrium in Poland in the years 1970–82. Annual personal money income exceeded the value of retail turnover of goods and services over the whole period. Given money demand for transactions, the excess between personal money income and the value of retail turnover mainly took the form of increases in savings (money and saving account) of the population. The growth of savings was increasing in 1971–3 and again after 1977. The main difficulty in the assessment of repressed inflation however lies in the measurement and interpretation of the 'desired savings ratio'. Any notion of forced saving or repressed inflation is to a certain extent arbitrary. But in a situation in which market imbalances and price distortions were growing, as was the case during the late 1970s and early 1980s, and given the money demand for transactions, and the supply and price levels in state retail trade, a considerable part of households' savings was involuntary saving (inflationary overhang)[10] in the sense that it resulted from the non-availability of desired consumer goods at state prices.

The growing economic instability from the second half of the 1970s, plus new developments in the techniques of disequilibrium econometrics, have produced extensive and diverse theoretical and empirical studies of shortages, market imbalances and inflation in the CPEs. The new literature provides additional insights into the working of the CPEs. But it has also provoked sharp controversies on issues such as the very nature of economic shortages, forced substitution, price and quantity adjustments, excess demand and the possibility of (demand) aggregation in the CPEs. Moreover, the use of diverse approaches and disequilibrium econometric techiques have produced various empirical results and interpretations, leaving a number of theoretical and computational problems to be resolved in the future.

For the sake of simplicity, the shortage and disequilibrium models in the CPEs can be divided into three groups:

1 The shortage models, developed by J. Kornai (1980, 1986a, 1986b), characterize the CPEs by paternalistic relations between superiors and subordinates, non-price control mechanisms, sellers' markets and soft budget constraints. The models assume that demand for most goods and services chronically exceeds supply, but reject the concept of aggregate demand and the possibility of its economic estimation.
2 The disequilibrium indicator models, developed, amongst others, by A. Welfe (1988, 1989) and W. Charemza (1989a, 1989b), assume *a priori* permanent excess demand and repressed inflation which are known to be positive and are subject to econometric estimation.
3 The testable excess demand models, developed by R. Portes and his associates (1980, 1987), and V. Dlouhy (1989), make use of demand and supply equations plus the minimum condition, but without any assumption concerning excess demand, which can be positive, negative or close to zero.[11]

Table 3.6 Personal money income, retail turnover and savings of the population, 1970–82

	1970	*1971*	*1972*	*1973*	*1974*	*1975*	*1976*	*1977*	*1978*	*1979*	*1980*	*1981*	*1982*
Personal money income (net of tax payment) in bill. zl.	489	543	626	717	824	933	1040	1169	1271	1397	1535	1996	3265
Percentage growth over previous year	–	11.0	11.5	14.5	14.9	13.2	11.5	12.4	8.7	9.9	9.8	30.0	64.8
Retail turnover (goods and services) in current prices (bill. zl)	469	504	564	636	729	832	947	1070	1162	1277	1399	1712	2690
Percentage growth over previous year	–	8.3	11.9	12.8	11.5	11.4	13.8	13.0	8.5	9.9	9.6	22.3	78.0
In constant prices of 1970 (bill. zl)	465	490	550	625	670	760	810	845	860	880	905	860	710
Percentage growth over previous year	–	5.3	12.2	11.8	8.9	13.4	6.5	4.3	1.8	2.3	2.8	−5.9	−17.4
Savings (end year, bill. zl)	171	198	239	300	370	435	486	538	600	675	766	1050	1440
Percentage growth over previous year	–	16.4	20.7	25.6	23.3	17.5	11.7	10.6	11.5	12.5	13.4	37.0	37.4

Sources: *Rządowy raport o stanie gospodarki* 1981: 109 and 127; J. Górski, *Gospodarka 1981* 1982: 47; *Rocznik Statystyczny 1984* 1984: 112, 115, 368.

Table 3.7 shows estimates of excess demand and shortages for Poland according to testable excess demand models (Portes-type), disequilibrium indicators (Welfe and Charemza) and Kornai-type shortage models (J. Burkett 1985). The magnitude of consumption excess demand estimates by Welfe and Charemza are significantly higher (except for 1972) than the estimates by Portes and Burkett. According to the Portes estimates, aggregate supply exceeded demand during three years (1976, 1977 and 1978) in the second half of the 1970s and excess demand in 1979 and 1980 was low. On the other hand, direct observations of the actual market suggested heightened excess demand and repressed inflation. The Portes view has been challenged by Nuti (1986), Winiecki (1985), Podkaminer (1988) and Charemza (1989b).

Table 3.7 Estimates of excess demand and shortages for Poland (in per cent of quantity transacted)

Year	*PQWY*	*WA*	*CW*	*BJ*
1957	−3.6	–	–	0.8
1958	−3.9	–	–	0.9
1959	1.0	–	–	1.0
1960	4.4	–	–	0.9
1961	1.4	9.4	11.2	1.0
1962	−2.0	7.9	0.4	0.9
1963	−0.6	7.8	3.3	1.1
1964	−1.6	6.8	2.5	1.3
1965	1.8	6.6	2.5	1.3
1966	1.3	7.5	2.8	1.3
1967	−0.7	7.0	3.6	1.0
1968	2.5	6.9	2.5	1.2
1969	0.2	6.6	3.5	0.9
1970	−1.0	4.2	2.6	0.9
1971	2.5	5.5	6.5	1.4
1972	7.0	6.2	10.9	3.7
1973	2.7	7.0	15.4	1.3
1974	1.2	6.8	17.7	1.0
1975	2.8	6.4	20.6	1.2
1976	−2.9	6.6	22.2	0.7
1977	−0.1	7.4	28.1	0.8
1978	−8.7	6.6	31.7	0.6
1979	1.2	6.5	38.5	1.0
1980	1.2	6.8	38.9	0.8
1981	–	16.2	36.0	–
1982	–	12.3	37.4	–
1983	–	6.2	31.1	–
1984	–	4.9	33.2	–
1985	–	8.4	39.6	–

Sources: PQWY: Portes *et al.* (1987); WA: Welfe (1988); CW: Charemza (1989a, 1989b); BJ: Burkett (1985).

INFLATION AND ECONOMIC COLLAPSE, 1980–2

Gierek's import-led growth strategy led to a relatively high dependence of current industrial production and investment on Western imports. But the economic growth in the 1970s failed to create a viable export sector so that a balance of payments deficit was a built-in feature of the economy. The debt–service ratio in hard currency increased from 34 per cent in 1976 to 75 per cent in 1979, constraining imports severely. From 1977, Western imports were cut erratically and drastically. For instance the volume of Western imports dropped on average by 2.7 per cent per annum in 1976–80 and by 24.1 per cent per annum in 1981–2. Imports of capital goods suffered the largest cuts (see Table 2.4).

The drastic cut in Western imports led to great shortages, whose impact was magnified by the operation of the so-called import bottle-neck multiplier causing a fall in the rate of industrial productive capacity utilization to 60–70 per cent, and a decline in industrial output in 1980–2. The overinvestment drive during the first half of the 1970s was followed by a slight fall of productive investment growth in 1976–8 and a drastic cut in 1979–82. As a result, the volume of frozen investment grew rapidly (see Table 1.7), accompanied by a considerable delay in the completion of investment projects, hence leading to a great loss of output. The productivity of fixed capital (net material product per unit of fixed capital) declined continuously after 1976 (see Table In.1), accompanied by a high raw material and fuel intensity of production.

In the summer of 1980, the workers' strike committees in Gdańsk, Szczecin and Jastrzęby demanded, amongst other things, more free Saturdays and a shorter working week. Finally the regime yielded to the miners' demands for free Saturdays throughout the year starting from 1 January 1981, a forty-hour working week and the immediate ending of the four-shifts (round the clock and seven days a week) work system in coal mining. The government's offer of considerably higher wages for voluntary work on free Saturdays and an appeal by Solidarność in August helped to moderate the fall in coal output, but it generated extra purchasing power. The cut in the average working week, which caused a drastic decline in mining production, coal output in particular, and exports, contributed to growing shortages and constraint of Western imports and imbalances. The militarization of the coal industry, following the declaration of martial law in December 1981, combined with favourable wage offers (such as special ration cards for scarce consumer goods) to coal miners, helped to restore coal output to near pre-crisis level by 1982.

The drastic cut in Western imports seriously hurt the industrial sector producing agricultural inputs. In addition to the bad weather conditions and inconsistent agricultural policy, the large fall in output and supply of agricultural inputs (fertilizers, pesticides, equipment and machinery) contributed significantly to the poor harvest of 1979–80.

The yearly average output of grain in 1979–81 was around 13 per cent and 20 per cent less than the yearly average output of grain in 1976–8 and 1975–7 respectively. The fall in potato output (besides grain an important component of food and animal consumption) was even worse. State procurement of grain and meat fell proportionally more than the output decline. The massive Western import of grain and animal feed could only temporarily halt the fall in animal products. For instance the annual output and procurement of meat in 1981–2 were respectively 20 per cent and 27 per cent less than the yearly average in 1979–80.[12] The drop in agricultural output was aggravated by the unwillingness of the farmers to sell more than a minimum amount of agricultural products to the state for worthless money. Both contributed significantly to a dislocation of basic food markets.

As a result of the large output decline in 1979–82, the volume of market delivery (see Table 3.3) and the sales of consumer goods (foods, beverages, non-food consumer goods and consumer services) dropped considerably in 1980–2. In 1982 the value of retail sales of food, alcoholic drinks and non-food consumer goods (at constant prices) was 22.2 per cent, 24.8 per cent and 20.1 per cent respectively below the level of of 1980.[13] This large drop in the supply of consumer goods contributed significantly to a collapse of the consumer market in 1980–2.

The gap between personal money income and the value of market supply of goods and services at current retail prices was widening in 1978–81. The gap grew particularly quickly from the second half of 1980 until the end of 1981. Total money income grew by 53.3 per cent in 1978–81 compared with a growth of only 18.7 per cent of the value of market supply at current retail prices during

Table 3.8 Personal money income and market supply of consumer goods, 1979–82 (in billion current złotys)

	1979	*1980*	*1981*	*1982*
Wages	858	959	1210	1755
Growth in per cent	9.2	12.0	26.2	45.0
Social payments (pension-benefits etc.)	169	194	258	630
Growth in per cent	17.3	14.9	33.1	143.9
Sale of private farms' products	269	266	370	614
Growth in per cent	8.0	−1.2	39.4	65.8
Other income	20.3	224	252	405
Growth in per cent	7.2	10.0	12.5	60.9
Personal money income	1498	1642	2090	3403
Growth in per cent	10.1	9.7	27.3	62.8
Market supply of goods (at current retail prices)	1357	1416	1496	2855
Growth in per cent	7.7	4.3	5.6	97.8

Sources: 'Bilans pieniężnych przychodów i wydatkow ludności', *Bank i Kredyt*, 7–8, 1982: 184; 'Bilans pieniężnych przychodów i wydatkow ludności w 1982 r.', *Bank i Kredyt*, 6, 1983: 177; *Rocznik Statystyczny 1983* 1983: 346.

the same period (see Table 3.8). In the third quarter of 1980 the value of market supply increased by only 1 per cent, personal money income increased by around 10 per cent; and in the fourth quarter, market supply dropped by 1.6 per cent, which was accompanied by a 12 per cent increase of personal money income (*Rocznik Polityczny i Gospodarczy 1981–3* 1984: 239). The consumer market worsened further when market supply (at current retail prices) increased by only 5.6 per cent in 1981, accompanied by a 27.3 per cent growth of money income. The consumer market disequilibrium was aggravated by panic buying and a flight from the zloty.

The share of wages in total personal money income varied between 52 and 68 per cent in 1978–82, reaching its highest share in 1980 and its lowest in 1982. Average money wages increased between 6–9 per cent annually in 1976–9, which slightly exceeded the average growth in the official cost of living indices, despite the rapid drop in the growth of labour productivity. The increase in wages and social payments agreed between the regime and the Interfactory Strike Committees in Gdańsk, Szczecin and Jastrzęby in the summer of 1980 was further reinforced by local Solidarność demands for higher wages and improved working conditions. Average wages increased by 13.5 per cent in 1980 and 27.4 per cent in 1981 combined with a large drop in the net material product, supply of consumer goods and labour productivity, which reinforced the inflationary spiral. The regime itself was partly to be blamed for the rapid increase of wages and social payments in 1980–1. It yielded to the demands for higher wages and social payments without a great struggle. It tried to use 'money illusion' in order to stop the workers from advancing political demands and also to reduce the psychological impact of the economic crisis.

The rapid growth of social payments (31.1 per cent) in 1980–1 was the result of a considerable increase of both average pensions (and social benefits) and the number of pensioners (and recipients of social benefits) following the government policy of encouraging early retirement and paid leave for young mothers to care for children. With an unchanged level of procurement prices, farmers' money income from the sales of agricultural products dropped in 1980 due to a bad harvest. With slightly better harvests and drastic increases in procurement prices of agricultural products in 1981 and 1982, farmers' money incomes rose by 33.1 per cent and 143.9 per cent in 1981 and 1982 respectively. However, the drastic procurement price increases combined with the shortages of industrial products led to a great fall in the volume of agricultural product sales,[14] thus reinforcing inflationary pressure.

The deficit of the state budget intensified inflationary pressure. The officially measured deficit rose from only 26 billion zlotys (2.1 per cent of total budgetary expenditures or 1.3 per cent of the net material product) in 1980 to 131 billion zlotys in 1981 (8.9 per cent of total budgetary expenditures or 6.1 per cent of the net material product).[15] Direct subsidies for food, non-food consumer goods and services (passenger transport and municipal services) amounted to 178 billion zlotys in 1979 (9.3 per cent of the net material product). They increased to 219 billion zlotys (11 per cent of the net material product) and to 288 billion zlotys (13.3 per cent of the net material product) in 1980 and 1981 respectively. Direct subsidies for consumer goods and services increased to 428 billion zlotys in 1982 but they made up only 9 per cent of the net material product.[16]

The pseudo-political and economic reforms propagated by the regime in 1980–1 left intact the monopoly control of the political and economic spheres by the *nomenklatura*. The redistribution of income through drastic cuts of productive investment in 1979–81, in order to protect consumption from a still greater fall, was not perceived as such by society. With the deepening economic and political crises, far reaching economic austerity and an orderly adjustment of income, consumption and prices commensurate with the large decrease in net material product seemed unlikely when society had no confidence in the regime.

By 1981 the regime opted for martial law and instead of seeking a political solution, it enforced a militarization of basic production and work discipline and a drastic increase of consumer prices, accompanied by a large drop in real wages and consumption. The volume of sales of consumer goods and services fell by 17 per cent in 1982. Although the gap between personal income and the value of market supply at current prices was narrowed by the drastic price rise in 1982, it was not eliminated.

CAUSES OR SOURCES OF INFLATION

The preceding description and analysis of inflation in Poland has elaborated implicitly on its various causes or sources. The elaboration, however, is unsystematic and incomplete. This part of the chapter will supplement the preceding description and analysis, focusing on major causes or sources of inflation in Poland during 1971–82. In Polish post-war economic writings on inflation one can distinguish two main approaches. The first approach interpreted inflation in terms of macro-economic (dis)equilibrium related to economic growth theories, such as questions of growth (dis)proportions between the value of the producer and consumer goods sectors, investment and consumption, money income and supply of goods, and imports and export. The second approach related inflation to basic features of the functioning (systemic features) of the CPEs (the 'expansive management system'), concentrating the analysis on the behaviour of enterprises generating phenomena like a permanent sellers' market, excess demand for labour and resources, and cost increases and shortages.[17]

The second approach had been influenced to a significant extent by the arguments and conclusions of the Hungarian economist J. Kornai who postulated that shortages and the permanent tendency of excess demand for resources, investment and labour, were determined by enterprises' 'soft budget constraint' and were systemically embedded in the CPEs. Shortages and excess demand for producer goods inevitably spilled over into the consumer goods market, generating inflation (J. Kornai 1980). Both approaches provide useful insights into the complex problems of inflation in the CPEs in general and in Poland in particular.

Gierek's economic growth strategy differed substantially from the strategies adopted during the two preceding decades. The high rate of growth of productive investment in the first half of the 1970s would have led to considerable realloction of resources from consumption to the investment sector, causing heavy inflationary pressure. However, because of large Western credits, which were anti-inflationary, in combination with simultaneous high rates of economic growth, the actual shift of resources was less. A high increase in the rates of growth of both investment and consumption, and a containment of heavy inflationary pressure as well, was made possible during the first half of the 1970s by the large Western credits and increase in production. But the overinvestment drive of the first half of the 1970s led to great investment tensions, inefficiency and waste. This was aggravated by the structural distortions of investment (the neglect of infrastructure, agriculture and consumer goods sectors and the lack of export orientation), a preference for costly new investment projects with long average construction periods and the rising fuel and (raw) materials intensity of production. The failure of the huge investment outlays to establish viable export and consumer goods sectors was one of the main sources of inflation in Poland.

The permanent 'insatiable investment hunger' in CPEs was significantly conditioned by the 'soft budget constraint' of the enterprises. The technique of 'hooking on to the plan', and the bargaining between the centre and enterprises over investment resources, material and wage funds (see Chapter 1), had encouraged excess investment demand and inflationary pressure, which were systemically embedded in the economy (J. Winiecki 1982; L. Podkaminer 1985).

The rapid growth of employment, average money wages and wage fund in the first half of the 1970s, which was partly caused by the high growth of investment and Gierek's policy of boosting the standard of living, led to a sharp rise of personal money income. The actual rates of growth of personal money income and wages exceeded the planned growth rates through the 1970s (Z. Fallenbuchl 1977a: 83; P. Dominiak 1981: 11). The existing wage system had a built-in mechanism for wage drift contributing to inflation. Enterprises strove for a larger wage fund than was necessary to carry out the planned targets and the central planning organs were not sufficiently resistant to this. Poland's record in controlling the wage fund and wage discipline in the 1970s and early 1980s was rather poor. This reflected partly the regime's political weakness *vis-à-vis* the workers and the policy of buying off discontent in order to avoid an explosion of the working class.

In general money wage increases are necessary to stimulate the growth of labour productivity, for the improvement of the quality of work and labour discipline. It was traditionally argued, however, that price stability requires that the average growth of money wages should be less than the average growth of labour productivity, a principle of income distribution which was promoted in economic textbooks into an 'economic law'.[18] It was also accepted by the central planners as a sound principle in regulating the distribution of money income, demand and the general price level.

Table 3.9 shows the average rates of growth of labour productivity and wages for the socialized industrial sector in Poland in the years 1971–9. From 1973, the rate of growth of money wages was systematically higher than the rate of growth of labour productivity, accompanied by rising cost of living indices. The ratio between the rates of growth of average nominal wage and labour productivity varied from 1.07 to 2.07 in 1973–8 compared to 0.60 to 0.80 in the 1960s. Based on past experience, the central planners' rule of thumb assumed that the 'optimal' ratio (a wage increase which would stimulate labour productivity and ensure price stability) varied between 0.7 and 0.8 (M. Kabaj 1980a: 129–31).

Under conditions of growing shortages and inflation, incentives will be distorted. Shortages and inflation tended to reduce the amount and quality of work performed by the workers (L. Podkaminer 1985: 140). Money wage growth would be largely considered by the workers as mere price compensation and it had little impact on labour productivity growth, amplifying the initial effects of wage increases and setting in motion an inflationary spiral (A. Welfe 1986: 113). During the period of the deepening economic crisis (1979–82) the relationship between the growth in money wages and labour productivity was fully distorted, where both average money wages and consumer prices were rising considerably, associated with a considerable fall in output and labour productvity.

Table 3.9 Growth of labour productivity and average wages in socialized industry, 1971–9

	Labour productivity	*Average set nominal wage*	*Indices of cost of living*	*Average real wage*	*Ratio of average wage growth and labour productivity*	
	Annual growth in percentage				*Nominal*	*Real*
1971	5.7	5.3	−0.2	5.5	0.93	0.96
1972	5.6	4.7	0	4.7	0.84	0.84
1973	8.5	9.1	2.6	6.3	1.07	0.74
1974	9.5	14.3	6.8	7.0	1.51	0.74
1975	10.0	13.6	3.0	10.3	1.36	1.03
1976	8.8	9.7	4.7	4.8	1.10	0.55
1977	6.2	7.1	4.9	2.1	1.15	0.34
1978	2.7	5.6	8.7	−2.9	2.07	−1.07
1979	−2.0	9.1	6.7	2.2	–	–
Annual averages						
1961–5	5.7	3.4	2.2	1.2	0.60	0.21
1966–70	4.3	3.4	1.6	1.8	0.79	0.42
1971–5	8.0	9.3	2.4	6.7	1.16	0.84
1976–9	3.9	7.9	6.2	1.6	2.03	0.41

Source: M. Kabaj, *Życie Gospodarcze*, 17, 25 April 1980.

On the whole, the effects of the world inflation of the 1970s on domestic retail price of consumer goods was limited. The increase in the consumer price indices was much less than the high rise in the unit prices of imported materials, fuels and consumer goods (Z. Fallenbuchl, E. Neuberger and L. d'Andrea Tyson 1977: 75–84). Domestic prices were insulated from world prices by means of the price equalization system, i.e. through payments of subsidies or taxes on imports and exports (see Chapter 2, p. 48). The gap between the rising import prices of inputs and the domestic prices of consumer goods contributed to the growing amount of subsidies. After 1977 the deterioration of Poland's terms of trade contributed to the fall in the rate of economic growth and supply, and indirectly reinforced inflation.

The hypothesis which maintains that excess demand inflation has the strongest impact on the price rises found support among many Polish economists (G.W. Kołodko 1987: 189; J. Winiecki 1986: 2–3; A. Topiński 1989). It was also generally admitted that in a 'sellers' market' situation, enterprises were able to shift the cost increases to the buyers. Production inefficiency, rising marginal cost due to natural constraints, lack of interest in cost reduction, 'soft budget constraint', etc. all tended to raise the costs of production. Unless they were covered by price subsidies, cost increases under cost-pricing formulae in their various forms were shifted automatically to price rises. Wholesale price reforms of capital and intermediate goods were introduced at intervals by the government in Poland (1971, 1978 and 1982) in order to adjust wholesale prices to cost increases.

CONCLUSION

Consumer price inflation (both the officially measured one and the hidden price rises) and repressed inflation manifested themselves in a combined fashion. Official consumer price inflation was insignificant during 1960–72, rising to a moderate level during the rest of the 1970s, and reaching the three-digit level in 1982. Hidden inflation was significant and it was growing in the 1970s and early 1980s. Both the existence and extent of repressed inflation are controversial. The descriptive literature and some econometric estimates, however, suggest that in the state sector repressed inflation was significant and was particularly large in 1977–82 (according to one econometric estimate) or 1981–2 (according to another). Gierek's import-led growth strategy and the rapid growth of productive investment during the first half of the 1970s both failed to establish a viable export and consumer goods sector, and contributed directly and indirectly to inflation. The systemic, built-in tendency to wage drift in the CPEs was reinforced in Poland by the regime's weakness *vis-à-vis* the workers and the policy of buying off discontent with money wage increase. This, together with the shortages and imbalances on the producer goods market and the systemic cost-increasing processes, contributed to the wage-price inflationary spiral.

4

AGRICULTURE

INTRODUCTION

This chapter deals with the agricultural sector in Poland in 1970–82, focusing analysis on the role of Gierek's agricultural policies in the generation of the economic crisis of 1979–82. It will describe and analyse the variation in Gierek's agricultural policies, the large and growing hard currency deficits in agriculture-related foreign trade, food consumption, discrimination against private agriculture and efficiency comparisons between socialized and private farming. In addition, this chapter will discuss certain structural features of Polish agriculture and related problems.

AGRICULTURAL POLICIES AND PERFORMANCES

When, in 1956, the Polish communist regime put an end to the limited collectivization drive of the early 1950s, it did not abandon the long-run aim of socializing agriculture. Putting the succession of good years and bad years of agricultural production of post-war Poland into a broader systemic and political perspective, observers noted the operation of a kind of 'political trade cycle'. This resulted from an ideological conviction about the long-run superiority of large-scale socialized farming over private farming, combined with specific reactions of the regime to changing economic and political situations. The Polish pattern of the state socialist 'political trade cycle' in agriculture was such that a short-lived boom in agriculture and an improvement in the living standards of the private farmers, which took place normally after several years of failure or stagnation, were sooner or later followed by a squeeze, particularly of private farmers.

In general, incentives and improvement in the living standards of the peasantry were inversely related to the strength of the regime. During periods of weakness, economic concessions were awarded to the private farmers, which were subsequently withdrawn with the growing strength of the regime (B. Mieczkowski 1978: 262; P. Hanson 1978: 553–6; M. Ellman 1979b: 143–7). Post-war agricultural development in Poland experienced a number of such cycles. The agricultural development and policies in 1971–82 formed a pattern characterized by initial concessions to the private farmers (1971–4), followed by a 'squeeze' of private agriculture (1975–7), a crisis and a return to a pragmatic approach (1978–82).

Rapid growth of agriculture, 1971–4

Agricultural output, especially livestock production was low during the second half of the 1960s. Harvests and livestock production were exceptionally bad in 1969–70. After the food-riots in December 1970, which were precipitated by an aborted price increase of food, the new leadership under Gierek adopted pro-consumption and pro-peasantry policies, and made a deal with the private farmers by offering favourable socio-economic incentives. The prices of agricultural products purchased by the state were increased and the supply of agricultural inputs (fertilizer, coal, animal feed, machinery and equipment) sold to the private farmers was also increased. Forced deliveries of grain, potatoes and milk were abolished whilst the rate of taxation paid by the farmers was reduced and was made less progressive. As a result, the profitability of agricultural production was improved.

Private farmers were included in the national health insurance system and retirement benefits for elderly farmers were introduced. A series of legal, administrative and economic measures were undertaken with the aim of facilitating the purchase or long-term lease of land. It was noted that in the early 1970s there was a revival of private farmers' interest in expanding their landholding and in buying land (Z. Kozlowski 1977: 27), and the government responded positively. The banks provided credit for the purchase of land surrendered by elderly peasants. Productive investment in private farming also increased significantly.

The agricultural sector and the private farmers responded positively to Gierek's pro-peasantry policy. Partly because of favourable weather conditions, the agricultural boom of 1971–4 was unprecedented in post-war Polish agricultural history and output increased at a rate which 'surpassed all expectations' (O'Hagan 1978). Record harvests were recorded. For instance, grain output increased from the low level of 16.3 million tons in 1970 to 19.9 million tons in 1971 and 23.0 million tons in 1974. The number of hogs increased from 13.4 million in 1970 to 15.2 million in 1971 and 21.5 million in 1974; and the number of cattle increased from 10.8 million to 11.1 million and 13.0 million during the same period. Average real income of the private farmers rose considerably.

Accelerated socialization of agriculture, 1975–7

As the economic and political crises of 1970–1 receded into the past, and with the strengthening of the regime, Gierek's pro-peasantry agricultural policy was gradually dismantled and replaced by more restrictive measures against private farmers. By late 1974, agricultural profitability and farmers' income were being squeezed as costs increased more rapidly than revenue. Real income fell and the productive investment of private farmers declined. The local government administrator ('naczelnik gminy'), who had virtually complete authority in his jurisdiction, intervened increasingly in the daily life of the peasantry (E. Cook 1984: 413). The role of village or commune self-government institutions such as agricultural circles ('kółka rolnicze'), cooperatives and other local elective councils was substantially reduced. Private farmers were increasingly discriminated against in the purchase and lease of land and in the distribution of agricultural inputs, whilst the tax burden increased.

In May 1974, the government passed a law on farmers' retirement benefits which required elderly farmers to surrender their land to the State Land Fund (PFZ) in exchange for pensions. Moreover, the state could confiscate uncultivated private land. Transfer of private land to the State Land Fund increased considerably. Under the banner of agricultural modernization and of stepping up the tempo of the 'socialist transformation' of agriculture, the socialized agricultural sector was expanded.

At the XVth Central Committee Plenary meeting in October 1974, it was decided, amongst other things, that land at the disposal of the State Land Fund should be transferred in the first place to the socialized farms. Socialized farms obtained the required investment grants and credits to take over the land surrendered by retired farmers. Private farms were at the bottom of the list of potential land recipients from the State Land Fund through lease ('XV Plenum KC PZPR' 1974: 47). By 1974 agricultural banks ceased to sell land controlled by the State Land Fund to private farmers and existing leases on land were either not renewed or prematurely terminated and turned over to socialized farms. Farmers' request to lease land from the State Land Fund were systematically turned down by local administrators, even when the land stood fallow.

The regime considered private land transfer to the socialized sector through the State Land Fund as a long-term instrument of structural change and socialization of agriculture. P. Jaroszewicz, the ex-prime minister, told the delegates at the VIIth Party Congress in December 1975 that the share of socialized agriculture in total agricultural land should increase from the current 21 per cent to more than 30 per cent in 1980 (J. Jaroszewicz 1976: 96). At the same Congress, Gierek triumphantly stated that 'for the first time in years' the socialist transformation of agriculture in Poland had progressed well. By 1977 the Ministry of Agriculture had developed, and passed down to the district level, guidelines for the socialization of agricultural land which envisaged about 44 per cent of agricultural land being socialized by 1990 (cited in E. Cook 1984: 410). The district plans for the socialization of agricultural land seem to have exceeded the above guide lines.

The amount of land controlled by the State Land Fund and sold to private farmers during 1974–6 dropped drastically in comparison with the period of 1971–3 (see Table 4.1). This is clear evidence of the efforts of the regime to force

Table 4.1 Land in the State Land Fund (in 1,000 hectares), 1960–82

	1960	*1965*	*1970*	*1971*	*1972*	*1973*	*1974*	*1975*	*1976*	*1977*	*1978*	*1979*	*1980*	*1981*	*1982*
Balance on 1 January	889.2	1016.9	1122.2	1084.7	1064.5	964.5	861.9	854.5	925.9	918.5	871.5	817.6	932.0	889.0	999.0
Total land acquired	233.6	229.9	154.8	157.2	117.0	128.9	246.3	375.0	326.8	240.8	232.6	239.0	205.0	308.0	145.0
of which from:															
state farms	39.8	4.2	15.0	25.7	13.7	24.2	17.3	10.2	9.2	15.1	12.6	2.0	4.0	136.0	55.0
private farms	36.2	68.9	111.2	117.3	90.2	104.7	224.0	358.9	311.4	209.9	182.4	202.3	162.0	45.0	37.0
Disposals total (durable)	149.6	193.3	192.3	117.4	224.8	231.5	254.5	304.6	335.5	287.9	294.0	286.7	251.0	204.0	285.0
of which to:															
state farms	26.7	64.9	106.4	93.1	100.5	71.8	106.1	117.4	110.7	74.5	82.2	70.3	37.0	7.0	7.0
collective farms	28.8	19.8	18.7	14.9	18.5	12.5	23.2	39.9	57.9	40.8	51.0	55.4	43.0	10.0	7.0
non-farm use	34.5	35.9	21.1	15.9	23.4	22.0	24.1	21.0	36.9	45.6	42.9	25.9	32.0	15.0	22.0
private farms	59.6	72.7	46.1	53.9	82.4	90.0	45.0	16.7	21.8	77.7	94.4	113.2	127.0	165.0	240.0
Balance on 31 December	973.2	1053.5	1084.7	1064.5	956.7	861.9	853.7	924.9	917.2	871.4	810.1	769.9	886.0	993.0	859.0

Source: *Rocznik Statystyczny* 1975, 1980 and 1984.

up the rate of the transformation of private agriculture through the takeover of private land surrendered by aged farmers.

Owing to a series of bad harvests, which were partly caused by unfavourable weather conditions, the livestock population declined. In order to prevent a further drastic fall in livestock production the government raised the imports of grain and fodder significantly. Socialist farming had a higher percentage of gross marketed output per hectare of agricultural land than private farming. Motivated both by a fear of the political consequences of a disruption in the production and supply of food (particularly meat, a sort of 'meat spectre' threatening political stability) and by an ideological faith in the efficacy of socialized farming to solve the food problems, the regime discriminated against private farming in the allocation of resources and expanded the livestock farming of the socialized sector.

Large and costly investment and other resources were expended on the construction and maintenance of large-scale socialized livestock farms which were highly grain intensive and heavily dependent on Western imports. On the other hand, the less capital and grain intensive private farms either gave up or reduced livestock production substantially either because of lack of fodder (due to discrimination in the allocation of fodder) or because it was unprofitable. According to an agricultural census made in 1977, about 35 per cent of private farms, many of them consisting of smallholdings, did not keep hogs and about 28 per cent were without cattle, most of them having given up livestock farming two to three years before the census (A. Bulak 1979). The government policy of keeping retail prices at a low level encouraged (small) farmers to buy livestock products (meat and dairy products) for their own consumption from the state shops. For instance, meat consumption from peasants' household slaughtering dropped from 16.9 kg per person in 1970 to 12.6 kg in 1975 and to 11.6 kg in 1980 (*Rocznik Statystyczny 1981*: 324).

The general hypothesis maintained by the regime, that accelerated socialization of agriculture would proceed without adverse effects on the agricultural output and productivity of private farming, was grossly contradicted by the facts. The increasing transfer of private land to socialized farms contributed to a shortage of animal feeds since the former was more oriented towards the cultivation of grain and potatoes (two important animal feeds) than the latter (B. Simatupang 1981b: 14–15). The discrimination against private farming in the sale or lease of land under the control of the State Land Fund, and the allocation of agricultural inputs, credit and subsidies, favouring the socialized sector contributed to an overall increase in input requirements per unit of agricultural product, a fall in agricultural output and a decline in the productivity of private farming. Due to uncertainties and lack of good prospects, private investment fell considerably. Because of a lack of prospects in private farming and the worsening income parity between agricultural and non-agricultural activities, the outflow of young people from agriculture was significant.

Economic crisis and a return to a pragmatic approach, 1978–82

The economy deteriorated rapidly during the last years of the 1970s. Because of the lack of investment funds, bad harvests and rapidly increasing domestic and external imbalances, the regime realized that it could not afford to continue the highly expensive policy of accelerated socialization of agriculture. A new agricultural policy began to emerge. Its aim was to increase production and ensure both the profitability of agricultural production and a higher income for the farmers that would narrow the income differentials between the urban and rural population and thereby slow down the exodus of the youth (W. Newcomb 1981). The specialized private farms (i.e. above average sized farms which specialized in a limited product assortment) were given priority in the allocation of agricultural inputs. Supply of agricultural inputs was tied to procurement contracts by which the state could ensure the supply of agricultural products. The restrictive land sale to private farmers was relaxed.[1]

The new agricultural policy failed, however, to dispel the distrust of the private farmers and to boost agricultural output. Average real income of the private farmers fell by 12 per cent in 1979–80 (*Rocznik Statystyczny 1981*: 350). Nevertheless, the annual average land sale to private farmers began to increase modestly from the low figures of 1974–7 (see Table 4.1). Gross agricultural output dropped by 1.4 per cent and 9.5 per cent in 1979 and 1980 respectively. The exceptionally bad harvests in both years (partly due to bad weather) and the growing workers' protest forced the regime to step up the imports of grain in order to prevent the collapse of the livestock population and production. But the severe shortage of hard currency and the balance of payments crisis led to a deep cut in Western imports of industrial raw materials and components, contributing to a considerable fall in the rate of output and supply of key agricultural inputs. This affected agricultural output adversely.

In parallel to the workers' struggle, which led to the establishment of the free trade union Solidarność, the private farmers began to organize Rural Solidarity in early 1981. The Rzeszów Agreement, signed in February 1981 between the government and representatives of the private farmers, stipulated amongst other things:

- the right of ownership and inheritance of the private farmers and the permanent status of private agriculture, guaranteed by law;
- private farmers' priority in land purchase from the State Land Fund;
- equal access to credit for all sectors of agriculture and an increase in farm credit;
- ensuring profitability of farming through favourable prices;
- an increase in the supplies of agricultural inputs of industrial origin to private farming.

The Rzeszów Agreement was a major break with the agricultural policy of the 1970s and on the whole it was a significant gain for private farming. The regime reluctantly officially recognized the private farmers' Solidarity ('NSZZ Rolników Indywidualnych "Solidarność"') as a trade union organization, which was dissolved (as were all independent organizations) after the declaration of martial law.

Under conditions of high inflation and shortage of industrial products, the farmers were prepared to sell only the amount of agricultural products absolutely necessary. In 1981, when the state doubled the purchasing price, almost one-quarter of private farms made no sales to the state and government procurement plans (especially for meat and grain) were unfulfilled (cited in CIA 1986a: 458). During martial law in 1982 the regime tried to maintain domestic market supplies by using a combination of threats and incentives. On one hand, the regime threatened the peasantry with grain requisitioning and sending the army to the countryside to encourage farmers to sell their products. On the other hand, the farmers were enticed to exchange grain for an interest-bearing 'grain loan', redeemable in 1983–5 on attractive terms, offering credit extension and sales of key agricultural inputs at subsidized prices to be tied to the procurement of agricultural products. Average real incomes of the private farmers dropped by 26 per cent in 1982 (*Rocznik Statystyczny 1983*: 281). The refusal to continue delivery of grain to Poland on soft terms, a part of the Western reaction to martial law, endangered the supply of fodder, which led to distress slaughtering of livestock. The deep economic crisis and the obstacles imposed by bureaucratic administration seriously constrained a comprehensive implementation of the Rzeszów Agreement.

EXTERNAL TRADE IN AGRICULTURE-RELATED PRODUCTS

The growth in livestock production was considerably higher than that in crop output in the 1970s. On average, crop output grew by only 0.9 per cent per year, as compared to the 3.7 per cent annual growth in livestock products. The disparity between the rates of growth of crop and livestock production led to a rapid increase in imports of animal feed. This was the reverse of the situation in the 1960s, when the rate of growth of crop output was higher than that of livestock products.

Traditionally, Poland's foreign trade balance with non-socialist countries in food products and agricultural commodities showed a surplus. Imports consisted mainly of grain, animal feed and tropical fruits. Poland paid for these imports by exporting quality livestock products (meat and meat products, and eggs) and it had profited from such exchange through greater employment opportunities in agriculture. Moreover, the hard currency trade surplus in agricultural products contributed to financing the badly needed imports of capital goods and raw materials from the West. From 1973 Poland became an increasingly significant net importer of food products and agricultural commodities. This mainly resulted from the rapid increase in Western imports of agricultural commodities (grain and animal feed). Moreover with the increasing role of agricultural imports from the Western countries, the role of CMEA countries as suppliers of agricultural commodities declined significantly.[2]

On average, imports of grain and high protein animal feed were 2.3 million tons annually in the years 1966–70 and they increased to 3.5 million tons annually in the years 1971–3. The combination of a moderate growth in imports of grain and animal feed, exceptionally good harvests and favourable incentives to the private farmers contributed to the rapid growth in livestock numbers in the years 1971–4. With the drop in arable output in 1975, followed by a series of bad harvests during the second half of the 1970s and early 1980s, a substantial increase in imports of grain and animal feed was needed if the regime was to rescue the livestock population from distress slaughtering and to maintain an adequate supply of livestock products.

The regime failed to adjust the growing food demand and consumption to the stagnating level of agricultural net production during the second half of the 1970s. Imports of grain and animal feed increased to an average of 6.4 million tons annually during 1975–7, and went up further to an annual average of 8.8 million tons during 1978–81. Imports of grain and animal feed at the end of the 1970s were about three times the volume of imports in the early 1970s. It was estimated that around 47 per cent of the growth in livestock production in the 1970s was attributable to grain and fodder originating from imports (Z. Grochowski 1979: 88–9). The Western credit sanctions on Poland in response to martial law led to a reduction in imports of grain and animal feed to 5.3 million tons in 1982, causing distress slaughtering and a significant drop in the livestock population.

The rapid growth in the hard currency deficits in agriculture-related trade in the years 1975–81 was visible evidence of the serious errors in Gierek's economic and agricultural policies. The government also failed to adjust the level of consumption of the highly subsidized food products (meat products in particular) to domestic crop production, whilst traditional agricultural exports were constrained by high domestic demand. Grain input requirements per unit of livestock product increased rapidly due to the increasing application of the so-called industrial method of animal feeding on socialized farms. Moreover, the drastic decline in the number of private farms keeping livestock production, where grain input was low and which had a high proportion of non-grain fodder (potatoes, sugar beets, and grass), contributed to a greater requirement for grain and high protein animal feed per unit of animal product. It was estimated that the partial shift of livestock production from private to socialized animal farming caused an additional consumption and import of at least 1 million tons of grain per annum (Z. Grochowski 1980). Moreover, the significant decline in output and supplies of key agricultural inputs of industrial origin during 1976–81,[3] contributed to the decline in arable output.

Table 4.2 shows the value of trade in agricultural products and foodstuffs with the non-socialist countries during the period 1960–82. Up to 1972 Poland

Table 4.2 Trade in agricultural products and foodstuffs with non-socialist countries (in million US$)[a]

	1960	*1965*	*1970*	*1971*	*1972*	*1973*	*1974*	*1975*	*1976*	*1977*	*1978*	*1979*	*1980*	*1981*	*1982*
Export	212.3	346.1	405.4	392.9	530.0	788.1	754.7	679.6	833.3	858.2	963.0	1048.0	1029.5	642.3	626.6
Import	180.3	285.9	280.2	325.2	415.8	791.8	952.7	1041.3	1490.9	1473.4	1725.5	1953.8	2425.4	2470.4	1261.7
Balance	+32.0	+60.2	+125.2	+67.7	+114.2	−3.7	−198.8	−361.7	−657.6	−615.2	−762.5	−805.8	−1395.9	−1828.9	−635.1

Source: *Rocznik Statystyczny Handlu Zagranicznego* 1975, 1978, 1980 and 1983.
Note: [a]Zloty dewyzowy are converted at the average annual exchange rate as provided by the Foreign Trade Statistical Yearbooks.

had a trade surplus in agricultural products and foodstuffs with the non-socialist countries. In 1970 the trade surplus amounted to US$125 million. The trade deficits in agricultural products and foodstuffs increased rapidly from US$200 million in 1974 to US$1.4 and US$1.8 billion in 1980 and 1981 respectively. Whereas in 1974 the trade deficit in agricultural products and foodstuffs accounted for only 9.2 per cent of the total hard currency trade deficit, the percentage rose rapidly to 176 per cent and 244 per cent in 1980 and 1981 respectively (see Table 2.10).

The following figures show the contribution of the large and growing hard currency deficits in Poland's agriculture-related trade (food products, agricultural commodities and investment goods for agriculture and food industry) to the increase in hard currency debt. In 1975–81, Poland's cumulative hard currency trade deficit from the agricultural-related sectors amounted to 25.5 billion złoty dewyzowy which was equivalent to around US$8 billion,[4] calculated according to the official exchange rate. During the same period the gross hard currency debt increased by US$17.1 billion (see Table 2.11). Thus on a very conservative estimate, around 47 per cent of the increment in hard currency debt in 1975–81 was accounted for by policy directly or indirectly relating to agriculture. If account is taken of the interest due on the agriculture-related debt, and if the counterfactual considered is the traditional agricultural export surplus, then of course the contribution of the agricultural-related sectors to the increase in debt was larger still.

FOOD DEMAND AND CONSUMPTION

The average share of expenditure on food, alcohol and tobacco (at current prices) in total private consumption declined from 56.4 per cent in 1970, food constituting 43.7 per cent, to 51.9 per cent in 1980, when food alone was 36.4 per cent (*Rocznik Statystyczny 1981*: 120). The share of expenditure on alcohol varied between 10–14 per cent. The more rapid rise of food prices relative to the prices of non-food goods and services from 1978 raised the share of food expenditure to 43.6 per cent in 1982 (*Rocznik Statystyczny 1983*: 106). By international standards the proportion of expenditure on food was high. Consequently a drawback or crisis in agricultural and food production would then have greater repercussions on standards of living and political stability.

Statistical studies on food demand and consumption in Poland indicate that the income elasticity of demand for food varied between 0.6–0.8.[5] Income elasticity of demand for individual food items varied considerably; it was high for quality foodstuffs like meat, meat products, eggs and dairy products, and low for food items like potatoes, grain products and sugar. For instance, it has been estimated that during the 1970s, the income elasticity of demand for beef was 0.9, for inferior food items like grain products it was −0.12 and for potatoes −0.18 (Z. Kozlowski 1980: 1286). By international comparison the growth of food demand in Poland was relatively high. According to studies presented at the

World Food Congress in Rome in 1974, food demand increased on average by 2.3 per cent annually in Poland during 1952–72, compared to 1.1 per cent in Austria, 1.2 per cent in Belgium, 1.1 per cent in Finland and 0.7 per cent in Great Britain during the same period (*Assessment of the World Food Situation*, United Nations, World Food Conference, Rome, 1974: 51). Two major factors, a high income elasticity coefficient (partly due to inadequate supply and relatively low prices of non-food products like housing, durable consumer goods, etc.) and a high growth of personal income, contributed to the high growth of food demand in Poland during the 1970s.

The Polish economy fluctuated sharply during 1970–82. According to official figures, the yearly average growth of per capita national net material product ('national income for distribution') at constant prices was 10.6 per cent in 1971–5. Subsequently, the absolute level fell. The average rate of decline was 1.1 per cent in 1976–80 and 11.4 per cent in 1981–2. Per capita overall consumption increased on average by 7.7 per cent yearly in 1971–5, of which food consumption increased on average by almost 4 per cent annually; they slowed down to 3.7 per cent and 1.8 per cent respectively in 1976–80 (*Rocznik Statystyczny 1983*: 74; *Rocznik Statystyczny Rolnictwa i Gospodarki Żywnościowej 1982* 1983: 336). The relatively low decline in the rate of growth of consumption compared to the absolute fall in the national net material product during the second half of the 1970s was made possible by a significant cut in investment. Vigorous adjustments occurred in 1981–2 when both investment and consumption dropped drastically.

The Polish diet improved considerably during the first half of the 1970s. The structure of food consumption changed significantly with a shift from low quality food items (potatoes, grains) to high quality food items (meat, dairy products and eggs). Per capita consumption of meat increased on average by 5.4 per cent annually in 1971–5, eggs by 2 per cent, and fat (including butter) by 1.8 per cent. At the same time, consumption of low quality food items like potatoes and grains dropped by about 1.6 per cent annually. Increase in per capita consumption of quality foodstuffs slowed down to almost 1 per cent annually in the second half of the 1970s. Due to a large drop in agricultural output and a drastic cut in grain imports by the end of 1982 per capita consumption of many quality food items dropped back to the levels of the early 1970s. For instance, per capita meat consumption dropped from 74 kg in 1980 to 58.5 kg in 1982 (see Table 4.3).

In the wake of the regime's overoptimism, and dizzy with the bumper harvests of 1971–3, the XVth Central Committee Plenary session of the Polish United Workers' Party (PUWP) in 1974 adopted an ambitious agricultural plan for the second half of the 1970s. The plan was referred to as a 'programme for the further improvement of the diet of the population and for agricultural development' for the second half of the 1970s and the 1980s ('XV Plenum KC PZPR', *Nowe Drogi*, 11, 1974). Agricultural output and food consumption targets for the second half of the 1970s were simple extrapolations of the extraordinarily good agricultural results of 1971–3. For instance, per capita

Table 4.3 Per capita consumption of selected agricultural products, 1960–82, and planned targets for 1980 and 1990 (in kg)

	1960	*1965*	*1970*	*1973*	*1976*	*1978*	*1980*	*1981*	*1982*	*1980*[a]	*1990*[a]
Grain and grain products	145	141	131	125	122	120	137	121	124	108	90
Potatoes	223	215	190	183	173	166	158	157	159	150	110
Vegetables	–	–	98	93.0	87.0	105	101	118	107	120[b]	145[b]
Fruits (excl. tropical fruits)	–	–	22.9	20.3	28.6	40.8	37.7	32.4	42.8	60[b]	80[b]
Meat	42.5	49.2	53.0	62.1	70.0	70.6	74.0	65.0	58.5	75–77	85–90
of which:											
Pork	25.6	29.5	29.2	38.8	34.5	36.5	37.2	31.7	31.9		
Fish and fish products	4.5	5.0	6.3	7.2	7.7	7.3	8.1	7.3	6.0	9.9	11–12
Edible fats (in trade weight)	15.6	17.5	20.8	22.3	23.5	24.8	24.8	24.6	21.5	24.5	26
of which:											
Butter	4.7	5.0	6.0	6.7	7.7	8.7	8.9	8.9	7.4	8.5	10
Other animal fats	7.4	6.8	8.2	8.4	8.0	8.1	8.1	7.3	6.8	8	7.5
Vegetable fats	3.5	5.7	6.6	7.2	7.8	8.0	7.8	8.4	7.3	8	8.5
Milk and milk products in litres (excl. butter)	227	233	262	263	263	264	262	257	247	310	340
Eggs (units)	143	162	186	200	214	219	223	227	200	230	270
Sugar	27.9	32.6	39.2	41.6	43.9	42.7	41.4	33.4	41.7	46	49

Sources: *Rocznik Statystyczny 1979*: 81; *Rocznik Statystyczny 1983*: 109.
Notes: [a]Projected figures, 'XV Plenum KC PZPR', in *Nowe Drogi* 11, 1974: 26;
[b]Fresh weight.

consumption of meat and milk was to increase from 62.1 kg and 263 litres in 1973 to 75–7 kg and 310 litres respectively in 1980; whilst per capita consumption of inferior food items like grains and potatoes was planned to fall during the second half of the 1970s.

The economic and material conditions underlying the bumper harvests of 1971–3 did not, however, exist during the second half of the 1970s. By 1973 the impulses of the economic incentives of the first years of the 1970s had already been exhausted, and instead of new and vigorous incentives aiming to boost agricultural output, the regime started to intensify a campaign of 'socialist transformation' of agriculture and discrimination against private farms. The success of the programme presupposed a rapid growth in the production of agricultural inputs of industrial origin (machinery, equipment, fertilizer, pesticides), for which tasks, however, Polish industry was structurally not suitable (A. Wós 1985: 314–16). Instead of the planned rapid growth, the production and supply of major agricultural inputs of industrial origin fell during the second half of the 1970s. The slight growth of food consumption in the second half of the 1970s was made possible by the large and growing imports of grain from the West.

The output and procurement of arable production deteriorated considerably from 1979. It was preceeded by a small output decline during 1975–8 and an agricultural boom in 1971–4. For example, the average output and procurement of grains varied from 20 million tons and 5 million tons respectively per annum in 1971–4 to 18.5 million tons and 5.2 million tons in 1975–8 which fell to an average of 16.9 million tons and 3.4 million tons per annum in 1979–82. Livestock production and procurement suffered less markedly initially due to large imports of grain from the West. But the exceptionally bad harvest in 1980–1 and a considerable drop in grain imports in 1982 led to a significant drop in livestock production. For example, meat production (i.e. slaughtering minus losses) fell from an average of 3.2 million tons per annum in 1979–80 to 2.6 million tons in 1981-2.[6]

Retail sales of all commodities in constant prices fell by 21.2 per cent, whilst the sales of foodstuffs fell by 22.3 per cent in 1981–2 (*Rocznik Statystyczny 1983*: 347). Faced with a large decline in both agricultural output and the output of industrial consumer goods, combined with a high growth in disposable income, panic buying and social opposition to market solutions, the regime was forced to introduce rationing of basic consumer goods in 1981.

Prior to the aborted price increase of basic foodstuffs in December 1970, Polish economists had discussed the issues related to consumption planning, the structure of consumption and relative prices. J. Pajestka, a leading Polish economist, complained about the irrational consumption structure and the high income elasticity of demand for food while the incremental capital–output ratio in agriculture was considered to be high. He suggested that the high share of food expenditure was largely due to price distortions which set prices of foodstuffs too low. He recommended raising the prices of foodstuffs, expanding non-food production (e.g. cars, televisions) and adopting economic measures aimed at achieving a shift in the structure of consumption away from foodstuffs towards manufactured consumer goods. Critics pointed out that because of price distortions (e.g. highly differential rates of taxation and subsidies) the result of the calculation and the cost-benefit criteria of production might be misleading.[7]

The core of Pajestka's reasoning about the irrational Polish consumption structure was repeated and maintained by the Polish authorities and many Polish economists. The failure of the aborted price increases of 1970 and 1976 and the implemented price rise of 1980, which provoked violent protests, was attributed to the 'failure of the workers to understand the need for equilibrium'. It was further argued that price distortions, i.e. the underpricing of food products[8] and state subsidies for food production and consumption,[9] increased in the 1970s, encouraging high growth in food demand and misallocation of resources.

L. Podkaminer, an economic adviser to the former government trade union, contested the prevailing 'conventional wisdom', offered an alternative explanation of Poland's consumer market disequilibrium during the past twenty years and an alternative prescription for restoring market balance. Judged by international standards, the findings of his model of Poland's consumer markets are that:

1 food products, clothing and footwear were overpriced or oversupplied at existing administered prices; while
2 housing (rents) and durables were underpriced or undersupplied at existing prices.

By international standards, paradoxically the relatively scarce goods (e.g. housing) were relatively cheap in Poland while the abundantly supplied goods like food were relatively expensive. Accordingly, consumer market disequilibrium was not caused by the low prices and limited supplies of food but by basically insufficient supplies of housing, durables and services, being provided at low prices. Unable to spend their money on (unavailable) housing, durables and services, people spent their income on food ('spillovers' or 'forced substitutions'). The underpriced (or undersupplied) non-food products were thus responsible for the high level of demand for food. Podkaminer's suggestions were that disequilibrium in consumer markets could have been redressed if prices and/or the supply of housing (rents) and durables had been raised combined with price cutting for foodstuffs.[10]

Podkaminer's analysis and conclusions contain a number of interesting ideas and insights into the working of consumer market disequilibria in Poland. The 'spillover' effects of unsatisfied demand for housing, durables and services clearly aggravated the observed food shortages. Black market prices of housing (rents) and scarce durables were far above official prices. Officials, who had easier access to luxuries, had a vested interest in keeping prices of housing (rents) and durables low. Food price increases (1980, 1982) provoked wage increases to compensate the fall in purchasing power without bringing consumer markets any closer to equilibrium.

PERFORMANCE COMPARISON BETWEEN PRIVATE AND SOCIALIZED FARMING

The long-accepted agrarian doctrine in state socialist countries held that there were two main advantages of socialized farming as compared to private farming:

1 elimination of the exploitation of labour by capitalists; and
2 advantages from economies of scales and efficient use of resources.

At least three groups of arguments need to be reconsidered in the context of this agrarian doctrine.

1 The significance of permanent employees in agriculture in Western Europe, for instance, is less than was predicted because of the viability of family farms. In Poland, only 3 per cent of the total number of private farms used paid labourers on a permanent basis, and 30 per cent of these were farms of a specialist nature, such as farms engaged in poultry farming (F. Kolbusz 1974: 196). The wages of seasonal help are high and family holdings have become more and more dominant in private farming.
2 Progress in agricultural mechanization (for example 'tractorization') is adjusted to the production needs of family farming, so that a farmer is able to cultivate a larger area without the help of permanently hired labour. A significant part of the labour used in family farming is underpaid ('self-exploitation').
3 There is a tendency to overestimate the advantages of economies of scale in agricultural production and to underestimate the diseconomies of scale in, for example, planning, coordination and management of socialized farming. For instance, the giant agricultural combines, comprising between 20,000 to 30,000 hectares, had absolutely no economic justification and were economically irrational (H. Laeuren 1977: 115–20; H. Philipp 1980: 345; J. Lewandowski 1983: 73–6).

Socialized farms were less efficient in the use of individual agricultural inputs such as fertilizer and animal feeds, compared with private farming. For instance, the average use of fertilizer per hectare of agricultural land on socialized farms was more than twice as high as on private farms. Moreover, the former were less efficient than the latter in fertilizer usage. On state farms in 1978, 95 kg NPK fertilizer (nitrogen, phosphates and potash) were required to produce one ton of grain, on cooperative farms 92 kg (NPK) and on private farms only 58 kg (NPK). It is estimated that about 10 per cent of the fertilizer allocated to state farms had a negative marginal yield (M. Miesczankowski 1980b; H. Płudowski 1980). Grain input requirements needed to produce one unit of livestock product grew in the 1970s. On average, approximately 65 per cent more grain was required in 1978 to produce one unit of meat equivalent on socialized farms than on private farms (B. Simatupang 1981c: 459).[11] Socialized farming was also less efficient than private farming in terms of the land–livestock production ratio.

In comparing the cost efficiency of private and socialized farming, the role of unpaid (or underpaid) labour as a part of the overhead costs of private farming was significant. Rychlik, cited by Kozlowski, states:

> The peasants' time devoted to management and to the maintenance of links with the outside world is not valued as an item of cost calculation. The latter, it has been found, involves an average of 75 days per year. State farms have to pay for all these functions although they spend less time per hectare to carry them out.
>
> (Kozlowski 1977: 31)

Prices paid by the state procurement agency for agricultural products were identical for both sectors. On the whole, private farmers had to cover their current expenses for production, investment and own consumption from revenue. In other words, using Kornai's (1980) terminology, the budget constraint was 'hard'. On the other hand, the 'state farms have proved on the whole unprofitable on the most favourable accounting methods' (Z. Kozlowski 1977: 30), and the losses were covered by state grants.[12] In Kornai's words, the budget constraint on state farms and collective farms was 'soft'.

A comparison between various categories of agricultural outputs (gross and net marketed output, gross production and value added, etc.) produced at different types of farms provides a better insight into the inter-sectoral performances. Moreover, it shows the negative effects of Gierek's agricultural policies on production.

Gierek's agricultural policy favouring socialized farming in the allocation of investment goods and agricultural inputs, particularly during the second half of the 1970s, was seen as a reliable instrument to direct products easily into state retail networks, hoping thereby to ensure sufficient food supplies. In the 1970s, the annual average of gross marketed output per hectare of socialized farming was 30 per cent higher than that of private farming. Nevertheless, the annual average of net marketed output[13] per hectare of private farming was between 14 and 23 per cent higher than that of socialized farming, with a growing discrepancy between the two types of farming during the second half of the 1970s (E. Cook 1984: 414–15; *Rocznik Statystyczny Rolnictwa i Gospodarki Żywnościowej* 1982: 197–8). The discrepancy between gross and net marketed output is a reflection of the government's policy of favouring socialized farms in the allocation of agricultural inputs.

Tables 4.4 and 4.5 give data on the yearly average value of gross production and value added at constant prices of 1977 over the period 1966–81, classified according to farm type. In both socialized and private farming the value of gross output per hectare of agricultural land was rising in 1966–80 with a slower growth rate during the second half of the 1970s. This was partly due to un-

Table 4.4 Gross production per hectare of agricultural land by farm type, yearly average, 1966–81

	1966–70	*1971–5*	*1976–80*	*1981*
		(1,000 constant zlotys of 1977)		
All farms	26.9	31.4	32.7	32.0
Socialized farms	22.7	28.3	30.9	27.2
of which:				
state farms	19.8	26.2	29.2	25.1
collective farms	27.3	35.6	37.5	32.4
agr. circle farms	7.9	18.2	22.7	16.9
Private farms	27.7	32.4	33.5	33.8
		Private farms = 100		
Socialized farms	81.9	87.3	92.2	80.5
of which:				
state farms	71.5	80.7	87.2	74.3
collective farms	98.6	110.0	111.9	95.9
agr. circle farms	28.5	56.2	67.8	50.0

Source: *Rocznik Statystyczny Rolnictwa i Gospodarki Żywnościowej* 1982: 205–6.

favourable weather conditions and bad harvests in the second half of the 1970s. Gross production per hectare of agricultural land from private farming was somewhat higher than from socialized farming (Table 4.4).

Value added per hectare of agricultural land from private farms was considerably higher than that from socialized farms. This partly reflected the difference in the efficiency and the techniques of production between the two sectors. The socialized farms purchased a great deal of necessary material inputs and they were more capital intensive. The private farms compensated for these resources by substituting the relatively abundant labour for scarce materials but also substituted to some extent self-produced agricultural inputs for inputs of industrial origins (Z. Kozlowski 1977: 30–2). This phenomenon was indicated by the low material costs and low capital depreciation per unit of output on private farms.[14]

The rate of value added per hectare of agricultural land in both socialized and private farms was declining, but the discrepancy between the two types of farming was growing. If the yearly average value added per hectare from so socialized farms was 45 per cent of the level of private farms in 1966–70, the relative disadvantage of the first compared to the second initially fell slightly to 42 per cent in 1971–5, but then dropped drastically to 24 per cent in 1976–80 and to only 7 per cent in 1981 (see Table 4.5).

A comparison between the rate of value added per worker classified by farm type during the 1970s also shows clearly the worsening performance of the socialized farms (E. Cook 1984: 416–17). The drastic deterioration in resource use coincided with the regime's drive to expand socialized farming, favouring

Table 4.5 Value added[a] per hectare of agricultural land by farm type, yearly average, 1966–81

	1966–70	*1971–5*	*1976–80*	*1981*
		(1,000 constant zlotys of 1977)		
All farms	11.2	11.7	10.4	9.8
Socialized farms	5.5	5.5	3.1	0.9
of which:				
state farms	4.2	4.6	3.4	0.2
collective farms	7.8	8.6	3.7	2.4
agr. circle farms	2.1	−2.9	−8.3	−10.8
Private farms	12.3	13.2	12.8	12.8
		Private farms = 100		
Socialized farms	44.7	41.7	24.2	7.0
of which:				
state farms	34.1	34.8	26.6	1.6
collective farms	63.4	65.2	28.9	18.8
agr. circle farms	17.1	–	–	–

Source: As Table 4.4.
Notes: [a]value added ('produkcja czysta') = gross output minus material costs (goods grown on the farms, off-farm purchases of goods and services) and capital depreciation.

socialized farms and discriminating against private farms in the allocation of resources, and with the increasing bureaucratization of agricultural planning. Resources were not used effectively by socialized farms and subsidies were growing fast. Despite discrimination against private farms, they performed better.

AGRICULTURAL STRUCTURAL FEATURES AND PROBLEMS

The private sector occupied the principal place in Polish agriculture despite the tendency for socialized farming to become more important in the 1970s. By the end of 1980, more than three-quarters of the gross value of agricultural output originated from private farms and about the same proportion of agricultural land was used by private farmers. Planning of private agriculture had to rely largely on economic incentives. Heavy reliance on administrative methods, as adopted during the second half of the 1970s, affected agricultural production adversely.

Poland's private farming consisted of about 3 million farms (excluding plots of up to 0.5 hectares), with a total area of about 15 million hectares of agricultural land in the mid 1970s. About 30 per cent of the farms were of less than 2 hectares which, together, represented approximately 6 per cent of the total agricultural land under private farming. About 30 per cent of farms were of more than 2 hectares and less than 5 hectares, representing approximately 20 per cent of the total land under private farming; and 26 per cent were of 5 to 10 hectares, representing 37 per cent of the total land under private farming and the remaining 14 per cent were of more than 10 hectares, representing 37 per cent of the total land (A. Szemberg 1980: 25–7). A slight improvement in the structure of private agricultue (e.g. an increase in the number of farms of more than 10 hectares and in the amount of land held by them) was noted in 1978–82. Even excluding farms with less than 2 hectares, the national average farm size did not exceed 6.5 hectares

Regional differentiation in the ownership structure of private land was considerable. Its origin can be traced back to Poland's pre-war history. The north-west region (voivodship Olsztyn, Koszalin, Szcecin, Zielona Góra) and the central-west region (Gdańsk, Poznan, Wrocław, Opole) have a relatively favourable land ownership structure, whilst the south-west and eastern regions (Katowice, Cracow, Kielce, Lublin) have small and highly fragmented land-holdings. This seriously limits the possibilities for agricultural modernization. Few changes took place in the land ownership structure of the private agricultural sector.[15]

Agricultural modernization, cost reduction and a viable level of income for the peasantry require a minimum size of landholding. Under Polish conditions a 'social minimum' income level, with agriculture being the main source of income for the family, would correspond to around 10 hectares farm size (E. Gorzelak 1987: 399). Therefore the government should provide strong economic incentives (credits for land purchase, tax rebate, priority in the allocation of resources, etc.) and help to encourage private farmers to expand and to consolidate their landholdings.

On the other hand, the average agricultural acreage of state farms, following the campaign of stepping up the tempo of socialist transformation of agriculture during the second half of the 1970s, increased to 4,000 hectares and more (H. Lauen 1977: 115–20). This megalomania led to increasing waste in resource use and diseconomies of scale.

Poland's industrial structure has always been unfavourable to agriculture. It is estimated that only slightly over 4 per cent of the industrial productive capacity was supplying agricultural inputs (A. Wós and Z. Mikołajczyk 1980), which limited agricultural modernization and investment. The socialized farms were disproportionally favoured in the allocation of investment funds and goods, receiving about 63 per cent of total productive agricultural investment in 1971–5 (a large part consisting of investment grants), whilst producing only about 9 per cent of the total agricultural value added! On the other hand, the share of private farms in total productive investment during the same period was approximately 37 per cent (largely originating from farmers' savings), whilst producing 91 per cent of agricultural value added. During the second half of the 1970s, private agriculture was increasingly at a disadvantaged position in the allocation of investment.[16]

In 1975, the average value of fixed assets per fully employed person in the socialized farms was approximately four times greater than the level on private farms. Moreover the structure of the capital stock of private farms was less favourable, having a relatively high proportional value of buildings whilst that of machinery was low. The stagnation of productive investment in private farms in 1975–7, which was followed by a slow growth during the following years, slowed down the progress of agricultural mechanization which was necessary to compensate for the rapid decline in and ageing of the labour force on private farms.

Subject to great difficulties in the definition and measurement of labour inputs in private farming, it is estimated that by the end of 1980 about 30 per cent of the total labour force was engaged in agriculture. According to certain estimates the total number of persons working in agriculture fell by 15 per cent during the 1970s compared to around 3 per cent decline in the 1960s. With around 40 per cent growth of employment in socialized agriculture, the number of persons engaged in private agriculture fell by about 24 per cent during the 1970s (*Rocznik Statystyczny* 1983: 51). The land–labour ratio in private farms was considerably less than in socialized farms; and in private agriculture the land–labour ratio on bigger farms (15 hectares and larger) was approximately seven times greater than on small farms (0.5–2 hectares). In general, the labour force on small- and medium-sized private farms was largely under-utilized, whilst on the other hand, a considerable number of relatively large farms suffered from labour shortage.

The quality of the agrarian labour force was rapidly deteriorating. The large exodus of young people from agricultural to non-agricultural activities aggravated the ageing process of the labour force in agriculture. Farming was highly unattractive (low income, heavy and long work with irregular working hours, low social status, etc.) to young people. The ageing process which plagued private farming was severe in the category of farmers who lived mainly or exclusively from agriculture. According to a survey made by the Institute of Agricultural Economics in Warsaw in the mid-1970s, almost 40 per cent of farms were run by farmers of 60 years old or more and, of these, more than 30 per cent were run by single old women. It should be added that the percentage of farms run by old people was considerably higher on small farms than on large farms (A. Szemberg 1980: 57; B. Simatupang 1981c: 462–3). In general it is unlikely that old farmers, especially those without successors, will be interested in capital investment and farm modernization.

It is interesting to note that the large fall in the number of persons engaged in private agriculture during the 1970s did not, however, lead to a significant concentration of landholding and production. The rapidly growing number of the so-called farmer-worker group (recruited largely from small farming), the ageing process of the agricultural population, the lack of long-run stable agricultural policies and the absence of strong incentives for private land concentration tended to preserve the small and fragmented structure of Poland's private agriculture.

CONCLUSION

The early pro-peasantry agricultural policy of the regime contributed significantly to the agricultural boom of 1971–4 and the rapid growth in the volume and quality of food consumption during the first half of the 1970s. This policy was followed by a squeeze on and discrimination against the private farms, accompanied by a rapid expansion of socialized farms, contributing to a decline in agricultural output and a worsening in the efficiency of resource use. A return to a pragmatic agricultural policy from the late 1970s, under conditions of a deepening economic crisis, did not succeed in reversing the decline in agriculture.

Poland raised Western grain imports considerably from 1975, keeping an adequate food supply to appease the growing consumption demands of a rebellious population. The hard currency deficits in agriculture-related trade contributed very substantially to the increment in Poland's Western debt.

Shortages of food were common throughout the period. They were not caused by a physical shortage of production. By international standards, food consumption in Poland was high. Throughout the period under study attempts to restore food market disequilibria by (aborted) price rises provoked worker protests and/or wage compensation.

The rapid deterioration in agricultural resource use coincided with a rapid expansion of socialized farms. Despite discrimination against them, private farms performed relatively better. The fast decline in the number and quality of persons engaged in private agriculture did not change the small and fragmented structure of Poland's private agriculture.

5

LABOUR SUPPLY

INTRODUCTION

In general, the aggregate growth of labour resources depends on a number of factors, such as population growth, changes in the age structure of the population, the participation rates of each group in employment, the average working hours per year, wage rates and labour mobility. The general tendencies governing the behaviour of each of these factors individually as well as their inter-relationships have varied over time. The scope of government policy to influence the behaviour of each of these factors has also differed. In the CPEs, the planner must provide short-, medium- and long-term labour resources estimates or forecasts for the construction of employment plans. They form a part of the overall socio-economic plans and specify, among other things, the necessary labour inputs to achieve the objectives of the plan, setting up 'labour balances' ('bilansy siły roboczej'). The government adopts certain socio-economic measures which attempt to regulate the supply of labour directly and indirectly in accordance with the basic objectives of the socio-economic plan.

This chapter will describe and analyse a number of important factors influencing the supply of labour in Poland, particularly during the 1970s and early 1980s. It will also deal briefly with certain aspects of labour quality (skill and education levels), professional aspirations and job (dis)satisfation of the labour force. It consists of sections dealing with the following issues: demographic factors, participation rates, working time, labour turnover and education levels of the work force. The next chapter will deal mainly with factors influencing the demand side of employment in Poland.

DEMOGRAPHIC FACTORS

The total population of Poland increased from 23.6 million in 1946 to 36.4 million in 1982, i.e. a growth of 54 per cent in more than three and a half decades, an annual average increase of 1.2 per cent. The annual rate of population growth varied considerably during the period. The population growth was exceptionally fast in the years 1946–55, then it slowed down from the second half of the 1950s. The downward trend in population growth was clearly visible in the 1960s, reaching its lowest rate during the second half of the decade. With an average annual growth of 1.3 per cent for the period 1950–70, Poland had the highest rate of growth of population among the European CMEA countries (M. Kabaj 1978: 3–5). This relatively high growth of population was the result of both a high birth rate and a declining death rate.

The exceptionally high birth rate in the years 1946–55 was even higher than the level observed immediately before the outbreak of the Second World War. There was, moreover, a great desire among the fertile age group to compensate for the large population losses suffered during the Second World War. The post-war 'baby-boom', however, began to slow down significantly in the 1960s, leading to a large drop in the birth rate. The annual average birth rate in the second half of the 1960s, the lowest birth rate noted in Poland after the war, was nearly one-half the average birth rate in the period 1951–5 (see Table 5.1). It is interesting, however, to note that the birth rate increased after 1969. Polish demographers attribute this to a change in the age structure of the female population favourable to women in the child-bearing age group, a shorter time-spread between the birth of the first child and subsequent birth(s) among relatively young mothers, and a compensating stream of births by working mothers in their thirties who limited their child-bearing in the 1960s (W. Kondrat and J. Mijakowska 1981: 8; M. Okólski 1983: 202–3).

In general, the birth rate in the countryside was much higher than in urban centres, although the gap between the two in Poland was narrowing. The large post-war migration of the rural population to urban centres, a high proportion of them consisting of relatively young people, has contributed significantly to the overall decline in birth rate. Rapid urbanization, resulting from the rapid industrialization process, brought important changes in the work and life pattern of the new inhabitants of the towns. These included new opportunities for

Table 5.1 Average annual natural increase in population, 1951–82

	Births	*Deaths*	*Natural increase*
		per 1,000 persons	
1951–5	29.8	10.7	19.1
1956–60	25.9	8.6	17.3
1961–5	19.1	7.6	11.5
1966–70	16.4	7.8	8.6
1971–5	18.0	8.4	9.6
1976–80	19.3	9.2	10.1
1981–2	19.2	9.2	10.0

Source: Z. Smoliński: 'Transformacja demograficzna w Polsce', *Wiadomości Statystyczne*, 25, 6, 1981: 6; *Rocznik Statystyczny* 1983: 42.

education and professional training, a growth in the participation of women in paid employment, housing difficulties, etc. All these factors contributed to an overall drop in the average birth rate.

The post-war death rate showed a steady decline up to the late 1960s, after which it increased. Some Polish demographers attributed this increase in the death rate largely to the process of the ageing of the population, i.e. a rising proportion of old people in the total population (J. Holzer 1979: 54; Z. Smoliński 1981: 6). This ignores, however, the increase in age-specific death rates. An increase of 36 per cent in the crude death rate in the years 1966–80 could not be related solely to the ageing of the population. Moreover, starting from the beginning of the 1970s, the average life expectancy at birth for both boys and girls fell (M. Okólski 1983: 190). According to certain estimates, the average life expectancy of a newly-born boy in the countryside declined by 1.46 years during the period 1974–9.

The large increase in the mortality rate of certain population groups (particularly men) of productive age assumed an alarming proportion. For instance, the mortality rate for men in the age group 35–54 years was between 36–50 per cent higher in 1979 than the lowest mortality rate noted since the war for this group in the mid-1960s.[1] For women, the highest increase in mortality rate noted was 8.6 per cent for the age group 25–9 years (J. Mijakowska 1980: 16). This increase in the mortality rate of men of productive age was unprecedented in its duration and scale in post-war Polish history. It became a typical phenomenon for the European CMEA countries, which so far has not been noted in other European countries (M. Okólski 1983: 214). The disparity in average life expectancy between men and women was growing.

A number of population studies and reports have indicated that the rise in mortality rates, particularly since the second half of the 1970s, was closely related to a deterioration in the general state of health of the population, worsening working conditions of workers and employees, and deteriorating health services (inadequate hospitals, shortages of medical equipment and drugs, etc.), reflecting the deepening socio-economic crises.[2] The rapid rise in the three major causes of death (cardiovascular diseases, cancer and accidents) among men 'in their prime'[3] is believed to be related to the rapid increase in environmental pollution, the widespread and rapid rise in cigarette smoking, high consumption of alcohol (with an estimated 4.5 million excessive drinkers), deterioration in the quality of food and impoverishment of the diet, and the increase of stress caused by hardships at work and daily life. It was not just coincidence that one of the demands made by the workers' strike and agreed upon in the Gdańsk Agreement in the summer of 1980 was to improve the working conditions of workers and employees, and to provide better health services and medical care.

The wave-like change in the growth of population determined the growth pattern and distribution of the working age group over a period of time. This, in turn, determined the supply of labour resources. Due to the high birth rate, up to (approximately) the mid-1960s, the annual increase in total population was higher than that of the working age group[4] and hence the proportion of the working age group in the total population during this period was falling. From the mid-1960s the annual growth of population in the working age group was higher than that of the total population, reflecting both the maturing of those born in the post-war 'baby-boom' and the decline in the birth rate. The annual average growth of population of working age during the period 1965–75 was nearly twice the rate of growth in the years 1950–60. In comparison with other European CMEA countries, Poland had the highest annual average growth of population of working-age in the period 1960–76 (J. Pietrucha 1979: 153). In the second half of the 1970s, the growth of the population of working age slowed down significantly. The large fluctuation in the growth of the working age population created considerable socio-economic problems, constraining the planners' choice of employment policy.

Internal migration formed an important resource in meeting the large labour demand of the non-agricultural sectors. Table 5.2 shows the average annual net migration from rural areas to urban centres for the period 1951–82. The drop in net migration in the second half of the 1950s was followed by a steady growth in the size of net migration. The average annual net migration was very large in the 1970s, and a number of Polish economists and demographers warned of the danger of an 'uncontrolled outflow' of young people, leading to demographic distortions (ageing, shortage of young women eligible for marriage, and depopulation in some regions) of the agricultural working population. Net migration to urban centres in the 1980s slowed down significantly due to a contraction in investment, construction and building activities, increasing housing shortages and the general economic crisis. Net migration to urban centres formed a high percentage of the total increase in urban population, influencing significantly the socio-cultural traits of the urban working people.

Table 5.2 Annual net migration into urban areas and annual increases in the urban population

Period	*Average annual net migration into urban areas (in thousands)*	*Average annual increase in urban population (in thousands)*	*Net migration as a percentage of urban population growth*
1951–5	112.1	564.8	19.8
1956–60	83.9	466.8	18.0
1961–5	100.6	256.0	39.3
1966–70	139.5	281.4	49.6
1971–5	187.6	388.4	48.3
1976–80	213.4	389.8	54.7
1981–2	155.9	294.6	52.8

Sources: Z. Fallenbuchl, 'Migration and Economic Development Under Socialism', in A.A. Brown and E. Neuberger (eds.), *Internal Migration* 1977: 312; *Rocznik Statystyczny* 1981: 31, 60.

Immediately after the war there was a mass external migration, largely due to the changes in Poland's borders. A second wave of external migration took place during the second half of the 1950s. On average net emigration was around 20,000 persons annually in the period 1960–70, i.e. less than 7 per cent of the total population growth (M. Olędzki 1978: 96; U. Fox 1977: 194–5). Net emigration abroad dropped to a low point in the first half of the 1970s. It was followed by a rise in net emigration, particularly among Poles of German origin, in the second half of the 1970s. The socio-economic and political crises in the 1980s encouraged new waves of external migration.

PARTICIPATION RATES

The growth of the labour force of an economy does not only depend on the increase in the population group of working age, but also on the level of participation of the population in (self-)employment or the work process. Participation rates are influenced by a number of complex socio-economic factors, such as social conventions, customs and willingness to work, the system of education and social security, and income and wage policy. In Poland the increase in labour resources was greater than the growth in population of the productive age group. It has been estimated that the increase of labour resources exceeded the growth of population of productive age by more than 600,000 in the period 1951–75.

The increase in the number of young people attending secondary schools and universities, accompanied by a slight decline in the participation rates of men in the labour force, were more than off-set by the rapid growth in female participation in the labour force (K. Dzenio and Z. Fiejka 1978: 123). The increase in female participation rates contributed significantly to the rapid growth of employment in non-agricultural activities. It has been estimated that approximately a quarter of the total increase in the labour force in the non-agricultural sector in the period 1951–75 originated in the increase in the female participation rate (M. Kabaj 1975b: 292).

Characteristic features of the changes in post-war employment in non-agricultural activities were the rapid increase in participation rates of women in the age group 25–59 years on the one hand and a considerable drop in the participation rates of females in the age group 15–19 years and post-productive age group on the other hand. If in 1950 approximately 62 per cent of females in the age group 25–59 years were 'economically active' ('pracujących')[5] for the whole economy, then the coefficient was only 36 per cent for the non-agricultural sectors. In 1970 the respective coefficients were 77 per cent and 68 per cent, and they were still rising up to the mid-1970s (K. Dzenio and Z. Fiejka 1978: 215). In non-agricultural employment, women have been over represented in unskilled labour and the low paid service sectors (education, health service, trade, etc.) and industrial branches (textiles, clothing, etc.) (M. Tatur 1979).

The participation rates of married women in non-agricultural activities increased exceptionally fast, from merely 13 per cent in 1950 to 68 per cent in 1970 and 75 per cent in 1975. By the late 1970s, Poland belonged to the group of countries with the highest rate of participation of married women in paid employment in the whole world (A. Kurzynowski 1979: 20–1). The combination of household work, bringing up children and paid employment created a tight schedule for working mothers. This was aggravated by the poor and inadequate social infrastructure (bad public transport, inefficient retail system, shortages of goods and services, inadequate facilities for childcare, etc.) and time-consuming household work.[6] Many economists and social scientists considered that the high level of participation in paid employment of women in the most fertile age group had exceeded the socially optimal level of rational reproduction of the population (M. Kabaj 1975b: 293; K. Knychała 1978: 26–7).

The rapid growth of female participation in paid employment in non-agricultural activities was also discussed within the general framework of the traditionally pursued maximum employment policy and the permanent insatiable demand for labour (including female labour) by enterprises arising from the systemic features of the CPEs (B. Fick 1970: 78–9). Moreover, the policy of maximum employment pursued, especially during the stage of forced industrialization, was closely associated with the policy of keeping the level and the growth of real wages per worker low (M. Ellman 1979a: 16–17).

A low level and slow growth of average real wages, on the one hand, and the necessity to make ends meet in the household budget or the desire to raise the standards of living, higher than those allowed by the low growth in real wages, on the other hand, had encouraged women to engage in paid employment. Surveys and public opinion polls on the motivations of married women seeking paid employment indicated clearly that the great majority of them who worked in non-agricultural activities did so in order to supplement their household income.[7] In this context it was suggested by a number of Polish economists, bearing in mind the slow growth in real wages in Poland during the 1960s, that a significant growth in average real wages of the main breadwinner, combined with a rationalization of employment, would have helped to discourage married women (especially mothers with young children) from taking paid employment (B. Fick 1970: 78–9; M. Nasiłowski 1974a: 175). But the endeavours of the regime to contain wage growth and overemployment were constrained by opposition from both households and enterprises. The households strove to raise their standard of living by means of increasing the number of gainfully employed members and the enterprises expanded their labour demand through hoarding to ensure plan fulfilment and bonuses (G. Feiwel 1974: 344).

Traditionally women have always been economically active in family farming in Poland. Women's work in private farming, besides the conventional, labour intensive household work, also includes working on livestock farms and field work, tasks which were hitherto carried out largely by men. The growing numbers of the so-called farmer-worker group, who combined non-agricultural employment with sideline agricultural activities, contributed to a feminization of labour in agriculture. A study of the utilization of working time by the agricultural labour force in private farming in the Cracow region in the 1960s, estimated that the share of women's labour in the total labour outlays comprised more than 50 per cent, whilst the share of men was 35 per cent and the labour of children constituted around 14 per cent (cited in K. Knychała 1978: 58–9). The average working day of women active in private farming, consisting largely of physical work because of the low level of mechanization, was long, varying between 12 and 16 hours (K. Knychała 1978: 58). It is obvious that the results of agricultural production depended to a large extent on the labour of women.

In general the increase in participation in employment was encouraged by the following factors:

- the rapid industrialization policy (maximum employment), coupled with low level and low growth of real wages;
- the income and wage policies pursued had made an increase in household income possible through more members of households (housewives) taking paid employment;
- the expansion of facilities for childcare (crèches, kindergartens, schools, etc.) and improved social legislation (equal pay for men and women, paid and unpaid maternity leave, as well as leave for mothers caring for sick children, etc.) enabled mothers to combine paid employment with bringing up a family.

Participation in paid employment was restrained by the following factors:

- the extension of the schooling and training period;
- the growing number of people included in the state pension scheme and the introduction of a flexible (early) retirement system;
- longer maternity leave and higher family allowances.

Table 5.3 sets out the variations and the trends in participation rates of the population, classified according to sex, age groups and economic sectors (agriculture and non-agriculture) on the basis of censuses of 1960, 1970, 1978 and 1984. Traditionally the participation rates of the population in (self-) employment in agriculture has been considerably higher than those in the non-agricultural sector. The contrast between the two is very striking when one compares the exceptionally high proportion of the population in the post-productive age group that has been classified as economically active in agriculture.[8]

The rising trend in the participation rates of the population of productive age in the non-agriculture sector (particularly women) stopped in the second half of the 1970s. For some sub-groups (e.g. women between 20–4 years, men and women between 55–64 years) the trend was reversed. A decline in the male participation in the non-mobile age group was probably due to the increasing number of disabled people (J. Adam 1982: 124), indicating the worsening of the health situation. The declining trend in participation rates had been accelerated by the introduction of paid leave of absence for young mothers to raise children, early retirement schemes in 1981–2 and the attraction of a rapidly expanded private sector, supplemented by moonlighting in 'informal' activities. The number of old workers and employees who opted for early retirement in 1982–3 was greater than anticipated.

WORKING TIME, ABSENTEEISM AND LABOUR TURNOVER

Up to 1981 the statutory working time in the socialized sector was eight hours daily (six hours on Saturday), or forty-six hours weekly, a stipulation originating in a law enacted in 1919. However, for certain groups of workers and employees nominal working time was actually shorter. For instance, for workers employed on around the clock production or a system of four shifts (e.g. coal miners) and workers employed in heavy work and jobs hazardous to health, the weekly average working time was less than the legally stipulated length. Furthermore, employees in certain branches of public administration, health services, insurance, teachers and scientists and so on had an average working week of forty-two hours, a regulation which ironically originated before the Second World War. On the whole, only around 2 million persons, or 19 per cent of the total employed in the socialized sector, had a shorter working week (J. Rosner 1981: 301; W. Szafarczyk 1982: 226). In comparison to the industrialized Western and other European CMEA countries, Poland had on average longer working hours. The workers in Poland considered a reform of statutory working time as necessary and long overdue.

The reduction in the average working time, occurring under workers' pressure, was mainly achieved by an increase in the number of vacation days per worker and an introduction of a limited number of free Saturdays in the 1970s.[9] The latter was granted, however, on the condition that certain requirements, such as fulfilment of the growth targets in labour productivity and no increase in overtime, were met by the enterprises. In many cases, additional free Saturdays did not lead to a shorter working week, but merely a rescheduling of the work time with greater intensity of labour and overtime because of the need to catch up the fall in output (W. Szafarczyk 1982: 227).

Workers' preference for more leisure time accompanied by a desire for higher standards of living, became increasingly strong in the 1970s (T. Stalewski 1976). This preference was significantly influenced by the shorter working week (free Saturdays) in the industrialized West. The stagnation and subsequent fall in real wages, particularly since the last years of the 1970s, reinforced the desire for more free time and a reduction in working time (D. Dobrowolska 1985). Planners and enterprise managers were in general unsympathetic to this desire. The economic motivations and incentives for introducing the necessary changes in investment, reorganization of work and planning end so on which would make shorter working time feasible without adverse effects on production, were absent.

Table 5.3 Participation rates[a]

Population	*Total*				*Non-agriculture*				*Agriculture*			
	1960	*1970*	*1978*	*1984*	*1960*	*1970*	*1978*	*1984*	*1960*	*1970*	*1978*	*1984*
Total economy	47.5	51.9	51.2	48.9	40.8	47.0	48.0	44.6	58.1	62.7	61.2	64.2
In the age group:												
pre-productive	3.2	2.1	1.1	0.7	1.7	0.8	0.7	0.3	5.8	4.9	2.2	1.8
productive	78.9	82.6	80.3	78.0	71.1	87.8	77.6	74.1	92.0	91.8	89.4	92.6
mobile[b]	78.8	82.3	81.7	82.0	73.1	80.2	80.9	80.5	90.6	88.6	84.6	88.6
not mobile[c]	79.0	83.3	77.2	69.7	65.6	74.5	68.7	58.6	94.1	96.6	96.3	97.9
post-productive	44.2	44.2	27.2	24.1	13.4	12.3	5.1	4.5	74.3	83.0	76.8	95.0
Male	55.4	57.7	57.4	55.1	54.0	56.0	55.3	51.7	57.8	62.0	63.8	66.5
In the age group:												
pre-productive	3.2	2.1	1.3	0.8	2.0	0.9	0.8	0.4	5.2	5.0	2.7	3.3
productive	93.2	90.6	87.8	85.0	89.4	89.1	86.0	81.8	96.8	95.1	94.1	96.5
mobile[b]	93.6	90.5	89.5	90.6	93.0	90.0	89.1	89.8	95.1	92.2	91.1	94.2
not mobile[c]	92.4	91.0	84.0	73.7	87.4	86.6	78.1	63.8	98.7	99.0	99.0	99.7
post-productive	59.7	56.4	34.9	29.7	24.8	21.9	7.9	5.8	87.6	91.3	86.4	98.3
Female	40.3	46.4	45.4	43.0	27.9	37.9	40.9	38.0	58.3	63.4	58.7	61.8
In the age group:												
pre-productive	3.2	2.0	0.9	0.6	1.3	0.8	0.6	0.3	6.3	4.9	1.7	1.4
productive	65.3	74.3	72.6	70.6	49.6	67.1	68.8	66.2	88.3	89.2	84.8	88.1
mobile[b]	65.5	74.1	73.6	73.1	52.8	69.6	72.7	71.3	87.5	85.8	77.8	81.9
not-mobile[c]	65.0	74.8	70.1	65.1	40.8	59.0	58.2	52.7	89.7	94.4	93.9	96.0
post-productive	38.2	39.0	23.3	21.7	9.6	8.7	3.8	3.9	68.4	78.9	71.1	93.2

Sources: *Rocznik Statystyczny* 1980: 41; *Rocznik Statystyczny* 1986: 46.
Notes: [a]according to population censuses, per 100 persons.
[b]Male and female in the age group 18–44 years.
[c]Male between 45–64 years old, and female 45–59 years.

Far reaching reforms in working time are usually the outcome of a persistent demand by the working people themselves. The huge protest of the workers in the summer of 1980 were to demand a shorter working week, free Saturdays, changes in the organization of working time and improved working conditions. The demands demonstrated the extent of the workers' dislike of exhausting long working hours and the desire to have more free time for physical and psychological regeneration. The general agreement between the regime and the protesting workers in Gdańsk, Szczecin and Jastrzęby stipulated a forty-two-hour working week and a limited number of free Saturdays for 1981, with a five day or forty-hour working week planned to be introduced in the future. In the Jastrzęby Agreement on work in coal mines, all Saturdays and Sundays were to be free as from 1 January 1981. If Saturday work was necessary, it was to be carried out on a strictly voluntary basis with higher pay. In view of the rapid economic deterioration, the workers responded positively to Solidarność's appeal to work in key industries (particularly coal mining) on the last eight free Saturdays in 1981, in exchange for extra pay and rations of meat (D. Mason 1985: 194–5).The four-shifts work system, work being carried out twenty-four hours a day underground in the coal mines and working on Sundays and holidays were very unpopular, and according to Polish sociologists, the system had distorted the normal rhythm of coalminers' family life.

The introduction of martial law on 13 December 1981 brought a militarization of important industries and plants (plants working under 'operational programmes', public utilities, armaments industry, etc.), prohibition of strikes, work on Saturdays and imprisonment of the leaders of Solidarność. The 'normalization' of the labour relationship under the aegis of martial law (suspended in 1983) contributed to an increase in the average industrial working hours per worker in 1982–3 compared to its lowest level in 1981.

Table 5.4 sets out the trend in average industrial working hours, non-utilized hours (sick leave, maternity leave, etc.) and holidays per worker in the period 1960–82. Both nominal and actual working hours per industrial worker dropped during the period. The average actual working time dropped by 16 per cent in the years 1960–82, mainly during the first half of the 1970s and in 1981 (both periods when the workers were politically strong). Overtime varied between 3.3 and 6.5 per cent of the normal working time; but overtime varied considerably between industrial branches, ranging for instance from 176 hours per worker per annum in the coal industry, to only twenty-three hours per worker per annum in light industry in 1979 (*Rocznik Statystyczny Przemysłu* 1980: 218–19). Irregular supply of inputs, power cuts, and a systemically built-in tendency to increase work intensity during the last part of a planning period enforced overtime work.

Non-utilized ('nie przepracowane') time due to sickness, maternity leave, and absence without leave, as distinct from vacation leave, was growing. Sick leave, constituting around two-thirds of the non-utilized working time, increased by 53 per cent in 1971–81, despite the regime's 'campaigns against absenteeism', such as control visits to those on sick leave, bonuses for low sick leave, etc. The rapid

Table 5.4 Working hours in socialized industry (production and development group per worker, 1960–82)

	1960		*1970*		*1975*		*1978*		*1980*		*1981*		*1982*	
	Hours	*Per cent*	*Hours*	*Per cent*	*Hours*	*Per cent*	*Hours*	*Per cent*	*Hours*	*Per cent*	*Hours*	*Per cent*	*Hours*	*Per cent*
Nominal working time	2346	100	2324	100	2255	100	2252	100	2238	100	2124	100	2123	100
Actual working time	2154	91.8	2062	88.7	1969	87.3	1952	86.7	1920	85.8	1763	84.0	1809	85.2
of which:														
nominal working hours	2057	87.7	1995	85.8	1890	83.8	1870	83.0	1842	82.3	1686	80.4	1697	79.9
overtime	97	4.1	67	2.9	79	3.5	82	3.6	78	3.5	77	3.7	112	5.2
Non-utilized working time[a]	161	6.9	169	7.3	201	8.9	21.4	9.5	226	10.1	243	11.5	236	11.1
of which:														
paid stoppages[b]	14	0.6	9	0.4	7	0.3	5	0.2	11	0.5	15	0.7	6	0.3
sick leave	93	4.0	112	4.8	142	6.3	159	7.1	163	7.3	171	8.1	171	8.1
maternity leave	–	–	10	0.4	22	1.0	22	1.0	22	1.0	19	1.0	20	0.9
absence without leave	11	0.4	7	0.3	5	0.2	4	0.2	5	0.2	5	0.2	4	0.2
vacation	128	5.4	160	6.9	164	7.3	168	7.5	170	7.6	175	8.1	180	8.4

Sources: *Rocznik Statystyczny Przemysłu* 1980: 216–17; *Rocznik Statystyczny* 1983: 62, 201.
Notes: [a]Does not include the reduction in hours for workers in the four-shift system, heavy work and hazardous working conditions.
[b]Stoppages due to shortage of power and materials and, since 1980, strikes are included.

growth in sick leave, including an increase in the number of days of work incapacity due to disease and accidents at work, in combination with a rapid increase in the number of employees suffering from occupational diseases, clearly indicated the deterioration of the state of health and the worsening conditions of labour in the 1970s.[10] Simple work clothing, gloves, protective masks and shoes were in short supply. Furthermore, there were great shortages in the investment resources, equipment and tools needed to ensure labour safety. According to a study by independent experts, close to 3 million persons in 1981 were working in places or had jobs which were heavy and injurious to health ('Raport a absencji chorobowej', *Życie Warszawy* 31 January, 1983). A survey among workers in three large plants (the steel factory Huta Warszawa, Gdańsk shipyard, Ursus tractor plant) in 1982–3 showed that poor health due to heavy work and health hazards was the main motivation of those who opted for early retirement (B. Synak 1984).

Absenteeism varied considerably between economic sectors, industrial branches, sexes, regions and age groups. For example, the construction and building sector had a high rate of absenteeism (a high percentage of the work force consisted of the so-called worker-peasant group). Industrial branches like energy and chemicals had a comparatively low rate of absenteeism. The textile and clothing industries (with a high percentage of the work force consisting of women) had a relatively high rate of absenteeism. Regional variations were also significant. For example, the voivodships Novosad, Cracowa and Tarnobrzeg, regions with a high percentage of the so-called worker-peasant group in total employment in non-agricultural activities, had a relatively high rate of absenteeism, particularly during harvest time. The frequency of sick leave was higher for young workers, although the average duration was shorter in comparison to the sick leave of older workers.

According to official statistics, non-utilized time constituted 10 per cent of nominal working time in 1978. A study made by a research institute under the Ministry of Labour estimated that in 1978 the enterprises' reserve in the form of non-utilized time, mainly due to defects in planning and bad organization of work, shortages and irregular supply of inputs, breakdown of power, etc. had varied between 20–30 per cent of the nominal working time (cited in D. Dobrowolska 1985: 211–12). The deepening of the supply crisis contributed to increasing production interruptions and dislocation of the rhythm of normal working time.

In general, labour mobility, requiring part of the labour employed in sectors, branches and plants having a low level of productivity to be transferred to those with a higher level, is a necessary condition for an optimal allocation of labour resources. In the early 1950s, during the large exodus of unskilled labour of peasant origin seeking employment in non-agricultural activities, the rate of labour turnover varied between 40–50 per cent per annum (L. Sobczak 1971: 229). The long-run rate of labour turnover subsequently stabilized at around 20 per cent per annum. Although Poland's rate of labour turnover was relatively low compared to the rate in certain Western economies, the regime complained about 'excessive' labour turnover. A Polish labour economist estimated that one-fifth of the number of persons who changed jobs could be considered as 'excessive' (M. Olędzki 1978: 200–1), much less than the claim of the regime. Other Polish economists suggested that various financial and administrative obstacles to labour mobility, together with shortages in housing and poor infrastructure, reduced labour mobility below its optimum level, making a swift restructuring of production favouring exports and consumer goods more difficult.

Table 5.5 sets out figures on labour turnover over the period 1965–82. Up to 1978 the total number of persons hired annually exceeded the number of persons leaving their jobs. In 1979–82, however, a reverse process occurred. The proportion of dismissal by enterprises out of an increasing total number of persons leaving their jobs had dropped considerably. Enterprises were increasingly less inclined to dismiss labour under conditions of a growing shortage of labour. On the other hand, the proportion of 'irregular discharges' ('porzucenie pracy'), i.e. leaving jobs without observing the regulations concerning termination of labour contracts, was increasing up to 1975. A high percentage of 'irregular discharges' involved young workers, demonstrating their dissatisfactions with their jobs. In general, young workers and employees were more mobile and changed their jobs more frequently than older persons. It was estimated that 50–70 per cent of the total number of dismissals and departures on the initiative of the employee during the first half of the 1970s involved young workers in the age group 18–25 years (M. Kabaj 1981: 154), whilst the percentage of this group in the total labour force in the socialized sector was much lower. Low remuneration, heavy work and bad conditions of labour, and lack of promotion prospects, were major reasons for changing jobs.

EDUCATION LEVEL, ASPIRATIONS AND FRUSTRATIONS OF THE LABOUR FORCE

The low level of socio-economic development and inadequate education facilities of pre-war Poland, plus the large losses of qualified and skilled personnel during the Second World War led to a great shortage of skilled workers, technicians, engineers and managers in the post-war economic reconstruction. The need for skilled labour and other qualified personnel expanded rapidly with the implementation of the forced industrialization programme initiated by the Six Year Plan (1950–5).

Enterprises and plants, industrial associations and (economic) ministries played an important role in the organization of on-the-job training and courses for skilled workers, technicians and managers. Particularly important was the large scale of on-the-job training for the newly employed workers, a large part of whom were recruited from the peasantry, which helped to meet the urgent need for semi-skilled and skilled labour. Production (coal mining) and investment (construction, building) were constrained by a shortage of skilled workers.

Table 5.5 Turnover of the labour force[a] in the socialized sector, 1965–82

	1965	*1970*	*1971*	*1975*	*1976*	*1977*	*1978*	*1979*	*1980*	*1981*	*1982*
Total number of persons hired (in 1,000) of which:	2004	2266	2448	2860	2885	2696	2608	2657	2336	2041	2440
men	1394	1549	1649	1813	1799	1724	1651	1672	1475	1251	1453
women	610	717	799	1047	1986	972	955	985	861	790	987
Total number of persons leaving their jobs (in 1,000) of which:	1729	2080	2032	2545	2623	2582	2566	2667	2365	2226	2686
Men	1268	1461	1453	1652	1687	1679	1665	1700	1512	1327	1611
Women	461	619	579	893	936	903	901	967	853	899	1057
Labour turnover rate[b] (%)	22.5	21.9	21.7	21.7	21.7	20.6	20.2	21.0	18.3	15.7	20.1
People leaving their jobs due to (%):											
Dismissals	24.1	16.1	12.1	6.7	7.0	5.9	5.3	4.6	5.1	–	–
Employees' initiatives	38.5	28.7	27.3	25.9	23.7	26.5	26.0	25.7	24.6	–	–
Irregular discharges	12.6	14.1	16.5	17.6	14.7	14.9	14.6	12.5	13.9	–	–

Sources: *Rocznik Statystyczny* of various years; *Zatrudnienie w Gospodarce Narodowej 1980* 1980.
Notes: [a]For the whole year, excluding part-time and seasonal workers and employees of the political and social organization.
[b]Total persons leaving their jobs in a given year as a percentage of total labour employed at the end of the preceding year.

Enrollment and graduation in general and vocational schools expanded rapidly. For instance, more than 1.2 million persons completed higher education, technical school and general secondary school in the years 1950–5 compared to 310,000 persons in the years 1946–9 (H. Dankowski 1975: 55).

Table 5.6 illustrates the progress in the level of formal education of the workers and employees in the socialized sector in 1958–82. At the end of the 1950s about three-quarters of the working people employed in the socialized sector had only an elementary education or less. Many of them were illiterate or semi-literate and recruited largely from the peasantry. By 1982 the proportion of working people employed in the socialized sector with an elementary education or less went down to about one-third. During this period the relative importance of semi-skilled and unskilled labour was significantly reduced. The absolute number and proportion of workers and employees in the socialized sector who had completed higher education, secondary (general and technical) schools and basic vocational schools increased considerably in the years 1958–82, particularly during the 1970s. Graduates from the secondary, technical and basic vocational schools, whose proportion in the total employment in the socialized sector increased from only 15 per cent in 1958 to nearly 50 per cent in 1982, formed the main core and source of recruitment of technicians and skilled workers.

The education level of the working people differed considerably between economic sectors. On the whole, the education level of the labour force in agriculture, especially in private agriculture, was very low in comparison to those employed in the non-agricultural sectors. According to the population census of 1970, there were only seventy per thousand economically active persons in the agricultural sector who had an education beyond an elementary level, compared to 460 persons in the non-agricultural sectors (cited in K. Dzenio 1975: 103–4). In private agriculture, the situation was worse. For instance, in 1970 it was estimated that 53 per cent of individual farmers had not completed elementary school (which was practically equivalent to no education at all), 42 per cent had completed elementary school and only 4 per cent had completed basic vocational education (M. Sulmicka 1975: 255–7). The majority of the graduates of agricultural colleges and secondary agricultural schools performed administrative jobs in towns! Unlike the rapid progress in the education of labour employed in the non-agriculture sectors (industry, construction and service, etc.) in the 1970s, the education level of agricultural labour practically stagnated. This low level of education, combined with the ageing of agricultural labour, constituted a serious obstacle to agricultural development.

Some argued that Poland's labour force in the non-agricultural sectors was over-qualified. For instance, the ratio of employment of personnel with higher technical education to total employment in the non-agricultural sector was higher in Poland than in a number of industrialized Western countries.[11] Furthermore, there was also widespread misallocation and irrational job assignments of engineers and other qualified personnel. Qualified personnel were

Table 5.6 Employment in the socialized economy by type of education, 1958–82

	Type of education					
	Total	*Higher*[a]	*Secondary*[b] *General*	*Technical*	*Basic vocational*[c]	*Elementary*[d]
	(in thousands)					
1958[e]	6350.8	239.9	275.5	438.6	522.0	4874.6
1964	7137.2	310.4	313.7	598.2	798.4	5116.3
1970	9312.0	501.6	526.1	1273.8	1589.2	5421.0
1975	11350.4	712.3	695.6	1875.6	2456.3	5610.6
1979	11661.5	891.2	746.3	2356.2	2766.9	4900.9
1981	11452.9	949.0	733.2	2456.9	2841.4	4472.4
1982	11193.9	972.9	720.6	2480.9	2872.6	4146.9
	(in percent)					
1958	100	3.8	4.3	6.9	8.2	76.8
1964	100	4.3	4.4	8.4	11.2	71.7
1970	100	5.4	5.7	13.7	17.1	58.1
1975	100	6.3	6.1	16.5	21.6	49.5
1979	100	7.6	6.4	20.2	23.7	42.1
1981	100	8.3	6.4	21.5	24.8	39.0
1982	100	8.7	6.4	22.2	25.7	37.0
	(indices (1958=100))					
1958	100	100	100	100	100	100
1964	112.4	141.9	113.9	136.4	153.0	105.0
1970	146.6	209.1	191.0	290.4	304.4	111.2
1975	178.7	296.9	252.5	427.6	470.6	115.1
1979	183.6	371.5	270.9	537.2	530.1	100.5
1981	180.3	395.5	266.1	560.1	540.3	91.7
1982	176.2	405.5	261.5	565.6	550.3	85.0

Sources: *Rocznik Statystyczny Pracy* 1971: 141; *Zatrudnienie w Gospodarce Narodowej* 1980: 3; *Rocznik Statystyczny* 1986: 70.
Notes: [a]University or equivalent education (4–6 years of studies after matriculation);
[b]Secondary education of general and technical type (4–5 years enrolment beyond elementary school);
[c]Basic vocational education (3 years of additional school beyond the elementary school);
[d]elementary schools (7–8 years or less).
[e]For 1958: 31 October 1958; 1964: 31 January 1964; the rest, end of year.

assigned to jobs which were not in accordance with their education or training. Studies and surveys have shown that between 30 and 50 per cent of engineers' working time was devoted to activities which did not require higher education or training at all, consisting mostly of simple, routine administrative tasks (M. Kabaj 1975a: 16; J. Tymowski 1982a: 104–10). Job assignments of economists were even worse. Technicians were frequently assigned to simple and monotonous jobs which were far below their professional competence and training. The widespread irrational use of qualified personnel was not only a waste of human resources and capital, but it also contributed to widespread discontent, dissatisfaction and frustration among qualified personnel, particularly among young employees and workers.

In CPEs enterprises and other labour employing institutions tended to overstate their demand for labour in general and for qualified personnel in particular, far exceeding the amount of labour required to carry out the plan targets. The hoarding and irrational use of qualified personnel had led to permanent labour shortages. Despite the rapid expansion in the number of graduates from technical schools and higher education institutions, the demand for them permanently outstripped supply (M. Kabaj 1975a: 11). This pseudo shortage of skilled and qualified personnel was mainly systemically determined, a built-in feature of CPEs.

It is often argued that because of the low level of wages, combined with the small wage differentials between the average salary of qualified personnel and the average wage of blue collar workers, enterprises tended to assign highly qualified personnel to jobs far below their skill and competence. In fact the wage differentials became even smaller in the 1970s. For instance, the ratio of average salaries of technicians and engineers in non-leading positions to average wages of blue collar workers fell from 1.5 in 1970 to 1.25 in 1979 and to less than one in 1981 (J. Tymowski 1982a: 104–10). This helped to encourage excessive demand for qualified personnel. Actually, enterprises did not pay the full cost of the 'reproduction of labour power', particularly the cost of training and educating qualified employees, which was covered largely by the state budget. It has been argued that a combination of a flexible wage system, enterprise autonomy to determine wage rates, and the introduction of a progressive tax on the wage bill or on employment representing the higher cost of education and training of qualified personnel, might reduce the excessive demand and irrational use of qualified personnel (M. Kabaj 1972: 281–9). There was no incentive, however, for enterprises to economize on qualified employees as long as they could shift the high labour costs to others (state subsidies, price rises, etc.) in an unreformed economic system.

The rapid growth of non-agricultural employment in the 1970s (particularly in industry and construction), supported by the rapid growth of young workers who joined the labour market for the first time as a result of the 'baby boom' of the late 1940s and the 1950s, led to a significant rejuvenation of the labour force. The percentage of young workers and employees (up to 29 years) in total employment in 1968 was 30.9 per cent, in 1973 it was already 37.3 per cent and in 1977 it went up to 38.1 per cent. The proportion of young workers and employees in industrial and construction sectors was higher than the overall average. For instance, the percentage of young workers and employees in the electrical and mechanical industries was 45.5 per cent in 1977. If persons up to 39 years old are included, the proportion of young workers and employees in total employment was over 60 per cent (M. Tatur 1983: 25–6). Furthermore the trend of concentration of industrial employment growth in large-size key industries (steel production, coal mining, shipyards and electrical industries, etc.) was reinforced in the 1970s.

The process of rejuvenation of the non-agricultural labour force occurred simultaneously with a rapid improvement in the level of education (see Table 5.6). This rapid progress in education was especially visible among young workers and employees. The percentage of young people in the group of skilled and qualified (secondary, general and technical education) personnel increased significantly in the 1970s.

Gierek's accelerated industrialization brought about a rapid growth in the number of young workers and employees with higher educational standards. They discovered the appeal of modern consumerism and youth life-style (modern music, dress, etc.) imported from the West, which they came to know through the mass media, contacts with family members living abroad and, for some, by means of personal encounters during a visit (or even having a job) in the West. Furthermore, Gierek encouraged aspiration towards higher consumption in the context of a strategy of depoliticization of the population and legitimation of the regime. In general, the young workers and employees had more self-confidence and were more critical of the authorities, compared to their parents who had experienced the hardships of the war or immediate post-war period and the ruthless rule of Stalin.

In an opinion poll conducted in 1973 about the hierarchy of social values, the question was asked as to which values are 'worth pursuing' in one's life. Both young and old respondents put 'happy family life' and 'prized workmanship' at the top. These two supreme values were supplemented by other values, which were ordered differently among the young and old respondents. Young respondents ranked 'possibilities for upgrading profession' and 'social acknowledgement' immediately after the supreme values, putting 'material comfort' on the fifth rank. Old respondents, on the other hand, ranked 'material comfort' and 'a quiet life' immediately after the supreme values (W. Adamski 1980). Young people's perceptions of material welfare were related normally to the desire to have a furnished flat and sufficient income to provide for basic needs (food, clothes, etc.), opportunities for travel and (further) education, combined with interesting work.[12] Other surveys and studies conducted by Polish sociologists in the 1970s more or less confirmed these findings. Family life and career (work) occupied top rankings, supplemented by welfare and education (M. Malikowski 1977; J. Poplucz 1981).

Young workers and employees, especially those with high educational standards, cherished high professional aspirations and expectations, looked forward to having interesting work and opportunities to put the acquired qualifications and skills into practice, and anticipated a high degree of job satisfaction. Beside its intrinsic values, education was generally conceived as a means to acquire skills and competence, which were instrumental in career promotion, higher income and social prestige. A confrontation with the employment realities meant in many cases that the acquired qualifications and skills were either not utilized at all or only partially used in the occupation or job. Opinion polls conducted in 1973 among young industrial workers showed that the degree of job satisfaction decreased with a higher level of education and training (K. Opolski and W. Wlodarski 1979). Earlier polls among engineers disclosed their high dissatisfaction and critical attitudes to their work and job assignments (J. Hozer, 1965).

Technical supervisors received less pay than blue collar workers on the highest pay scale. In general, the technical intelligentsia considered that education was devalued as disclosed by a growing discrepancy between earnings, social prestige and education level. Young employees graduating from higher education (engineers, economists, etc.) were earning less than blue collar workers of comparable age (S. Marczuk 1981: 135). On the other hand, wage and income differentials, inequality in the distribution of scarce goods and services, and privileges were increasing, particularly during the second half of the 1970s, which are largely thought to be unrelated to work quality, performance and skill. The link between individual inputs of labour and occupational achievements and qualifications was disrupted, violating the perceived socialist principle of pay according to work.

Various opinion surveys conducted in the 1970s have shown that a high proportion of the respondents consisting of young workers and employees initially had the opinion that workmanship, skill, education and training were important in determining the level of income and individual career prospects. They soon discovered, however, that other factors, such as having a good place in the 'informal network' of friends and system of protection, family connections, a good relationship with the superiors, cunning and smartness, and Party membership, etc. were decisive for individual career prospects, higher income, the distribution of scarce goods and social advancement (M. Malikowski 1977; S. Marczuk 1981; M. Jarosz 1985). Such a situation, which has been identified by sociologists as a state of anomie (i.e conditions in which the system of standards and expectations is in disarray), discouraged the motivation to produce high quality work. Good and solid work did not pay and were not rational. This situation caused widespread frustration, uncertainty and made the workers helpless. They were forced to adjust themselves to the discipline of the 'informal networks' and to participate in the process of the so-called pseudo-work ('działalność pozorna') where every one is pretending to work. This generated waste, inefficiency, disorganization and widespread frustration. The failure of the economic and employment systems to meet the occupational and economic aspirations and expectations of the qualified and skilled personnel contributed significantly to the workers' protests in the summer of 1980.

CONCLUSION

The state of health of the population in general, and the working population in particular, was deteriorating, especially from the second half of the 1970s. The working conditions (work safety, labour protection and hygienic conditions, etc.) were worsening; and a significant proportion of the workers were doing work which was heavy and injurious to health. The average working week in Poland was comparatively long and the preference among workers and employees for a shorter working week (free Saturdays) was firmly revealed in the 1970s. The rising trend in the participation rates of married women, which may have exceeded the socially optimal level, was reversed by the end of the 1970s. The four-shifts work system in coal mining was very unpopular. The post-war 'baby boomers', maturing in the late 1960s and 1970s, with higher educational standards and more professional training, had high occupational and consumption aspirations and expectations. The failure of the employment system and the economy to meet both aspirations and expectations contributed significantly to the emergence of the workers' protests in the summer of 1980.

6

LABOUR POLICY

INTRODUCTION

Economic crisis and recession in the industrialized market economies and Third World countries are characterized by widespread bankruptcies, closure of plants and high unemployment. In the late 1970s and early 1980s, Poland experienced a deep economic crisis and recession which were comparable to – and in certain fields (foreign debt, for instance) were worse than – the economic depression of the 1930s. By the end of 1982, net material product, investment and output per worker (according to official statistics) were respectively 23.5 per cent, 45 per cent and 20 per cent less than in 1978 (*Rocznik Statystyczny* 1983: 69, 155). Nevertheless, the yearly average employment level in the socialized sector remained stable in 1978–81; only in 1982 did the yearly average employment drop by 4 per cent and after that it remained stable. Neither bankruptcies nor plant closures took place.

Full employment was accompanied by acute labour shortage and gross under-utilization and misallocation of labour in the workplace. Enterprises and state non-profit institutions tended to hoard labour and to keep high labour reserves; the incentives to economize on labour were weak. This chapter will describe a number of significant factors influencing demand for labour, the drive towards full employment, employment policy and regulations. In addition, it will discuss problems concerning the relationship between full employment, the rationalization of employment and the resolution of the economic crisis.

THE DRIVE TOWARDS FULL EMPLOYMENT

The concepts of full employment, unemployment, disguised unemployment, etc., are closely related to certain socio-economic systems, i.e. they are systemically determined. Strictly speaking, the concept of employment refers only to the act of hiring labour as expressed for example in the wage/salary relationship. One of the main features of European state socialist economies was the prevailing tendency towards, or state of, full employment,[1] which was combined with labour under-utilization and labour redundancy ('unemployment on the job').

Full employment in the state socialist economies was not of a temporary nature. Once full employment was achieved, it remained stable and durable, guaranteed by job security. Provided that one was not involved in political activities directed against the state or criminal offences, legal provisions regulating dismissals were such that it was very difficult to dismiss workers for incompetence or make them redundant. Moreover, some groups of workers were protected against dismissal (the handicapped, pregnant women, etc.).

In the economic literature dealing with employment in state socialist economies, one can distinguish broadly two views which attempt to explain the drive towards full employment and eventually labour shortage in such economies.

The first view (M. Ellman 1979a; D. Granick 1987) treats full employment as a goal of economic policy. It attributes full employment to the striving of the regime to keep the highest possible rate of economic growth through mobilization of labour reserves and high growth of productive investment ('extensive economic growth strategy'), substituting scarce capital with abundant labour and keeping wages low. The striving was magnified in Poland by political and social pressure to create more employment opportunities in view of the inherited high rural, regional and urban unemployment, a high growth of population of productive age and a growing desire among women to participate in paid employment.

The second view is that full employment and labour shortage follow necessarily from the economic system. Kornai, the Hungarian economist, one of the main advocates of this view, argues that 'if the system is resource constrained, an almost unlimited investment hunger and expansion drive *must* prevail, and the potential reserve labour *must* be absorbed sooner or later' in employment (J. Kornai 1980: 126; emphasis in original). The lack of Keynesian effective demand did not form an obstacle to steady, high growth of output and employment in state socialist economies. At the macro-level the limits to sustained high growth in output in a resource constrained economic system were basically the physical constraints (the supply side) and the limits of social tolerance (slow growth or even a drop in consumption and real wages) associated with a certain pattern of accelerated economic growth.[2]

Summarizing the experience of economic development of the state socialist countries, one can list four main factors which contributed to the high rates of growth of employment and the maintenance of full employment.

1 The restriction of the principle of production for profit through the employment of the workers even when their wages were below the value of their marginal product.
2 The policy of large investment programmes, concentrating on the expansion of production capacities, normally coupled with a low level and slow growth in wages.
3 Capital intensive production techniques in basic production processes

combined with labour intensive variants for auxiliary works and services (internal transportation, loading, etc.), establishing a compromise between capital intensive and labour intensive production techniques.

4 A rapid expansion of the so-called 'quaternary sector' (education, health services, state administration and cultural activities, etc.) which were largely labour intensive activities.

(M. Ellman 1979a: 12–18; J. Kornai 1980: 262)

In general, the drive towards full employment and labour shortage was the result of both the striving of the regime to achieve a high rate of economic growth through massive investment and the systemic factors inherent in the state socialist economies. Since the late 1970s, however, the influence of the first factor in Poland turned out to be much less than the second, because of the drastic cut in investment and slow economic growth.

The drive towards and the state of full employment in Poland can be illustrated statistically in at least two ways. First, Table 6.1 shows the growth of population, working age population and employment (including self-employment) for the period 1950–82. Total employment (part-time workers are converted into full–time equivalents) increased from a yearly average of 10.2 million persons in 1950 to 17.4 million persons in 1981, i.e. a growth of 7.2 million (71 per cent), comprising an increase of 7.9 million (164 per cent) in the socialized sector and a decline of 0.7 million (12 per cent) in the private sector. The total growth in employment exceeded both the rates of growth of population and population of productive age. The drop in employment in private agriculture was more than compensated by the growth of employment in the socialized sector. The post-war increase in employment in the socialized sector absorbed not only the growth of population and the population of productive age but also part of the redundant labour in agriculture and labour reserves (unemployed, married women, etc.) in the urban centres. The economic crisis of 1979–82 and the government measures against threatened unemployment led to a drop of employment in the socialized sector in 1982 and a limited change in the composition of employment favouring employment in the non-agricultural private sector. The regime, however, remained committed to full employment.

Second, the central and local statistical offices regularly published the number of people seeking work and the number of vacant jobs registered at the local labour offices. Table 6.2 gives the figures for the economy as a whole. The data should, however, be treated with certain reservations. It is a well-known fact that the majority of people seeking work did not register themselves at the local labour offices. In fact, there was no legal obligation to register,[3] and little financial incentive to do so, since unemployment benefits hardly existed. It is safe to assume that the number of unemployed registered at the labour offices was a gross underestimation of the real number of unemployed, whilst the number of registered vacant jobs was an overestimation of the actual situation, since enterprises tended to overstate their demand for labour.[4] Nevertheless, the

Table 6.1 Total population, working-age population and employment, 1950–82

	1950	*1960*	*1965*	*1970*	*1975*	*1978*	*1980*	*1981*	*1982*
Total population (1,000)[a]	25035	29795	31551	32568	34185	35061	35735	36062	36399
1950 = 100	100.0	119.0	126.0	130.4	136.5	140.0	142.7	144.0	145.4
Working-age population (1,000)[b]	14481	16271	17058	18324	19962	20828	21202	21409	21547
1950 = 100	100.0	112.4	117.8	126.5	137.8	143.8	145.2	147.8	148.8
Employment + self-employment (1,000)[c]	10186	12401	13521	15175	16572	17109	17325	17420	16996
1950 = 100 of which:	100.0	121.7	132.7	149.0	162.7	168.0	170.1	171.0	166.9
Employment in socialized sector (1,000)[d]	4823	7194	8531	10325	12202	12632	12718	12720	12184
1950 = 100	100.0	148.9	176.6	213.7	252.5	261.4	263.2	263.7	252.6
Labour force in private sector (1,000)[c]	5354	5207	4990	4850	4370	4477	4607	4700	4812
1950 = 100 of which:	100.0	97.3	93.2	90.6	81.6	83.6	86.0	87.8	89.9
Labour in non-agricultural activities (1000)[c]	313	336	351	442	469	533	603	648	699
1950 = 100	100.0	107.3	112.1	141.2	149.8	170.2	192.6	206.3	233.3
Private farming (1000)[d]	5041	4871	4639	4408	3901	3943	4004	4054	4113
1950 = 100	100.0	96.6	92.0	87.4	77.4	78.2	79.4	80.4	81.6

Sources: *Rocznik Statystyczny* 1975, 1983; *Zatrudnienie w Gospodarce Narodewej 1980* 1980.
Notes: [a]end of year, based on population censuses in 1950, 1960, 1970 and 1978 and estimates of the Main Statistical Office;
[b]men, 18–64 years and women, 18–59 years;
[c]yearly average part-time labour is converted to fully employed equivalents;
[d]based on population censuses and estimates.

Table 6.2 Poland: persons seeking work and vacant jobs, 1955–82

	Persons registered as seeking work (in 1,000)										*Number of vacant jobs per person seeking work*	
Year[a]	*Total*	*Men*	*Women*	*Skilled workers*	*Unskilled workers*	*White collar workers*	*Youth up to 18 years*	*Total*	*Men*	*Women*	*Men*	*Women*
1955	30.6	10.7	19.9	4.1	14.3	7.6	4.6	46.4	39.2	7.2	3.7	0.4
1960	37.4	7.5	29.9	4.4	26.1	4.3	2.6	46.5	39.7	6.8	5.3	0.2
1961	40.6	7.6	33.0	4.8	29.4	3.6	2.9	54.6	46.7	7.9	6.1	0.2
1962	46.2	6.5	39.7	3.9	36.4	2.7	3.3	54.5	46.7	8.2	7.0	0.2
1963	60.4	13.6	46.8	7.8	44.5	3.9	4.3	25.6	21.5	4.1	1.6	0.1
1964	65.4	10.1	55.3	7.6	46.3	5.4	6.1	44.4	36.6	7.8	3.6	0.1
1965	62.0	7.5	54.5	7.3	48.6	6.0	5.1	52.9	40.8	12.1	5.4	0.2
1966	57.6	5.4	52.2	6.9	41.3	5.9	3.9	64.2	50.6	13.6	9.4	0.3
1967	52.0	4.6	47.4	6.2	36.5	6.8	2.5	58.2	46.3	11.9	10.0	0.3
1968	53.1	3.8	49.3	6.3	35.3	8.8	2.7	76.7	60.8	15.9	16.0	0.3
1969	71.1	6.8	64.3	10.1	42.2	16.2	2.6	33.6	24.7	8.9	3.6	0.1
1970	79.4	8.1	71.3	12.8	49.8	14.6	2.2	39.5	31.0	8.5	3.9	0.1
1971	81.7	6.8	74.9	12.3	52.1	14.7	2.6	84.2	64.8	19.4	9.5	0.3
1972	51.8	2.5	49.3	7.4	35.2	7.9	1.3	93.4	68.8	24.6	26.7	0.5
1973	28.1	1.3	26.8	4.2	19.1	4.2	0.6	146.9	105.7	41.2	81.3	1.5
1974	19.0	1.7	17.3	2.8	12.5	3.3	0.4	77.7	51.7	26.0	30.4	1.8
1975	15.2	2.5	12.7	3.1	7.7	4.2	0.2	94.6	64.5	30.1	25.8	2.4
1976	13.6	3.0	10.6	3.1	6.6	3.8	0.1	82.7	58.3	24.4	19.4	2.3
1977	11.7	2.5	0.2	2.3	5.5	3.7	0.2	97.8	69.5	28.3	27.8	3.1
1978	9.2	2.2	7.0	1.8	3.8	3.5	0.1	92.4	66.0	26.4	30.0	3.8
1979	6.4	1.2	5.2	1.2	2.9	2.3	0.0	128.5	91.5	37.0	76.3	7.1
1980	9.7	3.0	6.7	2.2	2.9	4.5	0.1	98.2	69.1	29.1	23.0	4.3
1981	26.0	14.0	12.0	9.0	6.0	11.0	–	119.0	80.0	39.0	5.7	3.3
1982	9.0	4.0	5.0	–	–	3.0	–	248.0	183.0	65.0	45.8	13.0

Sources: *Rocznik Statystyczny* 1965, 1973, 1976, 1980, 1983.
Note: [a]end of year, registered at Labour Office of the local administration units.

official statistics of persons seeking work and vacant jobs for the period 1955–82 indicated the growing shortage of labour and the following interesting points.

- The demand for labour fluctuated considerably over the period under consideration. With the exceptions of 1963–5 and 1969–70, when employment growth was tightly restricted by an employment stop, the number of vacant jobs exceeded the number of people seeking work. The gap between vacant jobs and people seeking work grew rapidly after 1971, an indication of the growing tightness of the labour market and the increasing labour shortage.
- The number of vacant jobs for men was always greater than the number of men seeking work, male labour having always been in short supply. Up to 1972 the number of women seeking employment was on the whole always greater than the number of vacant jobs for women. The excepionally rapid growth of investment in the first half of the 1970s, the large demand for labour in general and the gradual exhaustion of the easily mobilized male labour reserves led to a shortage in the female labour market.
- The majority of the unemployed consisted of unskilled labour of which a high percentage were women.
- Despite the large drop in net material product and investment in 1979–82, the number of vacancies was still much higher than the number of persons seeking work.

Regional disparities in the labour market had long existed. Highly industrialized regions like Upper Silesia or industrial agglomerations in major cities like Warsaw and Łódz suffered from acute labour shortages, particularly a large shortage of male labour. On the other hand, underdeveloped regions (the eastern part of Poland) and small towns suffered unemployment, especially among women. Moreover, regional imbalances between supply and demand for labour in the 1970s was aggravated by demographic factors. A high proportion of the growth in manpower in the years 1971–5 took place in less developed regions and rural areas, whilst demand for labour was concentrated in the industrialized regions and major towns (E. Marek 1972: 117). Social and political pressures on government for more jobs to cope with local unemployment in the underdeveloped regions were considerable.

Despite the overall tendency towards full employment, misallocation of labour between economic sectors, branches or plants was common in the economy. Certain type of services, where demand exceeded the supply, like trade, catering and public health, were undermanned and the services could not be improved due to labour shortages. On the other hand, employment in public administration, e.g. white-collar jobs in planning, management and the political bureaucracy, was excessively high.

EMPLOYMENT POLICY, 1950–70

After the successful completion of the post-war rehabilitation and reconstruction as laid down in the Three Year Plan (1947–9), the regime embarked on the ambitious industrialization programme of the Six Year Plan (1950–5). Planning and economic growth were geared to the Soviet economic model. The rapid growth of both industrial investment (especially in heavy industry) and the fast expansion of non-agricultural employment (especially in industry) formed the basis of the economic growth. The increase in employment in the socialized sector was planned to grow from 3.7 million persons at the end of 1949 to 5.9 million persons at the end of 1955, i.e. a planned growth of employment of 60 per cent in six years.

The policy of maximum employment pursued by the regime, particularly during the period of forced industrialization in the first half of the 1950s, occurring under conditions of labour abundance, low wages and scarce capital, contributed significantly to the generation of high rates of economic growth and productive investment (J. Pajestka 1961; Z. Knyziak 1964). Existing productive capacity was utilized more intensively, requiring, therefore, additional employment. It has been estimated that at least 30 per cent of the growth in industrial output in 1951–6 was attributed to improved utilization of the 'old' production capacity (Z. Knyziak 1964: 87). Implementation of the policy of forced industrialization was facilitated by the imposition of the 'extensive economic growth strategy' and centralized planning system. From the social point of view, the policy of maximum employment offered new opportunities and social advancement to the unemployed in towns, redundant rural labour, seasonal workers, the landless and poor peasants.[5]

The rapid employment policy had serious negative effects such as overmanning of plants, labour hoarding, poor labour discipline and inflation. Historically, overemployment preceded the state of full employment and shortage of labour. According to some estimates, for instance, at least half a million of the newly employed in the non-agricultural sector, i.e. about 20 per cent of the growth in industrial employment in 1950–5, were actually redundant (J. Meller 1977: 63). An overemployment bias was not only characteristic of the early phase of industrialization under conditions of large labour reserves but also of the later stage of economic development.

Growth in real wages lagged far behind the over-optimistic target of the Six Year Plan (1950–5). In 1952–3 a considerable fall in real wages occurred, combined with high inflation and the rationing of consumer goods.[6] Labour turnover was high.

The workers' riot in Poznan in 1956, precipitated by the government decision to raise the work norm in the machinery tool plant Ciegelsky in Poznan, intensified the crisis of Stalinism and restored Gomulka's leadership. Average real wages and the standard of living increased considerably in the second half of the 1950s, mainly because of the strong and violent pressure of the workers for wage rises. The 'Polish October' movement brought temporary political, social and economic revival. The rate of growth of productive investment, particularly investment in heavy industry, dropped significantly. This temporary shift in investment priority favouring the consumer goods sector was closely related to the necessity of coping with the increase in real wages and consumption (M. Nasiłowski 1974a: 176). The harvests in the second half of the 1950s were good, having been favourably influenced by the decollectivization of agriculture. The supply of labour declined significantly due to a fall in the growth of population of productive age, a temporary fall in the participation rate of women in paid employment and the attraction of private farming. The relatively slow growth of employment in the socialized sector in the second half of the 1950s (the planned growth of employment was 1.3 million compared to an actual growth of 0.6 million persons), combined with an improvement in both the standard of living and the political environment, contributed to a high growth of labour productivity.

The Five Year Plan (1961–5) was drawn up with the assumption that labour supply was quite limited, similar to the labour market in the preceding five-year period. However, labour supply and social pressure for more jobs were greater than assumed. The actual growth of employment in the socialized sector amounted to 1.3 million persons in the years 1961–5, i.e. about 500,000 persons (or 66 per cent) more than planned. From the end of the 1950s the regime decided to step up the rate of productive investment, particularly in the capital goods sector and industries producing raw materials, encouraging a rise in the demand for labour.

The creation of a sufficient number of new jobs was one of the main issues raised during the preparation of the Five Year Plan (1966–70). In 1966–70 the size of the population of productive age increased by more than 60 per cent compared to the preceding five-year period. A growth of employment in the socialized sector of 1.5 million persons was planned, i.e. 18 per cent growth. Actually the 1970 employment target (i.e. end of the Plan period) was already achieved in 1968. The government's rigorous administrative measures to freeze employment growth in 1969–70 led to growing frictional unemployment.

According to official figures, the annual rates of growth of net material product and labour productivity in the 1960s were 6.1 and 4.3 per cent respectively, whilst average real wages increased annually by only 1.8 per cent (Table 6.3 and J. Meller 1977: 158). In fact, actual average real wages probably stagnated because of hidden inflation. No doubt the low wage policy enabled the economy to spread the available wage fund over as many workers as possible and hence maximize employment (M. Ellman 1979a: 16–17). On the other hand, the low wage policy contributed to a rising pressure on people (especially married women) to take jobs, labour hoarding, inefficient use of labour through substitution of labour for capital and a slow growth in labour productivity. Moreover, the low wage policy helped to generate labour discontent and frustration.

Table 6.3 sets out macro-economic indicators for the period 1951–70. For the period 1956–70, on the one hand, the annual average rates of growth of employment and gross capital stock were rising, whilst, on the other, the annual average rates of growth of net material product and labour productivity were falling. The average share of capital accumulation and investment in fixed capital in the (national) net material product was rising whilst the average share of individual consumption was falling.

It has been argued that the increase in capital output ratio and a drop in the growth of average labour productivity, particularly apparent during the second half of the 1960s, were clear indications of the growing inefficiency in the uses of labour and capital. This was thought to be linked with the growing irrationality of the so-called extensive economic growth strategy[7] and the increasing ineffectiveness of the traditional, centralized planning and management system to stimulate efficiency in the uses of resources.

The appeal for a more rational use of capital and labour, linked with the necessity for a switch from extensive to intensive economic growth strategy and for economic reform became louder. However, Gomulka was against economic reform and preferred instead the programme of industrial modernization and restructuring formulated in 1968, whose main aims were to raise the falling rates of growth of the economy and labour productivity.

EMPLOYMENT POLICY, 1971–82

The VIth Party Congress, held in December 1971, was under strong social and political pressure to visibly improve consumption, to modernize industry and moreover to create more jobs to provide employment for the rapidly increasing

Table 6.3 Selected macro-economic indicators, 1951–70

	1951–5	*1956–60*	*1961–5*	*1966–70*
Average annual rates of growth (%)				
Net material product (in 1961 prices)	8.6	6.5	6.2	5.9
Employment in the national economy (excluding the peasant economy)	5.6	2.0	3.2	3.2
Labour productivity (material production outside agriculture in 1961 prices)	4.6	5.7	4.8	3.8
Gross capital stock (in 1960 prices)	2.2	3.2	3.6	5.0
Average share of net material product (%)				
Accumulation	23.7	22.7	25.0	28.0
Fixed capital investment	15.2	15.4	18.3	21.6
Individual consumption of the population	69.6	69.8	65.8	62.4

Sources: *Struktura Gospodarki Narodowej* 1969; *Rocznik Statystyczny* 1971; *Rocznik Statystyczny Pracy 1945–68* 1969; Z. Fallenbuchl 'Industrial Structure and the Intensive Pattern of Development in Poland', *Jahrbuch der Wirtschaft Osteuropas*, 4, 1973: 247.

number of young people entering the labour market. The Congress fixed higher growth targets, in comparison to the preliminary targets laid down in Gomulka's economic guideline, for net material product, productive investment, consumption and real wages for the period 1971–5.

One of the main aims of Gierek's new economic development strategy was to achieve 'full and rational employment'. It was estimated that in 1971–5 around 3.5 million young people, compared to 3.2 million in 1966–70, and only 2.1 million in 1961–5, would join the labour market for the first time. It was also estimated that around 1.7 million older workers and employees would retire in the first half of the 1970s.[8] The Five Year Plan (1971–5) targeted a growth of employment in the socialized sector by 1.8 million persons, i.e. about 300,000 more than the growth in 1966–70. The social pressure for more new jobs was strong.

The exceptionally high increase in productive investment during the first half of the 1970s generated a large demand for labour and a high growth of employment. Productive investment was, moreover, oriented to the construction of new investment projects or plants which in general required more direct labour per investment unit in comparison to investment for modernization of existing plants. Local pressure for more jobs in regions where unemployment was high (like the voivodships of Białostok, Kielecki, Lubelski, etc.) forced the government to allocate special funds for the creation of new jobs in small-scale industries, handicraft, and services, etc. (J. Górski and M. Kabaj 1973: 211). The improvement in the supply of working capital (raw materials, fuel, industrial components, etc.) supplemented by small investment outlays, initially enabled the economy to intensify the utilization of existing productive capacity bringing additional demand for labour.

With a rapid decline in easily mobilizable labour reserves, a growing regional disparity in the supply of and demand for labour and a widespread phenomenon of labour hoarding by enterprises, the labour market became increasingly tight, particularly in the industrial agglomerations of Warsaw, Upper Silesia and Gdańsk. Male labour was in exceptionally short supply, and it was hard to find manual labour, particularly for heavy work. According to official statistics, at the end of 1970 there were 3.9 vacancies for every one man registered as seeking work at the labour offices for the whole economy; in 1972–5 the number of vacancies per male job seeker rose to between 25.8–81.3 (see Table 6.2).

The rate of utilization of productive capacity (including the newly established and modernized plants) was sub-optimal and falling partly because of the shortage of labour (M. Kabaj 1975a). This can be illustrated by a decline in the utilization of shifts in state industry. The shortage of labour in relation to the volume of fixed capital was clearly illustrated by the difficulties in securing a sufficient number of workers for the second and, even more so, for the third shift (Z. Fallenbuchl 1982: 42–3). In general the extent of labour substitution by capital seemed to be less than was economically justified. Labour deficits, however, occurred simultaneously with under-utilization and misallocation of labour due to bad planning, poor organization, labour hoarding and high labour absenteeism. These difficulties encouraged enterprises to insure themselves against fluctuations in the supply of inputs (raw materials, fuel, power, industrial components, etc.) and variations in production targets, a situation which in turn further intensified labour shortage.

Employment growth in 1971–5 exceeded the employment plan, the greater part of the excess being attributed to the explosive growth of employment in the construction sector (M. Kabaj 1975a), which was closely related to the exceptionally high growth in productive investment. The rapid growth in demand for labour in non-agricultural activities encouraged extensive migration to urban centres. The average annual net migration to urban centres in the 1970s was high, constituting on average more than 50 per cent of the total growth in urban population. The government relaxed the policy of residential restrictions on migrants settling in the cities. Due to the housing shortage in the cities and the low income of the peasantry from farming, a substitute form of migration, rural–urban commuting, a phenomenon linked with the so-called farmer-worker group, was increasing rapidly.[9] The participation rate of women in the urban centres continued to grow during the first half of the 1970s.

The Five Year Plan (1976–80) targeted a growth in employment for the whole economy of 1.1 million persons compared to 1.9 million in 1971–5. The projected increase in employment was less than the estimated growth of population of productive age in the second half of the 1970s. The new employment priority would favour sectors producing for exports, trade, catering, transportation and the private sector, instead of traditional priority sectors like heavy industry and construction. Employment in the construction sector was planned to fall by 80,000 persons in 1976–80 compared to an increase in employment of 214,000 in the preceding five-year period.

The volume of investment was planned to grow much less compared to the exceptionally rapid growth of investment in the first half of the 1970s. The current investment policy was to favour outlays for the modernization and replacement of obsolete plants, a completion of the growing volume of unfinished investment projects and an encouragement of labour-saving investment. The Five Year Plan (1976–80) forecast unrealistically that the bulk (85–90 per cent) of the 48–50 per cent targeted growth of industrial production would originate from rapid growth of labour productivity.[10] The plan assumed better utilization of productive capacity (especially in the newly established plants), more rational employment through relocation of labour from low labour productivity branches or plants to higher productivity ones, and greater economies in the use of raw materials, fuel and energy. It was the explicit hope of the government that the growth in the capital–labour ratio and the improvement in labour quality (better education and training etc.), combined with 'further improvement in the system of functioning' of the economy would contribute towards rapid growth in labour productivity.

The planned increase in labour productivity, improvements in the utilization of existing productive capacity, rational employment and greater economies in the use of raw materials, fuel and energy for the second half of the 1970s were all based on an over-optimistic and false assessments of the actual growth potentialities of the economy. The severe constraints imposed by Gierek's arbitrary economic policy (excessive investment, over-indebtedness, anti-peasantry measures, etc.), chaos in planning and the systemic defects of the CPEs had been underestimated in the design of the Five Year Plan (1976–80). The domestic and external imbalances, growing cumulatively in the second half of the 1970s, threw the plan into economic disorder and dislocation. The rise in meat prices in the summer of 1980, accompanied by a stagnation or fall in real wages (for certain income groups) triggered the huge national protests and workers' strikes that led to the fall of Gierek and the establishment of Solidarność.

One of the main characteristics of Gierek's 'new economic strategy' during the first half of the 1970s was the rapid growth of money income (wages) accompanied by a relatively stable price level. The slow growth of consumption and real wages in the 1960s, and the violent workers' protests in 1970–1, had forced Gierek to concede a substantial rise in consumption in order to placate the rebellious industrial workers. The regime believed that 'consumerism' would function both as a decoy for political legitimacy and as a stimulus for higher labour productivity.

The relationship between consumption (real wages) growth and increase in labour productivity in a CPE was highly complex and indirect. A successful relationship between consumption growth and an increase in labour productivity depended on many factors, such as the relationship between the rulers and the ruled, the planning system, the working conditions, the wage system and wage differentials, and the availability of consumer goods. The effectiveness of increases in money wages as a means of stimulating growth in labour productivity had declined steadily since 1973 (M. Kabaj 1980b) and the situation deteriorated dramatically during the years 1979–82. With the growing open and repressed inflation, the quality of labour supply (discipline, morale, etc.) deteriorated and the workers considered increases in money wages as a mere compensation for price increases, thereby reducing the importance of money wages growth as an incentive to stimulate labour productivity (see Chapter 3).

The growth of money and real wages fluctuated sharply and erratically in 1970–82. According to official figures the average real wages increased by 7.1 per cent per annum in the first half of the 1970s, i.e. about four times the annual growth in average real wages in the 1960s and more than twice the growth target set in the Five Year Plan (1971–5). The economy deteriorated, however, at a growing speed from 1976 when the regime did not succeed in stopping the downward spiral. According to official statistics, the annual growth in average real wages fell to 1.8 per cent (in 1979 real wages dropped by 2.7 per cent) in the second half of the 1970s. Because of a wide margin of statistical error and manipulations, real wages were actually falling for a large section of the workers and employees, particularly in the last years of the 1970s (Z. Czajka 1981: 38).

The growth in productivity per worker was declining and with the deepening of the economic crisis productivity per worker dropped significantly from 1979. Due to growing inflation, the workers were pressing for higher wages to offset the price rises, feeding further inflation. Average monthly money wages in the socialized sector increased by 44 per cent, whilst net material product and labour productivity at constant prices fell by 21 per cent and 16 per cent respectively in 1979–81. A dramatic turn occurred in 1982 when, according to official figures, average monthly money wages rose by 51 per cent and real wages dropped by 25 per cent (see Table In.1).

The forecast growth of the population in the productive age range was greater than the employment growth targeted in the Five Year Plan (1976–80). In order to provide jobs for the young people entering the labour market and to meet the commitment to full employment, the regime offered incentives to old workers, employees, farmers and mothers with small children to withdraw from paid employment. By 1980 the number of persons taking early retirement and working mothers opting for leave to raise their small children increased considerably compared to 1975 (B. Simatupang 1983a: 17–19). When the regime was concerned about possible unemployment as a result of the economic crisis and reform of 1982, it further encouraged early retirement, paid leave for mothers and employment in the private sector. Employment in the state sector fell by 536,000 persons (around 4 per cent) in 1982 (mostly manual workers), accompanied by an increase in employment in private business of 112,000 persons (around 24 per cent). Some of the workers who left state enterprises found jobs in private business. The official employment figure for the private sector seems to underestimate the true level, since the 'second economy' was expanding fast.

ECONOMIC REFORMS AND LABOUR REGULATION

Poland attempted three major reforms of the traditional state socialist economic model: in 1956–7, 1973–5 and 1982. Each was introduced under pressure from deep socio-economic and political crises. Central planning was relaxed and was combined with enterprise autonomy, a deal with the peasantry and the encouragement of private business. In the first two economic reforms, retreat and recentralization of planning followed with the consolidation of the regime, creating the conditions for a renewed crisis (J. Staniszkis 1984: 248–77). The failure of the 1982 economic reform led to a complete loss of power and the Polish United Workers' Party disintegration. Chapter 9 of this book will describe and discuss the regime's efforts to reanimate the stagnated economic reform of 1982 (an undertaking known as the second stage of economic reform) from 1987 and its complete failure. The question of labour regulation (determination of employment, wages, bonus, etc.) occupied a crucial place in all reform endeavours.

The deep crisis of Stalinism gave rise to the 'Polish October' in 1956 and economic reform. Agriculture was decollectivized, the workers' councils (which emerged initially as a grassroots workers' movement) participated in enterprise management, and the number of binding instructions was reduced. Real wages and consumption were raised significantly. The question of employment and wage regulation occupied an important place in the 'Polish model' discussions in 1956–7. Kalecki, for example, feared that if enterprises were free to allocate the wage-bill and profit-related bonus without any binding plans for average wages or number of employed, enterprises could cut employment, leaving no alternative employment opportunities for the dismissed (M. Kalecki 1982: 99–101).[11] With the decision to step up the rate of productive investment from the final years of the 1950s, the consolidation of the regime, the fear that liberalization might get out of hand and threaten the dictatorship of the nomenklatura, the logical conclusion drawn was the need for a recentralization of planning and control (M. Ellman 1989: 60–1).

A Party–government committee on the modernization of the system of functioning of the economy and state (the so-called Szydlak Commission), was set up by Gierek in January 1971 when the regime was in the middle of a deep crisis, and in 1972 it presented its report (which was, however, never published). During this period, the economic and political situation had changed in favour of the regime and therefore the regime was less interested and in no hurry to introduce important changes. By the time the limited economic reform, known as 'management by parameters' (or the 'system of large economic organizations', Wielkie Organizaje Gospodarcze or WOG), was introduced in 1973–5, Gierek's leadership was already firmly consolidated.

The main aim of the WOG reform was to steer the industrial associations ('zjednoczenie') and enterprises towards achieving the targets set by the central plan with the help of 'economic parameters' (profit and tax rates, interest rates, prices, etc.). The number of binding administrative instructions was reduced, giving more room for decentralized decisions on employment, wage-bill, prices and investment to the large economic organization units. The central planners expected that by charging interest rates on capital (credits and fixed assets) and by raising labour costs (labour tax and an increase in social contribution), economies in the uses of resources and a curb in excess demand for investment and labour would be encouraged.

Under the WOG system, the wage bill was linked to value added and managerial bonus was related to net profit. Wages and bonuses would grow if value added increased, either by producing more saleable goods or by reducing costs given the price level. Labour hoarding and overmanning were to be discouraged, since by shedding redundant labour and raising average wages, fewer workers would share the same wage bill. The slogan was: 'Less employment – higher labour productivity – higher wages.' The benefits of labour-saving progress would lead to an increase in the wage bill through the norm R, which related changes in the wage bill to changes in value added brought about by cost reduction.[12] Therefore, the determination of the coefficient R was an extremely important policy instrument in the hands of the central planners.[13]

The WOG reform was intended to encourage economies in the use of labour by charging a 20 per cent tax on the wage bill and an increase in social security contributions from 15.5 per cent to 20 per cent. The labour tax was a charge on net profit, thereby affecting management bonuses. In this context, the labour tax was to provide a correction to underpriced labour, which should be higher than the going wage level, a sort of shadow price for labour (P.T. Wanless 1980: 36–7). The higher price of labour would encourage substitution of labour by capital.

The expectation that the large industrial organizations and enterprises would economize on labour by releasing excess labour and use that part of the wage bill saved for wage increases was not realized. Industrial associations and enterprises easily found ways to finance both employment growth and wage increases through subsidies, credits ('soft budget constraint'), and price increases of their output, finding it advantageous to keep a large labour reserve. On average, labour costs constituted only 16 per cent of the total industrial costs, making substitution of labour for capital unprofitable (M. Kabaj 1981: 72). If an enterprise opted to reduce labour and accordingly raise the average wage, it ran the risk of receiving a smaller wage bill for the next year and would be worse off compared to other enterprises who kept their labour reserves (M. Kabaj 1981: 76). In a situation where the supply of raw materials, power, fuel and other industrial inputs were irregular, leading to frequent production interruptions, it was prudent to keep high labour reserves so as not to endanger the fulfilment of production targets at the risk of losing the bonus.

The growing inflationary pressure and market disequilibrium since the end of 1973 helped to undermine the WOG reform. It was, however, the political resistance to the reform, i.e. the strivings of the Party-state bureaucracy and other interested groups at central and regional levels to maintain and to strengthen 'the system of monoarchy' in the exercise of political and economic power (W. Brus 1985: 205), which was crucial for the failure of the WOG reform. Bureaucratic intervention, administrative instructions and so on became more frequent and the 'suspension' of the WOG reform in 1976, which was followed by its 'modification' in subsequent years, represented a retreat from the system of parametric regulation.

The emergence of Solidarność and the free discussions in 1980–1 about the causes of the socio-economic and political crises and ways to resolve them, produced different economic reform projects written by the Party-state commission, professional bodies and universities. The official reform project was outlined in the document *Kierunki Reformy Gospodarczej*, approved by the IXth Party Congress in July 1981.

The main idea of the reform of 1982 was enterprise autonomy, involving workers' self-management and enterprise self-finance, accompanied by a reduction in Party controls. The central plan was no longer to contain directives (except in a number of key sectors, defence, and the fulfilment of international agreements); it was to indicate macro-economic trends and proportions. The economy would operate on the principle of central planning with a built-in market mechanism, and enterprises would prepare their plans autonomously, guided by profit maximization. Remuneration of the personnel would depend significantly on an enterprise's financial result (profit). Prices would in principle ensure a balance between supply and demand. During the transitional period certain products (basic consumer goods and industrial inputs included in the 'operational programmes' and 'government orders', etc.) and hard currency would be allocated centrally.[14]

Workers' self-management was an essential component of the economic reform as envisaged in 1981. Workers' councils were granted the power to co-appoint directors of the enterprises on a competitive basis (except for the appointment of directors of the key industries), to determine enterprise plans and to distribute profits. After a temporary suspension of workers' councils during martial law, they were reactivated, but their authority was significantly curtailed. In the reform model, the state still retained responsibility to provide full employment in the macro-economic sense. It abandoned, however, the promise that the employment offered would reflect each employee's qualifications and would be where the worker already lived or in the enterprise where the worker already worked (W. Baka 1983: 101–2). The government expected a relocation of workers because it assumed that enterprises would discharge redundant labour. The state would handle this by creating new jobs and retraining workers. This was to be financed from the newly established retraining fund (the fund for employment and professional activization, FAZ).

Under the reform of 1982, employment was supposed to be regulated indirectly and based on three sub-systems: the financial results (gross profits or losses) of enterprises; the taxation system; and the wage bill determination (including retained profit for distribution to the work force). Enterprises were supposedly free to fix the wage bill and to decide the level and composition of employment. The government hoped to encourage enterprises to economize on labour effectively through wage regulation and incentives (taxation and charges). Enterprises were subjected to three forms of taxation: turnover tax, that is, percentage tax on value of gross output; tax on inputs used (taxation on labour, land, buildings and capital); and two new direct taxes: 'income tax', which is actually a tax on profit, and a tax on wage payment (FAZ) growth beyond a certain threshold, both having progressive rates.

The taxation on profits and wage payments was to co-determine the size of the wage bill and retained profit for distribution, and thereby regulate employment indirectly. In view of the large market disproportion, inflation, monopoly, and the great economic inequalities between enterprises, both forms of taxation also had individual goals such as neutralizing inflation, siphoning off windfall profits, and offsetting large inter-enterprise wage inequalities. Several of these aims are irreconcilable with the goal of promoting efficiency. It soon turned out that the initially highly progressive rates of taxation on profits became counter-productive, discouraging output expansion and cost reduction, and penalizing efficient firms (M. Kabaj 1984: 388–9). The progressive tax on wage payment (FAZ), which was initially levied on growth in average wages, encouraged the hiring of labour at wages below the enterprise average wages, and hence intensified shortages in the labour market. The rates of progressive taxation of both profits and wage payments were softened in the following years (B. Simatupang 1988: 289).

Two inconsistent trends could be observed in the system of wage regulation. Due to high inflationary pressure (partly caused by money wage rises), the authorities were inclined to set a highly progressive rate of taxation on the growth in the wage bill, and hence reduce the incentives for greater effort. On the other hand, managers strove to relieve the pressure of the highly progressive wage bill taxation through an extensive system of vertical bargaining between enterprises or representatives of an industrial branch and higher authorities over tax and tax reductions, subsidies, the cost of production and prices, etc.,[15] so that they could afford to pay wage increases that at least would correspond to the prevalent wage rises in more or less similar industrial branches. The major aim was to prevent labour drain due to significant wage differentials.

Labour shortages in the state sector were aggravated by the government's encouragement of early retirement among elderly workers and employees, and of prolonged maternity leave, (self-)employment in private business (handicrafts, small industries, trade, services, and so on), and private farming. These measures were undertaken in anticipation of expected high unemployment due to economic crisis and economic reform.

In the early 1980s the regime was inclined to opt for ineffective administrative regulations of labour, such as labour rationing in certain provinces, priority allocation of labour to key branches and plants, restrictions on changes of job, 'anti-parasite' and 'anti-alcohol' campaigns, and 'work-attestation' procedures, in response to the (pseudo) taut labour market, instead of pursuing the path of consistent economic reform (B. Simatupang 1988: 296). The stagnation in economic reform, combined with the errors made in employment policy, exaggerated the role of (pseudo) labour shortages as major barriers to output growth. Moreover, acute housing shortages and poor transport put heavy constraints on the extent of labour relocation and regional mobility of labour. Under such conditions the mechanism of economic coercion enforcing economies in resources and labour was scarcely operating.

FULL EMPLOYMENT AS A PROBLEM. ARE AN 'UNEMPLOYMENT SCARE' AND AN 'ECONOMIC CRISIS' REMEDIES?

The policy of maximum employment pursued by the regime contributed significantly towards the generation of high rates of economic growth and investment growth during the period of forced industrialization in the 1950s, and promoted social and cultural advancement of the rural underemployed as well. Moreover, it was argued that the rapid expansion of the relatively small number of the pre-war industrial workers would strengthen the political and social base of the socialist state (O. Lange 1961: 180). Full employment also meant in general an improvement in the economic position of the workers in the labour market, a sort of 'seller's market' *vis-à-vis* the employer (the state). In general, competition among labour for jobs was low and, once employed, job security was high.

It was, however, well known that the state of full employment, generated by both maximum employment policy and the systemic features of the CPEs, caused serious socio-economic problems. Labour hoarding by enterprises, labour shortages and slow technical progress and innovations were widespread. It was commonly admitted that full employment, job security and labour shortages affected the effectiveness and productivity of employed labour unfavourably. Labour discipline and morale were low. High rates of labour absenteeism and labour turnover were thought to be positively correlated with labour shortages and a large number of vacancies. Politicians, economists and managers complained about the low morale of the workers and employees, for example drunkenness on the job, theft and shoddy work. There was a lack of motivation to produce good workmanship, quality products and services.

The traditional argument was that in principle there was no conflict between the objectives of full employment and rational employment in state socialism. It was maintained that 'it is not possible to carry out rational employment without the policy of full employment' (J. Górski and M. Kabaj 1973: 171) in the state socialist economy. It was argued further that with the exhaustion of easily mobilizable labour reserves (urban and rural unemployed, housewives, etc.), the priority of employment policy should be shifted from maximization to rational employment (B. Fick 1970; M. Kabaj 1972).

The new or rational employment approach should emphasize the relative scarcity of labour, its real high social costs[16] and the necessity of economizing on labour. A rational employment approach should put the right person in the right job, correct the widespread irrational job assignments of engineers and highly skilled personnel, and rectify the misallocation of labour between economic sectors and activities (E. Marek 1972: 114–15; J. Górski and M. Kabaj 1973: 213–25; M. Kabaj 1981: 81–8). This call for a rational employment approach was a basic component of the envisaged switch from the strategy of so-called extensive economic growth to intensive growth.

Periodically the government organized administrative campaigns against overemployment, but in general the results were unsatisfactory. For instance in 1969–70, when the economic and political situation was at its low point in combination with a high growth of labour supply, the government ordered an employment stop, and the dismissal of a large number of industrial employees was envisaged for the early 1970s (G. Blazynski 1980: 4). Had Gomulka's 'selective industrial development' been implemented, combined with the high growth of labour supply in 1971–5, it might have led to greater unemployment (H. Król 1971). Unofficially it was argued that the creation of an 'industrial reserve army' (the unemployed), thus generating a general fear of losing one's job, might contribute to an improvement of labour discipline, reduce absenteeism and encourage a stable work force (B. Fick 1970: 58–9).

The idea and the suggestion of creating an 'industrial reserve army' reappeared in the late 1970s. In 1978, there was a public discussion on the need to create an 'industrial unemployment reserve', as a way to deal with lax labour discipline. It was provoked by a letter from a group of leading industrial managers, printed in the weekly *Polityka*, a rejoinder by its editor and the reactions of the readers (*Polityka* 1978: 30 September, 21 October, 4 November, 11 November, 25 November, 2 December). The managers' letter complained that the main barrier to technical and economic progress in factories was the disregard of the 'most elementary principle of labour discipline' by the workers. Referring to the high labour productivity in industrialized capitalist countries, the authors of the letter assumed that a significant correlation exists between unemployment and high labour efficiency in a capitalist economy. The question was raised whether it would also not be desirable in Poland 'to create a thin layer of unemployed, whose mere existence would have forced others to work more precisely and conscientiously?'. The letter advised the authorities not to be frightened by the 'hard' line called for in the letter, adding that many leading industrial managers shared this view.[17]

In a rejoinder, one of the editors recognized the significance of the issues raised by the managers, but rejected the 'hard' line called for in the letter. It was underlined that large-scale unemployment would lead to greater social tensions and conflicts, which would not solve labour indiscipline, and reminded the readers at the same time of the uprising of the workers in December 1970. It was added that labour efficiency and discipline could be raised by an improvement in the organization of work, better planning, and rewarding good work and penalizing bad work (*Polityka*, 30 September 1978). It is interesting to note that during the debate, the phrase economic reform was not mentioned at all.

In a wider context, the question of unemployment was raised again during the economic and political crisis of 1980–2, and the discussion over ways to resolve the crisis and consequences of the economic reforms. The spectre of high unemployment was believed to be threatening Poland due to economic crisis and the envisaged economic reforms. The questions of unemployment and the retraining and relocation of the redundant labour were discussed under the euphemism of 'labour regrouping' ('rozmieszczenie pracy'). According to national sample surveys in 1980 and 1981 on popular notions of social justice (full employment, ceilings on earning and income differentiation), the overwhelming majority supported full employment and limits to earnings (L. Kolarska-Bobinska 1985: 318). Unskilled and semi-skilled workers feared the threat of unemployment most.

Unemployment threats, that is the creation of an 'industrial reserve army', announced on a number of occasions, have throughout the period under discussion remained only verbal threats. Rationalization of employment, by making the system more flexible, and dismissal of redundant labour and their relocation into more profitable sectors or activities, were inconsistent with a basically unreformed state socialist economy.

According to a familiar pre-Keynesian thesis, economic crises play an essential role in capitalist dynamics. They re-established the dominant position of dynamic capitalist enterprises by disciplining both labour and the commodity producers. Unemployment forces the workers to submit to the dictates of their employers, to reduce their wage demands and abandon their opposition to changes in labour processes. Bankruptcies lead to a scrapping of surplus capacity and a concentration of capacity and finance in the hands of strong and dynamic firms that can take advantage of the next upswing. Technical progress creates new investment opportunities and this, together with the fall in prices of primary commodities, leads to an upswing in industrial profits and investment.

Under state socialism these mechanisms did not work. Labour discipline was not raised during the crisis since large-scale unemployment did not emerge, partly because of the strong opposition of the workers. This was particularly serious since there were systemic factors that ensure a low level of labour productivity (J. Kornai 1980). For systemic reasons, dynamic and financially sound enterprises did not emerge to lead the next upswing. Hence, whereas a capitalist crisis creates the conditions for technical progress, the restructuring of production and a new upswing in economic growth, a socialist crisis, at any rate under the conditions prevailing in Poland, led only to a temporary improvement in the economic situation.

CONCLUSION

The Polish People's Republic successfully tackled the unemployment and underemployment that characterized pre-war Poland. However, the economic policies and economic system that achieved this (extensive growth and directive planning) had their own characteristic problems. The Polish labour scene in the 1970s and early 1980s was marked both by full employment and by labour hoarding, misallocation of labour and (pseudo) labour shortages. This situation resulted from the interaction of the economic system, economic policies and the economic environment. The labour shortages were made worse by measures taken by the regime in the light of anticipated unemployment and economic reform.

Rationalization of employment was hindered by the stagnation of economic reform. The latter was facilitated by fundamental features of the economic environment (for example, vested interest opposition to a market economy, the relationship between the government and the population, the high debt burden, etc.). The regime was more inclined to adopt administrative measures to deal with labour shortages and indiscipline than to pursue the difficult path of economic reform and appropriate economic policies. The reliance on administrative measures in the early 1980s formed the basis for a new crisis in the late 1980s. Throughout its history, the Polish People's Republic had failed to combine full employment with an efficient use of labour. Under state socialist economic conditions, unlike those typical of capitalism, the crisis did not affect the labour market in a way that contributed to long-run growth.

7

THE VIEWS OF POLISH ECONOMISTS

INTRODUCTION

The cyclical fluctuation of post-war Poland and the recurrence of socio-economic and political crises (1956, 1970 and 1980–1) have been extensively analysed by both Polish and Western social scientists. An economic crisis was perceived as the outcome of a mechanism characterizing the CPEs which tended to over-investment and hence to overheating the economy, producing disproportions and tensions. A declining rate of economic growth, despite a rising rate of growth of investment, accompanied by a fall in the standard of living and effectiveness of capital plus growing shortages of consumer and producer goods, were common features of an economic crisis situation. An economic crisis was a moment of rejection by the society and the economy of the hitherto pursued high and unbalanced growth policy. It was a moment of heightened contradiction between, on the one hand, the systemic mechanism which produced economic disproportions or tensions and inevitably encountered severe growth barriers and, on the other hand, the decision of the regime to suspend temporarily the working on the 'self-destructive logic of the system' with the main aim of easing the tensions. An economic crisis may develop into a political crisis where the workers' protests play a key role. A drastic cut in investment growth, a reallocation of resources favouring the consumer goods sector, a considerable rise in real wages and standards of living, which were normally accompanied by change in the Party-state leadership and a programme of economic and political reforms, were the commonly adopted adjustment measures of crisis management, stabilization and recovery.

The idea that socio-economic and political crises were necessary for the survival and development of really existing socialism in general and of Poland in particular had been underlined by a number of Polish and Western social scientists (J. Staniszkis 1979: 172–8; W. Lamentowicz 1982: 117–31; J. Gross 1979: 148–50). They hold the view that crises were functional in reducing the tensions ('regulation through crisis' or 'learning by crisis'), instrumental in the process of economic and political adaptation to changing environments, and provide a mechanism for economic and political recovery.

This chapter will briefly and selectively survey the writings of Polish economists on the economic crisis of 1979–82, focusing on the discussion of the nature and causes of the crisis. The chapter consists of two parts, followed by a brief conclusion. The first part is a brief review of Polish dissident writings before August 1980 on the approaching economic crisis in the last years of the 1970s. The second part examines the various economists' writings after the establishment of Solidarnośc. The 'odnowa' period produced a large number of books, reports, pamphlets, and articles of varying quality, dealing with the crisis.

POLISH DISSIDENT WRITINGS BEFORE AUGUST 1980

Official censorship was one of the key instruments of the regime to make the media responsive to the wishes of the Communist Party and to control the minds of the people.[1] Shortcomings in the socio-economic and political system of really existing socialism, errors in Gierek's economic policy, relevant political issues and the rapid deterioration of the economy in the last years of the 1970s were taboo subjects for the public media. Basic economic information and statistics (e.g. the size of foreign debts, debt service, the number of accidents at work, etc.) were either not published and classified as 'state secrets', or falsified to suit the propaganda purposes of the regime (M. Ellman and B. Simatupang 1982). Gierek's notorious 'propaganda of success', i.e. claiming success no matter what economic deterioration befell Poland, was practised on a wider scale with the increasing economic failings in the second half of the 1970s. The worse the situation became, the less the official media were allowed to present reality. Official censorship intensified the lack of feedback, isolating the leadership from the population and contributing to growing dissonance between the official propaganda and reality.

Polish dissident intellectuals attempted to build an alliance with the workers, helping the families of the arrested workers who participated in the June 1976 strikes in Radom and Ursus after the announcement of price increases for basic necessities. They provided legal aid during the trials and disseminated information about human rights violations. Defying the official censorship, the dissidents started to publish a series of unofficial publications, describing and analysing the worsening socio-economic and political situation. Underground publications worked illegally under conditions of continuous harassment and experienced severe difficulties in securing printing equipment and materials. The dissident movement was not confined to a few intellectuals. It aimed to penetrate society with true information and encourage critical thinking and independent action. Dissident writings described and analysed the failings of the system of CPEs, explained the major causes of the worsening state of the economy, social life and policy, and outlined alternative solutions.[2] The links between dissident and established or official intellectuals (experts) were never broken and in certain instances they were close. An important role was played by the so-called buffer group of intellectuals, who circulated in both communities, supporting the dissidents with writing, information and reports without being members and at the same time were allowed to keep their professional position (J.L. Curry 1984: ix).

The regime's monopoly on information was partially broken by the independent dissident publications, and the official media became more and more discredited and ultimately lost almost all credibility in the eyes of society. It was not surprising that the Gdańsk workers, organized through the strike in the summer of 1980, demanded freedom of expression and publication for independent publishing and access to the mass media for all groups, and also called for accurate and complete information. For the Communist Party leadership, losing control of the media was one of the most frightening concessions the workers demanded, and hence the Party fought hardest against it.

Nearly all dissident writings published before the outbreak of the workers' strike in August 1980 and selected for our brief survey[3] acknowledged the positive achievements (the substantial rise in real wages and consumption, full employment and industrial modernization, etc.) of Gierek's rule during the first half of the 1970s. This positive appraisal of Gierek's rule did not, however, contradict the major conclusion drawn by dissident economists that the Polish economy was in a state of crisis. They underlined both the cyclical and structural features of the economic crisis, and its complex nature as well, disclosing the socio-political, ideological and moral dimensions of the economic crisis (*Uwagi* 1979: 8; *Diagnoza* 1979: 61; S. Karol 1978: 74). Contrary to the regime's argument, which attributed the deterioration of the Polish economy to unfavourable external conditions (world oil crisis, economic recession in the West, poor weather conditions, etc.), the dissident economic writings underlined the primacy of internal factors (errors in economic policies, incompetence of the leadership, failings of the command economy, etc.) for causing the economic crisis. The undemocratic and authoritarian political system was commonly singled out as a major cause of the economic crisis (*Uwagi* 1979: 22; M. Vale 1981: 13). Another conclusion common to the dissident writings was that the Polish 'planned' economy was virtually unplanned, drifting into what was paradoxically called a state of 'planned chaos'; that is, an economy which was neither regulated by an orderly and consistent central plan, nor by market forces. The growing income disparities, the ubiquity of privileges, the corruption of the elite in the Party-state bureaucracy and the absence of a relationship between income level and economic achievements were all strongly condemned in the underground publications. A political upheaval (general strikes, demonstrations and violence) was predicted as a result of a worsening of the socio-economic situation.

The political composition and orientation of the Polish dissidents were not homogenous. Despite the fact that a certain convergence of views over economic and political crises could be observed among the Polish dissidents, they nevertheless differed considerably among themselves over many basic issues. The controversy concerned at least three main problems:

1 a debate over the major cause(s) of the economic crisis;
2 the scope, feasibility and viability of economic reforms (the question of 'reformability') of a command economy;
3 the kind of economic measures required to restore domestic and external balances.

The diagnosis of the Polish economic crisis in the dissident writings produced two major diverging views over the main cause(s). The first view explained the economic crisis as being largely due to systemic failings of the command economy, an anachronistic system of detailed directives, addressed to enterprises, specifying what, how much, in what way and for whom to produce. Wages and premiums were related to the degree of fulfilment of the directives and targets at the enterprise level. The systemic failings of the command economy led to low effectiveness of labour and capital uses, high cost of production and poor product quality, lack of competitiveness of export production and an aversion to innovations (*Uwagi* 1979: 13–14). The second view underlined the key role of long-run, structural economic disproportions, generated by the regime's 'preference and priority' in the allocation of investment (resources) favouring heavy industry, as an autonomous 'crisis-generating factor' ('czynnik kryzysogenny') of the command economy. It was admitted that the prevailing system of central planning and regulation of the economy had contributed to the deepening of the economic crisis, but it did not have an autonomous role in the generation of the economic crisis (*Diagnoza* 1979: 63). The command economy, a copy of the Soviet model and imposed on Poland in the last years of the 1940s, was a powerful instrument in the hands of the Communist Party, aiming to maximize economic potential as the required base for political and military rule of the regime (J. Bartecki 1978: 13, 40). This produced a strong lobby of pressure groups, established within the Party-state bureaucratic hierarchy and striving for a perpetuation and rapid expansion of heavy industry (steel, energy and machinery-tool production, etc.) and armament production, at the cost of the consumption goods sector, housing, agriculture and services.

Regarding the question of 'reformability', the authors of the *Uwagi* memorandum advocated an alternative system of economic regulation instead of the prevailing administrative planning. This was a sort of Hungarian type of economic reform with a planning system with a 'built-in market mechanism', enterprise autonomy and workers' self-management. Economic reform was projected to be combined with political reforms (a curb on censorship, the political upgrading of the representative organs, a democratic electoral system, free trade unions, etc.), operating within the context of a prevailing political system and accepting the 'leading position of the Communist Party' (E. Lipinski 1979: 8; *Uwagi* 1979: 24–8).

The *Uwagi* provoked sharp controversy and criticism among the dissidents. The suggestion of support for a 'Polish Kadar' was considered to be inadequate, since it did not demand the kind of 'institutional solutions' and changes which would safeguard civil rights (A. Zawada 1978). Viable political reform must establish an institutionalization of social pressure which 'can force the evolution of the political system which is essential for economic improvement' (E. Ryabarska 1978). Other dissidents, who had no intention of outlining reform projects under the prevailing political system, were more critical about the issue of whether it was politically and psychologically appropriate for dissidents to address the regime for an implementation of economic reforms and a 'minimum programme' (i.e. a wage freeze, a price increase of basic necessities, etc.) to restore economic balance at the cost of the standard of living of the workers (*Diagnoza* 1979: 64–5). Nearly all dissident writings which favoured economic reforms had postulated the thesis that viable economic reforms should be developed in parallel with changes in the 'monocentric order' of the communist polity. The main controversy concerned the basic issue of the 'reformability' of Poland's command economy, which was politically and economically dependent on the Soviet Union. A positive criticism of the *Uwagi* memorandum emphasized that if workers' self-management and far-reaching economic reforms were to be viable, economic reforms should not be confined to mere changes in the system of planning and regulations, the decentralization of decision-making, the socialist market, etc. Substantial changes in 'the ownership relations of the means of production', or real pluralism in the ownership of means of production, including a considerably greater scope for the private economic sector and capital, were considered necessary for viable economic reforms (*Diagnoza* 1979: 66–7).

On the question of the kind of economic measures that were necessary, the authors of the *Uwagi* memorandum advocated an urgent crash economic programme to cope with the rapidly growing domestic and external imbalances, and the rising burden of servicing the hard currency debts. The projected programme should include 'certain cuts in the volume of aggregate demand of the population' and a freeze or cut in real wages for certain groups through a non-compensated price increase of consumer goods. The measures were thought to be a part of a broader economic and political reform package (*Uwagi* 1979: 31–6). This suggestion provoked a chain of critical responses from fellow dissidents. Some rejected the measures outright, arguing that it was tactically and politically incorrect and harmful as well for the dissidents to support the regime's incomes policy of tightening the workers' belts, in effect letting the workers pay for the gross incompetence and corruption of the Communist Party leadership (*Diagnoza* 1979: 67–8). Others were inclined to support an unpopular belt-tightening incomes policy to rescue the economy from its wretched state, hoping that political and economic reforms would bring democracy and economic recovery (S. Karol 1978: 78). Contrary to official wage statistics, average real wages had in fact virtually stagnated for the period 1977–9 and, for certain income groups, they probably had dropped.

Many of the basic ideas, arguments, conclusions, and the alternative reform proposals discussed in the dissident economic writings of the second half of the

1970s reappeared and were discussed openly in the media and scientific journals after the establishment of Solidarność. The official media discussions, which appeared after the signing of the Gdańsk Agreement in 1980, were forced to admit the failure of Gierek's economic policy. Certain hypotheses and conclusions drawn by the dissident economists became part of official and mainstream economic analyses of the systemic shortcomings of the command economy and of the etiology of the Polish economic crisis.

SELECTED POLISH ECONOMISTS' VIEWS ON THE ECONOMIC CRISIS OF 1979–82

The Polish economic collapse of 1980–1, the workers' protests, the establishment of Solidarność and the paralysis of official censorship created favourable conditions for creative inquiries and stimulated free discussions on the extent, nature and causes of the ongoing socio-economic and political crises. Moreover, the analysis of the Polish economic crisis was greatly facilitated by greater access to more reliable and accurate economic information and statistics. This change was symbolically represented by a television interview with M. Krzak, a former Minister of Finance, on 24 August 1980, when he revealed for the first time that Poland's debt to the West amounted to US$20 billions. This information, like many other relevant statistics, had previously been classified as a 'state secret'.

The public had demanded full and truthful reports from the government and the Party on the state of the economy, and an explanation of the causes and circumstances which had led to the deep economic crisis. The government was under strong popular pressure to take measures to stop the economic decline and the severe shortages, and to implement socio-economic and political reforms. The Party-government commission for economic reform was set up in September 1980. Lively discussions and controversies among economists, experts and professional bodies produced at least seven economic reform projects and another six sets of proposals in 1980–1, all of which were considered by the commission (D.M. Nuti 1986b: 1). The official reform project, Kierunki Reformy Gospodarczej ('the direction of economic reform'), based on the principles of enterprise autonomy (independence, self-finance and workers' self-management) was passed by the IXth Party Congress in July 1981 and later on by the parliament. A series of new laws and acts were passed in 1981–2, providing a legal framework for the implementation of the economic reform.

After considerable delay the government submitted a draft report on the state of the economy to the parliament in May 1981. The draft was heavily criticized by the economic commission of the parliament, the trade unions and the media. After having been rewritten by a team of five Polish economists headed by Cz. Bobrowski, the final version of the *Rządowy raport o stanie gospodarki* ('Report of the state of the economy') was published in July 1981. The *Raport* admitted that the economic crisis was not only caused by gross errors in Gierek's economic policy, the incompetence of the leadership and declining efficiency in the use of labour and capital, but was also due to systemic shortcomings of CPEs.

Following up the IXth Party Congress resolutions, in September 1981, the plenary Central Committee meeting appointed a Party commission with the task of examining the causes and circumstances under which socio-economic and political crises had emerged periodically in post-war Poland. The commission was headed by H. Kubiak, a 'liberal' Politbureau member. The final version of the *Kubiak Report*[4] was at last released in the spring of 1983, one and a half years after the declaration of martial law and the suppression of the opposition. It represented a conservative trend in the general etiologies of the Polish crises where subjective factors, like 'deformations in the method of exercising power, errors in management and administration, neglects in the field of socialization, and lack of consistency in combatting the opponents' of socialist order, occupied a paramount place (*Kubiak Report* 1983: 60). An explanation of the crises as due to functional breakdown, errors and voluntaristic factors implied that the foundations of the really existing socialism and their structure were basically sound. Therefore, pressure for crucial economic and political reforms was considered unjustified and indeed as needing to be countered. This 'counter-reformist' official etiology considered in general that the appointment of a new leader and changes in policies were sufficient to resolve the crises.

The next sections of the chapter will concentrate on the discussions and controversies over various explanations of causes of the economic crisis of 1979–82, presented by Polish economists after August 1980. It is based on a selected number of books, essays and pamphlets.

Gierek's investment leap and rapid consumption growth

W. Kuczyński's book *Po wielkim skoku* (*After the Great Leap*) was initially circulated as a dissident publication in Poland. It was a transcript of a cycle of lectures delivered to the Polish Association of Sociologists in the spring of 1979, and was published in 1981 by the state publishing house. The author was a former member of the Commission of Experts advising the Interfactory Strike Committee of Gdańsk during the negotiations with the government in August 1980. Kuczyński attributed the economic crisis to two main factors: gross errors in Gierek's economic policy; and systemic shortcomings of the centrally planned economy ('patologie gospodarki centralnego planowania'). Futhermore, the interaction of both failings had reinforced the negative effects. Disputing the government's assertion that the economic crisis was caused mainly by unfavourable external factors (deterioration of the terms of trade, Western economic recession, etc.), the author examined Gierek's investment leap in the first half of the 1970s, domestic and external economic imbalances, the instability of the agricultural policy and the failure of the WOG economic reform.

The leap in the growth of productive investment during the first half of the

1970s, concentrated largely in industry, was unprecedented since the time of the forced industrialization drive of the Six Year Plan (1950–5). This determined the main features of Polish economic development in the 1970s and 1980s. Gierek's investment leap was the result of several important factors:

1 over-optimistic and ambitious economic growth aspirations of the central organs and of the lower economic/administrative units;
2 a built-in expansive mechanism of the investment system, driving actual investment growth beyond initial plans;
3 the lack of an adjustment mechanism which would redress misallocation in investment speedily (W. Kuczyński 1981: 75).

Moreover, when Gierek took over the Party leadership, he was facing strong pressure from the bureacratic lobby around heavy industry (e.g. the steel industry, engineering, coal mining, etc.) demanding more investment funds, partly as a reaction against the threat of investment cuts planned in Gomulka's strategy of 'selective industrial development' (W. Kuczyński 1981: 83–4).

Unlike Poland's past economic growth patterns, Gierek's investment leap occurred simultaneously with a rapid growth of real wages and consumption, particularly meat consumption. The outbreak of the workers' violent protest in December 1970, triggered by a sharp price increase of basic necessities, led to the fall and replacement of the Gomulka leadership by Gierek. The withdrawal of the announced price increase and the provision of a significant increase in the standard of living, in conjunction with a guarantee of existential or social security (full employment, job security, etc.), were the only accepted solutions to restore a minimum required confidence among the workers, when genuine economic and political reforms were not on the political agenda (W. Kuczyński 1981: 80–2). J. Wiatr, a former director of the Institute of the Basic Problems of Marxism-Leninism, stated explicitly that instead of reforms, Gierek offered people a quick increase of earnings through money borrowed from the West without regard to the consequences (J. Wiatr 1982: 20).

The new Party leadership was convinced, after a brief hesitation, that a renewal of the political and economic systems (various types of self-government, decentralization and marketization of economic decisions, etc.), normalization of the relationship with the Catholic Church and liberalization in science, culture and mass media were politically unfeasible. This rejection of a reform course by Gierek, which would have been aimed at restoring an appropriate relationship between the regime and society, was based on the conviction among the ruling elite that any change should not alter the leading position of the Communist Party in politics, the economy and society (W. Kuczyński 1981: 81).

The room for economic and political manoeuvre was tight when economic growth had slowed down considerably and the burden of servicing the Western debt was increasing fast in the second half of the 1970s. Politically, Gierek was not in a position to carry out a consistent incomes policy, such as a freeze in the growth of real wages and consumption, without antagonizing the workers and disturbing social peace. Similarly, an orderly deep cut in investment, which was to occur simultaneously with a restructuring of investment in accordance with new priorities (agriculture, exports and consumption) and quick-yielding and modernization investments, would encounter strong opposition from the bureaucracy (W. Kuczyński 1985: 35). What was left for the Gierek leadership to undertake were inconsistent and poorly implemented stop-gap measures against the increasing economic imbalances (such as the so-called economic manoeuvre, sugar rationing and parallel meat retailing in 'commercial shops' at higher prices, etc.). Gross investment was still growing up to 1978 and it was only in 1979 that investment fell by 8 per cent, with a more than proportional decline in small and medium enterprises which produced largely for the market.[5] By the end of the 1970s the economy was heading for economic and political crises.

The collapse of the economy from the second half of 1980 till the end of 1982 was the climax of the crisis caused largely by Gierek's errors in economic policy and the systemic shortcomings of the administrative economic system, exacerbated by an accumulation of particular adverse factors (a drastic fall in coal output and Western imports, bad harvests, etc.). Kuczyński argues against the government's interpretation, which blamed the alleged destructive strivings of Solidarność (strikes, unrestrained demand for higher wages, etc.) for causing the economic collapse (W. Kuczyński 1985: 58). High inflation and severe shortages followed by strong workers' demands for wage increases (to which the government gave way) led to greater inflation.[6] The buying spree and the flight from the zloty, fuelled by the growing inflationary gap and the lack of confidence in the value of the zloty, contributed to the collapse of the consumer goods market in 1980–2.

Gierek's 'new economic strategy' and economic voluntarism

J. Górski's booklet, *Gospodarka 1981: Problemy załamania i rozwoju* (*The Economy in 1981. Problems of its collapse and development*), locates the major causes of the economic crisis in the sphere of errors and distortions in Gierek's economic policy, poor economic achievements and the world economic recession. Górski considers that Gierek's striving to accelerate the rate of economic growth in the first half of the 1970s contained 'certain rational elements'. Higher economic growth was both 'necessary' and 'feasible' in view of the falling growth trend of the 1960s, the rapid growth in the population of productive age and the considerable improvement in the supply of industrial raw materials (e.g. copper, sulphur, fertilizer, etc.). Górski emphasizes, however, that the conditions for Gierek's economic 'big leap' were absent (J. Górski 1981: 5–6).

The rate of growth of both investment and real wages was excessive in the first half of the 1970s. The first was attributed mainly to the lack or weak control of the central organs in investment allocation, giving way to the 'pressure of the regions and industrial branches' for more investment funds and imports, leading to severe investment tensions and a rapid decline in the effectiveness of investment (J. Górski 1981: 7–9). The increase in real wages was similarly excessive in relationship to the growth of both net material product and labour productivity. This fact was largely conditioned by the slow growth of real wages in the 1960s, the need to compensate for the backlog in consumption and Gierek's desperate efforts to 'bribe' the rebellious workers with a tangible growth of consumption in exchange for political tolerance towards the regime and his leadership 'at any price'. Being a victim of his own 'propaganda of success' and guided by the imperative of political survival, Gierek was forced to take more Western credits to finance the growth of consumption (e.g. large imports of Western grain) in the second half of the 1970s, at a time when Polish economic growth was falling and the world economic situation was deteriorating (J. Górski 1981: 13–14). By the end of the 1970s the Polish economy was manoeuvred into a crisis situation, caused by an accumulation of unfavourable factors (an unrealistic programme of industrial modernization, domestic and external imbalances, the rapid increase of the debt service ratio in hard currency, bad harvests, etc.) which all occurred more or less simultaneously.

Despite the rapid deterioration of the economy in the last years of the 1970s, Górski considers that, in fact, the general economic situation and consumption level in early 1980 were not so severe as to vindicate the outbreak of massive protests and strikes in the summer of 1980. He notes, moreover, that the economy had improved slightly, and claims that the VIIIth Party Congress held in February 1980 had prepared an economic austerity programme. Had the government acted resolutely and cut both investment and consumption sufficiently, the effects of the economic deterioration could have been confined to manageable proportions. A 6–7 per cent cut in consumption in 1980 could have reduced domestic imbalances considerably, enabled hard currency exports to grow strongly, maintained sufficient confidence of the Western banks in Poland's credibility and hence made an orderly debt rescheduling possible (J. Górski 1981: 32–4). Economic voluntarism, a paralysis of the political leadership and a weakening of Gierek's credibility in the eyes of both the Party elite and the masses made a realization of a programme of economic austerity politically unfeasible and socially unacceptable. The regime was substantially weakened by the political crisis, strikes and the demands of the workers (for higher wages, a shorter working week, etc.) supported by Solidarność. The regime succumbed to the demands of the workers, contributing directly and indirectly to the drastic fall in industrial output, exports and imports, to growing inflation and severe shortages, which led ultimately to the collapse of the economy in 1981 (J. Górski 1981: 36–45).

Górski's diagnosis of the economic crisis of 1979–82 dismisses the general hypothesis which blames systemic defects of the command economy for making an economic crisis inevitable or likely. According to him:

> The crisis which broke out in August 1980 was exclusively the result of

errors in economic policy, committed already in the first half of the decade. That this was not caused by shortcomings of really existing socialism has been clearly demonstrated by the economies of Hungary and German Democratic Republic, which cut their rates of economic growth, as happened in all the developed world, but nevertheless have functioned reasonably well.

(J. Górski 1981: 59)

Viewed from a historical perspective, he further argues that central planning had also functioned quite well in Poland. Therefore, the disfunctions of the economy in the 1970s could not be attributed to the systemic defects of really existing socialism, but were mainly due to Gierek's unrealistic economic growth strategy, irresponsibility, incompetence, corruption and the demoralization of the leadership (J. Górski 1981: 11). It was the alleged deformation of socialism, but not state socialism itself, which was responsible for the economic crisis. Górski's explanation of the economic crisis of 1979–82 is conservative, basically similar to the official etiology of the crises, formulated in the final version of the *Kubiak Report*, which blamed Gierek's voluntarism ('the bad leadership syndrome'), unjustified demands on the workers and the extremist fraction of Solidarność for wrecking the economy.

Growing discrepancy between the state's development mission and the rising consumption aspirations of the masses

J. Pajestka's booklet, *Polski kryzys lat 1980–1981* (*The Polish Crisis of 1980–1981*), was one of the first diagnoses of the Polish crisis, written in the middle of its climax. The ideas and arguments contained in the booklet are developed further in his book *Kształtowanie procesu rozwoju* (*The Formation of the Development Process*). Pajestka was one of the leading Polish economists, a Vice-Chairman of the State Planning Commission until 1979 and an expert adviser to the government during the Gdańsk negotiations in August 1980. According to him, state socialism was essentially an attempt to embody the ideology of progress by a communist minority group who were determined to use state power as a lever for social and economic transformations.[7] Historically the major aim of economic planning was to promote rapid growth through a mobilization of investment resources and manpower by the state ('etatism'). Contrary to the expectations of classical Marxism, socialist revolutions occurred in economically underdeveloped regions. In accordance with Lenin's well-known thesis, it was the Communist Party which was to undertake 'the historical task of capitalism', that is to develop the productive forces following the revolutions in underdeveloped countries.

A deliberate shaping of the future development of the economy by the state was traditionally deeply-rooted in the ideology of socialist planning. The pursuit of an ambitious goal of the 'state economic development mission' by means of enormous investment outlays and mobilization of manpower was greatly facilitated by nationalization of the basic means of production ('the commanding heights' of the state sector) and the centralization of planning and management decisions. The state development mission succeeded in overcoming the pre-war backward Polish economy, a sort of 'conservative development' achievement (W. Brus and T. Kowalik 1983), but lacked a built-in mechanism which enabled it to adjust to changing needs. It generated a huge backlog in consumption and technical innovations for civilian purposes. The command economic system led to prevalent misallocation of labour and resources, inefficiency and waste (J. Pajestka 1983: 137–9). As a result, labour productivity growth was low and was accompanied by a rising capital output ratio and a high fuel and raw materials intensity of production.

Both the official ideology of state socialism and the evidence of higher consumption levels in the industrialized West fanned the consumption aspirations of the Polish people. According to Pajestka, the post-war experience of really existing socialism had demonstrated that socialism released broad and strong consumption aspirations among the people while failing to generate sufficient motivation for economic progress. This tended to lead to a 'degeneration of aspirations', that is, aspirations evolve into demands addressed to the state, and a general perception develops that the satisfaction of consumer needs depends on state and political decisions, instead of economic results (J. Pajestka 1983: 156–63). When economic growth had to slow down because a high rate of growth of investment and employment was no longer feasible, the gap between the state development mission and consumption aspirations grew. Under such circumstances, 'the contradiction between the state economic development mission and the consumption aspirations of the population' was bound to become intense. Critical momentum of the contradiction tended to precipitate the outbreak of regular crises (1956, 1970, 1980–1) in post-war Poland (J. Pajestka 1983: 141–7).

The failure of the economy to meet the rising consumption aspirations and expectations was attributed mainly to 'failings in the system of functioning of the economy' (J. Pajestka 1983: 154). Three basic defects in the socialist economic system are explicitly mentioned:

1 the mechanism of satisfying consumer needs, as exemplified by the functioning of the market for goods and services, was perverse, causing great vexation and demoralization in society;
2 the whole system of economic regulation was ineffective, manifesting itself in the form of large waste in resource use, slow innovation and faulty coordination of various activities of economic units;
3 the whole system of functioning of the economy mistreated people as members of the socialist community, refusing them the opportunity to satisfy the need for participation, co-responsibility and creativity.

(J. Pajestka 1981: 43–6)

Pajestka expresses the view that the systemic failings of the command economy exacerbated the fundamental contradiction between the ambitious goals of the state economic development mission and the rising consumption aspirations of the people in the 1970s.

Pajestka's general diagnosis of the post-war Polish crises is supplemented by an examination of the specific socio-economic and political environments prevailing in the 1970s which co-determined Gierek's economic policy. In retrospect – according to him – the rationale for the intensified development mission of the state during the 1970s was 'increasingly less justified' (J. Pajestka 1983: 148) as the country had made considerable progress in its industrialization effort. The intensified development mission of the state in the 1970s served the interests of the power elite more than it reflected the historical necessity of economic growth, supported by the people (J. Pajestka 1981: 30–1). The Gierek leadership, which replaced Gomulka after the violent protests of the workers, needed economic success urgently. Visible consumption growth was necessary in order to avert further riots and to regain conditional legitimacy. The use of coercion, a mechanism which had long been used to maintain state control, had increasingly played itself out. In this context the workers must be assured that the intensified development mission would not be achieved at the expense of the standard of living.

The regime under Gierek presented itself as a 'philanthropic state'. Propaganda focused on what the state 'gave' to the people and how good it was, instead of encouraging society to show readiness for hard work and sacrifice. A 'degeneration of aspirations' was progressing rapidly in the 1970s. While failing to pursue consistently the required 'systemic and institutional reforms and turn about in the general orientation of economic growth policy' in the 1970s (J. Pajestka 1983: 150), the regime opted for a substitute in the form of huge indebtedness to the West to finance the ambitious industrial modernization programme and rapid growth of consumption, thus creating the conditions for the outbreak of economic crisis at the end of the 1970s.

Pajestka believes that in a reformed socialist economy, the role of the state should be drastically reduced, leaving the bulk of economic decisions to autonomous enterprises and market mechanisms. A policy of high economic growth through state mobilization of investment would have no chance of success. He expresses the hope that economic growth would be shaped by general consensus, reconciling the contradiction between the logic of development and material needs of the population (J. Pajestka 1983: 264–84). Economic reform is seen as incompatible with a traditionally conceptualized development mission of the state.

Increasing constraints to economic growth and 'negative adaptations'

W. Herer and W. Sadowski, in their essay 'Bariery wzrostu – anatomia załamania gospodarczego' ('Barriers to economic growth – anatomy of the economic collapse'), discuss the economic crisis of 1979–82 in terms of rising barriers to economic growth experienced since the second half of the 1960s, their disregard and the negative responses of Gierek to these constraints. The growth barriers manifested themselves mainly in a 'declining marginal rate of return to investments', particularly in economic sectors and industries producing primary products, accompanied by growing raw material and fuel intensiveness of production, and rising foreign trade constraints (W. Herer and W. Sadowski 1985: 353–60). They seem to suggest that this 'law of declining marginal rate of return to investment' was somehow related to a worsening in the 'technical-natural conditions' of production in the primary sector (W. Herer and W. Sadowski 1985: 361). The authors focus their crisis analysis on the responses of the Gierek leadership to the rising growth constraints and an examination of possible alternatives which could have prevented the outbreak of the economic crisis.

In their view, the industrialized Western countries (West Germany, France and Great Britain, etc.) had in general reacted postively to the rising economic growth barriers and the oil crisis during the 1970s. They succeeded in restructuring production and cutting the fuel and raw materials intensity of production substantially in conjunction with a considerable slow-down of economic growth and mass unemployment. Hungary also reduced the growth of the economy and consumption in the 1970s, but without introducing unemployment. Gierek's leadership, on the other hand, instead of responding positively, had opted for 'negative adaptations' to the increasing growth constraints, 'seizing the barriers through storming', stepped up investment growth substantially, financed by Western credits, and hence had overheated the economy further (W. Herer and W. Sadowski 1985: 364–5). The negative adaptation to the increasing growth barriers in the first half of the 1970s was, they believe, the major cause of the deep economic crisis of 1979–82.

Within the perspective of economic crisis analysis, both authors are of the opinion that the Polish economy had great potentiality and untapped opportunity in the late 1960s and early 1970s. At that time, the environment for initiating economic reforms was favourable. This was due to the high growth of raw materials production in the Soviet Union (Poland's main supplier), good access to Western capital and export markets, a stable domestic market with reasonable public confidence in the value of the zloty ('good money') and a high rate of production growth of fertilizer production following the completion of a number of chemical plants in Poland. Had economic reforms been carried out consistently, then 'gains of non-investment factors of economic growth' could have been activated and realized. They would then have led to a reduction in the raw materials, fuel and import intensiveness of production. Should it be considered necessary to step up productive investment growth in the future in order to modernize production structure and to accelerate economic growth, then these steps must be initiated only after economic reforms had been institutionalized (W. Herer and W. Sadowski 1985: 365–7).[8]

Capital accumulation and net investment in fixed assets amounted to 28 per cent and 22 per cent of the national net material product ('national income for distribution') in 1970, compared to 24 per cent and 17 per cent in 1960, all expressed in 1961 prices (*Rocznik Statystyczny* 1971: 133). It is maintained that the rate of investment in 1970 was sufficiently high and there was actually no objective urgent economic need to boost investment growth as Gierek did in the early 1970s. What was needed was economic restructuring and investment regrouping, that is, efforts of measures aiming to improve the effectiveness of production and investment, even at the expense of a temporary slow-down of economic growth. Instead of opting for a reverse sequence of economic growth strategy, Gierek stepped up the rate of productive investment drastically in 1971–5 and indeed missed the opportunity to pursue a sound alternative programme of economic growth. Gierek's so-called strategy of accelerated development in the 1970s exacerbated the initial growth barriers and produced, moreover, new and more threatening growth constraints (debt trap, hard currency import dependency of industrial and agricultural production, poor export performance, etc.) which brought Poland into deep economic crisis at the end of the decade.

It is doubtful, however, whether the economic and political environments were as favourable at that time this hypothesis assumes. Positive conditions for economic reforms, both at home and abroad, hardly existed at that time (R. Bugaj and T. Kowalik 1986: 54–5). Neither a strong political will nor social pressure from below demanding economic reforms were observable. The economic and political environments at home (growing shortages, particularly meat products, and the weakening of the 'liberal' fraction in the Party since 1968, etc.) and abroad (the invasion of Czechoslovakia in 1968, the stagnation of economic reforms in Hungary in the early 1970s, etc.) were much less favourable to economic reform than assumed.

The primacy of the producer goods sector and economic crises

A. Müller's essay analyses Gierek's policy of accelerated economic growth against the economic policy background of the growth proportions of 1950–80, and underlines the historical roots of the economic crisis of 1979–82. According to him, 'The present crisis is not only the result of errors in economic policy, mistakes or simple corruption of the Gierek leadership, but it has already been growing for decades' (A. Müller 1985: 99). It is admitted that Gierek's errors and distortions in economic policy did contribute to the collapse of the economy in 1980–1, but the roots of the economic crisis were deeply embedded in the late 1940s and early 1950s when Poland was forced to copy the Soviet economic model of forced industrialization. These had at least two main characteristics: (i) a drift toward high rates of productive investment; (ii) a strong investment preference for the development of the producer goods sector or heavy industry. The rapid growth of heavy industry (steel, coal and machine-tools production), stimulated by the Cold War in the 1950s, had contributed to the strengthening of the armament and military–industrial complex in the economy and politics (A. Müller 1985: 118).

Poland's heavy industry economic growth orientation of the 1950s and the 1960s had its own momentum and dynamics determining the subsequent pattern of development of the economy. According to Müller: 'The nature, proportions and rates of economic growth during the first period of industrialization and of the sixties have exerted deep influence on economic proportions of the seventies' (A. Müller 1985: 190–1). The large flow of Western capital and technology during the first half of the 1970s, with the exception of a brief interruption in 1971–3, had not modified the investment preference and the structure of production.

The distribution of national income favouring productive investment with investment preference in the heavy industry sector tended to petrify and to magnify the initial economic disproportions, reinforcing the deformation in the structure of production. First the heavy industry growth orientation tended to reproduce or to perpetuate the initial economic disproportions in the following planning period or production cycle as a result of the socio-economic inertia. Second, the heavy industry growth orientation generated strong (in)formal pressure groups in the state and Party bureaucracy, successfully pursuing their own group interests in bargaining for more investment and resources for the development of the heavy industry complex (A. Müller 1985: 116). The reproduction of the unbalanced growth pattern seemed to be inevitable when economic mechanisms of investment verification, like the self-regulating market mechanism, were absent and other socio-political mechanisms of investment verification, like feedback-loops from society, were normally very weak.

At critical junctures economic disproportions had led to repeated collapse in the growth of the standard of living or consumption, generating grave social and political conflicts. Economic disproportions were the major cause of the post-war economic and political crises (A. Müller 1985: 116). In order to reduce the tensions, the regime was forced temporarily to make economic and political concessions to the population such as a rapid growth in real wages and consumption, more investment in the consumption sector (light industry, agriculture, etc.) and promises of economic and political reforms and cultural liberalization. After regaining the lost ground and achieving political consolidation, the regime restored the traditional distribution of national product, stepping up the rate of productive investment with a renewed preference for the development of heavy industry (A. Müller 1985: 130–1). Thus it prepared the conditions for the next economic and political crises.

The heavy industry growth orientation had contributed to the distorted phenomenon of production for the sake of production, a sort of self-consuming or self-propelling economic growth in state socialism. Overestimating the significance of ideology in economic decision-making, Müller attributes the distortions in economic policy and growth pattern to Stalin's economic growth doctrine which postulated the primacy of producer over consumer goods (A. Müller 1985: 191). In the 1970s, particularly in the second half of the decade, production was increasingly capital, raw materials and fuel intensive, causing poor hard currency export performance and lack of competitiveness of Polish industrial exports.

The failure to get away from the heavy industry growth orientation seemed to be endemic. The powerful bureaucratic pressure group around the heavy industry complex strongly opposed the investment cut in the steel and coal industries in 1969–70 as envisaged in the aborted programme of Gomulka's selective industrial development (A. Karpinski 1986: 153–4). Jaroszewicz's economic crash programme ('economic manoeuvre'), set up after the failure to cut consumption growth through a price increase of consumer goods in 1976, did not achieve its main aim of restructuring industrial investment and production to favour consumption, hard currency exports and industries producing inputs for agriculture. When industrial investment outlays were cut drastically in 1979–82, inter-branch reallocation or restructuring of investment represented not so much the 'preference of development' but rather the 'preference of protection' of certain branches like the coal and fuel industries, steel production and other allied industrial branches (W. Walkowiak 1983: 36–8). The 'investment arteriosclerosis', supported by the strong lobby around heavy industry, succeeded in preventing a restructuring (including complete abandonment) of the distorted pattern of unfinished investment projects in the first half of the 1980s.

Falling share of intensive growth factors and economic crisis

M. Nasiłowski, who specializes in theories and empirical studies on economic growth and income distribution in socialist countries, discusses the economic crisis by examining changes in the significance or contribution of individual growth factors (labour, labour productivity, capital and non-investment, etc.) in shaping the post-war economic development of East European countries. The run-down of extensive factors (massive investment and man-power) of economic growth, occurring more or less since the middle of the 1960s, and the accompanying great difficulties in activating intensive factors of economic growth (technical innovations, labour productivity growth, etc.), were the main characteristics of economic development in Poland and other CMEA countries. The supply of raw materials and fuel became increasingly short, and their cost of production was rising. Output tended to be more raw materials, fuel and capital intensive which required a corresponding structure of production to serve this trend. This unfavourable growth trend was reflected in the fact that the 'growth of labour productivity occurred at the expense of a continuous rapid growth in capital–labour ratios' (M. Nasiłowski 1985: 419). This finding was briefly characterized as a 'declining trend in the share of intensive factors' (A. Müller 1985: 15) in the economic growth of the Eastern European socialist countries, including Poland.

'The administrative system of planning and management' (M. Nasiłowski 1985: 420), introduced at the end of the 1940s and early 1950s, succeeded in boosting the rate of economic growth for some time. But the system reinforced arbitrary decisions in the allocation of resources, paralyzed initiatives from below and strengthened bureaucratization and distortions of economic life such as the underreporting of available production capacities or reserves at the disposal of economic units, manipulations of targets, poor product quality, etc. Nasiłowski maintains that the major cause of the substantial fall in the rate of economic growth and efficiency in resource use in the second half of the 1970s was 'the administrative system of central planning and management', which had hardly changed (except in Hungary) since it was introduced (M. Nasiłowski 1985: 421). The weak position of the central authority and the crisis of confidence in the society–state relationship forced the regime to make large economic and political concessions (free trade unions, consumption protection and rapid growth of money wages, etc.) to society, which tended to deepen the economic crisis at the time when the economy started to break down from the end of 1979 (M. Nasiłowski 1985: 423–6).

Nasiłowski pleads for a radical change in modes of thinking and explores ways to transform the present type of 'state-bureaucratic' system into 'democratic socialism'. The key concept for crucial reforms of the political and economic institutions is based on the idea of 'socialization of the state'. The reforms should comprise new institutions and guiding principles like 'self-governing and free trade unions', guarding the interests of the society concerning the distribution of national income and the working conditions of labour; a 'federation of consumers', protecting their interests against the monopolistic position of the producers; a definite division of powers between parliament ('Sejm'), government and the Communist Party, where the first should become a 'genuine mouthpiece of public opinion, upholding legality and exerting full control over the executive' (M. Nasiłowski 1985: 446–8). Furthermore he pleads for a 'socialization of the state-owned means of production',[9] based on an optimal mix between managerial professionalism and workers' self-management of the economic units, whilst the 'socialization of central planning' should help towards a 'debureaucratization' of the decision-making process, combined with 'pluralism' (state, cooperative and private, etc.) in the ownership of the means of production (M. Nasiłowski 1985: 448–53). It is hoped that political and economic reforms could help to get Poland out of the deep crises and achieve durable improvements in the efficiency of resource use if they were carried out consistently.

CONCLUSION

From the second half of the 1970s Gierek's 'propaganda of success' and the official censorship of the media contributed to the rising dissonance between the worsening socio-economic and political reality and the optimistic official propaganda. Dissident intellectuals, attempting to build an alliance with the workers, partially succeeded, with their critical underground media, in breaking the regime's monopoly of information, the credibility of which was declined rapidly with the worsening of the state of the economy. In examining this worsening situation, the dissident economic writings forecast the approaching economic crisis, analysing its major cause(s) and feasible economic policy alternatives or reforms. Basic ideas, arguments and conclusions drawn by dissident economists in the 1970s became part of the mainstream economics of crisis etiologies after August 1980.

The economic collapse of 1980–1, the establishment of Solidarność, the paralysis of censorship and the desire for truth created favourable conditions for objective inquiries into the extent, nature and causes of the socio-economic and political crises, and a discussion of programmes of economic recovery and reforms. At least four main determinants of the economic crisis can be identified in the writings of Polish economists:

1 the systemic shortcomings of really existing socialism were identified as a major cause of an increasing misallocation and inefficiency in resource use, making it unable to meet the growing needs of the society;
2 deformation in the economic structure (heavy industry growth orientation in particular) generating technical, socio-economic and political distortions which continuously reproduced economic disproportions;
3 defects in functioning due to errors in economic policies, voluntarism and bad leadership;
4 the collapse of Gierek's strategy of legitimation through satisfaction of consumers' aspirations.

The first two etiologies pleaded for far-reaching reforms of the socio-economic and political systems whilst the third was satisfied with a repair of the system, combined with changes in economic policy and leadership.

8

LEGITIMACY

INTRODUCTION

The word 'legitimacy' has been interpreted and conceptualized in many different ways, involving a variety of problems and being discussed in different political contexts. If one starts the discussion with Sternberger's general definition of legitimacy as 'the foundation of such governmental power as is exercised both with a consciousness on the government's part that it has the right to govern and with some recognition by the governed of that right' (D. Sternberger 1968: 244), then legitimation in communist states can be seen as the process of articulating the validity of the elite's authority to govern and its efforts to acquire and to secure that validity in the mind both of itself and of the ruled. Elite self-legitimation and legitimation at the mass level are two distinct but related aspects of the legitimation process. The focus on the ruling elite makes sense in Soviet-type societies which were characterized by a centralized and hierarchically organized political structure with the Communist Party occupying a leading position in political, economic and social institutions.

A number of Western observers have questioned the relevance and the use of the legitimacy concept in examining the realities of East European states. The assumption is that only liberal democratic regimes command legitimacy and that legitimacy, therefore, was absent in communist states. The traditional 'totalitarianism' approach presupposes the absolute monopoly power of the Communist Party and the state. The use (or threat) of terror or coercion was the main instrument of securing compliance. Under such a situation logically there was little need for an articulation of the validity of the right of the regime to rule. Using different analytical perspectives, Wright, for example, also rejects the legitimacy conceptualization and argues that an analysis of power politics 'gives us far more purchase on the realities of state socialism than the category of legitimacy' (M. Wright 1984: 115). The elite's requirement to validate its rule at mass level has a low priority in the state socialist system; and according to Jowitt, this was the view of the Soviet regime cadres who were 'concerned more with public awe than public legitimation' (K. Jowitt 1983: 282).

Pakulski's reflection on Max Weber's legitimacy theory and Soviet-type societies has also questioned the relevance of the concept of legitimacy. He concludes that conceptualization of 'legitimacy proper' (such as 'obedience is recognized as a duty' or 'persons exercising authority are lent prestige') is not appropriate for the analysis of compliance in such societies. Instead it is argued that the relative stability of the political and social order as well as the occurrence of mass dissent can be better explained in terms of 'conditional tolerance'. This results from the assessment of costs and benefits of (in)subordination, particularly with regard to the strategic groups in the society. The modes of acquiring and securing compliance (quasi-legitimacy), their mixture and components have changed over time (J. Pakulski 1986: 45–6). Authors examining legitimacy problems in Soviety-type societies, such as Rigby, Fehér, Markus, Zaslavsky and others, hold more or less similar views when they underline the key importance of economic performance and welfare policies in securing regime legitimation in the post-Stalinist period. Legitimation is then regarded as conditional on the regime's ability to produce a society with basic existential security and satisfied consumers. Gierek's strategy of consumer satisfaction for acquiring and securing legitimacy was a vivid example.

There were sufficient reasons for thinking that the ruling elites in Eastern European states were not indifferent to their legitimation. It is a truism that a legitimate rule is more effective than an illegitimate one. Furthermore, it could permit unpopular but necessary measures like substantial price rises for basic foods and necessities without provoking riots and political crises (P. Lewis 1984a: 3–4). Failure to acquire and to secure legitimation, either because of the weakness of its base, shortcomings in the satisfaction of consumer aspirations or the declining efficiency of the economic system, became a matter of acute importance for the regime. This had been clearly demonstrated by the recurrent political crises in post-war Poland, particularly by the deep socio-economic and political crisis of the first years of the 1980s. The breakdown of the legitimation process was closely linked with the socio-economic and political crisis.

A number of Polish sociologists and economists have attempted to comprehend the Polish crisis of the early 1980s in terms of mass perception of the growing responsibility of the state for the provision of welfare in enhancing the legitimacy of the regime, and its failure to meet these expectations. Failing to keep welfare provision in accordance with mass expectations was considered as a breach of promise for a 'better tomorrow' (J. Staniszkis 1984; W. Kuczyński 1981). From this perspective the political crisis was related to the collapse of the legitimacy of the state, which was partly attributed to the lack of 'traditional legitimacy' and a 'rationality crisis' (A. Jasinska-Kania 1983). The obvious falsity of Gierek's 'propaganda of success' had exacerbated the legitimation crisis.

This chapter will briefly describe and discuss several factors (history, ideology and institutionalization process) underlying the tenuous legitimation base of the communist rule. Further, a short description and discussion of Gierek's strategy of legitimation through consumer satisfaction will follow. The chapter ends with a brief discussion of the systemic strains and stability of the state socialist system.

Acknowledgement of the relevance of the legitimacy approach, however, should not lead to an exaggeration of its role in understanding the political realities of Eastern European states in general and of Poland in particular.

LEGITIMATION, IDEOLOGY AND INSTITUTIONALIZATION

Generalization of the evolution of the Leninist political system has underlined the correlation between the stages of development of the communist regimes and corresponding modes of legitimation. During the first stage, called the takeover period of the communist rule, mass submission was guaranteed by the threat and/or use of coercion. In the second stage of development, called the period of the regime's consolidation, legitimation stressed the future benefits, combined with attempts to create the appearance of law and order. The third stage of development, which presumably started from the middle of the 1960s, and is called the system of inclusion (reproduction), was characterized by the use of a more subtle form of cultural domination through the promotion of particular values and norms (K. Jowitt 1975; J. Pakulski 1986: 51–4). It was acknowledged that repression would work effectively only during a relatively short period. Moreover, the social and political costs for the upkeep of terror and coercion could be best utilized for the support of desirable social and economic goals. The post-Stalinist modes of legitimation changed significantly with greater emphasis on 'covert' legitimation based on common sense and pragmatism. A central issue at the stage of inclusion remained the question of the ideological definition of the Communist Party and its political role. Finally, the fourth stage, that of collapse, which began in Poland in 1979–82, was one of delegitimation through economic crisis.

The Polish communist revolution, which in the popular mind was a foreign (that is, Russian) transplant and antagonistic to Poland's national identity, had been entirely unable to legitimate the communist rule in the society since its beginning (J. Fiszman 1975: 132–5). Attempts to legitimate the communist rule in Poland had encountered 'negative feedbacks' (from the Catholic Church, Western-oriented intellectuals, etc.) or obstacles far greater than any East European states had ever faced (W. Brus 1984: 86–7). They partly stemmed from specific Polish historical development, politics and culture. The history of Polish–Russian antagonism, generated by almost 150 years of partition of Poland, with Czarist Russia as one of the three partitioning powers, was intensified by the Polish–Russian war (1920–1). The list of injustices felt by the Poles, inflicted by the Soviet Union both during and after the Second World War, was long. The Soviet invasion of Poland, at the time when its defence against the German aggressor was collapsing (in accordance with the secret Molotov–Ribbentrop protocol); the Katyn massacre of Polish army officers; the unwillingness of the Red Army to help in the heroic Warsaw uprising; and the Soviet annexation of Poland's eastern provinces were all serious grievances The fact that communism was brought by the Russians, guided formally by Marxism-Leninism, an ideology whose principles were basically at variance with the outlook of the Catholic Church, contributed to the weak legitimation of the communist rule (P. Lewis 1982: 131–2). Polish communists never succeeded in their efforts to tap nationalism and traditionalist ideology as sources of legitimacy.

Staniszki's explanation of the weak legitimation argued that this stemmed from the old tradition (during partition, German occupation, etc.) of Polish society's propensity to form a counter-community by establishing an elaborate structure of self-help (particularly in times of crisis) against what were perceived as illegitimate power holders. This tradition of polarization between state and society, which had transformed itself into a confrontation during crisis times, is considered to have lasted until recently (J. Staniszkis 1979: 185). Post-war modernization and social transformation of Poland had succeeded only partially in assimilating this latent tendency to form a counter-community against the communist state. Four major factors have contributed to the relative autonomy of the society against the state:

1 the survival and development of private agriculture, which helped to limit the influence of the bureaucracy on life in the countryside;
2 the existence of the influential Catholic Church;
3 the Western orientation of Polish intellectuals;
4 a strong tendency for self-preservation in the Polish society.

(A. Szczypiorski 1979: 21–32)

The idea of a society independent of the state has gained strength with the establishment of autonomous bodies independent of the state's control.

The discussion of the relationship between ideology and legitimation can be conducted at different levels. First it is concerned with the question of the role of official ideology in the legitimation process of communist states, including the question of the role of official ideology in the promotion of values and norms in society. Next comes the question as to whom ideology is aimed at. Here a distinction is made between official ideology for elite self-legitimation and a set of beliefs, ideas, etc. circulating among the population over whom the elite rules.

There seems to be a consensus of opinion among Western observers that official ideology had not succeeded in penetrating the mind and transforming the popular mentality in Eastern European society in accordance with socialist values and norms. Taras' study on the development of Poland's state ideology in the years 1956–83 has confirmed the thesis of the 'end of ideology' and its failure to promote values and norms in Polish society. Official ideology (particularly during Gierek's leadership) failed in three respects: it contributed to the spread of the myth of socialism; it was increasingly divorced from social reality; and it did not fulfil the historic goal of promoting values and norms expected of it (R. Taras 1984: 256).

Taras' study has also shown that no durable results were produced by the stop-gap measures taken by the leadership of the Party at the level of operative ideology (a set of explanations and justifications of the policy formulated) involving areas such as inner-party democracy, industrial democracy, state–church relationship and science and culture in response to the socio-economic and political crisis. The history of state socialism in Poland can be characterized as a protracted ideological crisis, interwoven with a cyclical occurrence of political crises (R. Taras 1984: 257–8). In four decades of communist rule, the official ideology was unable to replace the widely held view that the communist system was imposed by an external force (the Soviet army) and that the system was un-Polish. The failure in ideological matters and the hostile public attitude towards official ideology were major factors contributing to popular discontent with the state socialist system. The official ideology in Poland completely failed to ensure the legitimacy of communist rule at the mass level.

In the discussion on legitimation processes in East European states, Western observers have noted that the task of the regimes was to legitimate themselves in the eyes of their own elite as well as in the eyes of the public. The first task concerns the question of the extent to which the regimes (leadership) were considered legitimate by the members of their own elite. T. Rigby and others have underlined the key significance of a viable relationship between the ruling group and its 'administrative staff' for the stability and legitimation of the regime. It is suggested that in state socialist systems elite cohesion and self-legitimation were more crucial than legitimation at the mass level (S. Bialer 1980: 194–5; T. Rigby 1982: 14–15; J. Pakulski 1986: 50–1). The 'administrative staff' belonged to the elite, consisting of 'strategic groups' in the Party–state structure and other institutions like the secret police, the army, groups of party apparatchiks, sections of the managerial strata and skilled workers, whose individual relative importance in the elite set-up had varied over time. The credibility of the regime in the eyes of its strategic groups was the key to the legitimation of both the Party and the state.

Party elite disunity introduced uncertainty and hesitancy in the exercise of power by part of the strategic groups (e.g. agencies of coercion) which could trigger off mass dissent and outbreaks leading to a delegitimation of the regime (leadership). Instances of political crisis and instability in Eastern European states were associated with the failure to achieve elite integration and to maintain effective control over the political apparatus and agencies of coercion. It has been suggested that the roots of the political crises in Hungary and Poland in 1956, which heralded mass dissent, lay in the deep disunity and fractional struggles within the communist elites, which followed changes in the Party leadership in the Soviet Union and in other CMEA countries after the death of Stalin (S. Bialer 1980: 195; J. Pakulski 1986: 50). According to this view the inability of the authorities to suppress the initial dissent due to elite disunity leads to even wider protests.

The role of legitimation in serving to integrate the elite and the complex institutions (e.g. the Communist Party) through which its rule was exercised must be significant. The importance of both normative integration of the Party elite and the tendencies for elite differentiation indicated the significance of self-legitimation and its close relationship with ideology. The stability of a communist regime was related to the 'prominence of the shared attachment to Communist (Marxist-Leninist) ideology amongst the leaders of the regime's institutions and its contribution to their integrated operation in the regime'; and the possible weaknesses of the regime 'could emerge with the declining strength of ideological attachment' (P. Lewis 1984a: 16–17). Whilst generally the party remained committed to the principles of Leninist democratic centralism, Taras notes the unstable feature and weakness of the Polish rulers' operative ideology in the struggle against factionalism and its role in the promotion of Party elite integration since 1956. Attention to party unity in the operative ideology had diminished during the Gierek period, particularly in the second half of the 1970s. Subsequently it 'was made inoperative with the emergence of Solidarity in 1980–1 when the rulers were required to countenance greater ideological and institutional pluralism in the PUWP, but it was reasserted forcefully with the imposition of Martial Law' (R. Taras 1984: 238). The process of an increasingly weakening role of ideology in the legitimation of the Polish regime was intensified following the abandonment of the reformist tendencies that had emerged in 1956.

The weakness of ideology in serving as a basis of elite legitimation and integration had been problematic for the Polish Party, which had the reputation for being particularly faction-ridden.[1] Specific organizational expedients and the mechanism of elite integration had been emphasized. One of them was known as the phenomenon of the 'carousel of cadres', i.e. a persistent movement of cadres from one position to another with little thought for their functioning and competence in order to foster a sense of common identity. Other mechanisms of elite integration had emphasized the significance of material incentives and privileges in securing the allegiance of members of the leadership and key Party officials (P. Lewis 1984a: 29–30; 1985: 45). These substitute devices for elite integration and mechanisms for the prevention of an outbreak of intra-elite conflict, developed in Gierek's time, initially succeeded in buying-off potential dissenters and defecters. In the long-run, however, they tended to undermine the legitimation of the regime, contributing to the disintegration of the whole Party apparatus in 1980–1. This illustrates how simultaneous pursuit of elite self-legitimization and legitimation at the mass level may be contradictory and lead to the achievement of neither.

The interactions between ideology and reality are complex and the outcome may be unpredictable and contradictory. Staniszkis observes that ideological legitimation may often become a trap for the ruling elite itself, constraining its freedom of manoeuvre and causing it to become a prisoner of its own mythologized legitimacy.[2] As a result, the ruling group may easily be blackmailed by its own executives (e.g. demand for more investment funds) or by the workers (e.g. demands for a price freeze of basic necessities or a wage increase). The ruling group considers that 'every strike by workers is a serious political problem for the ruling group due to the myth of the Party as the vanguard of the working class' (J. Staniszkis 1979: 168) and the fears that the strike may spread rapidly. In the perception of the workers, the correlation between their own labour and remuneration was insignificant and the actual levels of wages, transfer payments and prices depended on the state's volition. This encouraged workers to demand wage increases and take part in action (including strikes) supporting such a demand, instead of trying to obtain pay increases by more effective work (W. Morawski 1984: 37).

The institutional reforms of the Party–state structure carried out by Gierek in 1973–5 failed to enhance the Party's control and its leading role in the processes of socio-economic development. The Party's ability to adapt itself to the new challenges posed by modern industrial societies and its degree of organizational coherence were declining (P. Lewis 1984b: 211–48). Central plan control over investment, wages and foreign trade was weakening considerably in the 1970s *vis-à-vis* the particularistic interests of the regional 'fiefdoms' and certain industrial branches (P. Bożyk 1983: 124–38), a phenomenon euphemistically described as 'open-ended' planning.

The Party's dominance over society was assured by its superiority within the overall Party–state complex, and this was effected in at least two ways. First, horizontally, the Party organs exercised authority over government and state organizations at the same level (e.g. the Political Bureau dominated the Council of Ministers). Second, vertically, a system of hierarchical control was exercised within the Party according to the principle of democratic centralism. Central control over occupancy of positions of importance was maintained, organizational discipline could be enforced and deviation from central policy was prevented. A key role in the process was played by the *nomenklatura*, a mechanism that served to institutionalize the control by the Party–state apparatus over society, counteracting any tendency for the emergence of autonomous social processes. The scope of *nomenklatura* extended to the most important appointments in almost every occupation: central and local government officials, managers of state enterprises and cooperatives, certain positions in the army and agencies of coercion, universities, leaders of the trade unions, youth and women's organizations, etc. (T. Itoh 1985; P. Lewis 1985).

The substitute devices for elite integration developed during the Gierek leadership in the 1970s led to low performance of the bureaucracies and tolerance or even encouragement of corruption of the rapidly expanding number of *nomenklatura* holders (T. Ash 1985: 6–7; P. Lewis 1985: 45; M. Hirszowicz 1986: 131–46). Compared to other Eastern European countries the *nomenklatura* system in Poland probably never functioned effectively, partly because of the weak basis of the legitimation of the communist system and the high prestige of the Catholic Church. The regime tried unsuccessfully to enforce its influence on the Church's personnel policy during the so-called investiture conflict with the Vatican. After 1956, however, the regime did not try this again. Unlike, for instance, the Orthodox Church in the Soviet Union, the Catholic

Church in Poland remained immune from the *nomenklatura* procedure. Since *nomenklatura* favoured and maintained the apparatchiks in the occupation of important positions, the system was considered unjust by a large part of the population in a society with an influential Church (T. Itoh 1985: 160–2; P. Lewis 1985: 44).

Non-party specialists and intelligentsia (e.g. DiP, that is 'Doświadczenie i Przyszłość', 'Experience and Future') criticized the *nomenklatura* procedure, requesting its substitution by a system based on the individual merits of the candidate. The workers' opposition to it was particularly strong during critical times. The demand for change in the *nomenklatura* procedure was included in the protocol of the Gdańsk Agreement of 1980 which stated that 'people in the leading positions are chosen on the basis of qualifications rather than Party membership' (A. Kemp-Welch 1983: 174). The establishment of Solidarność removed the *nomenklatura* procedure from such important institutions as the trade unions. Other institutions, like the Polish Writers' Association, students' organizations and universities, were contaminated.

The idea of workers' self-government, which was initially encouraged by the government's draft of economic reform, acquired spontaneous mass support from the second quarter of 1981. This resulted in the establishment of democratic self-governing bodies in many enterprises. Poland had a long and rich tradition of workers' self-government movements (1945, 1956). The controversy over the competence of the workers' council in the appointment of enterprise directors (which was the domain of *nomenklatura*) was one of the key issues in the dispute between Solidarność and the state, involving a basic feature of the 'leading position of the Party'. The 'open conspiracy' (e.g. overpoliticization of the workers' self-government) of part of Solidarność, the power vacuum and the deep economic crisis resulted in the imposition of martial law at the end of 1981.

Was a lack of an alternative to the communist system a part of the legitimation process? A lack of an alternative, other than state socialism with the Communist Party occupying a leading position, seemed in the pre-perestroika period to be a major source of political stability in Eastern European states (including Poland) which were dependent on the Soviet Union. The 'geo-political'[3] formula of Polish communist rule looked straightforward. When the masses threatened the monopolistic position of the Party and Soviet hegemony, the Polish communists simply argued, 'We rule because this is the only system, and we are the only authorities, the Soviet Union would accept' (J. Pakulski 1986: 46; F. Fehér, *et al.* 1983: 138). The Polish communist elite exploited the generally accepted impossibility of leaving the socialist camp by reminding the population that it was the communists who saved the nation from a repetition of the Hungarian tragedy of 1956 and the invasion of Czechoslovakia of 1968, using a veiled slogan like 'better us than the Russians'. It should be added that part of the non-communist elite (the Catholic Church, intelligentsia, etc.) had joined the regime during crisis times in its quest to prevent an uncontrolled outburst which might have provoked a Soviet invasion. The use of the 'geopolitical' formula for legitimation automatically led to a collapse in the legitimation of the Polish communists and the loss of power when the 'new thinking' and perestroika become official doctrine in the USSR.

The growing contradiction between the 'open conspiracy' of part of the Solidarność leadership and the 'self-limiting' nature of the workers' revolution (J. Staniszkis 1984) occurred simultaneously with the deepening of the power vacuum. This was caused by the disintegration of the state administration and the PUWP, torn by deep internal conflicts, and confronted with the open defiance of the working class in conjunction with the dramatic deterioration of the economy ('supply crisis'). As a result, the legitimation of the regime collapsed completely and the danger of an open confrontation between Solidarność and the state increased rapidly. Jaruzelski's regime presented the imposition of martial law as an extraordinary measure with the main aims of preventing the alleged threats of civil war and preserving Poland's 'raison d'etat' ('racja stanu') through the suppression of Solidarność by force. In the eyes of the ruling elite a limit had been reached and the system's institutional structure was threatened, particularly the monocentric power of the Party and its political control over the economy. Martial law restored the system with the 'identity of real socialism and re-established institutional legitimation', but these simultaneously 'precluded social legitimation' (A. Rychard 1987: 48–9).

THE COLLAPSE OF GIEREK'S LEGITIMATION STRATEGY

Analyses of techniques or modes of legitimation occupy an important place in the discussion of political legitimacy in Soviet-type societies. Legitimation techniques like the 'paternalistic mode of legitimation' (F. Fehér 1982; M. Markus 1982), 'organized consensus' (V. Zaslavsky 1982) or 'consumerism' (A. Pravda 1981) have emphasized the key importance of the satisfaction of the needs of the population as the basis for the regime's legitimation. The basic idea is how to acquire compliance through economic performance and consumer satisfaction. The constituent components consist of a mixture of welfare policies, such as full employment, social mobility, job security, access to basic health care and education, and last but not least a steady growth of consumption. Their provision is expected to generate conditional tolerance towards the regime and a feeling among many strata that it is worth obeying commands and renouncing political freedom in exchange for existential security and a steady improvement in the standard of living.

The fall of Gomulka and the rise of Gierek's leadership was precipitated by the workers' revolt in Trojmiasta at the end of 1970, instigated by the government decree to raise the price of basic necessities. The 1960s were characterized by a virtually stagnant growth of consumption, a political malaise and growing inter-elite conflicts in the Party, particularly during the second half of the decade. The textile-workers' strike in Łódz in early 1971 forced Gierek to rescind the price rise and promise a substantial increase in consumption.

According to Pravda, the tacit 'social compact' between the Gierek leadership and the population following the workers' revolt contained three major elements. First, the population expected certain social benefits from the regime, including job security, full employment and a relatively equal wage distribution. Second, there were improvements in consumption, a better supply of goods and services at relatively stable prices. Third, in return, the population accepted compliance with the political system, though not necessarily with a high degree of commitment (A. Pravda 1981: 163). The provision of basic security of every day life plus a steady rise in the standard of living with stable prices, in exchange for tolerance and obedience to the new leadership plus a forfeit of workers' basic political rights, were the key elements of the 'unwritten contract' between Gierek and the workers (W. Kuczyński 1981: 80–3).

Gierek's strategy of accelerated economic growth and a 'trade-off of consumerism against depoliticization' (M. Hirszowicz 1986: 91), presented in conjunction with the vision of a 'second Poland', was enthusiastically welcomed by the population. People believed that living conditions would improve visibly from year to year. The rapid growth of the consumption aspirations of the Poles was also fanned by Gierek's 'propaganda of success'. The rapid growth of consumption in the period 1971–6 may rightly be called a 'consumption revolution', if one compared it with the virtually stagnant growth of consumption during the 1960s. In particular, the increase in meat consumption, a politically sensitive issue, was impressive. Popular assessment of living conditions and confidence in the political leadership during the first half of the 1970s, as reflected in the public opinion polls organized by the government, was positive. Moreover, the regime had succeeded in depoliticizing the population (D. Mason 1985: 43–6). Reliance on continued economic success as the basis of political legitimation automatically meant, however, that legitimacy would decline if economic performance deteriorated.

By the end of 1975, the debt service ratio in hard currency had already reached a critical level. The government planned to boost Western exports, to slow down imports, particularly imports of grain, whilst keeping a high growth of Western imports of capital goods and industrial semi-finished goods. In the summer of 1976, the government announced a significant price increase of basic necessities with the aim of stopping further growth in consumption, but it was withdrawn within twenty-four hours under the pressure of the workers' protests. As a result the regime was demoralized. The workers considered the envisaged freeze in consumption growth and the price rise as a breach of promise whilst the Pyrrhic victory of the workers forcing the government to rescind the announced price rises considerably reduced the chance of an orderly management of the approaching crisis. The government's crash programme ('economic manoeuvre') failed to boost production for the domestic market and exports; and the drastic cut in Western imports led to a disruption in the supply of goods and production. For the first time since 1960, average real wages (according to official figures) dropped by nearly 3 per cent in 1978, compared to an annual growth of 7 per cent in 1971–6; a year later the net material product declined by 2.3 per cent. Poland was heading towards both socio-economic and political crises.

As has been noted previously, the significance of ideology in elite self-legitimation and integration was progressively weakening in the 1970s. The ideology deficits and the factionalism were compensated by organizational expedients of the Party–state complex and generous material incentives accorded to the strategic groups. These consisted of benefits and privileges (the special allocation of scarce goods and services such as cars, housing, medical treatment and vacations, etc.), high pay and security of tenure. Gierek extensively utilized material incentives, privileges and corruption for securing the allegiance of members of the elite and key Party–state officials.[4] These techniques of securing elite self-legitimation proved to be counter-productive on a national level and ultimately had a destabilizing effect.

The Gierek leadership developed a corporatist technique of economic group representation and protest absorption through control of the distribution of wage funds, bonuses, privileges and resources, using selectively different standards and criteria. The distribution principle of 'to each according to his usefulness to the authorities' (A. Rychard 1987: 51) came into play. By buying-off certain strategic groups which had a high potential for disruptive political mobilization (e.g. coal miners in Silesia, secret police, etc.), the ruling elite could neutralize dissatisfaction and play-off one group against another so that relative and temporary stability could be preserved (J. Staniszkis 1984: 66–7). This technique of protest absorption led to growing social segmentation and fragmentation, as well as income inequalities between regions, industrial branches and social groups, which depended largely upon an individual group's bargaining power ('siły przebicia') *vis-à-vis* the centre of power. On the other hand, the ruling elite became vulnerable and easily made itself a target of blackmail. Due to a rapid decline in the net flow of Western capital and economic deterioration, Gierek's corporatist technique of group representation and protest absorption had lost its efficacy by the end of the 1970s. It collapsed completely when the striking workers in Trojmiasta, Silesia and Szczecin were united and refused to confine their demands to the economic sphere but extended them to include fundamental political rights such as free trade unions and the right to strike.

Various groups of dissidents, proto-oppositions and critical intellectuals such as the KOR (Workers' Defence Committee), DiP (Experience and the Future), the Flying University and others had cropped up during the second half of the 1970s (particularly in the last years of the decade). They were active in the presentation of alternative views and information through underground publications and unauthorized lectures and meetings. Some of them (KOR) were instrumental in the formation of workers' and other self-help organizations. Gierek did not succeed in isolating the proto-oppositions and dissidents partly because of the deterioration of the economy and the pressure of Western public opinion.

Some of the apparatchiks, and in particular those in the agencies of coercion, became restless. For instance, the deep frustration of the security police was reflected in the so-called Pyja case in Cracow in the summer of 1978, when a student-KOR supporter was beaten by the police with the intention of polarizing the situation and provoking hard measures against dissidents. Dissatisfaction among part of the high Party apparatus and factional fights had developed intensively during the last years of the 1970s (G. Sanford 1983: 36–40). There was also widespread dissatisfaction in the rank and file of the Party. Party disunity and the factional fights reflected the lack of confidence among part of the Party elite in the ability of Gierek to solve the worsening economic and political problems. This constrained Gierek's possibilities of managing the approaching economic and political crises; and the fall of Gierek's leadership occurred under conditions of mass disobedience and Party elite delegitimation.

The so-called 'crisis of distribution' in the late 1970s and early 1980s was considered as a breach of promise. According to societal perception, two main aspects of the distribution crisis could be distinguished. First the inability of the political elite to provide goods and services in accordance to consumers' expectations. Second the growing unequal distribution of income and goods (services), favouring high Party bureaucrat and state officials, was considered contrary to the socialist principle of income distribution according to labour. As long as the overall standard of living was rising, privileges, income inequalities and even corruption were largely ignored. But with the stagnation of income and rising shortages of goods, income inequalities and privileges became increasingly the targets of criticism and resentment. Failure to meet the required growth of consumer goods and services in accordance to consumers' expectations and to ensure the distribution of income in conformity with egalitarian values led to a loss of credibility and legitimacy of the regime in the eyes of the population (W. Adamski 1985: 21–3). The collapse of Gierek's strategy of legitimation by means of consumer satisfaction was exacerbated by the general weakness of the legitimacy of communist rule in Poland, errors in economic policy, the efficiency crisis and the systemic defects of state socialism.

LEGITIMATION STRAINS IN STATE SOCIALISM

Formulated in a simplified manner, there is in Western society a relatively clear division between the economic and political spheres. Ruling is seen commonly as belonging to the domain of politics. The principles of both the leading role of the Party and the predominance of politics over economics had ensured that in Soviet-type societies economic and political decisions were difficult to separate. In Soviet-type societies the state carried out economic policy with the main aim of strengthening and consolidating its power.

A transition from market economies to state socialism had brought additional strains to legitimating the regime. As Pakulski observes, 'the "invisible hand" of market and tradition has been replaced by the "visible hand" of the party agencies' (J. Pakulski 1986: 54). As a result, certain legitimating strategies were precluded, while at the same time the actual responsibilities of the Party agencies had increased dramatically. Many processes which were once resolved automatically and were considered as 'natural' (e.g. price rises) in market economies, and hence did not need legitimation, in state socialism required justification.

In general, state socialism was more likely to generate political conflicts than market economies, and hence overstrain the regime, irrespective of the levels of economic development. Hirszowicz notes that, 'Communist economies have a high potential for generating conflicts between the rulers and the ruled. Communist bureaucrats carry out incomparably more functions in regulating and coordinating economic and social activities than past forms of government' (M. Hirszowicz 1986: 10). The Party and state bureaucrats were held responsible for nearly all outcomes which the population see as unjust and harmful.

Gierek's strategy of legitimation through economic growth and satisfaction of consumption encountered two basic constraints: a long-run decline in the system's economic efficiency; a continual rise of societal consumption aspirations. The economy, however, lacked the capacity to generate a momentum of its own for technical innovations and a sustained satisfaction of the backlog in consumption. The 'import-led growth' strategy of the 1970s, financed largely by Western credits, did help to compensate temporarily for the missing factors. But the debt trap and the irrationalities in resource use, which arose from the unreformed economic system, had generated a deep socio-economic and political crisis by the early 1980s.

In general, the use of economic policy for the purpose of strengthening and consolidating political power in state socialism had several negative aspects. First any important conflict within the economic sphere involves political authorities or Party agencies who initiate and control the processes. Because of the absence of a self-regulating mechanism and the insignificant role of autonomous and horizontal linkages, important conflict between groups must be referred to the main centre of power. Second the declining efficiency of the economic system ('rationality crisis') and the inability to plan economic development tended to undermine the authority of the state (B. Misztal 1985: 107).

Theoretically, economic reforms could remedy the negative aspects of state socialist economy through an improvement in the efficiency of resource use and a better adjustment of production to consumption needs. But marketization and decentralization of economic decisions would potentially endanger political power, interpreted in a traditional perspective, by loosening the Party–state control over its source of legitimacy, that is, the economy. The three major attempts by the PUWP (Polish United Workers' Party) at economic reforms (1956, 1973 and 1982) confirmed the basic dilemma (M. Ellman 1989: 60–3). Economic reforms were constantly required but they were repeatedly rejected.

The basic dilemma and destiny of the Polish economic reforms of 1973–5 is rightly formulated by the Polish sociologist, Rychard:

> the destiny of the changes is the resultant of two conflicting tendencies – to

> preserve the continuity of the political system, and to enhance the efficiency of the economic system. In effect, the shape of the reform becomes inconsistent, reflecting the contradictions between politics and economics.
>
> (A. Rychard 1980, cited in W. Brus 1985: 205)

The resistance of the Party–state bureaucracy at central and regional levels put an end to the WOG (large economic units) economic reforms. Opposition to their withdrawal was absent, as had also been the case with the economic reforms of 1956.

A number of studies of the political economy of abortive economic reforms in Poland since 1956 have underlined the paramount importance of political factors (the leading role of the Party, *nomenklatura* and politicization of economic decisions, etc.) in determining the destiny and failures of the economic reforms (M. Morawski 1984; W. Brus 1985; T. Kowalik 1986). In state socialism, the economy was a sub-system of the political system. It is concluded, that a depoliticization of the most important economic decisions was a necessary and a minimum requirement for viable economic reforms (W. Morawski 1984: 43–8). This obviously presupposes far-reaching reforms of the political system which were not politically feasible prior to perestroika.

CONCLUSION

The collapse of Gierek's mode of legitimation through consumer satisfaction was determined by the general weakness of the legitimacy of communist rule in Poland and errors in economic policy, in conjunction with the legitimation strains of state socialism, an unrestrained rise in consumers' aspirations and a decline in the system's economic effectiveness. One hoped-for tool of legitimation, the formal ideology, turned into a trap, constraining the freedom of manoeuvre of the ruling elite itself. The simultaneous pursuit of elite self-legitimization and legitimation at the mass level was contradictory and led to the achievement of neither.

9

THE AFTERMATH OF THE ECONOMIC CRISIS

INTRODUCTION

This chapter deals with the aftermath of Poland's deep socio-economic and political crises of 1979–82, covering the period from 1983 till the establishment in 1989 of the first non-communist government in the former Warsaw Pact countries, headed by Mazowiecki from Solidarność. The chapter will describe briefly the regime's efforts to 'normalize' the relationships between the state and society, its policies aimed at reviving the economy from the deep crisis and its reforms of the political and economic systems. From the end of 1986 the regime was increasingly subjected to heavy economic and political strains. During the last years of the 1980s, market disequilibrium and inflation were rapidly growing, reflecting the deepening socio-economic and political crises.

In the past, the crisis-ridden post-war Polish economy had relied, reasonably successfully, on the mechanism of 'regulation through crisis' to bring temporary stabilization and reproduction of state socialism through political concessions, reduction of investment tension and reallocation of resources favouring consumption. The interaction of factors emerging at the second half of the 1980s, such as the changing configuration of domestic political forces, Gorbachev's perestroika, the decomposition of state socialism and the exhaustion of economic and political reserves, however, had undermined substantially the curative effects of 'regulation through crisis'. The emerging political breakthrough offered new opportunities and solutions to the deepening Polish crises of the late 1980s which lay beyond state socialism and made a transition to a market economy feasible. The reproduction of state socialism was replaced by a collapse of the regime.

ECONOMIC PERFORMANCE IN 1983–9

Jaruzelski's regime introduced martial law on 13 December 1981. It officially lasted till 21 July 1983. Although martial law was introduced primarily for political reasons, it helped to bring an end to the chaotic economic life of 1981. The regime was trying to 'normalize' labour and work discipline. From the economic point of view the regime aimed to reach certain basic short-run goals:

1 to stop the downward spiral of output and to initiate economic recovery;
2 to impose a realistic incomes policy (drastic price increases of products and services, a sharp cut in real wages and consumption, deep cut in grain imports, etc.) commensurate with the large fall in net material product, domestic imbalances and inflation;
3 to achieve a trade surplus with the West and in this way try to convince Western creditors that Poland could manage economic austerity and partly meet its debt-servicing obligations.[1]

As a response to martial law the West imposed economic sanctions on Poland, causing *inter alia* drastic cuts in Western imports, and hence dislocation of supply and production. A greater orientation of Poland's foreign trade towards the Soviet Union, pursued after the declaration of martial law could not compensate for the large drop in Western imports of industrial inputs. The regime declared an implementation of economic reform starting from the end of 1981. The severe supply constraints, however, limited the possibilities of realizing economic reform. Moreover, the heavy political pressure to increase ouput according to the traditional pattern of production and resource allocation was inconsistent with the process of economic reform.

The increase in coal output (an extremely important product for domestic fuel and energy consumption and also for export) from the low level of 163 million tons in 1981 (1980 = 193 million tons) to 189 million tons in 1982 was the first success story of Jaruzelski's military rule. Western exports could be raised from their lowest point by a partial restoration of coal output. The 'price' of this success, however, was high. Average employment in coal mining increased by nearly 5 per cent to a total of 400,000 persons in 1982. Saturday working was obligatory. In exchange for greater labour efforts the miners obtained high wage increases, better rations of consumer goods and access to privileged shops supplied with scarce goods. The costs of coal production increased considerably and, despite the large price increase, coal subsidies grew fast (Z.M. Fallenbuchl 1984: 518–19). On an annual basis the net material product in constant prices fell by 5.5 per cent in 1982 with August having the lowest output level. After that, output began to recover.

In 1982 the authorities prepared a Three Year Plan (1983–5) which outlined a moderate economic recovery programme. The draft plan was constructed in three variants involving alternative rates of economic growth, distribution of income between consumption and investment, state budget and investment allocation between economic sectors, production branches and regions. The draft was submitted for 'social consultation' through discussions in the media and social and political organizations. The revised draft was submitted to the Sejm (parliament) and the final Three Year Plan was passed in April 1983. According to the planning reform, both central authorities and enterprises would set their own plans independently. Under the new system, certain central plan goals were simple forecasts. Other targets, like the centrally fixed investment plan, state budget expenditures, deliveries to the CMEA trading partners and allocation of important products and foreign exchange, were centrally determined and binding. Similar to traditional central planning, the aggregation of enterprise plans deviated significantly from the central plan targets, with the former demanding larger inputs (labour, fuel and materials) and wage funds (A. Karpinski 1986: 310–12).

Under the new system, central authorities, in principle, would not issue obligatory production targets to individual enterprises. Since the market mechanism was not functioning, price distortion, shortages and excess demand were widespread. Moreover, central authorities manipulated 'economic instruments' (credits, taxation rates, subsidies, distribution of enterprise profit, state fixed prices and rules of price fixing, procurement of materials) plus 'informal pressure', to persuade enterprises to make decisions in conformity to the priorities of the central plan. The final result was the outcome of a process of 'bargaining' between the central authorities and the enterprises.

Table 9.1 shows selected targets of the Three Year Plan and its realization. The rates of growth of domestic (produced) and national (distributed) net material product, industrial production sold and gross agricultural production and consumption exceeded significantly the plan targets in 1983–5. But by 1985

Table 9.1 The Three Year Plan, 1983–5, and its realization

	Plan growth in per cent 1983–5	*Realization in per cent 1983–5*
Domestic net mat. product[a]	10.1–11.7	15.7
National net mat. product[a]	8.5–10.1	14.6
Industrial production sold of which:	14.3	16.3
industrial consumer goods	19.2–22.0	17.6
gross agricultural production	7.3–7.5	9.8
Total exports of which:	17.7	23.4
capitalist countries	24.7	24.5
Total imports of which:	12.3	23.1
capitalist countries	22.2	34.3
Consumption	8.5–10.9	13.2
Employment (state sector)	−0.6	0.9
Industrial labour productivity	17.8–19.8	18.9
Money income	57.0	85.9
Cost of living	36.0	61.2
Real wages (state sector)	3.0–5.0	5.1
Investment in fixed assets	4.9	29.2

Source: A. Karpinski, 'Ocena wykonania planu trzyletniego na lata 1983–1985 i wnioski na przyszłość', *Gospodarka Planowa*, 6, 1986: 238.
Note: [a]Domestic net material product = 'produced income' in Marxian terminology; national net material product = 'national income for distribution' = domestic net material product + balance of current account of balance of payment.

they were still below the pre-crisis (1978) levels. Total exports and imports grew faster than plan targets. This relatively high economic growth occurred after the deep depression of 1979–82 and under conditions of limited supplies of fuels and raw materials and Western economic sanctions. The authorities congratulated themselves and they were reasonably optimistic over Poland's prospects of economic recovery. Moreover, they falsely argued that the three-year economic reform contributed favourably towards the high economic growth through more efficient use of labour, capital, raw materials and fuels.

The realization of the Three Year Plan showed, however, serious shortcomings. The production of industrial consumer goods and exports to the West were significantly below target. The critical aim of the plan, to reallocate inputs and to restructure production towards consumption and (Western) exports, was not fulfilled. Imports were mainly geared to support domestic final demand. For instance, a 45 per cent growth in hard currency import of industrial supplies in 1982–5 generated only 9 per cent growth of hard currency manufacturing exports over the same period (B. Wojciechowski 1986: 4–5). Output was still traditionally orientated towards the production of industrial supplies and capital goods to feed heavy industry. The growth of money incomes (money wages) was high and it exceeded the plan considerably. After a four-year continuous drastic fall, investment in fixed assets increased rapidly in 1983–5, exceeding the plan targets. Open and suppressed inflation were still high, and they were considerably higher than forecast.[2] In short, inflation, domestic and external imbalances, rigidity of production structure and highly inefficient use of labour and resources continued to plague the economy.

Contrary to what the Polish authorities maintained, the high rates of economic growth in 1983–6 resulted mainly from the utilization of 'shallow growth reserves' and favourable weather conditions. The four-year economic reforms failed to bring favourable changes in the micro-economic behaviour of enterprises towards efficient use of labour and resources, reduction of costs of production and improvement of product quality (J. Pajestka 1986: 391–3). During this period work discipline had improved somewhat, following the deep political turmoil of 1980–1, and the declaration of martial law at the end of 1981, which was accompanied by an extension of average working hours (prohibition of strikes, work on Saturdays and less absenteeism).[3] This contributed to greater use of the highly under-utilized production capacity. The composition of imports changed significantly with a higher percentage of industrial inputs and raw materials at the expense of a large drop in imports of capital and consumer goods. Particularly important for the economy was the exceptionally high growth of arable production during this period, due to favourable weather conditions. All these factors, individually and collectively, contributed substantially to the relatively rapid economic recovery in 1983–6 (R. Bugaj 1986).

By the time the authorities began to carry out the Five Year Plan (1986–90), passed by the Sejm on 18 December 1986, economic growth was falling, accompanied by growing domestic and external disequilibrium. The Five Year Plan aimed to pursue a sustained and balanced economic growth with structural change in production oriented towards exports and consumption. It was intended to keep the annual rate of inflation in single figures. The formulation of the Five Year Plan had to take into account a series of severe inter-locking constraints:

1 short supply of labour due to unfavourable demographic factors;
2 limited supply of raw materials and fuels;
3 difficulties in cutting costs of production due to poor state of fixed assets, a large part of which were obsolete and needed to be replaced ('decapitalization');
4 a large part of planned investment was allocated for the continuation of unfinished investment projects started during the 1970s, with high material and fuel intensity;
5 heavy environmental pollution (high contamination of water and air, destruction of forests etc.);
6 large hard currency debt and heavy burden of debt servicing.

As a result of the tight supply of labour and resources, economic growth during the period 1986–90 had to rely on more efficient use and allocation of resources through intensive utilization of labour and existing productive capacity, improvement in the quality of production, reduction in cost of production, economies in raw materials, fuels and electricity.[4] But a critical and strategic question was whether these goals should be achieved by introducing consistently far-reaching economic reforms with greater reliance on market forces or by a return to traditional administrative planning. Both targets and instruments of implementation of the Five Year Plan were formulated in a 'traditional manner'. The plan assumed a strengthening of central government controls over the economy, further expansion of heavy industries, especially coal mining and energy production, greater integration into the Soviet economy and the promotion of the interests of the central bureaucracy (D.K. Rosati 1991: 26). The conflict between the two approaches continued to dominate Poland's economic debates in the second half of the 1980s until the establishment of the Solidarność-dominated government of Mazowiecki (Z. Fallenbuchl 1991: 18–19).

The growth of net material product declined to 1.9 per cent in 1987. The slow down in output growth was largely due to a fall in agricultural output, stagnation in imports, labour shortages and slow growth in construction (KRG 1988b). During the second half of 1986 the growth of industrial production was already falling significantly and it would be difficult to sustain a high industrial growth for 1987 when the supply of inputs was taut. The rapid growth in after-tax profit left at enterprises' disposal in 1987 led to a considerable increase in demand for raw materials, machinery and equipment and thereby contributed to growing inflation and investment tension (K. Lutostański 1988: 57–62), accompanied by consumers' panic buying in the last quarter of 1987. In 1988 there was a short-lived reanimation of economic growth, largely due to high growth of Western imports of industrial inputs which made greater utilization of productive capacity possible (K. Lutostański 1989: 3) and a slight recovery in agricultural production. Imbalances, inflation and shortages however were rising fast, following the price–income operation (an official term for the large administered price increases for consumer goods and services) in early 1988, which triggered a wave of strikes in May and August.

In the light of those problems and the constraints on economic growth the targets of the Five Year Plan (1986–90) for the remaining two years (1989–90) were officially revised in 1988 (S. Kuzynski 1985: 9–13). Later on the Plan was completely abandoned when the economy was in a recession and the government had lost control over the economy. In 1989 coal output dropped significantly largely due to miners' lack of interest in working on Saturdays, whilst the output of the fuel industry declined significantly due to a considerable fall in crude oil imports from the Soviet Union. Labour shortages, strikes in a number of industries and a fall in domestic production of raw materials and imports of industrial inputs (steel and chemical products) led to a fall in supply of inputs, economic dislocation and recession (M. Misiak 1989). For the first time since 1983, investment dropped in 1989. Political uncertainties encouraged a 'wait and see' attitude among managers. The economic recession of 1989 was accompanied by rapidly accelerating increases in prices, wages and the budget deficit.

After a decline of about a quarter in the net material product between 1979–82, net material product grew on average by 4.9 per cent annually during the period of 1983–6. Annual average growth fell, however, to 2.1 per cent in 1987–9 accompanied by high inflation, shortages, economic chaos and a recession in 1989. On the whole, Poland's economic recovery in the 1980s proceeded slowly. By 1989 total net material product was 1 per cent below the pre-crisis (1978) level and in terms of per capita production it was 8.5 per cent less. The outcome of the economic recovery was uneven between production sectors and economic activities. The pre-crisis levels of industrial output sold and gross agricultural production were attained earlier; and by 1989 they were 10 per cent and 2 per cent respectively above the pre-crisis levels. By 1989 total exports and imports exceeded by nearly one-third and more than one-quarter the pre-crisis levels respectively, of which exports to capitalist countries surpassed by one-fifth. On the other hand, however, imports from capitalist countries lagged behind the pre-crisis level by nearly one-sixth. Furthermore, by 1989 the gross value of accumulated total fixed assets was four-tenths above the pre-crisis level, indicating a grossly wasteful utilization of capital. Total gross investment in fixed assets in 1989 was one-fifth below, whilst personal consumption (according to the over-estimated official statistics) was one-tenth above the pre-crisis levels (see Table 9.2).

The size of the hard currency trade surplus (largely achieved at the expense of

Table 9.2 Selected basic indicators of economic development, 1983–9 (percentage growth with respect to previous year in constant prices)

	1983	1984	1985	1986	1987	1988	1989	1989 as per cent 1978	FYP (1986–90) yearly average growth	Yearly average growth 1986–9
Domestic net mat. product[a]	6.0	5.6	3.4	4.9	1.9	4.9	−0.2	99.0	3.0–3.5	2.9
National net mat. product[b]	5.6	5.0	3.8	5.0	1.8	4.7	0.1	93.5	2.6–3.2	2.9
Industrial production sold	6.6	5.6	4.1	4.4	3.4	5.3	−0.5	110.0	3.3	3.1
Gross agricultural output	3.3	5.7	0.7	5.0	−2.3	1.2	1.5	102.0	2.2–2.5	1.3
Imports of which:	5.2	8.6	7.9	4.9	4.5	9.4	1.5	126.0	2.4	5.1
socialist countries	6.5	6.0	5.7	6.4	4.3	1.9	−3.4	141.0	5.0	2.3
capitalist countries	7.2	13.4	10.5	3.2	4.7	18.3	6.4	80.5	4.0	8.1
Exports of which:	10.3	9.5	1.3	4.9	4.8	9.1	0.2	131.1	4.9	4.7
socialist countries	6.5	7.4	7.0	8.7	4.8	8.0	0.1	210.1	7.9	5.4
capitalist countries	14.9	12.4	−3.6	1.5	4.7	10.1	0.3	124.0	4.7	4.1
Gross investments	9.4	11.4	6.9	5.1	4.2	5.4	−2.4	80.1	4.7	3.0
Personal consumption	6.0	3.8	2.2	5.0	3.0	3.3	0.8	109.7	1.6	3.0
Monthly nominal wages (soc. sector)	24.5	16.3	18.8	20.4	21.3	81.9	291.8	4256	–	103.8
Consumer prices	23.1	15.7	14.4	17.3	25.5	59.0	259.5	4000	–	90.3
Monthly average real wages (soc. sector)	1.1	0.5	3.8	2.6	−3.5	14.4	9.0	106.4	–	5.6
Average employment in soc. sector	0.0	0.3	0.6	0.8	−0.2	−1.1	−1.4	95.7	–	−0.4
Economic effectiveness:										
productivity of fixed capital[c]	3.4	2.7	0.3	2.6	−0.9	1.7	−2.9	–	–	–
labour productivity[d]	6.7	5.7	3.1	4.8	2.4	5.8	0.1	–	–	–
fixed capital per employee	3.3	2.9	2.7	2.3	3.5	3.8	3.7	–	–	–

Sources: B. Dobiegala-Korona 1987: 185–91; K. Lutostanski 1989: 2.

Notes: [a]'Produced income' in Marixan terminology;
[b]'national income for distribution';
[c]income produced per unit of fixed capital;
[d]labour productivity in the sphere of material production.

low growth in Western imports) and the level of personal consumption (largely achieved at the expense of lower growth in investment and Western exports) in the 1980s were unsatisfactory both to the Western creditors and to the Polish population at large. The first failed to bring significant new Western credits to finance the badly needed growth of imports of capital goods to modernize the economy and the second was insufficient to elicit political support of society for the regime.

INVESTMENT INEFFICIENCY

After the drastic and haphazard cuts of investment in 1978–82, investment in fixed assets started to grow from 1983. By 1983 total investment in fixed assets was only 60 per cent of the pre-crisis level. By 1985 investment went up to 71.2 per cent of the pre-crisis level, which was about 20 per cent of the gross domestic product. According to a World Bank study, such a rate of net investment was sufficiently high to achieve a steady, moderately high rate of economic growth and to implement desirable production restructuring. Because of inefficiency and low return to investment, however, economic recovery proceeded slowly. The 'investment arteriosclerosis', supported by various interest groups, particularly the strong lobby around the heavy and armament industries (fuel and energy, steel and engineering, etc.), succeeded in preventing a restructuring (including amongst others complete abandonment) of a majority of the distorted unfinished investment projects, inherited from the Gierek period (see Chapter 1). A high proportion of investment outlays was expended for the continuation of the unfinished investment projects of the Gierek era. Nearly 60 per cent of the state sector's outlays on fixed investment in 1982–5 was expended on projects started before 1982. Only a small part of investment was allocated to replacement and modernization of obsolete capital stock. By 1985 this ratio went down to 40 per cent and completion of the old 'investment portfolio' was projected to be attained by the end of the 1980s. A large part of the unfinished investment projects had a long gestation period with a high raw materials and fuel intensity of production.

The Three Year Plan (1983–5) projected a marginal increase (4.9 per cent) of investment in fixed assets for the whole plan period. Actual investment, however, rose by nearly 30 per cent, reflecting the traditional over-investment drive in CPEs. Investment growth was nearly two times the growth in net material product in 1983–5, but in the following years the disparity between the rates of growth of investment and net material product was far less. Investment outlays in the state sector systematically exceeded plan targets. This high investment growth did not, however, result in a faster rate of investment completion. The value of investment projects brought on stream was far below the planned targets and was deteriorating in the second half of the 1980s. Moreover investment was spread too thinly. The actual gestation period of investment projects became longer, while the total cost of investment in progress and the value of frozen investment were growing rapidly (B. Kierski 1988: 2–5). The actual costs of investment projects rose fast and nearly all increases in investment cost could be shifted to higher prices of the projects (S. Kuzinski 1988: 1–3).

Both the low rates of investment projects completions (particularly in the industrial sector) and the small investment allocation for modernization and replacement of obsolete fixed assets led to rising disinvestment ('decapitalization') in the stock of physical capital in the 1980s. As a result, a growing proportion of the capital stock, particularly machinery and means of transportation, was already worn out by wear and tear. It became obsolete, unreliable and caused frequent break-downs, produced poor quality output and operated with high costs of production (Z. Stępniowska and D. Segala-Górniaszek 1988: 16–21). According to a sample survey of enterprise managers in 1987, the poor quality of the capital stock ('decapitalization') was ranked as the third, after labour and input shortages, most important constraint on an increase in the volume of production (H. Bartczak and A. Bogus 1988: 27).

The rate of return on completed investment projects was very low. According to a World Bank estimate on investment return for forty-four projects (nine were from the power and mining industries), the weighted average payback period was fifty years (an internal rate of return of less than 2 per cent) for the whole sample. For centrally financed projects the payback period was eighty-one years (an internal rate of return of less than 1.2 per cent) and for the enterprise-financed projects, the payback period was almost nine and a half years (an internal rate of return of less than 10.6 per cent) (The World Bank 1987: 43–4). It should be added, however, that the low financial return on investment projects partly reflected government policy of setting domestic prices of fuel and energy far below world levels. This pricing policy encouraged waste of energy and fuel and it made investment in energy saving and fuel conversion highly unattractive.

The Five Year Plan (1986–90) projected a higher growth of investment compared to the growth in net material product, with higher growth of investment in the so-called material sector. Investment in the industrial sector was to account for about one-third of the total investment in the socialized sector. About three-fifths of the total industrial investment was scheduled for allocation to the fuel and energy sector and the engineering industry, in contrast to modest investment in the light and food processing industries. An important element of the investment planning was the Industrial Restructuring Programme, comprising forty-four projects, which was intended to act as a vehicle for industrial modernization, creating industrial linkages and a base for hard currency export promotion.

The investment and industrial restructuring plan had been criticized by many Polish economists[5] as well as the World Bank. It was criticized because planned sub-sectoral distribution of industrial investment would reinforce the heavy industry (fuel and energy, steel, and engineering, etc.) structural bias of Polish industry and the high capital and energy production intensity. About one-third of the total industrial investment was planned to be allocated to the fuel and energy sector just in order to have a small rise in coal output for the second half of the 1980s. On the other hand, more economical investment for energy saving and conversion was insufficient. It was estimated that the cost of extracting an additional ton of hard coal was around three times higher than the cost of economizing one ton in the economy (P. Glikman 1986.). The investment programme paid little attention to investment projects that could have a high return in the short run. Furthermore the planned rapid growth of investment in engineering industries was concentrated on projects which would produce goods in excess supply worldwide, with unsophisticated techniques of production, little international appeal and competitiveness (The World Bank 1987: 49–50). Insufficient investment for the renovation and modernization of chemical, light and food processing industries would put greater strain on domestic consumer markets and Poland's capability for export.

According to the blueprint of the economic reform, autonomous enterprises' investment, financed through profits, depreciation and bank credits, should play a major role. Highly insufficient capacity of construction and building industries, shortages and government procurement of capital goods (and raw materials) severely limited enterprises' investment opportunities. Fiscal policy in the 1980s took a large share of the profits and depreciation from profit-making enterprises and allocated them to loss-making enterprises. The share of enterprises' investment in total investment in state and cooperative sectors, however, was growing in the 1980s.[6] But it should be noted that part of the formally classified enterprise-financed investment projects were actually centrally determined. The actual scope of autonomous enterprise investment decisions was still limited.

Throughout the years 1983–8, investment grew faster than net material product. As a result of the poor economic result of 1987 and the increasing investment tension (T. Wojciechowski 1989: 110–14), the Economic Advisory Council (KRG) and the Planning Commission advised the goverment to revise the investment programme contained in the Five Year Plan (1986–90). Both recommended a significant slow down of total investment growth by cutting investment in the fuel (coal) and energy industry (through, for example, complete or partial abandonment of certain projects in coal mining and electrical plant) and steel plants.[7] Under pressure from the workers' strikes in the spring and summer of 1988, the government was forced to allocate more investment to the light and food processing industries at the expense of a substantial drop in investment in the fuel and electrical power industry. In 1989 total gross investment fell by 2.4 per cent; and the cut was particularly large in sectors like construction, transportation and agriculture, and the fuel and electrical power industries.[8]

INFLATION

Following a consumer price increase of more than 100 per cent and a drop in average real wages of about one-quarter in 1982 (both occurring under martial law), inflation dropped to 22 per cent in 1983 and to between 16–18 per cent in 1984–6. The supply of consumer goods improved somewhat from 1983 and the number of rationed goods was reduced. The rapid rise in prices in the second half of the 1980s, however, was in sharp contrast with the aim of the Five Year Plan (1986–90) of reducing inflation to below 10 per cent at the end of the Plan. In 1987 the official measure of consumer prices rose by 26 per cent. After the price income operation in early 1988, consumer prices increased by 60 per cent in 1988. Despite the rising rate of open inflation from 1985, shortages and market imbalances were growing, a situation known as 'shortageflation', i.e. a combination of rising inflation and shortages (G.W. Kołodko and W.W. McMahon 1987: 189–90; G.W. Kołodko 1990: 764–5). In 1989 inflation accelerated rapidly to 259 per cent on an annual basis and starting from August it entered a hyperinflationary stage, accompanied by economic anarchy and recession.

The low effectiveness of investment (long gestation periods, low rate of completion of investment projects, etc.) exacerbated inflation. Moreover, investment allocation had discriminated against the production of consumer goods. It was estimated that only 10 per cent of the total investment for the continuation of unfinished industrial projects in 1983–4 was allocated to the development of consumer goods industries (G.W. Kołodko 1987: 225–7). Output growth was also heavily constrained by the limited supply of raw materials and fuel, and the low import capacity of the economy due to insufficient exports in combination with a relatively high burden of debt servicing. A deterioration of market supply was moreover aggravated by the distortion in the structure of production and the misallocation of resources. This fact was reflected in the falling share of industrial consumer goods in total value of industrial production. For instance, the share of consumer industrial products declined from 33 per cent in 1984 to 25.4 and 24.2 per cent of total sales of industrial production in 1987 and 1988 respectively (A. Karpinski 1988: 63–5; W. Bien 1989: 4–5). The underfulfilment of plan production and state procurement of animal products in the second half of the 1980s aggravated the food supply problems.

Unlike capitalism, there was no serious conflict between firms' managers (as employers) and employees over demands for wage rises at enterprise level. Managers did not in principle oppose workers' demands for wage increases, since the major aims of state enterprises were survival and labour peace. This implied that firms tried to minimize internal conflicts by offering wage increases at a level which would be at least equal to the general price rise of consumer goods (P. Dziewulski, *et al.* 1987: 204–9). Directors of state enterprises were more interested in keeping ample labour reserves ('labour hoarding'), enterprise peace and prevention of strikes and they behaved more or less like trade union leaders (J. Staniszkis 1989: 26–7). The labour market in Poland in the 1980s was aggravated by the unfavourable demographic factors and the early retirement scheme of 1981. There was a growing number of workers who shifted employment from the state to the private sector. Competition among state enterprises and between state and private sectors forced state enterprises to offer reasonably high wage increases in order to prevent the departure of employees.

Despite the high and progressive tax on wage increases beyond a certain threshold (either in the form of the old FAZ or the new PPWW version), enterprises could shift wage increases to buyers in the form of price rises through the formula of cost-plus-pricing and/or by virtue of their monopolistic position. Moreover, enterprises could negotiate with the centre either for tax exemptions and price subsidies or cheap credits from the bank to finance wage increases. Wage increases, in fact, had no clear relationship with economic performance or productivity of enterprises or industries.[9] In general, the budget constraint of state enterprise, using Kornai's terminology, was 'soft'. Large enterprises were not allowed to fail in the 1980s. A bankruptcy law was introduced in 1983, but up to 1989 less than fifty liquidation procedures were initiated – all for fairly small firms. Even when these procedures began, it took several years of 'rehabilitation' attempts before a firm could be closed (S. Johnson 1991: 131–2).

The traditional financial control by the centre of money and credit flows was maintained, *inter alia*, through the system of enterprises' separate 'purpose account', i.e. money or funds which could be used only for the allowed purposes. For instance, enterprises' wage funds could not be used for investment purposes. Starting from the mid-1980s, state enterprises had more opportunities to circumvent the strict division between accounts, for example by subcontracting out certain work to private firms (often owned by the managerial staff of the state enterprises) and by employing enterprises' own fixed assets and workers who were working beyond the daily eight hours' working time.[10] Under such arrangements, state enterprises could use investment funds to pay wage increases and thereby evade the wage fund ceiling and high tax on wage increases (S. Johnson 1991: 133–4). After 1988, central control of enterprise wage funds was abolished, giving them more opportunities of determining their own wage fund.

Despite the existence of plans for credit and money supply, monetary policy was, in general, accommodating. If, for instance, investment outlays exceeded the plan, or if enterprises suffered from unplanned losses, the bank and state budget normally provided the additional credits and subsidies (G.T. Jędrzejczak and K. Kalicki 1991: 102). Budget deficits were financed by interest free loans supplied by the central bank and money printing. In the 1980s, the real rates of interest were negative. The nominal rate of interest was below 10 per cent until 1988. In 1989 it rose to 87 per cent. Enterprises used bank loans to finance higher wages. According to the World Bank's estimate, the value of transfers to state enterprises due to negative interest rates and generous credit policy amounted to about 10 per cent of GDP. Most of this transfer was financed by a rapid depreciation of households' deposit holdings denominated in złoty (cited in S. Johnson 1991: 135). The flight from domestic currency and the use of hard currency as a stable unit of account and a safe store of value led to an increase in the velocity of money circulation and inflation.

According to official statistics, average money wages in the socialized sector and the cost of living increased by 21.1 and 26 per cent respectively in 1987 whilst average real wages fell by 3.7 per cent. The decline in average real wages in privileged industries like coal mining, electrical power and steel was greater, varying to between 7 and 10 per cent. The level of average real wages in 1987 was still around 20 per cent below the level of 1980 (*Rocznik Statystyczny* 1988: 126). In the last quarter of 1987 market supply deteriorated further, partly due to panic buying as a result of the rumours that drastic consumer price increases were imminent following the referendum on economic reform held in November 1987. As a basic component of the realization of the second stage of economic reform and the stabilization programme, food prices were raised on average by 40 per cent on 1 February 1988, plus a steep price rise of gasoline and diesel oil. The government offered a flat monthly wage price compensation of 6,000 złoty (i.e. about 19 per cent of the average industrial money wages), an offer which was close to the demand made by the official trade union. Like the consumer price rises of 1970, 1976 and 1980, the 1988 price increase triggered workers' protests and strikes in the spring and autumn of 1988, demanding higher wage increases. The regime succumbed to the wage pressures, precipitating further the price–wage inflationary spiral (see Table 9.3).

Inflation in 1988 was considerably higher than originally planned. The price–income operation planned to cut average real wages by 5–6 per cent for 1988. But average money wages and the cost of living index increased (on an annual

Table 9.3 Monthly changes of retail consumer prices and money wages in state sector, 1988–9 (percentage from previous month)

	1988			*1989*	
	Prices	*Wages*		*Prices*	*Wages*
January	3.7	+1.8		11.0	+0.0
February	17.2	+25.8		7.9	−4.1
March	5.7	+1.1		8.1	+43.6
April	7.1	−5.8		9.8	−5.7
May	2.4	−1.5		7.2	−5.8
June	2.9	+1.4		6.1	+3.5
July	3.2	+5.5		9.5	+9.6
August	0.6	−1.9		39.5	+66.5
September	2.8	+15.4		34.4	+31.1
October	2.6	+14.9		54.8	+25.2
November	3.8	+2.5		22.4	+15.3
December	4.9	+27.6		17.7	+29.6
December 1987 to December 1988	72.9	+125.6	December 1988 to December 1989	639.6	+466.4

Source: Central Statistical Office (GUS) and National Bank of Poland (NBP), as reported in Z. Polański (1991: 357).

basis) by 81.9 and 59.0 per cent respectively in 1988; and despite growing market shortages official statistics noted an increase in average real wages by 14.4 per cent (*Rocznik Statystyczny* 1989: 149). Public opinion polls, however, showed that the majority of the respondents believed their standard of living to be falling. The wage policy of 1988, moreover, showed that the higher the rate of inflation the stronger the demand for wage increases. Due to the political weakness of the regime, it conceded to the workers' demands, fearing disorder and revolt. The regime considered money wage increases as a lesser evil ('money illusion'), a substitute for the more dangerous political demand for the legalization of Solidarność and political pluralism (J.W. Wiktor 1989: 22).

Aside from 1981 (when the budget deficit was around 10 per cent of the GDP), the budget deficit in the period 1982–8 was low (averaging 1.5 per cent of the GDP). During this period, the budget expenditure as a percentage of the GDP fell from 3.7 per cent in 1983 to 0.2 per cent in 1988 (A. Wernik 1990: 74–5). In 1989, however, the budget deficit rose rapidly to around 7 per cent of the GDP, financed by central bank loans and money printing. Both the rapid rise of the budget deficit and the form of deficit financing contributed to the high inflation in 1989. The new law on corporate taxation (enacted in early 1989) proved to be a revenue loser for the budget.

The rapid growth in the budget deficit in 1989 was also part of the overall political process, as had been the fall of the Messner–Sadowski government in autumn 1988, the Round Table discussion of February–March 1989 and the June parliamentry elections. This process was analogous to the 'political trade cycle' in the West. Rakowski's communist government attempted to put together an electoral coalition with the United Peasants' Party and thereby hoped to gain the votes of the peasantry by raising considerably the purchase prices of agricultural products to the so-called income-parity levels. The pre-election increase of wages by 45 per cent in March 1989, particularly wage rises for employees in the public sector which were partly politically motivated, contributed to the budget deficit (J. Staniszkis 1991: 58–9).

On an annual basis consumer prices rose by 244 per cent in 1989, but calculated on a monthly basis from December 1988 to December 1989, prices rose by 640 per cent (see Table 9.3). Besides the wage inflation (i.e. wage indexation to protect real wages against rising inflation as stipulated in the Round Table agreement), the 'marketization of the food economy' (i.e. the abolishment of state monopoly purchase of agricultural products and food price subsidies in August 1989) and high złoty devaluations in 1989, all together contributed to the hyperinflation from August 1989, which was only ended by the drastic Balcerowicz economic stabilization programme in 1990.

EXTERNAL ECONOMIC RELATIONSHIPS

Since 1982 Poland had a hard currency trade surplus, increasing from US$0.40 billion in 1982 to US$1.5 billion in 1984. Then the trade surplus fell steadily to

US$1.1 billion in 1986 and US$0.9 billion in 1988 and only US$0.2 billion in 1989. The Five Year Plan (1986–90) projected, however, a steadily rising trade surplus, reaching to between US$2.0 and US$2.4 billion by 1990. The Polish economy seemed to be unable to generate a sufficiently large hard currency trade surplus to regain international creditworthiness. The surplus since 1982 was, however, in contrast with the hard currency trade deficits throughout the period of 1972–81. But the trade surplus was achieved largely by a contraction in the total value of hard currency trading, particularly in the form of a severe cut in imports, and not by boosting exports. The value of hard currency imports and exports (in current prices) in 1983 was only 49.4 and 67.9 per cent respectively of the levels of 1980. By 1989 the value of hard currency imports was still around 9 per cent below the import level of 1980, whilst the value of exports exceeded the export revenue level of 1980 only slightly (see Tables 2.10 and 9.4). In real terms hard currency imports and exports in 1989 were considerably below the levels of 1980.

Throughout the 1980s, the current account in hard currency was in deficit. The deficits on current account fluctuated sharply, varying between US$3.1 billion in 1981 and US$0.40 billion in 1987. The steady growth of net individual transfers from US$375 million in 1983 to US$1.4 billion in 1988 helped to ease the deficits on current account. Poland's outstanding gross debt in hard currency increased from US$24 billion in 1980 to US$40.8 billion at the end of 1989, largely caused by the capitalization of the unpaid interest. According to official Polish sources, the ratios between interest paid and interest due in hard currency in the 1980s showed a steady decline from 0.68 in 1981 to 0.55 in 1983 and to between 0.46 and 0.31 in the period of 1984–9 (as reported in K. Kalicki 1991: 130), whilst average principal payments amounted to around 10 per cent of the principal due.[11]

Hard currency debt indicators throughout the 1980s show how grave Poland's debt situation was. The net debt/export ratios in hard currency hovered between 4.7 (in 1982) and 5.7 (in 1986), showing clearly that Poland was highly over-indebted. The debt service ratios fell from 1.88 in 1981 to 0.76 in 1988, whilst the net interest payments as a percentage of exports also decreased from 78 per cent in 1981 to 39 per cent in 1988, largely as a result of a series of debt reschedulings (K. Kalicki 1991: 130). Despite a series of debt rescheduling agreements with Western private banks and the Paris Club creditors, the debt service burden constrained sustained economic growth. In the early 1990s outstanding debts and debt service due were expected to grow fast. It seemed that continuous debt restructuring could not solve Poland's mounting debt. After the collapse of the communist regime, Poland obtained a one-half reduction of the US$33 billion public debt owed to the members of the Paris Club, conditional on an acceptance of an economic programme to be negotiated with the IMF. Poland is hoping to negotiate a similar rate of debt reduction with Western private banks.

Poland's trade deficits in non-convertible currency with the CMEA countries,

Table 9.4 Current balance in convertible currencies (million US$), 1983–9

	1983	*1984*	*1985*	*1986*	*1987*	*1988*	*1989*
Exports (fob)	5404	5828	5768	6226	6920	7911	8113
Imports (cif)	4317	4372	4594	5108	5878	6991	7987
Balance of trade	+1087	+1456	+1174	+1118	+1042	+920	+126
Services receipts	639	343	585		756	760	808
Services payments	607	437	602	709	793	850	1019
Services balance	+32	−94	−17	−80	−37	−90	−211
Transfer balance	+375	+472	+764	+944	+1049	+1433	+1232
Interest receipts	153	183	168	183	212	270	409
Interest due	2884	3112	2612	2739	3016	3096	3474
paid interest	1430	1065	1234	1152	924	954	1075
unpaid interest	–	–	1378	1587	2092	2142	2403
off. rescheduled	–	–	828	87	2067	1557	145
arrears	–	–	550	1500	25	585	2222
Interest balance	–	–	−2444	−2556	−2804	−2826	−3069
Balance of current account	−1350[a]	−1139[a]	−523	−574	−392	−563	−1992

Sources: H. Gabrisch, 'Die Perspektive der Westwirtschaftsbeziehungen Polens', *Forschungsberichte*, 113, 1986, Wiener Institut für Wirtschaftsvergleiche, Vienna: 123; *Poland: Reform, Adjustment and Growth*, The World Bank, 1987: 89; *Rocznik Statystyczny* 1990: 152–3.
Note: [a]Corrections based on official statistics.

nearly all with the Soviet Union, varied between 500 million transferable roubles and 1.6 billion transferable roubles during the period 1981–7. The unfavourable terms of trade with the Soviet Union (mainly due to oil price increases) during the first half of the 1980s contributed significantly to the trade deficits. In the last two years of the 1980s, Poland's trade in non-convertible currency produced surpluses. Poland's efforts to substitute its Western import deliveries through a reorientation of its foreign trade toward the CMEA countries had only a limited success. Industrial production was dependent on the import of industrial supplies from the West, whilst trade and aid possibilities from the CMEA countries were limited.

At the end of 1987 Poland's debt to the CMEA countries amounted to 6.6 billion roubles and it then fell slightly to 5.8 billion roubles at the end of 1989. The rouble debt burden was relatively small compared to the hard currency debt, and the terms of repayment were soft. Nevertheless, repayments of non-convertible debt would lay additional burden on Poland's limited export capability. Moreover, the Soviet Union was insisting on an improvement of the low quality of Poland's major export, engineering products, and an export mix which contained a higher proportion of 'hard products', i.e. products which were exportable to the West (B. Slay 1988:184–5). The economic dislocation of the Soviet Union during the last years of the 1980s led to a decline in exports of raw materials and industrial supplies to Poland, affecting production adversely.

The failure of Poland to obtain sufficient new Western loans since 1982 (due to the lack of creditworthiness and rather than to credit sanctions imposed by the West after the declaration of martial law, as the Polish goverment initially maintained) led to a sharp constraint on hard currency imports. More often than not, Poland had to pay cash for hard currency imports and in certain cases down-payments were required. Hard currency imports were thus highly dependent on Poland's poor export performance. Poland did not succeed in boosting hard currency exports to the extent that would have restored its creditworthiness in the eyes of Western creditors.

With a high proportion of investment expended on the completion of investment projects in infrastructure – fuel, energy and raw material industries having long gestation periods – the scope of production restructuring in the medium term towards export orientation was very small. Because of the slow growth (or stagnation) of fuel and raw materials output, in combination with a persistently high fuel and raw materials intensity of production, Poland was forced to cut or slow down the growth of traditional export of raw materials and fuel to the West. The industrial modernization programme of the Five Year Plan (1986–90), which aimed to boost industrial production and exports to compensate for the stagnation in traditional exports products to the West, seemed to have failed to achieve its goals. The 'small restructuring' programme of 1985, which provided partially interest free loans in hard currency to finance enterprise investment in export projects, tax relief, etc., had only minor effects (C. Boffito 1988: 159). On the whole, the role of enterprise investment in export-oriented projects remained small. In 1987 it constituted only 9 per cent of the total value of investment in progress (J. Piotrowski 1988: 9–10). On the whole, incentives to invest in exports among enterprises were weak.

Under conditions of growing internal shortages and excess demand, domestic markets were far more attractive for producers and traders than the more competitive export markets. There was strong competition between domestic and export markets for certain products such as coal, agricultural products and products of light industry. Judged from macro-economic perspectives, the possibilities of restraining domestic demand (e.g. a fall or freeze in real wages and consumption) for the purpose of boosting exports were very small due to strong opposition from the workers (E. Lustacz 1988: 89; M. Misiak 1988: 7). Due to ageing and obsolete industrial fixed assets, Poland was also becoming less able to supply competitive manufacturing products to the West and its share in the total Western European import of manufactures was falling.

Persistent high inflation, price distortions and an overvaluation of złoty, in combination with the large scope of central discretions over foreign trade, made a large part of exports unattractive and unprofitable for the producers. During 1982–5, for instance, domestic prices rose by 228 per cent, whilst the złoty–dollar exchange rate was only devalued by around 172 per cent in the same period (A. Parkola and R. Rapacki 1986: 5). Price distortions were also growing in the 1980s. Despite a series of price increases, the levels of domestic prices of internationally tradeable raw materials and fuel were still too low, lagging behind the level of transaction prices (J. Piotrowski 1986: 14–15). This led to a distortion in Poland's export specialization, concentrated as it was on raw materials and fuel intensive production instead of high labour and skill intensive production.

As a result of the distortion in prices and foreign exchange rates, the central authority had to apply various specific export incentives (profit tax reliefs, price equalization and subsidies, foreign exchange retention, lower tax for wage increase, etc.) or simple directives in order to encourage producers to export. This led to arbitrary bargaining between the central authorities and enterprises instead of parametric planning with a market mechanism as visualized in the economic reform blueprint. Despite certain progress in economic reform, the Polish foreign-trade mechanism remained largely unreformed. The central allocation of imports and foreign exchange, enterprise participation in operational programmes and government orders, and informal pressure from above were the dominant instruments (B. Slay 1991: 199; C. Boffito 1988: 155–6).

Within the framework of the realization of the second stage of economic reform (from mid-1987), the government introduced a series of changes in the organizational structure and system of regulation in foreign trade. The main aim was to reduce price distortions and to establish economic linkage between domestic and export production, greater freedom for foreign trade enterprise decision making and more emphasis on regulation through economic parameters. The government decided to liberalize the criteria for granting concessions and permits for state and private enterprises to engage directly in foreign trade and to allow more freedom in choosing trading partners. For instance, the number of enterprises, cooperatives and individuals with direct trading rights increased from 430 at the end of 1986 to 1,007 at the end of the first half of 1988 (J. Piotrowski 1988: 3–4). The scope of the so-called 'commodity competence' of the foreign trade enterprises was drastically reduced and competition was encouraged.

The government also decided to adjust the foreign exchange rate (i.e., to devalue) more frequently in line with the rising cost of export production in order to ensure that 80 per cent of the exports to both payment areas would be profitable. It was intended that the scope of transaction prices for internationally tradeable commodities should become larger at the expense of administrative prices ('ceny urzędowe'), aiming to establish a linkage of domestic prices of primary products with world market prices. Price subsidies for manufacturing were to be reduced, with a unified agricultural export subsidy, whilst relief on profit tax and tax on wage increases of enterprises working for exports were to be limited. The legal status of the hard-currency retention account was to be changed into ownership rights of the exporting enterprises; and the scope of the hard currency auction, to be organized by the Export Development Bank at higher exchange rates than the official one, was to be expanded (A. Parkola and R. Rapacki 1987: 3–8; M. Deniszczuk 1988: 3–5; J. Sobota 1989: 4–6).

Cost increases of export production in 1987–8, however, were not sufficiently compensated by devaluation of the złoty so that the basic goal of achieving profitability for 80 per cent of the exports could not be realized (J. Sobota 1989: 5). According to a survey of forty large enterprises producing for export conducted in 1988, a large majority of them considered the level of foreign exchange rates too low and that the devaluation of the złoty could not keep up with increases in domestic prices (J. Piotrowski and K. Stępinska 1989: 5). Nevertheless, the more than 60 per cent devaluation of the złoty against the US$ in 1988, probably contributed positively to the high growth of hard currency exports in that year. Devaluation could not, however, prevent a fast growth of hard currency imports in 1988, partly due to high domestic excess demand. In 1988, the exchange rate for the US$ traded at auctions organized by the Export Development Bank varied between 95.5 and 270 per cent above the official rate (J. Sobota 1989: 6). The share of hard currency imports financed through enterprises' own foreign exchange was increasing.

The official złoty exchange rates were on the whole over-valued which was reinforced partly by the continuation of administrative price control. The gap between the black market and the official exchange rate was widening. The black market exchange spread rose from around 250 per cent in the early 1988 to more than 500 per cent by September, but after that the spread dropped drastically. From 1989 the złoty was devalued several times, falling from 500 złoty in January to 1,000 złoty in August and 5,240 złoty for US $1 in December (A. Berg and J. Sachs 1992: 129–30). The devaluation of the złoty was particularly large during the last quarter of 1989 (the average exchange rate in October was around 1,970 złoty to US$1). This period should be treated as the last phase of the preparation for złoty (internal) convertibility at an overshoot exchange rate of 9,500 złoty for US$1 starting from 1 January 1990, which formed an integral part of the Balcerowic economic stabilization package.

ECONOMIC REFORM

Chapter 6 described and discussed briefly the circumstances and the basic ideas underlying the economic reform of 1981–2 and its components such as the principles of enterprise autonomy involving workers' self-management and enterprise self–finance, planning with a built-in market mechanism and regulation with the help of economic instruments. That description focused attention on labour regulation under the reform system, its modification in the course of reform implementation, the stagnation of the reform and its failure to bring about efficient use and allocation of labour, natural resources and investment.

The early thrust of the economic reform in 1982–3 was followed by an overall slow progress, stagnation and backlash by 1986 (Z. Fallenbuchl 1988: C. Jozefiak 1989; K. Crane 1991). The Polish United Workers' Party (PUWP) and the government admitted this fact and from the spring of 1987 they attempted to re-animate the reform project of 1981–2 and to give new impulse to the reform process, an undertaking known as the second stage of the economic reform. This section of the chapter will present a brief overall evaluation of the reform process in the 1980s, its successes and failures.

The Xth Party Congress in the summer of 1986, which formally declared for a continuation of the economic reform course outlined in 1982, cautiously spoke of a second stage of economic reform. This was followed by further discussion and debates on economic reforms among economists. The World Bank Report (1987) and Gorbachev's perestroika gave further stimulus towards a revival of economic reform. In April 1987 the Party and government commission for economic reform published an extensive 'Theses on the second stage of economic reform', and it was submitted for discussion. In May of that year a law on a referendum about economic reform was passed by the Sejm, the first time in the history of Poland that a proposal for economic reform was subjected to a referendum. If the outcome of the referendum were positive, the regime could hope to strengthen its legitimacy to carry out the harsh measures associated with economic reform. In July a bill on the promotion of the economic activities of the small–scale private sector, cooperatives and private persons, making it easier to start a business, was passed. In October 1987 the reform commission published the 'Programme for the realization of the second stage of economic reform',[12] and it was subsequently passed by the Sejm.

The basic reasoning behind the second stage of the economic reform is as follows. The main aim of the reform was to improve as quickly as possible the efficiency of resource use (to achieve a rational and highly innovative behaviour of economic subjects). This presupposed economic reform, and this would function well only under market equilibrium. Hence the first step was to establish market equilibrium. To achieve this basic aim a set of measures in the field of pricing and monetary and fiscal policies were designed (H. Gabrisch 1989: 180–2). The *Theses* also advocated that an increase in the supply of goods was necessary for achieving market equilibrium and part of the reform process, a goal which, however, was hardly feasible under the then prevailing structural and supply constraints. Given these constraints, the official view was that market balances would be achieved mainly by price increases and constraints on income. The *Programme* pointed out three basic aims of the planned price and income operation of 1988: (i) drastic reduction of consumer price subsidies; (ii) removal of price distortions; and (iii) restoring market equilibrium.

If conceptually the reform of 1982 had been confined largely to the state sector, the second stage of the reform advocated an expansion of the private and cooperative sectors, which should operate in a stable and economically attractive environment. Private and cooperative sectors were to be treated on an equal footing with the state sector. The *Programme* strove to create a mixed economy, consisting of state, cooperative and private sectors, which would embody planning and genuine markets for consumer goods, raw materials, capital and labour. A competitive environment was to be promoted by the establishment of new enterprises, the break up of large monopolistic corporations into small enterprises and an anti-monopoly law. Traditional elements of central planning were to be severely limited and central allocation of raw materials, intermediate products, capital goods and foreign exchange would be eliminated. The banking system was to be reformed. The central bank was to become an instrument in the execution of government monetary and fiscal policies and to supervise the activities of the commercial banks. Competition among commercial banks was to be promoted, and it was intended to create a capital market. The bankruptcy law, which was passed in 1982, would be applied more stringently.

With the passing of the *Programme* in October 1987, a bill on the reorganization of the central administrative organization, in particular the reorganization of the production branch ministries, was adopted by the Sejm. Ministries of mining and energy, metallurgy and machine building, chemical and light industries were dissolved and instead a new ministry of industry, covering part of the old production branch ministries, was set up. The reorganization of the central administrative organization, which was also part of the 1982 reform blueprint but was never implemented, was intended to help to promote enterprise autonomy and to reduce the influence of the traditionally strong lobbies of the coal, steel and machinery industries. It was also expected that the influence of the Ministry of Finance would be greatly enhanced.

Judged by the law passed in May 1987 governing referenda, which required that a majority of the eligible voters was needed for approval, the November

1987 referendum rejected economic reform. The regime, however, could claim a certain success since the majority of the voters participating supported both reform options presented at the referendum. The government proceeded with the price income operation and other reform measures, and opted for a more cautious price reform than initially planned. The basic issue, however, was not so much on the support for economic reform presented in the referendum but whether the population had enough political confidence in the ability and the will of the regime to carry out economic reform, in view of the past failures and the perceptions of major obstacles in reforming the state socialist economy (J.P. Mcgregor 1989: 223–6). The gloomy economic situation had reinforced the scepticism regarding the government's will and ability to pursue consistently economic reform. Moreover, public opinion polls suggested that a high percentage of the public came to identify economic reform with price rises and a fall in the standard of living.

Under strong pressure from workers demanding wage increases, demands which were supported by a wave of strikes to which the regime succumbed, the price income operation of February 1988 failed completely. The government lost macro-economic control over the economy, leading to an acceleration of inflation and increasing economic distortions (see Table 9.3). The inability of the government to resist wage increases reflected the basic political weakness and tenuous legitimacy of the regime. People did not trust the regime. They were not confident that the cost of economic reform (e.g. a temporary decline in real wages and standard of living) would not be wasted in a treadmill of reforms without any chance of sustained improvement. The economic deterioration and the second wave of strikes in August 1988 had two far-reaching political consequences. First, with the Catholic Church acting as intermediary, a meeting between Cz. Kiszczak (the former Minister of Internal Affair) and Lech Walesa took place at the end of August 1988, wherein the latter was asked by the regime to help to end the strikes, in exchange for a promise of a round table meeting between the government and Solidarność or opposition. The second consequence was the fall of the Messner–Sadowski government in September 1988 which had been the architect of the price income operation. It was replaced by a government headed by M.F. Rakowski, the former Secretary of the PUWP.

The new government adopted a consolidation plan, which outlined a crash economic programme for 1989–90 and guidelines for the first half of the 1990s. This actually meant an abandonment of the Five Year Plan (1986–90) for the last two years of the plan period. The consolidation plan aimed at stopping the economic recession, improving market supply, housing and slowing down inflation. The encouragement of private activities and enterpreneurship, a greater utilization of existing production capacity and stronger reliance on the market mechanism were to be strongly stimulated in order to achieve the plan goals (M. Misiak 1988). The Rakowski government reconfirmed the economic reform course. It also provided new impulses for economic reforms, particularly in the forms of new laws and institutional changes (a two-tier banking system, abolition of obstacles to start new economic activities, equality of all economic sectors, liberal law on foreign investments, etc.) which eliminated the impediments for private economic activities. Limited internal convertibility of the złoty was introduced and private individuals were allowed to open foreign exchange offices. In early 1989, the system of centrally allocated inputs and obligatory distribution, with the exception of certain essential products, was abolished (T. Wojciechowski 1989). In August 1989 the government abolished price subsidies for food products and agricultural inputs of industrial origin, and earlier the state monopoly purchase of agricultural products was abolished.

The deepening economic crisis in 1988–9 was accompanied by growing economic anarchy. The failure of the price income operation in early 1988 reinforced inflation, shortages and imbalances. As a part of the round table politics (February–March 1988) and the general election of 4 June 1989, the Rakowski government tried to bribe the votes of the workers and peasantry by granting high growth of both wages and purchase prices of agricultural products. Also because of the election, for instance, the government let wages increase even faster than was implied in the wage indexing formula (B. Milanovic 1992: 519).

The weakening of the central organs and their inability to provide the means for survival for a large part of the *nomenklatura* at lower levels led to a crisis of obedience and control. Defiance and rebellion towards superiors among managers of the state firms and local administrators became widespread in 1988–9; disobedience and open rebellion were no longer risky (S. Johnson 1991; J. Staniszkis 1991: 86–9). For instance, managers disobeyed the instructions to limit wage increases or price rises. In their efforts to ensure survival, part of the *nomenklatura* tried to set up joint enterprises with foreign capital and private firms, either related to the state sector or operating independently, using their old connections and networks. Others made arrangements with local authorities or opposition forces; and others simply waited for the situation to settle down. The general outcome was bureaucratic anarchy and administrative disorganization.[13]

Both the design of the economic reform and the process of reform itself contributed to economic anarchy and collapse in 1988–9. Aside from the political weakness of the regime, the price income operation of 1988 was bound to fail since the economic reform was not comprehensive. The złoty was overvalued, the trade regime remained practically unchanged, price control was pervasive and real interest rates were negative (B. Milanovic 1992: 515–16). The piecemeal and fragmented character of the economic reform process itself tended to paralyse central economic regulation and control. At the same time, the inadequacy and ill-functioning of the market mechanism (the lack of competition, non-existing capital and labour market, etc.) was unable to set in motion market equilibrating forces.

BREAKTHROUGH AND THE TRANSITION TO A MARKET ECONOMY

Traditionally the mechanism of 'regulation through crisis' was instrumental in the process of managing economic and political recovery from crises and it succeeded in reproducing state socialism (see Chapter 7). This section will discuss and analyse briefly the changing circumstances, environment and causes which explain why, unlike in the past, 'regulation through crisis' in the last years of the 1980s failed to bring economic and political stabilization and a reproduction of state socialism. Material exhaustion of the extensive economic growth factors, decomposition of state socialism and a loss of economic control had undermined severely the efficacy of crisis management. The interactions and configuration of newly emerging domestic and international forces generated a political breakthrough and unprecedented opportunities which contributed to the collapse of state socialism and made a transition to a market economy feasible.

Growing disinvestment ('decapitalization'), obsolescence and ageing of the stock of physical assets; the rapidly growing size of the hard currency debt and the burden of debt servicing; the economic crisis in the Soviet Union in the last years of the 1980s which constrained the import of supplies; a growing labour shortage facing the state sector – all these factors taken together had severely limited Poland's possibilities of extensive economic growth in the 1980s. Despite differences in approaches and scope of analysis, a number of Western and Polish social scientists examining the socio-economic and political development of Poland came to a more or less similar conclusion that the process of 'decay of the socialist economic system' (J. Rostowski 1989), 'disarticulation of the socialist mode of production' (J. Staniszkis 1989: 34–6 and 124–6) or 'decomposition of state socialism' (B. Kaminski 1991: 162–93) were proceeding quickly in the 1980s. Common to this phenomenon was the growing importance of the official private sector,[14] the 'second economy',[15] the mixed state-private firms,[16] a widespread escape from the złoty into hard currency by using the dollar as a stable unit of account and store of value,[17] accompanied by a growing withdrawal from political institutions and apathy.

Jaruzelski's efforts through cooption and inclusion of part of non-communist individuals and groups into advisory and consultative institutions such as the Patriotic Movement for National Rebirth (PRON) of 1982, Constitutional Tribunal (1985), Social Consultative Council to the President (1986) the appointment of an Ombudsman for civil rights (1987) had failed to broaden public and political support for the regime. Subsequently the regime launched the idea of a democratization of the political system through a dialogue with the 'constructive opposition'. A growing number of economists, party and state leaders, and the public as well seemed to have come to the conclusion that economic reform could not succeed without substantial political reform. It was argued that far-reaching political reform was a precondition for economic reform and the willingness of the society to accept the social costs of reform as well (W. Morawski 1988: 97; see also Chapter 7). This conviction became more obvious and urgent when the workers rejected the price income operation of February 1988 and wave of strikes ensued (B. Kaminski 1991: 201–7).

The idea of a reform of the political system through a dialogue with the 'constructive opposition' found positive responses among both the reformist faction of the Polish United Workers Party (PUWP) and part of the leadership of Solidarność. The leadership of the Party needed a broadening of its legitimation base for carrying out economic reform, which was denied to the Party by the November 1987 referendum. For Walesa a legalization of the trade union Solidarność and eventually political pluralism would offer greater opportunities for developing his own social and political activities. At this stage of development both groups were 'united by a feeling of responsibility for social peace by their support for economic reform being imposed from above'. The reformist faction of the PUWP leadership needed the opposition 'as a shock absorber of social tensions and a source of impulses (challenges) for the routinized, inert, and nonsteerable executive power apparatus'. The opposition, in turn, was 'willing to play this role in exchange for the legalization of trade-union pluralism and even limited political pluralism' (J. Staniszkis 1991: 94–5).

Although the Round Table agreement between the regime and the opposition, concluded on 7 April 1989, was rather vague and was subject to various interpretations, it produced, however, the first political breakthrough, consisting of at least three political 'trade-offs':

1. the legalization of the trade union Solidarność in exchange for the stabilizing influence of the opposition;
2. a change in the constitution with a creation of a new, powerful institution in the President, chosen from the ranks of the Communist Party, in exchange for a reduction of the 'leading position of the Party', where the President was to occupy the role of a balancing force and guarantor of some sort of continuity *vis-à-vis* Moscow;
3. a semi-free election to the Sejm[18] and a free election to the Senate in exchange for the opposition's sharing responsibility for the difficult decision on economic reforms.

(J. Staniszkis 1991: 77–8; 198)

In purely economic terms, the Round Table agreement reaffirmed the commitment of the regime to proceed consistently with economic reform, to expand market supply at the cost of the armament industry, to support economic restructuring and expansion of the private sector, market oriented pricing and general principles of the distribution of the social cost of the economic reform, including an 80 per cent wage indexing of the price increases (P. Pysz and W. Quaisser 1989).

Both the reformist faction of the PUPW and the leadership of Solidarność miscalculated the political situation, the mood of the population and the depth of the political crisis in the Soviet Union before and during the time of the Round Table. The leadership of the PUWP, under the then prevailing political situation, misjudged the significance and meaning of the election of June 1989 for the Sejm and Senate. In the eyes of the voters, the election of June 1989 was turned into a referendum on communist rule in Poland (J. Holzer 1990: 22–3). This mistake was confounded by the wish of the Party to set up a national list, consisting of reformist leaders of the PUWP without a counter-candidate, which required more than 50 per cent of the votes for its direct election. At this stage, the leadership of Solidarność still did not question in principle the implicit formula of the 'leading position of the Party', though it would be weakened. Its position had some resemblance to the idea of the 'self-limiting' revolution of 1980. Moreover, the leadership of the opposition probably had overestimated the significance of a legalization of Solidarność.

The standpoint of the Moscow leadership was one the big uncertain factors in Poland's political development. The 'geopolitical' formula as legitimation of Polish communist rule had been long accepted not only by the communists, but also by part of the non-communist elite (see Chapter 8). Gorbachev had supported Jaruzelski's reform policy from the beginning and perestroika provided more room for manoeuvre and opportunities for the PUWP to undertake autonomous domestic political initiatives. But the Polish communist elite was also aware of the fact that under perestroika the Soviet Union most probably would not apply the Breznev Doctrine if communist rule was challenged legally by domestic opposition. This meant that the 'geopolitical' legitimation of Polish communist rule was severely undermined. This was a radical breakthrough in Poland's politics and offered completely new opportunities to the opposition.

The political consequences of the defeat of the PUWP in the June election was not initially fully understood by the PUWP leadership when Jaruzelski, in accordance with the Round Table agreement and thanks to the opposition, was elected by the Sejm to become President by a one vote majority.[19] The leadership of the PUWP still tried to propose Cz. Kiszczak to head a new government. The overwhelming victory of the opposition and the humiliating defeat of the candidates of the national list of the Polish United Workers Party (PUWP), the break away of the PUWP coalition partners (the Democratic and the United Peasant parties), the intensifying conflicts between different factions within the Moscow ruling elite and the power vacuum at the centre of the empire all contributed to a breach and a reformulation of the Round Table agreement.

At this stage, a revolutionary political breakthrough occurred. In view of the emergence of a completely new domestic and international political situation, the opposition reviewed and reformulated its old standpoint. Although the opposition at that time did not have a clear political programme and was facing a communist-dominated bureaucracy and armed forces, it launched bold and revolutionary political slogans ('who wins the election forms the government' or 'your president – our prime minister'), claiming that under the present configuration of political forces the opposition should form the government. The leadership of the PUWP was completely demoralized and it ultimately joined a Solidarność-based coalition government in mid-September 1989, led by Mazowiecki. After a brief period of indecision, the new government rejected any 'third road' experiment, and starting from 1 January 1990, it implemented a drastic economic stabilization plan (freeing prices, balanced budget, tight money and credit policy, convertibilty of złoty and wage restrictions) and a transition to a market economy.

CONCLUSION

Economic growth was relatively high in 1983–6, following the deep economic recession of 1979–82. In 1987–9, however, economic growth slowed down significantly. On the whole economic recovery proceeded slowly in the 1980s. By 1989 net material product was still 1 per cent below the pre-crisis (1978) level and in terms of per capita production it was 8.5 per cent less. Economic reform failed to bring efficient use of the falling and limited supply of labour and resources in the economy, a reduction in costs of production and market balance.

A high proportion of investment in the 1980s was expended for the continuation of unfinished investment projects started before 1982. A high proportion of them had a long gestation period and a high raw materials and fuel intensity. The low rates of investment project completions and the small investment allocation for modernization and replacement of worn-out fixed assets led to rising disinvestment. The rate of return on completed investment was low. A high percentage of industrial investment for the second half of the 1980s was allocated for the development of fuel and energy production; on the other hand, investment for fuel and energy saving (and conversion) was insufficient.

The yearly rate of inflation – according to underestimated official statistics – fell to 22 per cent in 1983 from more than 100 per cent in 1982. Inflation fell to between 16–18 per cent in 1984–6 but since then inflation accelerated from 26 per cent in 1987 to 259 per cent in 1989. Starting from August 1989 the economy entered a hyperinflationary stage which was terminated by the drastic Balcerowicz economic stabilization programme in 1990. Inflation was accompanied by growing shortages. The price income operation of February 1988 precipitated worker protests and strikes demanding high wage increases and generating a price-wage inflationary spiral. Subsidies, money supply and credit were rising fast. The rapidly growing budget deficit in 1989, largely politically motivated, fuelled further inflation.

After 1982, Poland had a hard currency trade surplus, rising from US$0.4 billion to US$1.5 billion in 1984. But in 1988–9 the trade surplus fell steadily to US$0.9 billion in 1988 and then to US$0.2 billion. The trade surplus in hard currency was achieved largely through a contraction in trade volume. Continuous and growing domestic imbalances, inflation, price distortions and overvaluation of the złoty made exports highly unattractive to producers. The Polish economy seemed to be unable to generate sufficient hard currency trade surplus to regain international creditworthiness and to attract new loans. The rapid growth of hard currency debt in the 1980s, largely due to the accumulation of unpaid interest, and the heavy burden of debt servicing were among the basic constraints on sustained economic recovery. The size of the rouble debt, nearly all of it owed to the Soviet Union, and the burden of rouble debt servicing, were relatively small. The growing economic dislocation and crisis in the Soviet Union during the last years of the 1980s affected the Polish economy adversely.

The early thrust of economic reform in 1982–3 was followed by a slow advance, stagnation and partial backlash by 1986. From 1987, the regime attempted to reanimate the reform process and to infuse new impulses into it, known as the second stage of economic reform. It advocated a rapid expansion of private and cooperative sectors which would be operating under favourable and equal conditions with state sector, and a creation of competitive environment and a reform in the banking system. The main aim of improving the efficiency of resourse use presupposed economic reform and this would function well only under market equilibrium. The failure of both the November 1987 referendum on economic reform and the price income operation of February 1988 triggered waves of strikes demanding high wage increases to which the regime succumbed, and this caused rapidly growing market disequilibrium and inflation. Inflation was further reinforced by the government's manoeuvres connected with the February–March 1989 Round Table talk between the regime and the opposition and the election of June 1989. Disobedience of employees toward their superiors, piecemeal and fragmented economic reform and the lack of a smoothly functioning market mechanism in Poland contributed to economic crisis and anarchy.

Exhaustion of the extensive economic growth factors, decomposition of state socialism and a loss of control over economic processes had undermined substantially the efficacy of the traditional 'regulation through crisis' in Poland. The idea that a far-reaching reform in the political system was a precondition for succesful economic reform had found greater response among the reformist faction of the Polish United Workers Party (PUWP) and part of the leadership of Solidarność after the failure of the price income operation of February 1988 and the ensuing waves of workers' strikes. The talks between the regime and the opposition produced a breakthrough in the form of three political 'trade-offs'. The overwhelming victory of the opposition and the humiliating defeat of the PUWP in the elections, the break away of the PUWP coalition partners, the growing conflicts between different factions in Moscow's ruling elite and the power vacuum in the Soviet empire contributed to a breach and reformulation of the Round Table agreements. For the first time in the history of the Warsaw Pact, a non-communist government was formed in one of its member states. The new government opted for a drastic economic stabilization plan and a transition to a market economy.

The communist regime did successfully stabilize the economic situation and partially 'normalize' the political situation after the deep crisis of 1979–82.

However, its long-standing lack of legitimacy, its loss of geopolitical support, its poor economic performance, its failed attempts to implement economic reform in 1987–8, the concessions it made to reach agreement with the opposition at the Round Table (1989) and in the hope of winning the elections, and the decomposition of state socialism, led to a new economic crisis in 1988–9. This time the crisis was resolved not by 'regulation through crisis' but by the collapse of the regime.

10

CONCLUSION

INTRODUCTION

Economic and investment growth in the Polish 'planned' economy proceeded in a recurrent cyclical movement caused largely by an interaction between the variation in economic policies, systemic and technical factors (the indivisibility of investment, the time gap between investment outlays and output growth and the 'echo effect' of investment cycles). The lower economic turning points of 1955–6, 1970–1 and 1981–2 were accompanied by political crises (violent workers' protests, changes in political leadership, etc.).

The longer duration and the greater amplitude of the economic and investment growth cycles in 1971–82 accentuated by the deep economic and political crises of 1979–82, indicated the grave state of the economy and polity. Polish economic development in 1971–82 can be roughly divided into three sub-periods. The first sub-period (1971–5) was an economic boom, characterized by great optimism, high rates of economic growth, investment, Western imports, real wages and consumption. The second sub-period (1976–8) saw a significant slow-down in the rates of economic growth, investment, real wages and consumption, and a stagnation in Western imports. The third sub-period (1979–82) was a time of deepening socio-political and economic crises leading to economic collapse and the declaration of martial law at the end of 1981.

Following the declaration of martial law, the communist regime initially succeeded in stabililizing the economic situation and in 'normalizing' the political situation. But because of the poor economic performance (particularly during the second half of the 1980s), the failed economic reform in 1987–8, the exhaustion of the extensive economic growth factors, the decomposition of state socialism, and the long-standing lack of legitimacy of the regime, a new economic crisis broke out in 1988–9. In the past the recurrent political and economic crises were necessary for the reproduction of state socialism in Poland and they were instrumental in the process of economic and political recovery. Unlike the previous crises, however, the economic crisis of 1988–9 led to a collapse of the regime.

GIEREK'S INVESTMENT LEAP AND INVESTMENT DISTORTIONS

Gierek's investment leap during the first half of the 1970s and the accompanying rapid consumption growth, which was necessary in order to bribe the rebellious workers, were made possible by the large Western credits. The investment leap was determined by the interaction of systemic factors (enterprises' unlimited demand for investment, 'hooking on to the plan', and 'soft budget constraint', etc.) and Gierek's ambitious 'new economic strategy' (industrial modernization, a boost for the falling rates of economic growth, investment pressure by heavy industry lobbies, full employment, etc.). Moreover, the regime misinterpreted the economic boom of the early 1970s, which was made possible by the exploitation of the so-called shallow economic growth factors and simple luck, and believed it due to Gierek's new economic policy and to have a relatively durable nature. These factors, taken together with the easy access to Western credits, encouraged the regime to continue the investment leap during the first half of the 1970s.

The over-investment drive, which exceeded the absorptive capacity of the economy, led to rapidly rising costs of investment, investment tensions, the extension of the investment gestation period, an excessively broad investment front, inefficiency and waste of investment resources. The production capacity of the building materials and construction industries was considerably short of investment demand. These problems were aggravated by the powerful lobbies around the heavy industry complex, which successfully bargained for more investment resources. The misallocation of investment between economic sectors, industrial branches and economic activities (neglect of infrastructure, agricultural and consumer goods sectors, lack of hard currency export orientation, discrimination against private agriculture and handicrafts, etc.) led to grave distortion of investment. There was a strong bias to expend more investment in the costly, prestigious new investment projects (e.g. Huta Katowica), having on average a longer gestation period, instead of quick-yielding and smaller investment projects for modernization, expansion and renovation of existing plants.

Investment and current industrial production were increasingly dependent on Western imports, whilst the volume of hard currency debt and the burden of debt servicing rose to critical levels by 1976, accompanied by insufficient growth of hard currency exports. The failure to enforce an orderly curb on the rapid consumption growth of the first half of the 1970s, as was envisaged by the aborted price rises of basic consumer goods in the summer of 1976, had adverse economic and political consequences. It accentuated the fact that the workers' support for Gierek's leadership was conditional on sustained high consumption growth. Growth of investment and Western imports was cut considerably after 1977 in an arbitrary manner. The failure of the so-called economic manoeuvre programme of early 1977 to reanimate the flagging economy and to redirect investments in accordance with the new investment priorities (promotion of Western exports, agricultural and consumer goods production and housing) led to further social tensions and economic deterioration.

The large investment fluctuation in 1971–82 (the over-investment in 1971–6 and large cuts in investment in 1979–82) caused great economic losses. Both the accumulated costs of investment in progress and the estimated costs of completing investment projects already started were growing rapidly after 1976. The rate of investment project completion was low, lagging considerably behind the targets. A growing proportion of the stock of physical capital, particularly in industry (light industry, chemical and building materials industries, etc.) became obsolete, high cost and worn out.

Due to investment distortions at the end of the 1970s, the structure of the unfinished investment projects was highly unfavourable (a long average construction period, high concentration in fuel and energy sectors, high hard currency import intensity, etc.). This structure was incompatible with the newly declared investment priorities such as agriculture and industries working for agriculture, exports, housing and economies in raw materials, fuel and energy. The restructuring plan of the unfinished investment projects was successfully blocked by vested interest groups, which maintained the investment arteriosclerosis in the economy in the 1980s.

THE FAILURE OF GIEREK'S IMPORT-LED GROWTH STRATEGY

Gierek's import-led growth strategy failed to generate the sustained growth in both hard currency exports and labour productivity necessary to meet the growing need for Western imports, the rapidly rising burden of debt servicing and the consumption aspirations of the population. Failure to meet these main goals led inevitably to the collapse of the strategy, leaving the economy with huge debts, unpaid debt servicing and deep economic distortions in the early 1980s.

In general exports received a low priority with an autarchic biased production. Poland's export capability was low in comparison both with the small CMEA countries and with market economies having a comparable level of economic development. Estimates of export ratios to gross national product varied between 9–13 per cent in 1966–82 in terms of US dollar prices. Effectiveness of export production, particularly with regard to export to non-socialist countries, deteriorated during the second half of the 1970s and early 1980s. A high proportion of investment projects developed (iron and steel, chemicals and building materials, etc.) had a high material, fuel and energy intensity of production and hence were import biased. Due to growing domestic imbalances and inflation, a growing proportion of exportable products was absorbed by domestic demand. The rapid growth of investment, and of imports of Western capital and technology during the first half of the 1970s, did not lead to an export boost as expected. Export performance in 1971–82, expressed in terms of elasticity of exports with regard to investment, was worse than export performance in the 1960s.

The modernization and expansion of the machinery and equipment industries, undertaken with the help of Western capital and technology, stimulated the export of manufactured goods to the CMEA countries. Instead of vigorously penetrating the competitive markets for manufactured goods of the industrialized West, Poland preferred the soft CMEA market. The European CMEA countries faced growing competition from the NICs in the OECD market for manufacturing exports from the second half of the 1970s and lost the battle. Poland's share in the OECD imports of machinery, equipment and other manufactures dropped in the late 1970s and early 1980s. The degree of Poland's export specialization, with the exception of a number of primary products (coal, sulphur and copper, etc.) and industrial products (ships, metal working machinery, rolling stock, etc.), was low.

The rapid growth of imports of machinery, production processes and licences from the West led to an increasing dependence of Poland's industrial production on hard currency imports of industrial inputs (raw materials, components, spare parts, etc.). The economy was highly material, fuel and energy intensive in comparison with industrialized Western countries. The excessive and erratic fluctuation in Western imports and their drastic cuts after 1977 led to under-utilization of industrial productive capacity and economic dislocation.

The large import of Western capital and technology in the 1970s did not lead (as expected) to a significant improvement in the structure of Poland's foreign trade. The export share of primary products (SITC:0–4) in total exports to the CMEA countries at current prices remained stable (about 18 per cent) in 1971–82. On the other hand, the import share of primary products increased from close to one-third of Poland's total imports from the CMEA countries in 1975 to close to one-half in 1982, mainly due to price increases of Soviet crude oil. The share of machinery, equipment and means of transportation (SITC:7) in Poland's trade with the CMEA countries was high. A high proportion of Poland's exports to the industrialized West consisted of primary products (coal, copper, agricultural products, etc.), intermediate industrial products and manufacturing with a relatively low degree of processing and poor quality, and having low unit values.

Domestic price and incentive systems were increasingly distorted. The planning and regulation of foreign trade and production relied increasingly on administrative measures, which were absolutely unsuitable for the purpose of boosting hard currency exports of manufactures. Import and export targets and hard currency allocation were increasingly determined by *ad hoc* bargaining and lobbying between the central planner, ministries, industrial associations and enterprises, the outcome of which depended mainly on the bargaining power, and political and personal patronage of the individual participants. The so-called open-ended planning, the mismanagement of the Western debts, the incompetence and irresponsibility of the highest Party and state leadership contributed significantly to Poland's balance of payments crisis.

The favourable international conditions and easy terms for substantial borrowing in the 1970s (East–West *détente*, economic recession in the West, liquidity of Western banks, the flood of petrodollars, the Western belief in the 'Soviet financial umbrella', etc.) encouraged Poland, like other European CMEA countries, to take large Western loans. In many cases, Western loans were supplied on the basis of insufficient information or economic analysis. Because of the high inflation prevailing in the industrialized Western countries, the Polish regime falsely believed that the real cost (interest rate in real terms) of borrowing would be very low or even negative, giving additional encouragement to take large Western loans.

A growing proportion of the new loans, contracted under more stringent conditions, were devoted to servicing the growing debts. This led to a tightening of the debt trap. The debt structure was deteriorating (falling average maturity, a growing proportion of commercial credits, etc.), aggravated by a fast rise in the rate of interest during the late 1970s and early 1980s and accompanied by a rapid decline of Poland's creditworthiness. The large fall in output (in coal production, manufacturing and agriculture, etc.) and high inflation in the early 1980s contributed to a drastic fall in exports, aggravating the balance of payments crisis which forced Poland to seek debt rescheduling. The Western credit sanctions, imposed after the declaration of martial law in 1981, put additional strains on the economy.

INFLATION

The slow growth in both average money wages and the price level prevailing in the 1960s was accompanied, however, by individual market imbalances (meat, furniture, durable consumer goods, etc.), shortages, unattractive product mix and poor quality of products. The critical economic and political situation in the late 1960s accentuated the negative impact of a decade-long decline in the rates of growth of net material product and labour productivity, which were accompanied by a slow growth of real wages, consumption and a rising rate of productive investment. The aborted price increase of basic foodstuffs in December 1970 precipitated the political crisis (violent workers' protests, the fall of Gomulka, etc.) which forced the new leadership under Gierek to freeze food prices and to boost income, wages and consumption.

The continuation of a relatively stable and low inflationary economic boom in 1971–3 was followed by growing consumer market imbalances, shortages, consumer price inflation and investment tensions. The insignificant official consumer price increases in the early 1970s rose to a moderate level during the remaining years of the decade and reached a three-digit level in 1982. Both hidden and repressed inflation were intense, the latter was particularly large in the early 1980s. It would be wrong to consider the vexations and frustrations resulting from queuing, shortages, forced substitution, bribery and privileges, etc. to be merely anecdotal.

The failure of Gierek's 'import-led' growth strategy to establish a viable export and consumer goods sector, combined with a lagging growth in labour productivity, contributed directly or indirectly to inflation. The systemic built-in tendency to wage drift in the CPEs was reinforced by the regime's weakness and the policy of buying off the workers with wage increases, which, together with the shortages and imbalances on the producer goods markets and the systemic cost increasing processes, all contributed to the wage-price inflationary spiral.

ZIG-ZAG IN AGRICULTURAL POLICIES

Agricultural development and policies in 1971–82 formed a closed cycle with a pattern similar to Poland's post-war 'political trade cycles'. The early pro-peasantry agricultural policy, which was preceded by bad harvests and food riots in 1970, contributed significantly to the agricultural boom of 1971–4 and a rapid growth of (food) consumption. With the growing strength and self-confidence of the regime, the policy was gradually reversed, by squeezing and discrimination against the private farms, accompanied by a rapid expansion of socialized farms. These measures contributed substantially to a decline in agricultural output and a deterioration in the efficiency of resource use. A return to a pragmatic agricultural policy from the late 1970s, under conditions of a deepening economic crisis till 1982, did not, however, succeed in reversing the decline in agriculture

From 1975, due to bad harvests, Poland increased Western imports of grain (and high protein fodder) considerably in order prevent the collapse of the livestock population and to ensure an adequate supply of food. Throughout the period under study attempts to restore food market imbalances by (aborted) price rises provoked workers' protests and/or wage compensation. Both the income elasticity of demand for food and the level of food consumption (by international standards) in Poland were high. The hard currency deficits in agriculture-related trade contributed very substantially to the growth in Poland's Western debts. Despite discrimination against private farms they performed relatively better than socialized farms. The large outflow of agricultural labour did not lead to an improvement of the small and fragmented structural features of Poland's private agriculture.

LABOUR SUPPLY, LABOUR QUALITY AND FULL EMPLOYMENT

The maturing of the post-war 'baby-boomers' in the 1970s, combined with a rising trend in the participation rates (especially among married women) in non-agricultural activities, led to a rapid growth in the labour supply and social pressure for more employment. These occurred together with a rejuvenation of the non-agricultural (industrial) labour force, a rapid improvement in the level of education and training and rising professional and consumption aspirations, particularly of young workers and employees. The widespread misallocation and misassignment of university graduates, engineers, technicians and skilled workers to simple, routine administrative and monotonous jobs caused discontent and frustration. Opinion polls showed that the degree of job satisfaction decreased with a higher level of education and training. The failure of the employment system and the economy to meet the rising professional and consumption aspirations of the workers and employees, especially the young, contributed to the emergence of Solidornośč and the workers' protests in 1980.

The state of health of the population, and of the working people in particular, was deteriorating from the second half of the 1970s. The large increase in the rate of mortality, in particular of men in the productive age group 35–54 years, due to the high consumption of alcohol, rapid growth of cigarette smoking, stress and enviromental pollution was alarming, reflecting partly the deepening socio-economic crises. Working conditions (work safety, labour protection and hygiene conditions, etc.) were worsening. A significant proportion of the workforce was doing work which was heavy and injurious to health. The average working week was comparatively long and in the 1970s the preference for a shorter working week was strong among the workers. The four-shifts work system was very unpopular with the coal miners. The time-schedule of working mothers was very tight, being aggravated by the poor infrastructure and the crisis in the supply of consumer goods and services.

The Polish People's Republic successfully tackled the unemployment and underemployment that characterized pre-war Poland. The economic policies (extensive growth, low wages, etc.) and the economic system (directive planning) that achieved full employment, however, had their own characteristic problems. Full employment was marked by widespread labour hoarding, misallocation of labour, pseudo labour shortages, poor labour discipline and slow growth in labour productivity. The labour shortages in the state sector in the early 1980s were made worse by measures such as early retirement, paid leave for young mothers and the expansion of private sector, taken by the regime in the light of anticipation of unemployment and economic reform.

Rationalization of employment was hindered by the stagnation of economic reform, and blocked by vested political and socio-economic interests. The regime was more inclined to adopt administrative measures to cope with labour shortages and labour indiscipline than to pursue the difficult path of economic reform and appropriate economic policy. Throughout its history the Polish People's Republic failed to combine full employment with efficient use of labour. The economic crisis in communist Poland did not contribute to a rationalization of employment, improvement of labour discipline and quality, partly because large-scale labour relocation and unemployment did not emerge.

ECONOMIC CRISIS ETIOLOGIES AND LEGITIMACY DEFICITS

The monopoly over and complete censorship of the mass media were key instruments in the hands of the regime in controlling the minds of the people, and it fought hard against popular demands for true information and a free press. Gierek's 'propaganda of success' and censorship of the monopolized mass media led to a growing dissonance between the worsening socio-economic situation after 1975 and the optimistic official propaganda. The underground media, spearheaded by a group of dissident intellectuals who sought an alliance with the workers, aimed to penetrate society with true information, encouraging critical thinking and independent actions. These dissidents succeeded to some extent in breaking the regime's monopoly of information.

The dissident writings underlined the worsening socio-economic situation after 1975 and forecast the approaching economic crisis, discussing the cause(s) of the crisis and economic policy alternatives (or economic reforms) to restore the growing domestic and external imbalances. After August 1980, the *odnowa* movement created favourable conditions for free discussion and inquiries into the causes, nature and extent of the crises, and offered alternative programmes to resolve the crises. Basic ideas, arguments and conclusions of the dissident writings became part of the mainstream economics of Poland's crisis etiologies after August 1980.

In the dissident and post-August 1980 writings of the Polish economists surveyed, at least four major determinants of the economic crisis can be identified:

1 the systemic shortcomings of the command economy causing misallocation of resources, waste and inefficiency;
2 deformation in the structure of the economy (e.g. heavy industry growth orientation) generating technical, socio-economic and political distortions;
3 defects in the functioning of the economy due to errors in economic policies, voluntarism and bad leadership;
4 the collapse of Gierek's strategy of substituting for legitimacy deficits the promise of continued economic success and the satisfaction of consumer aspirations.

These four determinants, together with the factors specific to the crisis years 1979–81 (bad harvests, the shorter working week, drastic cuts in Western imports, high inflation, etc.), generated the crisis of 1979–82.

The legitimacy of the Polish communists was always tenuous. There are a number of reasons for this. One was the historical antagonism between Poland and the Soviet Union (resulting from Czarist Russia being one of the three partitioning powers of Poland between 1772–1918, the Polish–Russian war in 1920–1 and a number of serious grievances of the Poles against the Soviet Union during the Second World War); another was the cultural discrepancy between the influential Catholic Church and Marxism-Leninism, and the Western orientation of Polish intellectuals. Yet another reason was the political isolation of the communist elite (a prevalent perception of the communist system being imposed by the Red Army at the end of the Second World War, the minority position of the Polish communists and the dictatorship of the *nomenklatura*). The abandonment of the use of terror and coercion as the main instruments in securing compliance in the post-Stalinist period, together with the incapacity of the regime to implement far-reaching economic and political reforms and the rapidly rising consumption aspirations of the population, underlined the key importance of economic performance and the satisfaction of consumer aspirations in securing legitimation. Gierek's strategy of political legitimation, which relied heavily on consumer satisfaction, was dependent on continued economic success.

The hope that official ideology would enhance the legitimacy of communist rule at mass level actually turned into a trap, constraining the freedom of manoeuvre of the ruling elite. Elite self-legitimation through high pay, security of tenure, privileges and the corruption proved to be counter-productive at national level and had a destabilizing impact.

The economic success and the high consumption satisfaction in the first half of the 1970s were to a significant extent financed by Western credits. The replacement of the 'invisible hand' of the market by the 'visible hand' of the Party in state socialism made the regime particularly vulnerable to economic outcomes, since people held the regime responsible for almost all outcomes considered as unjust and harmful. Barring crucial economic and political reforms, Gierek's legitimation strategy was bound to break down under conditions of medium- and long-run decline in the system's economic efficiency (being compounded by errors in economic policies) and the unrestrained rise in consumer aspirations.

AFTERMATH OF THE ECONOMIC CRISIS OF 1979–82 AND THE COLLAPSE OF STATE SOCIALISM

Jaruzelski's regime introduced martial law in December 1981 and it lasted until July 1983. Martial law helped to bring an end to the chaotic economic situation of 1981. Economic growth was relatively high in 1983–6, but in 1987–9 it slowed down significantly. On the whole, economic recovery proceeded slowly in the 1980s. By 1989 net material product was still 1 per cent below the pre-crisis (1978) level and in terms of per capita production it was 8.5 per cent less. A high proportion of investment in the 1980s was expended for the continuation of the unfinished investment projects started before 1982, and a high proportion of them had a long gestation period and a high raw materials and fuel intensity of production. The rate of investment project completions and the rate of return on completed investment were low, accompanied by misallocation of investment between economic sectors and industrial branches.

Inflation (according to underestimated official statistics) fell from more than 100 per cent in 1982 to 22 per cent in 1983, and in 1984–6 inflation fell further to between 16–18 per cent. However, inflation accelerated continuously from 22 per cent in 1987 to 259 percent in 1989, and in August 1989 the economy entered a hyperinflationary stage, accompanied by growing shortages. After 1982 Poland had a hard currency trade surplus which was largely achieved at the cost of a contraction in trade volume. The Polish economy seemed to be unable to generate a sufficient hard currency trade surplus to regain international creditworthiness and to attract new loans. The rapid growth of hard currency debt, due to the accumulation of unpaid interest, and the heavy burden of debt servicing imposed heavy constraints on sustained economic recovery.

The early thrust of economic reform in 1982–3 was followed by a slow advance, stagnation and partial backlash. From 1987 the regime attempted to reanimate the reform process, which was known as the second stage of economic reform, advocating a rapid expansion of the private sector, price liberalization and the creation of a competitive economic environment. The failure of both the November 1987 referendum on economic reform and the price income operation (consumer price increase) in February 1988 triggered waves of strikes demanding high wage increases, which caused disequilibrium and shortages. Inflation was reinforced by the government's effort to bribe the votes of the workers and the peasantry, granting high increases of wages and procurement prices of agricultural products, connected with the February–March 1989 Round Table talk between the regime and the opposition and the election of June 1989. Disobedience of employees toward their superiors, piecemeal and fragmented economic reform and the lack of a smoothly functioning market mechanism in Poland contributed to economic crisis and anarchy in 1988–9.

The idea that a far-reaching reform of the political system was a precondition for successful economic reform found a greater response among the reformist faction of the Polish United Workers Party (PUWP) and part of the leadership of Solidarność after the failure of the price income operation in 1988 and the ensuing waves of strikes. The talks between the regime and the opposition produced a political breakthrough:

1. the legalization of Solidarność;
2. the creation of a powerful office of the Presidency, to be occupied by a communist;
3. the holding of a semi-free election to the Parliament and a free election to the Senate.

The overwhelming victory of the opposition and the humiliating deafeat of the PUWP in the elections, the break away of the PUWP coalition partners, the growing conflicts between different factions in Moscow's ruling elite and the power vacuum in the centre of the former Soviet empire contributed to a breach of the Round Table agreements and a new political breakthrough, making the formation of a non-communist government feasible. The new government opted for a drastic economic stabilization plan and a transition to market economy beginning in January 1990.

SUMMARY

The dramatic Polish economic crisis of 1979–82 can be explained by the interaction of Gierek's economic policy, the administrative economic system, the international economic environment, the tenuous legitimacy of the Polish communists and the specific circumstances of 1979–81. The policy was based on a misreading of the favourable results of 1971–3, and a misjudgement of likely real international interest rates and was shattered by working–class opposition in 1976 and 1980 and the economic incompetence of the leadership. The administrative economic system ensured that the economy would remain inefficient, that much of the investment would be wasted, that agricultural policy would be partly counter-productive, and that exports would not rise sufficiently to make the economic policy viable. The international economic environment first tempted Poland with substantial loans at favourable terms in the early and mid-1970s and then, when Poland had fallen into the debt trap, injured Poland with rising interest rates in the late 1970s and early 1980s. The tenuous legitimacy of the Polish communists forced Gierek to meet the workers' protests of 1970 with consumption increases, to rescind the price increases of 1976 and capitulate before the workers' protests of 1980. The specific circumstances of 1979–81 naturally influenced the way the crisis manifested itself.

The initial success of the regime in overcoming the crisis of 1979–82 was only temporary. Its longstanding lack of legitimacy and the loss of geopolitical support, its poor economic performance, its failed attempt to reform the economic and political systems in 1988–9, and the decomposition of state socialism, led to a new economic crisis in 1988–9. Unlike the past crises, this crisis was not resolved by 'regulation through crisis', but by a collapse of the regime.

NOTES

1 INVESTMENT

1 For an extensive survey of Polish economists' writings on investment cycles see P. von der Lippe, 'Investitionszyklen in Polen – ein Literaturbericht und statistische Berechnungen', *Diskussionbeitrage*, 19, Universität Essen, 1980 (mimeographed).

2 Dziewulski and Maciejewski are less definite about the economic gain which would be obtained from unbalanced growth in comparison to balanced growth:

> It is obviously very difficult, if not impossible to arrive at a uniform evaluation of the phenomenon of overinvestment and the cyclical character of the investment process. So far, there has been a lack of empirical evidence that in the case of socialist countries, unbalanced economic growth entails more benefits than balances growth in the long run.
>
> (P. Dziewulski and A. Maciejewski 1980: 221)

3 A Western student of Polish investment cycles has pointed out that using the actual changes in rates of growth of the economy and investment has a number of disadvantages, such as too high a level of fluctuations and over-sensitivity to change in the previous year, the fact that no reference could be made to 'trend' or 'normal' level and the inability to distinguish endogenous cycles from random fluctuations (see P. von der Lippe 1980a).

4 Genuine political and economic reform with a lasting character seems to be incompatible with the principle of the 'leading role' ('kierownicza rola') of the Party and the traditional relationship between Party and state was considered (by the Party's leadership) to be the only form compatible with socialism. Hence, radical economic reform had to wait until the Party lost power in 1989. Moreover, when Gierek took over the leadership of the Party, the forces opposing reform and liberalization were strong. Gierek's credibility was barely sufficient to prevent further escalation of riots, let alone to defend the increase in prices of basic consumer goods. Under such circumstances, the room for manoeuvre was narrow and consumption growth was the only condition acceptable to the workers for tolerating the new leadership (W. Kuczyński 1981: 80–2).

5 For a more detailed description and analysis of plan targets and their modifications see S. Albinowski (1981: 357–61) and D. Kostyrka (1982: 68–71).

6 The figures are calculated from *Rocznik Statystyczny 1983*: 155–6 and *Rocznik Statystyczny Handlu Zagranicznego 1983*: 5.

7 'Investment expansion is ... "sanctioned" by the appraisal system of the economic organizations, which are called upon to reward the fulfillment and overfulfillment of the plan tasks. Investments are the easiest way to implement the socio-economic

tasks contained in the plan' (P. Dziewulski and A. Maciejewski 1980: 220).

8 The notion of investment tension comprises at least three interrelated components:
a) total investment claims always surpass prescribed investment quotas, i.e. a tension between claim and quota;
b) many approved investment projects cannot be carried out within the planned material balances, building and construction balance and the time-table;
c) the officially approved investment plan cannot be fully satisfied by the supplies of producer goods, the construction and building capacity.

9

> Nearly all claimants underestimate costs. The investors have an interest in underestimating costs since the chances of acceptance of the project are greater if expected costs are relatively smaller. The discrepancy between estimated costs and actual is not of the order of 2 to 5 per cent.... The average may be about 20 to 30 per cent, and a discrepancy of 50 per cent is not infrequent. A part of this discrepancy is connected with rises in prices, while another part reflects *actual physical inputs* exceeding estimates.
>
> (J. Kornai 1980: 196; emphasis in original.)

10 The table shows that the proportion of expenditure on machinery and equipment grew relative to the share of construction and installation in total ivestment in 1961–80.

	Fixed prices 1 January 1977 and in per cent			
	1961–5	*1966–70*	*1971–5*	*1976–80*
Total investment of which:	100	100	100	100
construction and installation	65.6	63.2	56.6	52.2
machinery and equipment	29.5	32.0	38.1	42.8
other	4.9	4.8	5.3	5.0

Source: *Inwestycje 1979*, Warsaw 1979, p. 9; Statistical yearbook of various years.

11 Normally the renewal of fixed capital in state socialist economies is carried out through a massive growth in new investments while old machinery and equipment are operated until their physical decay. In industrial, capitalist countries, however, the growth in new investments is accompanied by an accelerated withdrawal of old machinery and equipment, taking into account not only the physical (technical) but also economic obsolescence of the fixed assets (P. Glikman 1982).

12 In a speech before the CC Plenary Meeting of the PZPR, the former prime minister Jaroszewicz declared: 'We should absolutely resist – by applying severe sanctions – every effort to undertake investment outside those which are stipulated in the plan, and also pseudo social works which serve as screen for (*note*: illegal) investment activities', ('II Plenum KC PZPR', *Nowe Drogi*, 2, 1976: 20). It was, however, common for many important and less important investment projects to be started outside the plan, although authorization was normally given retrospectively.

2 EXTERNAL ECONOMIC RELATIONSHIPS

1 Total value of final products is equal to the value of domestic end-uses of the products consisting of personal and collective consumption, investments, changes in inventory and exports.

2 The degree of export specialization is measured by comparing Poland's export struc-

ture to the total CMEA export structure. Export products are classified into three groups: a) products whose share in Poland's exports is less than the share in the CMEA exports; b) products whose share in Poland's exports is equal or up to three times the share in the CMEA exports; c) products whose share in Poland's exports is greater than three times the share in the CMEA exports. Studies show that the proportion of the first group was increasing whilst that of the third group was falling in 1975 in comparison to 1965 (P. Glinski 1980: 9–11).

3 The foreign exchange multiplier was calculated on the basis of the cost of export production required in order to obtain one unit of foreign currency by export. It should be noted, however, that the rates were kept secret and remained unpublished for nearly ten years until 1981. (For a more extensive description and analysis, see E. Böhm 1985: 98–117.)

4 Import subsidies, after the deduction of import taxes, reflecting the difference between domestic price and transaction price, constituted only 19 per cent of the value of Western imports of basic raw materials in 1973; they rose rapidly, however, during the next two years to 44 per cent and 43 per cent in 1974 and 1975 respectively. It should be noted that import price subsidies were not confined to basic raw materials; it was estimated that import subsidies accounted for around one-quarter of the total value of Western imports in 1975 (E. Böhm 1985: 91–3).

5

> The central authority was . . . not consistent as far as foreign trade was concerned. Every year it assumed a growth of exports and a constraint of imports; but every year ministries and enterprises were exempted (from export tasks) under various pretexts like the products were needed for the domestic market, the targets set based on 'self-financing in foreign trade' were incorrectly fixed etc. At the same time the central authority, driven into the corner by ministries and enterprises, had allowed extra imports. Generally, it was forced to do so under threats of a production stop due to the lack of industrial components, raw materials etc.
>
> (P. Bożyk 1983: 126–7)

6 A former top economic adviser of Gierek's in the 1970s described the open-ended planning as follows:

> A large number of investment projects were started 'frantically' outside any plan and material balance. The Ministries started constructing plants without restraint, local authorities started building swimming pools, sporthalls, and office buildings, etc. Open-ended planning gave the impression that decision-makers were allowed to undertake all sort of activities outside the plan.
>
> (P. Bożyk 1983: 114)

7 Industrial associations or enterprises, which received hard currency import credits for investment purposes to establish new plants or to expand production capacity within the system of self-financing in foreign exchange, were obliged to repay part of the credits in the form of hard currency exports. Within a relatively short time the scheme failed completely, largely because of the ability of managers to bargain for a substantial reduction or exemption from the obligation to export the products to the West on the grounds of a rapidly growing domestic demand, shortage of inputs and delays in commissioning investment projects, etc. (See E. Böhm 1985: 144–64; S. Jędrychowski 1982: 83–7).

8

> A modernization of industrial productive capacity with a simultaneous increase in the standard of living requires the use of foreign credits. This makes

a realization of the economic reconstruction programme feasible, while keeping that part of national income for distribution corresponding with the social aims fixed ahead. So far we have not utilized these possibilities appropriately.

(Jaroszewicz at the VIth Party Congress, *Nowe Drogi*, 1972 1: 123).

3 INFLATION

1 The rapid growth of capital accumulation resulted in socially and economically critical rates during 1951–5. In 1953 the official rate of capital accumulation was 38.2 per cent (which was an underestimation of the actual capital accumulation due to the underpricing of producer goods), and the bulk of the accumulation went to productive investment to develop heavy industry or the so-called 'A' sector including armaments industries. It was estimated that in 1950–4 on average 15 per cent of the national income per annum was expended for military and armaments purposes (M. Müller 1985: 106 and 204).

2 According to official statistics, the indices of real wages in 1970 stood at 146 (1960=100) for Romania, Bulgaria at 143, Czechoslovakia at 127 and the USSR at 134; the Polish index of real wages was only 119 (cited by W. Brus 1982: 134).

3 *VII Zjazd Polskiej Zjednoczonej Partii Robotniczej; 8–12 grudnia 1975: Podstawowe materialy i dokumenty* 1975: 107.

4 In 1974 the government announced a cut in the interest rate on saving deposits from 5 to 4 per cent, making saving less attractive. The fall in households' savings ratio in 1975–7 occurred at a time when the rate of both official and hidden inflation was significantly growing (J. Winiecki 1986: 213; G. Kołodko 1987: 194–5).

5 According to a survey of the Central Statistical Office, per capita consumption at constant prices in workers' households fell by 16.8 per cent (food consumption fell by 6.8 per cent) in 1982. At the same time, however, consumption per capita of alcoholic drink and cigarettes increased by 13.6 per cent and 10.7 per cent respectively. Households of the other social groups (pensioners, worker-peasants, etc.) showed similar consumption behaviour (*Zróżnicowanie Dochodów, Kosztów Utrzymania i Spożycia Gospodarstw Domowych w 1982r* 1983: 45–6).

6 Apart from theoretical and methodological difficulties in making estimates of consumer price indices under conditions of permanent shortages, forced substitutions, bribery and black markets, the regime's statistical manipulations contributed to a growing gap between society's perception of price rises and the government's, which helped to discredit the latter entirely. Polish statisticians had pointed out the serious defects of official statistics (L. Zienkowski 1982: 2; A. Luszniewicz 1982: 18–21). It was not just coincidence that one of the provisions of the Gdańsk charter in 1980 was the adoption of indexed wages and the need for objective cost of living indices to be calculated by autonomous research institutions.

7 For an extensive and critical survey of various estimates of hidden inflation in CMEA countries, see: D.M. Nuti 1986a: 48–54.

8 Nuti remarks that queues may get longer because of an improvement rather than a worsening of the state of supplies. This is expressed in a Polish joke: 'Do you often have queues as long as these?' 'No, not very often. Only when there are goods in the shops' (D.M. Nuti 1986a: 54). A plausible argument made by a number of Polish economists contends that the rise in household savings ratios in 1971-3 was not a sign of growing repressed inflation. On the other hand, the rise in savings ratios after 1977 was considered as a sign of growing repressed inflation (A. Wernik 1984b: 26 and 30; P. Bożyk 1983: 90–1). Portes offered a reverse interpretation, suggesting that the fall in the savings ratio in Poland in the second half of the 1970s 'may

indicate the re-establishment of equilibrium' in the consumer market (R. Portes and D. Winter 1980: 155).

9 According to the official figure, which was an underestimate, the value of goods sold for hard currency, expressed in złoty at current prices in 1975, was only 2 per cent of the total sales of state retail trade. For certain goods, however, sales in hard currency was important. For example, about 12 per cent of the total sales of new cars in 1970 was for hard currency and its share went up rapidly to about 50 per cent in 1975 (*Rocznik Statystyczny* 1976: 361). It was estimated that in a number of large towns, more than 10 per cent of the total flats 'released for use', which was equal to about one-third of the total flats allocated by housing cooperatives in the second half of the 1970s, were sold for hard currency (W. Brus 1979a: 45).

10 Polish economists made a distinction between inflationary gap ('luka'), i.e. the part of personal income which was not covered by the sales of goods and services in state trade, and inflationary overhang ('nawis'), i.e the part of monetary balances (saving accounts and cash) accumulated out of past inflationary gaps that would, at given prices, have been spent on goods and services that were unavailable in state trade. By mid-1981 around 500 billion złoty (one-quarter of personal income) was estimated as inflationary overhang (W. Herer and W. Sadowski 1981).

11 For an extensive survey and analysis of the various schools of economic shortage and disequilibrium modelling in the CPEs, see C. Davis and W. Charemza 1989; W. Charemza 1989.

12 The figures for agricultural output and procurement are taken from *Rocznik Statystyczny* 1981: xxxix.

13 *Rocznik Statystyczny* 1983: 347.

14 According to certain estimates, the price elasticity of supply of certain agricultural production in Poland such as barley, potatoes and hogs for 1973–83 was negative (Z. Krasinski, H. Mruk and H. Szulce 1985: 95–7). The farmers were inclined to sell a very limited amount of agricultural products which fetched a high price, just sufficient to purchase the short supply of consumer goods and agricultural inputs in 1981–2.

15 The actual state budget deficit in 1981 was greater than that officially measured, since the withdrawal of 156.6 billion złotys reserve, accumulated in previous years and deposited at the central bank, was regarded as state revenue (*Rocznik Statystyczny* 1983: 70, 78.)

16 The figures are calculated from the Statistical Yearbook of various years. See also Z. Krasiński *et al.* 1985: 62–8. Due to price distortions and widespread subsidies for inputs, the extent of subsidies for consumer goods and services using subsidized inputs could only be roughly estimated.

17 For an extensive exposition and survey of Polish writings on theories of inflation in Poland, see Z. Polański 1987: 1283–1302.

18 See B. Minc 1961: 423–5.

4 AGRICULTURE

1 K. Barcikowski, the Minister of Agriculture who resigned (in protest) in 1977, but who did not dispute the long-run aim of socialized agriculture, criticized the restriction of land sales to private farmers and refuted the regime's arguments.

> It is not true that there is a shortage of [private] farmers who would like to expand their farms and agricultural output. All surveys made in the villages have shown, that a large percentage of good farmers, who invest and develop livestock farming, seek the opportunity enlarge their landholdings in order to

increase the output of fodder. However, the farmers often encounter artificially created obstacles, which simply force them to give up the idea of purchasing land.

(K. Barcikowski 1977: 25).

2 The share of the CMEA countries in total import value of food products and agricultural commodities declined from 35 per cent in 1970 to only 13.5 per cent in 1980 (*Rocznik Statystyczny Handlu Zagranicznego* 1981: 6–7).

3 For instance, the output of commercial fertilizer and chemical components for high protein animal feed fell by around 18 per cent during 1976–81, and the output of pesticides and tractors dropped by around 18 per cent and 19 per cent respectively during 1979–81 (*Rocznik Statystyczny Rolnictwa i Gospodarki* Żywnościowej 1982: 4).

4 Poland's accumulated trade deficit in hard currency from the agricultural-related sector in 1975–81 included trade in capital goods for agriculture and the food industry (*Rocznik Statystyczny Rolnictwa in Gospodarki Żywnościowej* 1982: 326).

5 According to Hunek's study, the income elasticity of demand for food was 0.77 in the years 1966–70 (T. Hunek 1975: 13), while other estimates were between 0.6 and 0.8 (Z. Kozlowski 1980: 1286; L. Beskid, 'Ewolucja konsumpcji w latach siedemdziesiątych', cited in J. Lewandowski 1983: 31). According to a Polish expert on food economy the high income elasticity of demand for food was 'one of the most alarming coefficients in our economy'. Under such conditions, complying with the growth in food demand would be extremely difficult even under a modest rate of economic growth (W. Szymanski 1979: 179).

6 The figures for agricultural output and procurement are taken from *Rocznik Statystyczny* 1983: xxxix.

7 For an extensive summary and analysis of the debate and arguments, see B. Mieczkowski 1975: 154–9. See also M. Ellman 1989: 239–42.

8 According to official statistics, retail prices of food products rose 1.33 times between 1970–8 compared to 1.35 times for non-food commodities. Meat prices at state shops were frozen up to 1977. However from 1978 food prices increased more rapidly than prices of non-food products; with a drastic increase of food prices in 1982 the price scissors between the two widened considerably (*Ceny Detaliczne 1971–1985* 1985: 2–3 and 6–7).

9 Budget subsidies for food production and consumption increased from 7.5 billion złoty in 1970 to 51.3 billion złoty in 1975, and they rose further to 163.9 billion złoty and 213.4 billion złoty in 1980 and 1981 respectively. Subsidies constituted 11.9, 25.3 and 29.7 per cent of the total value (wholesale prices) of food production in 1975, 1980 and 1981 respectively. The drastic price rise of food in 1982 cut the proportion of subsidies to 12.4 per cent of the total value of food production. More than two-thirds of the budget subsidies for food were earmarked for meat and dairy products (Calculated from various Statistical Yearbooks and E. Gorzelak 1987: 274).

10 See L. Podkaminer 1982: 423–31; L. Podkaminer 1986; L. Podkaminer 1987: 509–12; L. Podkaminer 1988: 43–60.

11 Calculated meat equivalent is equal to 1 kg meat = 1 kg eggs = 6.67 l. milk = 0.28 kg raw wool (Z. Grochowski 1979: 88).

12 Yearly average budgetary subsidies to socialized farms in current złoty amounted to about 63 billion in 1978–80, of which about 44 billion was allocated to state farms. It was estimated that the percentage share of subsidies to total sales of basic agricultural products of the state farms grew from 21.8 per cent in 1971–2 to 36.9 per cent in 1977–8, reflecting a growth in operating losses (A. Wós 1985: 155–7). To further lighten the financial load of the state and collective farms, debt obligations were often written off (E. Cook 1984: 415).

13 Net marketed output is equal to gross marketed output minus the value of off-farm purchase of feed and other inputs of agricultural origin.

14 For every 1 złoty value added from socialized farms in 1976, an outlay of 7.32 złotys on material inputs (including capital depreciation) were required, of which 4.12 złotys were off-farm purchases. For every 1 złoty value added from private farms, the corresponding outlays amounted to 1.80 złotys, of which 0.53 złoty was off-farm purchases (see L. Rzeńdowski 1980).

15 According to a Polish agricultural economist:

> An outstanding characteristic of the agrarian structure of private farming in Poland is its stagnation. The structure has not changed since 1950.... During the same period, tremendous changes have taken place in the agrarian structure of private farming in Europe and the whole world. It finds expression in the growth of the average size of the farms and a concentration of land.... In this respect our private farms are left far behind.
>
> (A. Szemberg 1980: 26).

16 Value added and productive investment in agriculture (yearly average of 1971–5 and 1976–80, in złotys of 1977).

	1971–5		*1976–80*	
	In million złoty	*Per cent*	*In million złoty*	*Per cent*
Value added of which:	226.168	100	199.047	100
Socialized farms	19.574	8.7	13.943	7.0
Private farms	206.594	91.3	185.104	93.0
Productive investment of which:	68.174	100	100.702	100
Socialized farms	42.696	62.6	72.471	72.0
Private farms	25.477	37.4	28.231	28.0

Sources: Calculated from *Rocznik Statystyczny Rolnictwa: Gospodarka Zywnościowa* 1980: 26; 1982: 111 and 204–5.

5 LABOUR SUPPLY

1 The table below shows the highest increase (in per cent being measured by a three-year moving average) of the age-specific death rates of men.

Age group	*Increase (in per cent)*	*Period*
30–4	19	1970–9
35–9	36	1966–79
40–4	42	1965–79
45–9	50	1965–79
50–4	36	1966–79
55–9	22	1966–79

Sources: M. Okólski 1983: 214; 1988: 127.

2 For more information over the deterioration of the state of public health in the 1970s, see J. Mijakowska 1981. For the deterioration of the working conditions and the health situation of the workers in the 1970s, see M. Tatur 1983: 56–68; for the deterioration of the health services, see L.F. Millard 1981 and KOR Document 1981.

3 The following table illustrates the increase (in per cent) in the three major causes of death (which accounted for around 72 per cent of total deaths) among men in their 'prime' during the period 1964–79.

Age group	*Cardiovascular diseases*	*Cancer*	*Accidents*[a]
35–9	70	4	70
40–4	83	17	69
45–9	105	34	90
50–4	67	37	74

Source: M. Okólski 1988: 131.
Note: [a]Including accidents at work, road accidents, poisoning and suicides.

4 Working age group or productive age group is defined conventionally according to ages. In Polish statistics, one of the three statistical notions of working-age population defines the productive age group for men between 18–64 years and for women between 18–59 years.

5 The Polish statistics measure and include in the 'economically active' ('pracujących') group those persons who are in paid employment or perform work which produces income, where part-time labour is converted to fully employed equivalents (M. Olędzki 1978: 82–3; *Rocznik Statystyczny* 1980: 50). This concept raises a number of problems. For instance, household work, raising children and caring for the sick are counted as 'non-economic' activities, while part of the domestic work of the members of a farmer's household is listed as an 'economic' activity.

6 A time-budget study of full-time working women in non-agricultural activities conducted at the end of 1960 estimated that on working days a woman worker spent on average nine hours and nineteen minutes on paid work (including commuting time to work), five hours and thirty-eight minutes on household tasks (including time spent on shopping), eight hours and five minutes on sleeping, eating and personal hygiene, leaving only one hour and ten minutes as free time (H. Strzeminska 1970: 261). A time-budget study of women working on night shift in the textile industry in Łódz, conducted in the early 1970s, reckoned that apart from the time spent on paid work, six-and-a-half hours daily were spent on household labour and only four-and-a-half hours were left for sleep (cited in M. Tatur 1979: 237)! The shortages of crèches, kindergartens and homes for old people were severe. It has been estimated that in the 1970s the available capacity of these facilities could satisfy less than one-tenth of the needs (A. Tymowski 1982b: 144–5). The deepening economic crisis from the late 1970s onwards led to longer time spent on shopping, queuing and commuting to work, etc., at the cost of free time, rest and sleep.

7

> Economic activity of women is, within certain limits, a function of the incomes and social policies. Surveys show that 77 per cent of women who began to work in the cities were motivated mainly by the desire to supplement the household income.
>
> (M. Kabaj 1975b: 293)

8 Due to the low household income of small farmers, their lack of successors and

inadequate pensions, a very high proportion of old farmers (72–98 per cent) is still forced to work. By the end of the 1970s nearly one in three private farms was managed by farmers over 65 years old (J. Lopato 1985). According to the 1984 population census, the proportion of old people who remained 'economically active' in agriculture was even growing, indicating the increasing ageing of agricultural labour. A Polish expert said: 'More than half of the women over 70 years old are still actively self-employed [in agriculture]. In [private] agriculture, occupational activities last until the moment when the person has completely lost the ability to work' (M. Olędzki 1978: 106). Although the population censuses have registered very low participation rates of old people in the non-agricultural sector, their engagement in 'non-economic activities', such as household work, caring for children, shopping, standing in queues and other 'informal' activities to supplement their meagre pensions, was widespread.

9 The length of vacation depended in principle on the duration of employment. The average length of vacation of industrial workers increased from sixteen days in 1960 to twenty-one days in 1979 (*Mały Rocznik Statystyczny* 1980: 105). A limited number of free Saturdays were introduced; six in 1974, twelve in 1975, but less during the second half of the 1970s (W. Szafarczyk 1982: 227).

10 According to official statistics, both the number of accidents at the work place and employees registered as suffering from occupational diseases increased by at least around 30 per cent and 82 per cent respectively in the 1970s compared to the figures of the preceding decade. Due to manipulation, lack of control and enterprises' bias to the under-reporting of accidents combined with the great shortages of medical inspectors and modern equipment to undertake extensive diagnosis, Polish experts estimated that the real numbers of accidents at work and victims of occupational diseases were between four to five times the official figure (A. Hansen 1984: 412–24).

11 The number of personnel with higher technical education per 10,000 employees in the non-agricultural sector:

Poland (1971)	196
Great Britain (1964)	69
West Germany (1959)	40
France (1962)	71
USA (1966)	58

See M. Kabaj 1975b: 18–19. Others argued that the ratio of employment of personnel with higher education to total employment in the non-agricultural sector in Poland (as in other CMEA countries) did not diverge significantly from that in the industrialized West. The employment structure in Poland did, however, differ considerably, having a much higher percentage of personnel with higher technical education (J. Tymowski 1982a: 83).

12 For an extensive review of 'life-aims', orientations and attitudes of young Polish workers based on empirical surveys conducted by Polish sociologists in the 1970s, see M. Tatur 1983: 91–102.

6 LABOUR POLICY

1 'Despite transitional, frictional, structural, seasonal, political and disguised unemployment, it seems . . . to be reasonable to describe the situation normally existing in the state socialist countries of "full employment"' (M. Ellman 1979a: 12).

2 Kalecki analysed the determination of growth rates in state socialist economies and the various barriers such as the slow growth in consumption incommensurate with

the population's expectation, labour shortage, foreign trade imbalances, etc., which were all connected with the policy of accelerated economic growth or technical modernization. See M. Kalecki 1963.

3 The law on 'social parasites' and the 'work shy', passed in 1982, obliged persons unemployed for more than three months to register at the local labour offices and to accept jobs offered.

4 According to estimates made by Western observers, the actual number of unemployed at the end of the 1960s was 4–6 times for men and 6–8 times for women the official unemployment figures (U. Fox 1977: 216–17). J. Górski, the former Vice-Minister of Labour, Wages and Social Affairs, noted that with reference to the labour market in the early 1980s, for practical purposes the official unemployment figures should be multiplied by four and the number of vacant jobs should be adjusted downwards (*Polityka*, 31, 1982).

5 Different estimates suggested that before the Second World War between a quarter and a half of the agricultural labour force was 'redundant' (see A. Zauberman 1964: 82–3; M.L. Carmelo 1968: 186–7).

6 Estimates of actual growth in average real wages for the period 1950–5 differ widely, ranging from zero growth to 28 per cent growth according to official statistics. L. Beskid estimates the growth in average real wages for the whole Six Year Plan at about 10 per cent with large fluctuations, ranging from a 13 per cent drop in 1953 to a 9 per cent rise in 1955 (see J. Meller 1977: 51–6). Rationing of scarce consumer goods, open and repressed inflation, black markets, etc. were widespread.

7 Extensive growth relies more on the growth of investment and employment as growth factors than on growth in labour productivity, technical progress and innovations, as in the case of intensive growth. For a more detailed and theoretical analysis of extensive and intensive growth see Z. Fallenbuchl 1973: 233–54; M. Nasiłowski 1974a: 71–83.

8 See the Prime Minister's speech at the IVth Central Committee Plenary Meeting published in *Nowe Drogi*, 4, 1972: 12–13 and E. Marek 1972: 114.

9 The so-called farmer-worker group, workers living in the country-side with farming as a sideline occupation, formed a reserve of cheap labour for the construction sector, light industry, etc., consisting largely of unskilled labour performing heavy, monotonous and, in some cases, jobs hazardous to health. It was estimated that the size of of the rural–urban commuting labourers increased from around 1.7 million persons in early 1968 (constituting around 20 per cent of the total number employed in the state sector) to more than 2.9 million persons at the end of 1973 (i.e. 27 per cent of the total number employed in the state sector). This phenomenon was common in the voivodships of Warsaw, Cracow, Upper Silesia and Opolski (Olędzki 1978: 183).

10 For more information on the aims and assumptions underlying the Five Year Plan (1976–80) see F. Kubiczek 1976: 1–9: and *Gospodarka Planowa* 1977: 61–8.

11 During a session of the experts' commission of the Council of Ministers, Kalecki jokingly said: 'For many years I was paid in England to conduct studies in order to eliminate unemployment, but here you are paying me in order to create it' (M. Kalecki 1982: 324).

12 In general the wage-bill formula could be expressed as follows:

$$F_1 = F_0 \left[1 + R\left(\frac{PD_1 - PD_0}{PD_0}\right)\right]$$

where subscript $_{0}$, $_{1}$ indicates the previous year and the current year;
F = wage bill;
PD = value added;
R = the norm relating changes in the wage-bill to changes in value added, $0 < R < 1$.

In general value-added represents the difference between sales and material costs and capital charges.
$PD = Sk - (Mk + K)$
where:
Sk = realized sales;
Mk = material cost of production (capital depreciation excluded);
K = capital repayment, interest charges and capital depreciation.
In general net profit could be expressed as follows:
$Z = FA - p + d + e + a - i - n - k$
where
Z = net profit;
FA = financial accumulation = realized sales minus material costs plus labour costs, depreciation and interest costs;
p = turnover tax and other sales taxes;
d and e = various subsidies paid to the producer to keep the price below the average cost of production;
a = windfall gains or losses to be removed;
i = tax on fixed assets;
n = tax on wage-bill;
k = repayments of investments credits.

13 For a more extensive description and analysis of the WOG reform, see D.M. Nuti 1980.

14 For an extensive description and analysis of the Polish economic reform of 1982, see S. Gomulka and J. Rostowski 1984: 386–405; B. Simatupang 1983b: 34–9; D.M. Nuti 1986b.

15 The economic or planning system that emerged from the reform of 1982 has been described by different authors as 'informal command planning' (S. Gomulka and J. Rostowski 1984: 401) or a system of 'authorizations and bargaining' ('uznaniowo-przetargowy'), where the centre and enterprises are constantly negotiating over the scope of 'government orders' or 'operational programmes', material supplies, hard currency, employment, prices, taxes and amortizations, subsidies and investment (W.I. Otta, 1985). The results of the negotiating process are often specific to individual enterprises or industrial sectors. The role of the vertical bargaining and individual norms prevented the emergence of a built-in market mechanism in the state industrial sector.

16 Because of the low wages policy, necessarily accompanying the drive towards full employment, and insufficient social and fiscal contributions paid by the firms, enterprises did not pay the total actual costs incurred for the 'reproduction of labour', such as the cost of training and education of the workers and employees, health care, old age pensions, etc. From the firms' point of view, labour costs were low, and hence they tended to discourage economies of labour.

17 In response to the letter of the managers, an anonymous worker-overseer from Cracow came up with a proposal 'to create a reserve of unemployed bureaucrats, half-educated engineers, negligent laboratory assistants, bad managers and political cadres. They are the source of every misfortune which destroy the result of the work of good engineers and economists and the workers as well' (*Polityka*, 11-11-1978).

7 THE VIEWS OF POLISH ECONOMISTS

1 For a good analysis and insight into the mechanism, rules and practices of censorship in Poland during the second half of the 1970s see: J.L. Curry 1984. This book is a collection of translated classified documents on censorship smuggled out to the West

in 1977 by a former censor in Cracow, supplemented by an introduction on the Polish media by the editor. The documents were published for the first time by the Polish emigré publishing house Aneks in 1977, smuggled back into Poland and reprinted afterwards by underground publishing networks.

2 For a comprehensive list of Polish dissident writings in the second half of the 1970s, see J.M. Preibisz and J.L. Curry 1981; P. Raina 1981. For a brief analytical survey of the economic writings of the Polish dissidents see W. Brus 1979b: 205–16.

3 This survey is based on the following published documents, reports and articles: A memorandum prepared by a group of anonymous economists who were close to the KOR (Committee for the Defence of the Workers), 'Uwagi o sytuacji gospodarczej kraju' (On the economic situation in Poland), 1978; a transcript of a discussion among economists on the economic situation in Poland and criticism of the above memorandum published as 'Diagnoza i programme' ('A diagnosis and a programme'), in *Droga*, 1, 1978, a monthly which was close to the KPN (Confederation for an Independent Poland); S. Karol, 'Dzień dzisiejszy i jutro polskiej gospodarki' ('The Polish economy today and tomorrow'), *Głos*, 7, 1978; A. Zawada, 'Program dla polskiego Kadara' (Programme for a Polish Kadar), *Głos*, 11–12, 1978; E. Ryabarska, 'Kto zreformuje gospodarke?' ('Who will reform the economy?'), *Głos*, 11–12, 1978; Z. Karlinski, 'Uwagi do uwag' ('Comments upon the comments'), *Głos*, 11–12, 1978. The first three publications listed above were reprinted in the quarterly *Aneks*, 20, 1979. Furthermore our brief survey covers also J. Bartecki's booklet, *Gospodarka na manowcach* (*An economy in disorder*), 1978, plus two reports on the DiP (Experience and the Future), 'Raport o stanie rzeczpospolitej i o drogach do jej naprawy – wersja wstępna' ('Report on the state of the republic and on the ways to renovate – preliminary version'), 1978 and 'Jak z tego wyjsc?' ('Which way out?'), 1980. An English translation of the two reports was published as *Poland: The State of the Republic*, M. Vale (ed.) 1981. The two DiP reports are based on questionnaires to and responses from more than sixty intellectuals, scientists and journalists representing a group of 'loyal oppositionists' having links with the communist party elite.

4 The full title of this is 'Sprawozdanie. Z prac komisji KC PZPR powołanej dla wyjaśnienia przyczyn i przebiegu konfliktów społecznych w dziejach Polski Ludowej' and was published in *Nowe Drogi* (special issue), May 1983: 6–78. For a good analysis of the *Kubiak Report* and the changing official interpretations of Poland's post-war crises, reflecting factional struggles in the leadership and the changing political situations, see R. Taras 1986.

5 The transcript of the secret hearings of the top members of the Gierek leadership before the Grabski Commission showed the inconsistency, weakness and utter incompetence of the leadership in coping with the growing political and economic difficulties in the second half of the 1970s. See G. Pomian (ed.) 1986.

6 The government partly bore the responsibility for the rapid increase of wages and inflation when it granted a wage increase to the workers in July–August 1980. The government was frightened and hoped that the workers would renounce political demands (W. Kuczyński 1985: 51).

7 W. Lamentowicz, in underlining the minority situation of Polish communists, speaks of a threefold minority position during their formation and strivings towards modernization: (i) the left as a minority in the political life of the entire country; (ii) the communists as a minority among several leftist currents; (iii) and finally the Stalinist doctrinaires as a minority among the Polish communists of the time 1986: 14–18).

8 The authors told us that they wrote a discussion paper outlining the above ideas and suggestions in the context of a 'nation-wide discussion' on economic growth strategies before the convocation of the VIth Party congress held at the end of 1971. The paper was accepted for publication in *Polityka* for March 1971 but the manuscript

was confiscated under the censorship laws and remained unpublished (W. Herer and W. Sadowski 1985: 395–6).

9 The distinction between nationalization ('etatism') and socialization of the basic means of production, based on the democratic participation of direct producers in the decision-making, is crucial to Brus's argument for economic and political reforms of really existing socialism (W. Brus 1975).

8 LEGITIMACY

1 G. Sanford, in a study of Polish communism, concludes that 'in spite of over 3 decades of power, the Communist leadership was never able to turn the PZPR into a wholly reliable instrument for Communist rule in Poland. There is reliable evidence regarding the split and faction-ridden character of the PZPR leadership, especially in times of crisis' (G. Sanford 1983: 36).

2 She observes that the 'so-called "ideological" legitimating arguments are more often traps for the ruling group itself, limiting its freedom of manoeuvre, rather than a catalyst for social involvement. The situation described above is the result of the abandonment of a utopian ideal, even for Party functionaries themselves. This ideal persists only as a magic system, with symbols used as the instruments of inter-organizational games and levers of particular interests ... their particular power lies in the way they ensnare the ruling group in its own legitimacy arguments. Caught in the trap of its own myths and rationalizations of previous activity, the ruling group is now easily blackmailed by those at executive levels' (J. Staniszkis 1979: 167).

3 An interview in the early 1980s with J. Berman, in political disgrace since 1956 but a former member of the PUWP's highest leadership, on the subject of the 'geopolitical' imperative, is illuminating. He accused M. Mikołajczyk, the former Prime Minister of the Polish government-in-exile in London and Deputy Prime Minister of the Polish Provisional Government of 1945–7, of lack of political insight. Mikołajczyk, according to Berman, was

> clinging to absurdities, imagining that we live on the moon instead of on the Oder and Vistula.... He refused to see that if the road of communication to Europe leads through Poland, the Soviet Union has to be certain that road won't be cut-off.... He wanted to deceive.... He wanted to pretend that Poland was Finland, but Poland could not have been Finland, because Finland lies in a different part of Europe. It doesn't pose a threat to the Soviet Union and it isn't a strategic road, and that is why it could be permitted methods of government of one sort or another; but that was something we could not permit ourselves.... I have said repeatedly that I would have to give Mikołajczyk an F in geography, because all he had to do was to look at a map and see where Poland was and how its fate depended on a given set of circumstances or a given distribution of power. Mikołajczyk couldn't grasp that the Soviet Union had to ensure that Poland was secure, in other words that it wouldn't rear up; and in a sense this meant that it had to be completely subordinated – yes, that's right, subordinated.
>
> (T. Toranska 1987: 276–8).

4 Generous pension provisions were decreed in 1972 for those holding major positions in the Party and state (Party secretaries at the central and provincial levels, ministers and vice-ministers, directors and deputy directors of central institutions, etc.) and the members of their families (P. Lewis 1984b: 30–1). A widespread and tacitly legitimized corruption and acquisitiveness among the state and Party bureaucracy (M. Hirszowicz 1986: 135–46) were further examples of this policy. The draft *Kubiak*

Report speaks of the 'practices common in the 1970s of allowing special, often undeclared, privileges and pay increases to the higher echelons of the *apparat*. . . . The system, centralised and bureaucratically run, preferred and rewarded obedience; it brought about an increase in privilege and injustice' (*Nowe Drogi 1983*).

9 THE AFTERMATH OF THE ECONOMIC CRISIS

1 For an extensive analysis of Jaruzelski's economic policy and achievement under martial law, see G. Blazyca 1985: 428–36; Z.M. Fallenbuchl 1984: 513–27.

2 For an extensive analysis of the realization of the Three Year Plan (1983–5), see A. Karpinski 1986b: 237–43; KRG 1986a.

3 The average utilized ('przepracowane') working time in socialized industry increased from 1,861 hours in 1982 to 1,903 hours in 1985, largely on account of a large amount of overtime, whilst non-utilized time due to sickness, maternity leave and absence without leave was falling during the same period. See *Rocznik Statystyczny* 1986: 76. The growth in labour productivity during this period was partly attributed to improved labour discipline; see KRG 1987a.

4 For a detailed description of the problems of the Five Year Plan (1986–1990) see Z. Szeliga 1985: 405–12; L. Ochocki 1987: 59–64; J. Pinkowski 1987: 64–8; Z.M. Fallenbuchl 1991: 17–37.

5 See among others: M. Nasiłowski 1985; KRG 1986b; J. Pinkowski 1987: 64–8.

6 In 1983, enterprises' investment constituted 48.6 per cent of total investment in the state and cooperative sectors, in 1985, 52.4 per cent and in 1989, 61.9 per cent. See *Mały Rocznik Statystyczny* 1987: 124 and *Rocznik Statystyczny* 1990: 238.

7 See KRG 1987b; KRG 1988a; T. Jezioranski 1988.

8 In 1989, total investment in the socialized sector at constant prices fell by 3.4 per cent; in the construction sector investment fell by 27.5 per cent, in transportation by 31.6 per cent, in communication by 7.8 per cent and in agriculture by 8.7 per cent. Total investment in state industry, however, grew by 3.8 per cent in 1989, but investment in coal mining fell by 22 per cent, in electric power industry by 17.5 per cent and in engineering industry 3.8 per cent. These falls were accompanied by considerable rise of investment in the chemical, light and food processing industries, varying between 20–39 per cent. See *Rocznik Statystyczny* 1990: 235 and 280.

9 A study of the garment industry showed widely varying levels of enterprise performance, but there was no necessary link between wage increases and labour productivity (D. Kopycińska 1987: 416–18). The former Vice-Premier Sadowski said: 'We have a list of firms, showing that during the last several months [of the first half of 1988] high increases of average wages were occurring at the same time as an absolute drop in output of sometimes up to 50 per cent' (cited in B. Brach 1988).

10 From about 1987 until the collapse of state socialism a version of privatization in the state sector, (making owners of the *nomenklatura*), developed in Poland. J. Staniszkis distinguished six forms of the combination of political power and private capital in production:

(i) due to shortages of inputs (e.g. labour and foreign exchange, etc.), fixed assets of the formally state-owned enterprises could be put to use by private firms set up by the managers of the state enterprises;

(ii) certain functions of the enterprises (e.g. computer programmeming and design) were to be done by private firms set up by the managerial staff and employees;

(iii) the leasing of selected departments of the state enterprises to private firms whose shares were often owned by persons associated with the managerial staff of the state enterprise;

(iv) firms owned by private persons and the Treasury;

(v) the participation of the managerial staff of the state enterprises in joint firms with foreign capital;
(vi) firms owned by political parties, trade unions and social organizations.

(J. Staniszkis 1991: 38–49)

11 According to official figures Poland paid US$18.1 billion (US$12.2 billion for interest and US$5.9 billion for principal payments) to service its hard currency debt over the period of 1981–9. Over the same period, Poland received US$8.7 billion in new loans, of which nearly one-half were in 1981 (K. Kalicki 1991: 119 and 128; I. Antowska-Bartosiewicz and W. Malecki 1992: 11–12). The regime considered that it had made sufficient sacrifices and that it deserved new and larger loans to help to step up growth of output and hard currency exports (Z. Kamecki 1988: 12–13).

12 The *Theses* were originally published in *Rzeczpospolita* (1987) 'Tezy w sprawie II etapu reformy gospodarczej – projekt', 17 April; The *Programme* was originally published in *Rzeczpospolita* (1987) 'Program realizacyjny drugiego etapu reformy gospodarczej (projekt)', 22 October. For an extensive analysis of the second stage of the economic reform, see, H. Gabrisch 1989: 175–90.

13 A similar situation occurred in Hungary when the Party lost control of the political and economic processes in 1989. See M. Csanadi 1991: 1085–99.

14 According to underestimated official statistics the share of private sector at current prices increased from 17.2 per cent of the net material product in 1980 to 19.2 per cent in 1989, of which 9.5 per cent was contributed by agriculture and 9.7 per cent by the registered non-agricultural private sector. Employment in the private sector increased from 4.6 million (26 per cent of total employment) in 1980 to 5.1 million (29.6 per cent of total employment) in 1989. The structure of employment (and output) in the private sector, however, changed significantly in the 1980s. Employment in private agriculture fell from 4 million in 1980 to 3.5 million in 1989, while employment in the non-agricultural private sector increased rapidly from 0.6 million to 1.5 million during the same period (*Rocznik Statystyczny* 1990: 93 and 121). New forms of private activities such as the 'Polonia' firms, joint ventures with foreign capital, mixed state–private companies and so on had developed in the 1980s.

15 Estimates of the value of the 'second economy' differed considerably among authors, varying from around 12 per cent of the disposable income in 1985 (M. Bednarski 1987: 21) to around 25 per cent of the disposable income in 1986 (A. Szablewski 1988: 80).

16 It was estimated that by mid-1990 about 10–20 per cent of the value of state fixed assets was privately owned by the former *nomenklatura* in Poland as a result of the privatization of the state sector under communist rule (J. Staniszkis 1991: x).

17 Whereas hard currency savings accounted for only 15.5 per cent of total savings accounts (at the black market rate of exchange) in 1983, in late 1987 they represented 56 per cent (cited in J. Rostowski 1989: 198).

18 In order to ensure an absolute majority in the Parliament, 65 per cent of the seats was reserved for the Polish United Workers Party and its allies (the Democratic Party and United Peasant Party), and only 35 per cent of the seats was reserved for non-Party candidates to be contested freely.

19 Under a completely different and new configuration of political forces, General Jaruzelski resigned from the Presidency and Lech Walesa was elected directly at the second round to become President of Poland in the autumn of 1990.

BIBLIOGRAPHY

Adam, J. (1982) 'Similarities and differences in the treatment of labour shortages', in J. Adam (ed.) *Employment Policies in the Soviet Union and Eastern Europe*, London: Macmillan.

Adamski, W. (1980) 'Typy orientacji życiowych młodego i starszego pokolenia Polaków', *Studia Socjologiczne*, 1.

—— (1985) 'Aspiracje – interesy – konflikt', *Studia Socjologiczne*, 2.

Albinowski, S. (1981) 'U źródeł załamania gospodarczego', *Gospodarka Planowa*, 7–8.

—— (1982) *Alarm dla gospodarki trwa*, Warsaw.

Aneks (1979) 'Diagnoza i program. Dyskusja o sytnacji gospodarczej' (hereafter *Diagnoza*), 20: first printed in *Droga* (1978), 1.

Aneks (1979) 'Uwagi o sytuacji gospodarczej kraju', 20 (hereafter referred to as *Uwagi*).

Antowska-Bartosiewicz, I. and Malecki, W. (1992) 'Foreign debt, foreign capital, stabilization and transformation', *Working Papers*, 22, Warsaw: Institute of Finance.

Ash, T. (1985), *The Polish Revolution*, New York: Vintage Books.

Askanas, B. and Laski, K. (1985) 'Consumer prices and private consumption in Poland and Austria', *Journal of Comparative Economics*, 9, 2: 164–77.

Baka, W. (1983) *Polska reforma gospodarcza*, Warsaw.

Bank i Kredyt (1982a) 'Biłans płatniczy PRL', 3.

Bank i Kredyt (1982b) 'Bilans pieniężnych przychodów i wydatków ludności', 7–8.

Bank i Kredyt (1983a) 'Biłans płatniczy PRL za rok 1982', 6.

Bank i Kredyt (1983b) 'Bilans peiniężnych i wydatków ludności w 1982 r', 6.

Barcikowski, K. (1977) 'Zadania w dziedzinie rozwoju produkcji roślinnej i hodowli oraz lepszego wykorzystania rezerw gospodarki rolnej', *Nowe Drogi*, 2.

Bartczak, H. and Bogus, A. (1988) 'Samodzielność przedsiębiorstw – niepokoje i nadzieje. Raport i badan', *Gospodarka Planowa*, 9.

Bartecki, J. (1978) *Gospodarka na manowcach*, Paris.

Bauer, T. (1978), 'Investment cycles in planned economies', *Acta Oeconomica*, 21, 3: 243–60.

Bednarski, M. (1984) 'Drugi obieg', *Życie Gospodarcze*, 35.

—— (1987) 'Gospodarka "drugiego obiegu" w Polsce', *Wektory Gospodarki*, 2.

Berg, A. and Sachs, J. (1992) 'Structural adjustment and international trade in Eastern Europe: the case of Poland', *Economic Policy*, 14: 117–73.

Bialer, S. (1980) *Stalin's successors: leadership, stability and change in the Soviet Union*, London: Cambridge University Press.

Bien, W. (1989), 'Jak zwalczać inflację?', *Gospodarka Planowa*, 8–9.

Blazyca, G. (1985) 'The Polish economy under martial law – a dissenting view', *Soviet Studies*, 38, 3: 428–36.

Blazynski, G. (1980) *Flashpoint Poland*, New York: Pergamon Press.

Boffito, C. (1988) 'Reforms and export promotion', in P. Marer and W. Siwinski (eds), *Creditworthiness and Reform in Poland*, Bloomington: Indiana University Press.
Boguszewski, J. (1979) 'Procesy inwestycyjne w latach 1971–1976', *Studia Finansowe*, 27.
Bojarski, J. *et al.* (1981) *Kryzys gospodarki polskiej*, Warsaw.
Bożyk, P. (1983) *Marzenia i rzeczywistość*, czyli anatomia polskiego kryzysu, Warsaw.
Böhm, E. (1985) *Die Krise des polnischen Aussenhandelssystems*, Hamburg: Verlag Weltarchiv.
Brach, B. (1988) 'Przyjemność systemowa', *Życie Gospodarcze*, 26.
Brus, W. (1975) *Uspołecznienie a ustrój polityczny*, Uppsala: Anets.
—— (1979a) 'Na marginesie "Uwag o sytuacji gospodarczej kraju"', *Aneks*, 20.
—— (1979b) 'Problemy gospodarcze polski', *Kultura*, Paris, 7–8.
—— (1982) 'Aims, methods and political determinants of the economic policy of Poland 1970–1980', in A. Nove, H.H. Hohmann and G.H. Seidenstecher (eds), *The East European Economies in the 1970s*, London: Butterworth.
—— (1984) 'O gospodarce Polski i bloku sowieckiego' interview in *Kultura*, Paris, 5.
—— (1985) 'The political economy of Polish reforms', *Praxis International*, 5, 2: 195–208.
Brus, W. and Kowalik, T. (1983) 'Socialism and development', *Cambridge Journal of Economics*, 7, 3–4: 243–55.
Budnikowski, A. and Misala, J. (1981) 'Polski eksport w latach siedemdziesiątych', *Handel Zagraniczny*, 2.
Bugaj, R. (1986) 'Dlaczego kryzys się przedłuża', *Tygodnik Powszechny*, 1.
—— and Kowalik, T. (1986) 'Kryzys polski w oczach ekonomistów', *Więź*, 10.
Bulak, A. (1979) 'Dlaczego nie chcą hodować?', *Życie Gospodarcze*, 11.
Carmelo, M.L. (1968) 'Unemployment in Socialist Countries: Soviet Union, East Europe, China and Cuba', Cornell University, Ph.D.
Charemza, W. (1989a) 'Disequilibrium modelling of consumption in the centrally planned economy', in C. Davis and W. Charemza (eds), *Models of Disequilibrium and Shortage in Centrally Planned Economies*, London: Chapman and Hall.
—— (1989b) 'Computational controversies in disequilibrium and shortage modelling of centrally planned economies', *Journal of Economic Surveys*, 3, 4: 305–24.
Chelinski, R. (1964) 'Etapowy charakter rozwoju gospodarczego w Polsce Ludowej', *Ekonomista*, 5.
CIA (1986a) 'Polish agriculture: policy and prospects', *East European Economies: Slow Growth in the 1980s*, 3, Washington: Congress Papers.
—— (1986b) 'Eastern Europe faces up to the debt crisis', *East European Economies: Slow growth in the 1980s*, 2, Washington: Congress Papers.
Cieslik, J. (1983) 'The regulation of technology transfer in Poland', *Osteuropa Wirtschaft*, 28, 3: 217–33.
Clapp, A. and Shapiro, H. (1986) 'Financial crisis in Eastern Europe', in *East European Economies: Slow Growth in the 1980s*, 2, Washington: Congress Papers.
Cook, E. (1984) 'Agricultural reform in Poland: background and prospects', *Soviet Studies*, 36, 3: 406–26.
Crane, K. (1986) 'Foreign trade decisionmaking under balance of payments pressure: Poland versus Hungary', in *East European Economies: Slow Growth in the 1980s*, 3, Washington: Congress Papers.
—— (1991) 'An assessment of the economic reforms in Poland's state-owned industry', in D. Kemme (ed.), *Economic Reform in Poland: The Aftermath of Martial Law 1981–1988*, Greenwich: Jai Press.
Csanadi, M. (1991) 'The diary of decline: a case-study of the disintegration of the party in one district in Hungary', *Soviet Studies*, 43, 6: 1085–99.

Culbertson Jr, W.P. and Amacher, R.C. (1978) 'Inflation in the planned economies: some estimates for Eastern Europe', *Southern Economic Journal*, 45, 2: 380–94.

Curry, J.L. (ed.) (1984) *The Black Book of Polish Censorship*, New York: Vintage Books.

Czajka, Z. (1981) 'Nieprawidłowości w polityce płac w latach 1971–1980', *Praca i Zabiezpieczenie Społeczne*, 23, 10–11.

—— (1982) 'Ocena systemu płac w latach siedemdziesiątych', *Studia i Materiały*, 5.

Czepurko, A. (1982) 'Kilka uwag w sprawie handlu zagranicznego', *Nowe Drogi*, 11.

Dankowski, H. (1975) 'Planowanie kształcenia kadr wykwalifikowanych na tle prognostycznych potrzeb gospodarki narodowej', *Polska 2000*, Wrocław.

Davis, C. and Charemza, W. (1989) *Models of Disequilibrium and Shortage in Centrally Planned Economies*, London: Chapman and Hall.

Dembowski, J. (1983) 'Energetyczna bariera wzrostu gospodarczego Polski', *Gospodarka Planowa*, 12.

Deniszczuk, M. (1988) 'Drugi etap czy kolejna runda?', *Handel Zagraniczny*, 2.

Dlouhy, V. (1989) 'Disequilibrium models of the Czechoslovak economy', in C. Davis and W. Charemza (eds), *Models of Disequilibrium and Shortage in Centrally Planned Economies*, London: Chapman and Hall.

Dobiegala-Korona, B. (1987) 'O Narodowym Planie Społeczno-Gospodarczym Polski na latach 1986–1990', *Gospodarka Planowa*, 5.

Dobrowolska, D. (1985) 'Wartość pracy i jej przemian we współczesnym spoleczeństwie Polskim. Próba diagnozy', *Studia Socjologiczne*, 3–4.

Dominiak, P. (1981) 'Płace w latach siedemdziesiątych', *Polityka Społeczna*, 9.

Droga (1978) 'Diagnoza i program. Dyskusja o sytnacji gospodarczej', 1 (hereafter *Diagnoza*); reprinted in *Aneks* (1979) 20.

Dubczynski, K. and Dytman, M. (1981) 'Produkcja i gospodarka materiałowa Polski na tle wybranych krajów', *Wiadomości Statystyczne*, 7.

Dudzinski, W. (1972) 'Czy stopa akumulacji nas uszczęśliwi?', *Życie Gospodarcze*, 47.

Dzenio, K. (1975) 'Demograficzno-zatrudnieniowe uwarunkowania prognoz kadrowych', *Polska 2000*. Kadry kwalifikowane w perspektywie lat 1990–2000, Wrocław.

—— and Fiejka, Z. (1978) 'Factors determining the size of labour force in Poland and long term changes in the structure of its use', *Oeconomica Polona*, 5, 2: 121–50.

Dziewulski, P. and Maciejewski, A. (1980) 'Nierównomierność inwestowania a ekspansja inwestycyjna', *Gospodarka Planowa*, 4.

Dziewulski, P. Mizielinska, W., Smuga, T. and Sobota, J. (1987) 'Zachowania przedsiębiorstw w 1 etapie reformy', *Gospodarka Planowa*, 6.

Ellman, M. (1979a) *Full Employment: lessons from state socialism*, Leiden: H.E. Stenfert Kroese.

—— (1979b), *Socialist Planning* (1st edn) Cambridge: Cambridge University Press.

—— (1989), *Socialist Planning* (2nd edn) Cambridge: Cambridge University Press.

—— and Simatupang, B. (1982) 'Odnowa in statistics', *Soviet Studies*, 1: 111–17.

—— and Simatupang, B. (1983) 'The Polish economic crisis', *Critique*, December, 16: 123–38.

Fallenbuchl, Z. (1973) 'Industrial structure and the intensive pattern of development in Poland', *Jahrbuch der Wirtschaft Osteuropa*, 4: 233–54.

—— (1977a) 'The Polish economy in the 1970s' in *East European Economies Post-Helsinki*, Washington: Congress Papers.

—— (1977b) 'Internal migration and economic development under socialism: the case of Poland', in A. Brown and E. Neuberger (eds) *Internal Migration: a comparative perspective*, New York: Academic Press.

—— (1981) 'The Polish economy at the beginnning of the 1980s', *East European Economic Assessment*, Washington: Congress Papers.

—— (1982) 'Employment Policies in Poland', in J. Adam (ed.), *Employment Policies in the Soviet Union and Eastern Europe*, London: Macmillan.

—— (1983) *East–West Technology Transfer: Study of Poland 1971–1980*, Paris: Organisation for Economic Cooperation and Development (OECD).

—— (1984) 'The Polish economy under martial law', *Soviet Studies*, 36, 4: 513–27.

—— (1988) 'Present state of the economic reform', in P. Marer and M. Siwinski (eds), *Creditworthiness and Reform in Poland*, Bloomington: Indiana University Press.

—— (1991) 'The 1986–1990 Five Year Plan: strategy and reform dependency', in D. Kemme (ed.), *Economic Reform in Poland: the aftermath of martial law 1981–1988*, Greenwich: Jai Press.

—— Neuberger, E. and d'Andrea Tyson, L. (1977) 'East European reactions to international commodity inflation', in *East European Economies Post-Helsinki*, Washington: Congress Papers.

Fehér, F. (1982) 'Paternalism as mode of legitimation in soviet-type Societies', in T.H. Rigby and F. Fehér (eds), *Political Legitimation in Communist States*, London: Macmillan.

—— Heller, A. and Markus, G. (1983) *Dictatorship over Needs*, Oxford: Basil Blackwell.

Feiwel, G. (1974) 'Causes and consequences of disguised industrial unemployment in a socialist economy', *Soviet Studies*, 26, 3: 344–62.

Fick, B. (1970) *Polityka zatrudnienia a płace i bodźce*, Warsaw.

Finanse (1982), 'Bilans płatniczy Polski w latach 1971–81', 6: 59

Fink, G. (1983) 'Poland's statistics on current account of the balance of payment in convertible currencies', (mimeographed) *Forschungsberichte*, 91, Vienna: Wiener Institut für Internationale Wirtschaftsvergleich.

Fiszman, J. (1975) 'Poland: the pursuit of legitimacy', in I. Volgyes (ed.), *Political Socialization in Eastern Europe*, New York: Praeger Publishers.

Fox, U. (1977) 'Beschäftigungsstruktur und Arbeitskräftepolitik in Polen', in H. Höhmann (ed.), *Arbeitsmarkt und Wirtschaftsplanung*, Köln: Europaische Verlaganstalt.

Frey, D. (1982) 'Co dzień milion', *Polityka*, 23.

Frouk, M. and Wierzbolowski, J. (1981) 'Specjalizacja międzynarodowa Polski a analiza i planowanie w warunkach kryzysu', *Handel Zagraniczny*, 10–11.

Gabrisch, H. (1983) *Polens krise und aussenwirtschaftliche entwicklung*, Hamburg: Verlag Weltarchiv.

—— (1986) 'Die Perspektive des Westwirtschaftsbeziehungen Polens', *Forschungsberichte*, 113 (mimeographed), Vienna: Wiener Institut für Wirtschaftsvergleiche.

—— (1989) 'The "second stage of the economic reform" in Poland', in H. Gabrisch (ed.), *Economic Reforms in Eastern Europe and the Soviet Union*, Boulder, Colorado: Westview Press.

Glinski, P. (1980) 'Kierunki specjalizacji polskiego eksportu. Próba analizy na przykładzie przemysłu elektromaszynowego', *Handel Zagraniczny*, 9.

Glikman, P. (1982) 'Odtworzenie i modernizacja środków trwałych a kryzys gospodarki polskiej', *Gospodarka Planowa*, 7.

—— (1986) 'Dekapitalizacja', *Życie Gospodarcze*, 32.

Gomulka, S. (1978) 'Growth and the import of technology: Poland 1971–1980', *Cambridge Journal of Economics*, 2, 1: 1–16.

—— (1986) *Growth, Innovation and Reform in Eastern Europe*, Sussex: Wheatsheaf Books.

—— and Rostowski, J. (1984) 'The reformed Polish economic system 1982–1983', *Soviet Studies*, 36, 3: 386–405.

Górski, J. (1981) *Gospodarka 1981: Problemy załamania i rozwoju*, Warsaw.

—— and Kabaj, M. (1973) 'Zatrudnienie i płaca a rozwój gospodarczy', in M. Kabaj (ed.), *Polityka Gospodarcza PRL*, Warsaw.

Gorzawski, W. (1985) *Bedeutung des Transfers westlicher Technologie nach Polen in den*

70er Jahren, Pfaffenweiler: Centaurus Verlagsgesellschaft.
Gorzelak, E. (1980) *Polityka Agrarna PRL*, Warsaw.
Gorzelak, E. (1987) *Polityka Agrarna PRL*, Warsaw.
Gospodarka Planowa (1977) 'Ciąglość polityki – nowe elementy jej realizaji (omówienia planu pięcioletniego na lata 1976–1980)', 2: 61–8.
Granick, D. (1987) *Job Rights in the Soviet Union: Their Consequences*, Cambridge: Cambridge University Press.
Grochowski, Z. (1979)' 'Mozliwości i warunki wzrostu produkcji rolniczej w latach 1981–1985', *Nowe Drogi*, 7.
Grochowski, Z. (1980) 'Skąd wziąć zboże i mięso?', *Życie Gospodarcze*, 41.
Gross, J. (1979) 'Thirty years of crisis management in Poland', in T. Rakowska-Harmstone (ed.), *Perspectives of Changes in Communist Societies*, Boulder, Colorado: Westview Press.
Gruczynski, M. and Kołodko, G. (1975) 'Regularność wahan tempa wzrostu gospodarczego', *Gospodarka Planowa*, 7–8.
Gruzewski, S. (1981) 'Jak zatrzymać ten proces?', *Handel Zagraniczny*, 3.
—— (1982) 'Eksport wciąz najsłabszym ogniwem – refleksje nad specjalizacją', *Handel Zagraniczny*, 9.
Guzek, M. (1980) 'Integracja gospodarcza krajów RWPG a racjonalizacja struktury przemysłu PRL', *Handel Zagraniczny*, 2.
Hansen, A. (1984) 'Ewolucja bezpieczeństwa i higieny pracy w latach osiemdziesiątych', in *Ewolucje polskiego systemu pracy w latach 1981–2000*, Warsaw, a collection of papers presented at the Conference on Employment System held in Jabloni in December 1981.
Hanson, P. (1978) 'Mieczkowski on consumption and politics: a comment', *Soviet Studies*, 30, 4: 533–6.
Herer, W. and Sadowski, W. (1981) 'Nawis inflacyjny: I. Zjawisko: mechanizmy; II. Reforma cen', *Życie Gospodarcze*, 32 and 33.
—— (1985) 'Bariery wzrostu – anatomia załamania gospodarczego', in A. Müller (ed.), *U zródeł* polskiego kryzysu, Warsaw.
Hirszowicz, M. (1980), *The Bureaucratic Leviathan*, Oxford: Martin Robertson.
—— (1986) *Coercion and Control in Communist Societies: the visible hand of bureaucracy*, Brighton: Wheatsheaf.
Holzer, J. (1979) 'Sytuacja demograficzna Polski – problemy i prognozy', *Nowe Drogi*, 2.
—— (1990) 'Polens Weg aus dem Kommunismus', *Aus Politik und Zeitgeschichte*, B.12–13: 17–28.
Holzman, F. (1974) *Foreign Trade under Central Planning*, Cambridge, Massachusetts: Harvard University Press.
—— (1960) 'Soviet inflationary pressure, 1928–1957: causes and cures', *Quarterly Journal of Economics*, 74, 2: 167–88.
Howard, D. (1976) 'A note on hidden inflation in the Soviet Union', *Soviet Studies*, 28, 4: 599–608.
—— (1980) 'Hidden inflation in the Soviet Union: a reply to Professor Rosefield', *Soviet Studies*, 32, 4: 580–2.
Hozer, J. (1965) 'Orientacje zawodowe inzynierów', *Studia Socjologiczne*, 1.
Hunek, T. (1975) *Wyżywienie, rolnictwo i wieś w Polsce*, Warsaw.
Iskra, W. (1972) 'Teoria wzrostu gospodarczego w podręcznikach ekonomi', *Nowe Drogi*, 12.
Itoh, T. (1985) 'Nomenklatura in Polen: Die Kontroverse um die Vorherrschaft der Partei (PZPR) im Staat und Gesellschaft 1980–1981', in D. Bingen (ed.), *Polen 1980–1984: Dauer Krise oder Stabilisierung*, Baden-Baden: Nomos Verlagsgesellschaft.
Jarosz, M. (1985) 'Frustracje młodych Polaków', *Studia Socjologiczne*, 3–4.

Jaroszewicz, P. (1976) 'Założenia społeczno-gospodarczego rozwoju kraju w latach 1976–1980', *Nowe Drogi*, 1.

Jasinska-Kania, A. (1983) 'Rationalization and legitimation crisis: the relevance of Marxian and Weberian works for an explanation of the political order's legitimacy crisis in Poland', *Sociology*, 17, 2: 157–62.

Jezierski, A. (1981) 'The stages of economic development in postwar Poland', *Studia Historiae Oeconomicae*, 15: 49–54.

Jezioranski, T. (1988) 'Jednak korekta pięciolatki', *Życie Gospodarcze*, 18.

Jędrychowski, S. (1982) *Zadłużenie Polski w krajach kapitalistycznych*, Warsaw.

Jędrzejczak, G.T. and Kalicki, K. (1991) 'The banking system and monetary policy', in G. Blazyca and R. Rapacki (eds), *Poland into the 1990s: Economy and Society in Transition*, London: Pinter Publishers.

Johnson, S. (1991) 'Did socialism fail in Poland?', *Comparative Economic Studies*, 28, 3: 127–51.

Jowitt, K. (1975) 'Inclusion and mobilization in European Leninist regimes', *World Politics*, 28: 69–96.

—— (1983) 'Soviet Neotraditionalism: the political corruption of a Leninist Regime', *Soviet Studies*, 35, 3: 275–97.

Jozefiak, C. (1989) 'The Polish reform: a tentative evaluation', in H. Gabrisch (ed.), *Economic Reforms in Eastern Europe and the Soviet Union*, Boulder, Colorado: Westview Press.

Kabaj, M. (1972) *Elementy pełnego i racjonalnego zatrudnienia w gospodarce socjalistycznej*, Warsaw.

—— (1975) 'Bariera zatrudnienia', *Życie Gospodarcże*, 41.

—— (1975a) 'Human resources and the development of Poland's economy in 1950–1990', *Oeconomica Polona*, 2, 3: 289–313.

—— (1975b), 'Próba weryfikacji założeń aktualnych prognoz zapotrzebowania na kadry kwalifikowne' in *Polska 2000*, Wrocław.

—— (1978), 'Manpower resources and employment in Poland 1950–1990', *Forschungsberichte*, 46, Vienna: Institut für Wirtschaftsvergleich.

—— (1980a) 'Efektywność wzrostu płac', *Nowe Drogi*, 2.

—— (1980b) 'Płacic za efekt, ale jak?', *Życie Gospodarcże*, 17.

—— (1981) *Ekonomika pracy*, Warsaw.

—— (1984) *System motywacji i płac w reformie gospodarczej*, Warsaw.

Kafarski, J. (1980) 'Ceny w handlu zagranicznym a system cen krajowych', *Handel Zagraniczny*, 3.

Kalecki, M. (1963) *Zarys teorii wzrostu gospodarki socjalistycznej*, Warsaw.

—— (1982) *Dzieła: Socjalizm*, 3, (collected works) Warsaw.

Kalicki, K. (1991) 'External disequilibrium and adjustment process', in G. Blazyca and R. Rapacki (eds), *Poland into the 1990s: Economy and Society in Transition*, London: Pinter Publishers.

Kamecki, Z. (1988) 'Zadłuzenia zagraniczne Polski', *Handel Zagraniczny*, 4–5.

Kaminski, B. (1991) *The Collapse of State Socialism: the case of Poland*, Princeton, New Jersey: Princeton University Press.

Karcz, Z. (1980) 'Jeszcze o sprawie zadłuzenia', *Handel Zagraniczny*, 12.

Karlinski, Z. (1978) 'Uwagi do uwag', *Głos*, 11–12.

Karol, S. (1978) 'Dzień dzisiejszy i jutro polskiej gospodarki', *Głos* (Warsaw), 7: reprinted in Aneks (London), 1979.

Karpinski, A. (1968) *Zarys rozwoju gospodarczego Polski Ludowej*, Warsaw.

—— (1986a) *40 lat planowania w polsce*, Warsaw.

—— (1986b) 'Ocena wykonania planu trzyletniego na lata 1983–1985 i wnioski na przyszłość', *Gospodarka Planowa*, 6.

—— (1988), 'Główne tendencje i zagrożenia w rozwoju gospodarki', *Nowe Drogi*, 7.

Kazmer, D. (1986) 'The adjustment of the Polish economy to the scarcities in the 1970s', in *East European Economies: Slow Growth in the 1980s*, 3, Washington: Congress Papers.

Kemp-Welch, A. (1983) *The Birth of Solidarity: the Gdansk Negotiations*, London: Macmillan.

Kierski, B. (1988) 'Zagrożenia inwestycji produkcyjnych', *Gospodarka Planowa*, 8.

Kindlarski, E. (1984) 'Sytuacja jest krytyczna (o uwarunkowaniach jakosci wyborów w przemysłe krajowym)', *Życie Gospodarcże*, 36.

Knychala, K. (1978) *Zatrudnienie kobiet w Polsce Ludowej*, Warsaw.

Knyziak, Z. (1964) *Czynniki wzrostu produkcji przemysłowej w Polsce 1950–1960*, Warsaw.

Kolbusz, F. (1974) 'Nowe elementy w ewolucji społecznoekonomicznej struktury chłopskiego rolnictwa', *Ekonomista*, 3.

Kolarska-Bobinska, L. (1985) 'Egalitaryzm społeczenstwa a szanse reformy gospodarczej', *Gospodarka Planowa*, 5.

—— (1991) 'Changing the Polish economy: social attitudes and interest 1980–1990', *Economic Systems*, 15, 1: 79–92.

Kołodko, G.W. (1979) 'Fazy wzrostu gospodarczego w Polsce', *Gospodarka Planowa*, 3.

—— (1986) *Cele rozwoju a makroproporcje gospodarcze*, Warsaw.

—— (1987) *Polska w świecie inflacji*, Warsaw.

—— (1990) 'Polska hiperinflacja i stabilizacja 1989-1990', *Ekonomista*, 6.

Kołodko, G.W. and McMahon, W.W. (1987) 'Stagflation and shortageflation: a comparative approach', *Kyklos*, 40, 2: 176–97.

Kondrat, W. and Mijakowska, J. (1981) 'Wielowariantowa prognoza demograficzna Polski do roku 2010', *Wiadomości Statystyczne*, 7.

Kopczynski, J. (1981) 'Perspektywy zdrowotne ludnośći', in J. Danecki (ed.), *Perspektywiczna Polityka Społeczna*, Warsaw.

Kopycińska, D. (1987) 'Wyniki ekonomiczne przedsiębiorstw przemysłu odzieżowego w pierwszym etapie reformy gospodarczej', *Gospodarka Planowa*, 10.

KOR Document (1981) 'The health of the Polish health system', *Critique*, 15.

Kornai, J. (1980) *Economics of Shortage*, I and II, Amsterdam: North-Holland Publishing Company.

—— (1986a) 'The soft budget constraint', *Kyklos*, 39, 1: 3–30.

—— (1986b) 'The Hungarian reform process: visions, hopes and reality', *Journal of Economic Literature*, 24 (December): 1687–1737.

KRG (1986a) 'Gospodarka w latach 1981–1985', *Życie Gospodarcze*, 14–16.

KRG (1986b) 'Konsultacyjna Rada Gospodarcza o NSPG 1986–1990: Uwagi do projektu', *Życie Gospodarcze*, 24.

—— (1987a) 'Gospodarka w 1986 r', *Życie Gospodarcze*, 7.

—— (1987b) 'Uwagi do założen CPR na 1988 rok', *Życie Gospodarcze*, 40.

—— (1988a) 'Rewizja inwestycji', *Życie Gospodarcze*, 18.

—— (1988b) 'Gospodarka w 1987 r', *Życie Gospodarcze*, 11.

Kosinski, B. (1981) 'O polityce płatmyczej Polski w nowym dziesięciolecue 1981–90', *Bank i Kredyt*, 3.

Kostyrka, D. (1982) 'Aspiracje społeczne i struktura płacowo-konsumpcyjna a wybór zadań planistycznych w latach siedemdziesiątych', *Gospodarka Planowa*, 2–3.

Kotowicz-Jawor, J. (1979) 'Presja inwestycyjna w rozwoju gospodarczym', *Gospodarka Planowa*, 3.

Kotowicz, J. (1985) 'Popyt inwestycyjny przedsiębiorstw w warunkach reformy', *Gospodarka Planowa*, 5.

—— (1986) 'Dekapitalizacja majątku trwałego w przemysłe', *Gospodarka Planowa*, 3.

Kowalewski, J. (1980) 'Wspólpraca przemysłowe krajów RWPG na przykładzie przemysłu elektromaszynowego', *Handel Zagraniczny*, 11.

Kowalik, T. (1986) 'On crucial reform of real socialism', *Forschungsberichte*, 122, Vienna: Wiener Institut für Internationale Wirtschaftsvergleich.

Kozlowski, Z. (1977) 'Socialism and family farming: the Polish experience', *Osteuropa Wirtschaft*, 22, 1: 21–36.

—— (1980) 'Pläne und Engpässe der polnischen Ernährungswirtschaft', *Osteuropa*, 30, 12: 1285–302.

Kraczewska, A. (1972) 'Błędy teorii – korekta praktyki', *Życie Gospodarcze*, 49.

Krakowiak, E. and Wojciechowski, B. (1984) 'Zdolność do eksportu gospodarki narodowej', *Studia Ekonomiczne*, 7, 7: 83.

Krasiński, Z. (1984) 'Reforma cen 1982 – wyniki i doświadczenia', in K. Bajan (ed.), *Reforma gospodarcza i jej wdrazanie*, Warsaw.

Krasiński, Z., Mruk, H. and Szulce, H. (1985) *Ceny a rynek*, Warsaw.

Król, H. (1971) 'Rozwój intensywny a zatrudnienie', *Trybuna Ludu*, 15 February.

Kubiak Report (1983) first published as 'Sprawozdanie. Z prac komisji JC PZPR powolanej dla wyjasnienia przyzcyn i przebiegu konfliktow spolecznych w dziejach Polski Ludowej' in *Nowe Drogi*, special issue, autumn.

Kubiczek, F. (1976) 'Program społeczno-gospodarczego rozwoju Polski w latach 1976–1980', *Gospodarka Planowa*, 31, 1: 1–9.

Kuczyński, W. (1981) *Po wielkim skoku*, Warsaw.

—— (1985), 'Katastrofa i przebudzenie', *Zeszyty Historyczne* (Paris), 72.

Kurzynowski, A. (1979) *Aktywizacja zawodowa kobiet zamężnych w Polsce Ludowej*, Warsaw.

Kuzinski, S. (1989) 'Zmiany narodowego planu społeczno-gospodarczego na lata 1986–1990 w częsci dotyczacey lat 1989–1990', *Gospodarka Planowa*, 4–5.

Kuzynski, S. (1987) 'Zmiany i zagrożenia w sytuacji inwestycyjne', *Gospodarka Planowa*, 7.

Laeuen, H. (1977) 'Polens Dorf in der Auflösungsperspektive der Partei', *Osteuropa*, 27, 2.

—— (1979) 'Unrühe unter Polens Bauern', *Osteuropa*, 29, 1: 53–67.

Lamentowicz, W. (1982) 'Adaptation through political crises in post-war poland', *Journal of Peace Research*, 19, 2: 117–31.

—— (1986) 'Die Legitimation der politischen Herrschaft in Polen seit 1944', *Berichte des Bundesinstitut fur ostwissenschaftliche und internationale Studien*, 23, Köln.

Lange, O. (1961) 'Zasada planowania gospodarczego', in *Pisma ekonomiczne i społeczne 1930–1960*, Warsaw.

Laski, K. (1979) 'The problems of inflation in socialist countries', *Eastern European Economics*, 17, 4: 3–84.

Leowski, K. (1980) 'Dynamika inwestycji produkcyjnych i nieprodukcyjnych', *Ekonomista*, 2.

Leslies, R. (ed.) (1980) *The History of Poland since 1863*, Cambridge: Cambridge University Press.

Lewandowski, J. (1983) *Strategia rozwoju rolnictwa*, Warsaw.

Lewis, P. (1982) 'Obstacles to the establishment of political legitimation in communist Poland', *British Journal of Political Science*, 12 (April): 125–47.

—— (1984a) 'Legitimation and political crises: East European developments in the post-Stalin period', in P. Lewis (ed.), *Eastern Europe: Political Crisis and Legitimation*, London: Croom Helm.

—— (1984b) 'Institutionalisation and political change in Poland', in N. Harding (ed.), *The State in Socialist Society*, Oxford: Macmillan in association with St Antony's College.

—— (1985) 'Institutionalization of the party-state regime in Poland', in B. Misztal (ed.), *Poland After Solidarity: Social Movement versus the State*, New Brunswick: Transaction Books.

Lipinski, E. (1979) 'Słowo wstępne', *Aneks*, 20.

Lippe, P. von der (1980) 'Investitionszyklen in Polen – ein Literaturbericht und statistische Berechnungen', *Diskussionbeitrage*, 19, Universität Essen.

—— (1980a) 'Investment cycles in Poland', *Berichte zum DFG-Forschungsvorhaben*, 4, Universität Essen.

Lopato, J. (1985) 'Ludzie starsi na wsi', in A. Piekara and J. Supinska (eds), *Polityka społeczna w okresie przemian*, Warsaw.

Lustacz, E. (1988) 'O "Raporcie" Banku Swiatowego – krytycznie', *Gospodarka Planowa*, 3.

Luszniewicz, A. (1982) 'Statystyka kosztów utrzymania w Polsce Ludowej', *Wiadomości Statystyczne*, 9.

Lutostański, K. (1988) 'Wyniki gospodarcze1987 r.', *Gospodarka Planowa*, 3.

—— (1989) 'Gospodarka Polski w 1988 r.', *Gospodarka Planowa*, 2.

Mcgregor, J.P. (1989) 'Economic reform and Polish public opinion', *Soviet Studies*, 41, 2: 215–27.

Macieja, J. (1978) 'Obniżenie materiałochłonności i energochłonności produkcji strategicznym zadaniem gospodarki w latach osiemdziesiątych', *Gospodarka Planowa*, 9.

Malikowski, M. (1977) 'Młodzież wobec naczelnych wartośći społecznych', *Studia Socjologiczne*, 3.

Marczuk, S. (1981) 'Młodziez akademicka i robotnicza wobec zróżnicowania społecznego w Polsce Ludowej', *Studia Socjologiczne*, 3

Marek, E. (1972) 'Problemy pełnego i racjonalnego zatrudnienia', *Nowe Drogi*, 7.

Markus, M. (1982) 'Overt and covert modes of legitimation in East European societies', in T.H. Rigby and F. Fehér (eds), *Political Legitimation in Communist States*, London: Macmillan.

Mason, D. (1985) *Public Opinion and Political Change in Poland, 1980–1982*, Cambridge: Cambridge University Press.

Meller, J. (1977) *Płace a planowanie gospodarcze w Polsce 1950–1975*, Warsaw.

Miastkowski, L. (1979) 'Problemy cen detalicznych w Polsce w latach 1971–1977', *Gospodarka Planowa*, 10.

Mieczkowski, B. (1975) *Personal and Social Consumption in Eastern Europe*, New York: Praeger Publishers.

—— (1978) 'The relationship between changes in consumption and politics in Poland', *Soviet Studies*, 30, 2: 262–9.

Mieszczankowski, M. (1980a) 'Kryzys w gospodarce – przyczyny i drogi wyjścia', *Nowe Drogi*, 12.

—— (1980b) 'O przemianach struktury agrarnej', *Życie Gospodarcze*, 1.

Mikołajczyk, Z. (1978) 'Gospodarka przemyslowych jednostek inicjujących w latach 1973–1975', in U. Wojciechowska (ed.) *Studia nad systemem wielkich organizacji gospodarczych 1973–1975*, Warsaw.

Mijakowska, J. (1980) 'Prognozowanie demograficzne. Problemy prognozowania umieralności', *Wiadomości Staystyczne*, 7.

—— (1981) 'Stan zdrowia społeczeństwa w latach siedemdziesiątych', *Wiadomości Statystyczne*, 4.

Milanovic, B. (1992) 'Poland's quest for economic stabilization, 1988–91: interaction of political economy and economics', *Soviet Studies*, 44, 3: 511–32.

Millard, L.F. (1981) 'The health of Polish health services', *Critique*, 15: 57–67.

Minc, B. (1961) *Ekonomia Polityczna Socializmu*, Warsaw.

Misiak, M. (1988) 'Powstrzymać spadanie', *Życie Gospodarcze*, 46.

—— (1989) 'W obliczu depresji', *Życie Gospodarcze*, 26.

Misztal, B. (1985) 'The state and the legitimacy crisis', in B. Mistral (ed.) *Poland after Solidarity: Social Movement versus the State*, Brunswick, Ohio: Transaction Books.

Monkiewicz, J. (1980) 'Rola licencji w polskim handlu zagranicznym w latach 1971–1978', *Handel Zagraniczny*, 7–8.

Montias, J. (1962) *Central Planning in Poland*, New Haven: Yale University Press.

Morawski, W. (1984) 'Reforma gospodarcza w Polsce', *Studia Socjologiczne*, 2.

—— (1988) 'A sociologist's look at public opinion, politics and reform', in P. Marer and W. Siwinski (eds), *Creditworthiness and Reform in Poland*, Bloomington: Indiana University Press.

Mujżel, J. (1975) 'Changes in price level in socialist economies', *Jahrbuch der Wirtschaft Osteuropa*, 6: 105–25.

Müller, A. (1985) 'Przyspieszony wzrostu gospodarczy w latach 1971–1975 a proporcje wzrostu w trzydziestoleciu 1950–1980', in A. Müller (ed.), *U źródeł polskiego kryzysu*, Warsaw.

Nasiłowski, M. (1974a) *Analiza czynników rozwoju gospodarczego PRL*, Warsaw.

—— (1974b) 'Warianty rozwoju gospodarczego Polski do roku 2000', *Gospodarka Planowa*, 8.

—— (1985) 'System gospodarczy – reformai perspektywy', in A. Müller (ed.), *U źródeł polskiego kryzysu*, Warsaw.

—— (1985a) 'Niewariantowe warianty', *Życie Gospodarcze*, 28.

Newcomb, W. (1981) 'Polish agriculture: policy and performance', in *East European Economic Assessment: Country Studies 1980s*, Washington: Congress Papers.

Nowe Drogi (1968) 'V Zjazd PZPR', 2.

—— (1972) 'IV Plenum KC PZPR', 4.

—— (1973) 'Krajowa narada aktywu Partyjnego i gospodarczego', 2.

—— (1974) 'XV Plenum KC PZPR. O dalsza poprawę wyżywienia narodu i rozwój rolnictwa', 11.

—— (1976) 'II Plenum KC PZPR', 2.

—— (1983) 'Sprawozdanie. Z prac komisji JC PZPR powołanej dla wyjaśniénia przyzcyn i przebiegu konfliktów społecznych w dziejach Polski Ludowej' (hereafter *Kubiak Report*), special issue, autumn.

Nuti, D.M. (1977) 'Large corporations and the reform of Polish industry', *Jahrbuch der Wirtschaft Osteuropas*, 7: 345–405.

—— (1981) 'The Polish crisis: economic factors and constraints', *The Socialist Register 1981*, London: Merlin Press.

—— (1986a) 'Hidden and repressed inflation in Soviet-type economies: definitions, measurements and stabilisation', *Contributions to Political Economy*, 5: 37–82.

—— (1986b) 'Poland: current development and prospects of economic reform', in *The Economies of Eastern Europe and their Foreign Economic Relations*, Brussels: Nato-Economic Directorate.

Ochocki, L. (1987) 'Polityka społeczna w latach 1986–1990', *Gospodarka Planowa*, 2.

O'Hagen, J. (ed.) (1978) *Growth and Adjustment in National Agriculture*, London: Food Agricultural Organisation (FAO).

Okólski, M. (1983) 'Demographic transition in Poland: the present phase', *Oeconomica Polona*, 2: 185–232.

—— (1988) *Reprodukcja ludności a modernizacja społeczeństwa*, Warsaw.

Olędzki, M. (1978) *Polityka zatrudnienia*, Warsaw.

Opolski, K. and Wlodarski, W. (1979) 'Młodzi robotnicy pryuczeni do pracy jako kategoria społeczno-zawodowa', *Studia Sociologiczne*, 1.

Otta, W.I. (1985) 'Gospodarka przetargów', *Życie Gospodarcze*, 35.

Pajestka, J. (1961) *Zatrudnienie i inwestycje a wzrost gospodarczy*, Warsaw.

—— (1965) 'Analiza niektórych aspektów polityki rozwoju ekonomicznego Polski', *Ekonomista*, 2.

—— (1981) *Polski kryzys lat 1980–1981*, Warsaw.

—— (1983) *Kształtowanie procesu rozwoju*, Warsaw.

—— (1986) *Gospodarka w procesie reformowania*, Warsaw.

Pakulski, J. (1986) 'Legitimacy and mass compliance: reflections on Max Weber and Soviet-type societies', *British Journal of Political Science*, 16, April: 35–56.

Parkola, A. and Rapacki, R. (1986), 'Polityka kursu walutowego w latach 1982–1985', *Handel Zagraniczny*, 4–5.

—— (1987) 'II etap reformy – propozycje rozwiązan w sferze handlu zagranicznego', *Handel Zagraniczny*, 4–5.

Philipp, H. (1980) 'Zur gegenwärtigen Lage der Lebensmittelversorgung und Agrarpolitik in der Volksrepublik Polen', *Agrarwirtschaft*, 29, 11: 340–7.

Pietrucha, J. (1979) *Podstawowe problemy teorii zatrudnienia*, Warsaw.

Pinkowski, J. (1987) 'Kilka refleksji o planie 1986–1990', *Gospodarka Planowa*, 2.

Piotrowski, J. (1986) 'Ceny w polskim handlu zagranicznym', *Handel Zagraniczny*, 9–10.

—— (1988) 'Drugi etap reformy gospodarczej w handlu zagranicznym po roku', *Handel Zagraniczny*, 9–10.

Piotrowski, J. and Stępinska, K. (1989) 'Rozwiązania systemowe a rozwój produkcji eksportowej w świetle badań ankietowych', *Handel Zagraniczny*, 7.

Piotrowski, Z. (1984a) 'Handel zagraniczny Polski w latach siedemdziesiątych', *Gospodarka Planowa*, 3.

—— (1984b) 'Zależność polskiego eksportu od importu zaopatrzeniowo-kooperacyjnego w latach siedemdziesiątych', *Handel Zagraniczny*, 10.

Płocica, A. (1970), *Strategia intensywnego rozwoju gospodarki*, Warsaw.

—— (1976) 'Potrzeby i efekty modernizacji zakładów', *Nowe Drogi*, 7.

—— (1986) 'Dekapitalizacja majątku trwałego i sposoby jej przeciwdziałania', *Finanse*, 37, 1.

Płowiec, U. (1979) 'Ewolucja metod kierowania handlem zagranicznym Polski w latach 1944–1979', *Handel Zagranyczny*, 7.

—— (1980) 'Powiązanie planowania bieżącego z działaniem systemu finansowego w handlu zagranicznym', *Handel Zagraniczny*, 3.

Płudowski, H. (1980) 'Komu brakuje nawozów?', *Życie Gospodarcze*, 9.

Podkaminer, L. (1982) 'Estimates of the disequilibria in Poland's consumer markets, 1965–1978', *The Review of Economics and Statistics*, 64, 3: 423–31.

—— (1985) 'Investment cycles in centrally planned economies: an explanation invoking consumer market disequilibrium and labour shortage', *Acta Oeconomica*, 35, 1–2: 133–44.

—— (1986) 'Persistent disequilibrium in Poland's consumer markets: some hypothetical explanations', *Comparative Economic Studies*, 28, 3: 1–16.

—— (1987) 'On Polish disequilibrium once again', *Soviet Studies*, 39, 3: 509–12.

—— (1988) 'Disequilibrium in Poland's consumer markets: further evidence on intermarket spillovers', *Journal of Comparative Economics*, 12, 1: 43–60.

Pohorille, M. (1982) *Tendencje rozwoju konsumpcji.* Postulaty i uwarunkowania, Warsaw.

Polański, Z. (1987) 'Zagadnienia inflacji w polskiej myśli ekonomicznej', *Ekonomista*, 6.

—— (1991) 'Inflation and the monetary system in Poland in the 1980s and the stabilization program 1990', *Osteuropa Wirtschaft*, 32, 3: 342–63.

Polityka (1978) 30 September, 21 October, 4 November, 11 November, 25 November, 2 December.

—— (1980) 'Raport doradców', 48.

Pomian, G. (ed.) (1986) *Protokoły tzw. Komisji Grabskiego. Tajne Dokumenty PZPR*, Paris.

Poplucz, J. (1981) 'Badania warunków kształtujących postawy zawodowe pracowników przemysłu', *Studia Socjologiczne*, 1.

Portes, R. (1977) 'The control of inflation: lessons from East European experience', *Economica*, 44, 173: 111–29.

—— (1981) *The Polish Crisis: Western economic policy options*, London: Royal Institute of International Affairs.

—— Quandt, R., Winter, D. and Yeo, S. (1987) 'Macro-economic planning and disequilibrium: estimates for Poland, 1955–1980', *Econometrica*, 55, 1: 19–41.

—— and Winter, D. (1980) 'Disequilibrium estimates for consumption goods markets in centrally planned economies', *Review of Economic Studies*, 47: 137–59.

Poznanski, K. (1986) 'Competition between Eastern Europe and developing countries in the Western markets for manufactured goods', in *East European Economies: Slow Growth in the 1980s*, 2, Washington: Congress Papers.

Pravda, A. (1981) 'East–West interdependence and the social compact in Eastern Europe', in M. Borstein, Z. Giłelman and W. Zimmerman (eds), *East–West Relations and the Future of Eastern Europe*, London: Allen and Unwin.

Preibisz, J. and Curry, J.L. (eds) (1981) *Polish Dissident Publications: an Annotated Bibliography*, New York: Praeger Publishers.

Programme (1987) first published as 'Program realizacyjny drugiego etapu reformy gospodarczej (projekt)' in *Rzeczpospolita* (1987b) 22 October.

Ptaszek, J. (1979) 'Specjalizacja i kooperacja produkcji między Polską a Związkiem Radzieckim', *Handel Zagraniczny*, 4.

Pysz, P. and Quaisser, W. (1989) 'Nach dem "Runden Tisch": Polens Wirtschaftsreform an der Wende?', *Osteuropa Wirtschaft*, 32, 3: 175–87.

Raina, P. (1981) *Independent Social Movements in Poland*, London: Orbis Books.

Rigby, T. (1982) 'Introduction: political legitimacy, Weber and Communist mono-organisational systems' in T. Rigby and F. Fehér (eds), *Political Legitimation in Communist States*, London: Macmillan.

Rosati, D.K. (1991) 'Poland: systemic reforms and economic policy in the 1980s', in G. Blazyca and R. Rapacki (eds), *Poland in the 1980s: economy and society in transition*, London: Pinter Publishers.

Rosner, J. (1981) 'Prognoza czasu pracy i czasu wolnego do roku 1990', in J. Danecki (ed.), *Perpektywiczna polityka społeczna*, Warsaw.

Rostowski, J. (1989) 'The decay of socialism and the growth of private enterprise in Poland', *Soviet Studies*, 41, 2: 194–214.

Rurarz, Z. (1972) 'Przesłanki przyspieszenia rozwoju kraju', *Nowe Drogi*, 10.

—— (1974) 'Jeszcze pól procenta', *Życie Gospodarcze*, 12.

Ryabarska, E. (1978) 'Kto zreformuje gospodarkę', *Głos*, 11–12.

Rychard, A. (1987) 'The legitimation and stability of the social order in Poland', in J. Koralewicz, I. Bialecki and M. Watson (eds), *Crisis and Transition: Polish society in the 1980s*, Oxford: Berg Publishers.

Rydygier, W. (1980) 'Złudzenia i rzeczywistość', *Życie Gospodarcze*, 41.

—— (1985) 'Pułapka zadłuzenia', in A. Müller (ed.), *U źródeł* polskiego kryzysu, Warsaw.

Rządowy raport o stanie gospodarki (1981) (hereafter *Raport*), Warsaw.

Rzeczpospolita (1987a) 'Tezy w sprawie II etapu reformy gospodarczej – projekt' (hereafter *Theses*), 17, April.

—— (1987) 'Program realizacyjny drugiego etapu reformy gospodarczej (projekt)' (hereafter *Programme*), 22 October.

Rzedowski, L. (1980) 'Słabe ogniwo?', *Polityka*, 43.

Sanford, G. (1983) *Polish Communism in Crisis*, London: Croom Helm.

Simatupang, B. (1980) 'Het inflatieprobleem in Polen (1970–1979)', *Internationale Spectator*, 34, 10: 577–85.

—— (1981a) 'De oorzaken van de economische crisis in Polen', *Economisch Statistische Berichten*, jrg. 66, 15 juli: 668–74.

—— (1981b) 'Polish agriculture in the 1970s: some problems', *Research Memorandum*, 8110, Dept of Economics, University of Amsterdam, Amsterdam.

—— (1981c) 'Polish agriculture in the 1970s and the prospects for the early 1980s', *European Review of Agricultural Economics*, 8, 4: 453–73.

—— (1982) 'Labour supply and quality in Poland in the 1970s and 80s', *Research Memorandum*, 8210, Dept of Economics, University of Amsterdam, Amsterdam.

—— (1983a) 'Poland: full employment and economic crisis', *Research Memorandum*, 8315, Dept of Economics, University of Amsterdam, Amsterdam.

—— (1983b) 'Economische hervorming in Polen', *Oost Europese Verkenningen*, December: 34–9.

—— (1983c) 'Aanbod en kwaliteit van arbeid in Polen', *Internationale Spectator*, 37, 4: 188–97.

—— (1984) 'Poland: investment and economic crisis', *Research Memorandum*, 8411, Dept of Economics, University of Amsterdam, Amsterdam.

—— (1985) 'Recente ontwikkelingen in de Poolse economie', *Economisch Statistische Berichten*, jrg. 70, 24 juli: 740–4.

—— (1986) 'Werkgelegenheid, werkgelegenheidsbeleid en ekonomische krisis in Polen', *Tijdschrift voor Politieke Ekonomie*, jrg. 10, 1: 63–84.

—— (1987a) 'Poland: external economic relationships and economic crisis (1970–1982)', *Research Memorandum*, 8715, Dept of Economics, University of Amsterdam, Amsterdam.

—— (1987b) 'Economic recovery in Poland? The Polish economy in 1982–1984', in G. Gandolfo and F. Marzano (eds), *Keynesian Theory Planning Models and Quantitative Economics*, II, Milan: Dott. A. Giuffre Editore.

—— (1988) 'Economic crisis and full employment: the Polish case', *The Journal of Communist Studies*, 4, 3: 282–300.

—— (1989) 'De Poolse economie in de jaren tachtig', *Economisch Statistische Berichten*, jrg. 74, 7 juni: 561–3.

Skibiński, L, (1979) 'Zarys rozwoju organizacji i systemu zarządzania w handlu zagranicznym', *Handel Zagraniczny*, 7.

Slay, B. (1988) 'Foreign trade reform since 1981', in P. Marer and W. Siwinski (eds), *Creditworthiness and Reform in Poland*, Bloomington, Indiana: Indiana University Press.

Smoliński, Z. (1981) 'Transformacja demograficzna w Polsce', *Wiadomości Statystyczne*, 25, 6.

Sobczak, L. (1971) *Rynek pracy w Polsce Ludowej*, Warsaw.

Sobczuk, T. (1979) 'Ceny transakcyjne i efektywność eksportu', *Gospodarka Planowa*, 3.

Sobota, J. (1989) 'System funkcjonowania gospodarki i efektywność eksportu', *Handel Zagraniczny*, 3.

Soos, K. Attila (1975) 'Causes of investment fluctuations in the Hungarian economy', *Eastern European Economics*, 14, 2: 25–36.

Sosnowski, Z. and Wojciechowski, B. (1984a) 'Problemy wspólpracy z zagranicą', *Studia Ekonomiczne*, 7.

—— (1984b) 'Importochtonność gospodarki narodowej', *Studia Ekonomiczne*, 7, 8: 107.

Stalewski, T. (1976) 'Badania wartości preferencyjnych w grupie robotników przemysłowych', *Studia Socjologiczne*, 2.

Staniszkis, J. (1979) 'On some contradictions of socialist society: the case of Poland', *Soviet Studies*, 31, 2: 167–87.

—— (1984) *Poland's Self-limiting Revolution*, Princeton, New Jersey: Princeton University Press.

—— (1989) *Ontologia socjalizmu*, Warsaw.

—— (1991) *The Dynamics of the Breakthrough in Eastern Europe: the Polish experience*, Berkeley, California: University of California Press.

Stanczyk, A. (1982) 'Wykorzystanie zdolności produkcyjnych w przemysłe', *Gospodarka Planowa*, 4.

Stępniowska, Z. and Segala-Górniaszek, D. (1988) 'Dekapitalizacja majątku produkcyjnego w latach 1980–1986', *Gospodarka Planowa*, 6.

Sternberger, D. (1968) 'Legitimacy', *International Encyclopedia of Social Sciences*, 9, London: Macmillan.

Strzeminska, H. (1970) *Praca zawodowa kobiet a ich budżet czasu*, Warsaw.

Sulmicka, M. (1975) 'Rolnictwo jako źródło rezerw siły roboczej', in *Polska 2000*, Wrocław.

Synak, B. (1984) 'Motywy przechodzenia na wcześniejsze emerytury', *Studia Socjologiczne*, 1.

Swierkocki, J. (1982) 'Handel zagraniczny w polityce gospodarczej w latach siedemdziesiątych – założenia i realizacje', *Handel Zagraniczny*, 5–6.

Szablewski, A. (1988) 'Przedsiębiorczość a rowój nie rejestrowanej działalności gospodarczej', *Gospodarka Planowa*, 3.

Szafarczyk, W. (1982) 'Zródła zwiększania czasu wolnego' in M. Pohorille (ed.) *Tendencje rozwoju konsumpcji*, Warsaw.

Szczypiorski, A. (1979) 'The limits of political realism', *Survey*, 24, 4: 21–32.

Szeliga, Z. (1976) 'Zmiana struktury cen', *Polityka*, 26.

—— (1985) 'Założenia planu 5-lietnego', *Gospodarka Planowa*, 7–8.

Szemberg, A. (1980) *Rolnictwo indywidualne w latach siedemdziesiątych*, Warsaw.

Szymanski, W. (1979) *Ceny a konsumpcja i produkcja żywności*, Warsaw.

Taras, R. (1984) *Ideology in a Socialist State: Poland 1956–1983*, Cambridge: Cambridge University Press.

—— (1986) 'Official etiologies of Polish crises: changing historiographies and factional struggles', *Soviet Studies*, 38, 1: 53–68.

Tarnowski, P. (1982) 'Polskie statki w mgle', *Rynki Zagraniczne*, 42.

Tatur, M. (1979) 'Merkmale der Erwerbstätigkeit der Frauen in Polen', *Osteuropa*, 29, 3: 220–37.

—— (1983) *Arbeitssituation und Arbeiterschaft in Polen 1970–1980*, Frankfurt: Campus Verlag.

Terry, S. (1988) 'External debt and the Polish leadership', in P. Marer and W. Siwinski (eds), *Creditworthiness and Reform in Poland*, Bloomington, Indiana: Indiana University Press.

Teske, G. (1981) 'Poland's trade with the industrialized West: performance, problems and prospects' in *East European Economic Assessment*, I, Washington: Congress Papers.

Theses (1987) first published as 'Tezy w sprawie II etapu reformy gospodarczej – projekt' in *Rzeczpospolita* (1987) 17.

Topiński, A. (1989) *Inflacja a funkcjonowanie gospodarki Polskiej*, Warsaw.

Toranska, T. (1987) *Oni: Stalin's Polish Puppet*, London: Wheatsheaf.

Tymowski, A. (1982a) *Problemy kadr wysoko kwalifikowanych*, Wrocław.

—— (1982b) 'Dylematy rodzinnych i zawodowych obowiązków współczesnej kobiety' in M. Jarosz (ed.), *Rodzina Polska lat siedemdziesiątych*, Warsaw.

Turcan, J. (1977) 'Some observations on retail distribution in Poland', *Soviet Studies*, 29, 1: 128–36.

United Nations (1974) *Assessment of the World Food Situation*, World Food Conference, Rome.

Vale, M. (ed.) (1981) *Poland: the state of the republic*, Reports by the Experience and Future Discussion Group (DiP), London: Pluto Press.

Wagener, H. (1982) 'The economics of socialism as an economics of shortage: a critical review', *De Economist*, 132, 4: 514–35.

Walkowiak, W. (1983) 'Procesy inwestycyjne w latach 1976–1981', *Finanse*, 1.

Wanless, P.T. (1980) 'Economic reform in Poland 1973–79', *Soviet Studies*, 32, 3: 28–57.

—— (1985) 'Inflation in the consumer market in Poland, 1971–1982', *Soviet Studies*, 37, 3: 403–16.

Welfe, A. (1988) 'Savings and consumption in a state of disequilibrium: estimates for Poland, 1961–1985', paper presented at the Econometric Society European Meeting, Bologna.

—— (1986) 'Modelling inflation and disequilibrium in consumer goods markets', *Oeconomica Polona*, 1: 93–114.

—— (1989) 'Savings and consumption in the centrally planned economies: a disequilibrium approach', C. Davis and W. Charemza (eds), *Models of Disequilibrium and Shortage in Centrally Planned Economies*, London: Chapman and Hall.

Wernik, A. (1984a) 'Polityka antyinflacyjna w Polsce w latach 1945–1970', *Finanse*, 5.

—— (1984b) 'Zjawiska inflacyjne w latach siedemdziesiątych', *Finanse*, 6.

—— (1990) 'Równowaga budżetowa a stabilizcji', in *Prace i Materiały*, Mimeographed, Warsaw: Instytut Finansow.

Wiatr, J. (1982) 'The sources of crisis', *Polish Perspectives*, 4: 9–21.

Wiktor, J.W. (1989) 'Dylematy polityki płac w Polsce (na przykładzie 1988)', *Gospodarka Planowa*, 10–12.

Winiecki, J. (1982) 'Cykle inwestycyjne a inflacja popytowa w gospodarce planowej', *Ekonomista*, 5–6.

—— (1983) 'Central planning and export orientation', *Oeconomica Polona*, 3–4: 295–312.

—— (1985) 'Portes ante Portas: a critique of the revisionist interpretation of inflation under central planning', *Comparative Economic Studies*, 27, 2: 25–51.

—— (1986) *Źródła inflacji w gospodarce rynkowej i w gospodarce planowej*, Warsaw.

Wisniewski, M. (1984) 'Gospodarka cienia', *Życie Gospodarcze*, 31.

Wojciechowski, B. (1977) *Handel zagraniczny a dochód narodowy Polski*, Warsaw.

—— (1981) *Importochłonność produkcji w Polsce.* Analiza gałęziowa, Institut Koniuntur i Cen Handlu Zagranicznego, Warsaw.

—— (1982) 'Importochłonność gospodarki Polski. Problemy ogólne i gałęziowe', *Handel Zagraniczny*, 4.

—— (1984a) 'Problemy współpracy z zagranicą', *Studia Ekonomiczne*, 7.

—— (1984b) 'Przemiany strukturalne a trudności importowe Polski', *Gospodarka Planowa*, 9.

—— (1986) 'Wpływ handlu zagranicznego na sytuacje gospodarcza Polski w latach 1982–1985', *Handel Zagraniczny*, 6.

Wojciechowski, T. (1989) 'Na progu wolnego rynku materiałowego', *Gospodarka Planowa*, 4–5.

Wojciechowskia, U. (1978) 'Załozenia, modyfikacje i kierunki doskonalenia systemu wielkich organizacji gospodarczych', in U. Wojciechowska (ed.) *Studia nad systemen wielkich organizacji gospodarczych 1973–1975*, Warsaw.

—— (1982) *Inwestycje i budownictwo w PRL*, Warsaw.

The World Bank (1987) *Poland, Reform, Adjustment and Growth*, 1, Washington: The World Bank.

Woś, A. (1985) *Ekonomiczne narzędzia sterowania rolnictwem*, Warsaw.

—— and Mikolajczyk, Z. (1980) 'Dla wszystkich rolników', *Życie Gospodarcze*, 44.

Wright, M. (1984) 'Ideology and power in the Czechoslovak political system', in P. Lewis (ed.), *Eastern Europe: Political Crisis and Legitimation*, London: Croom Helm.

Wrzaszczyk, T. (1977) 'Kierunki dalszego rozwoju gospodarki', *Nowe Drogi*, 1.

Zaslavsky, V. (1982) *The Neo-Stalinist State: ethnicity and consensus in Soviet society*, New York: Harvester.

Zauberman, A. (1964) *Industrial Progress in Poland, Czechoslovakia and East Germany*, London: Oxford University Press.

Zawada, A. (1978) 'Program dla polskiego Kadara', *Głos*, 11–12.

Zienkowski, L. (1979) 'Dochód narodowy w trzydziestopięcioleciu 1945–1978', *Gospodarka Planowa*, 6.

—— (1982) 'Ceny – pięta Achillesowa statystyki', *Wiadomości Statystyczne*, 1.

OFFICIAL STATISTICS

Ceny Detaliczne 1971–1985 (1985), Warsaw.

Inwestycje 1979 (1980), Warsaw.

Mały Rocznik Statystczny of various years.

Rocznik Statystyczny of various years.

Rocznik Statystyczny Handlu Zagranicznego of various years.

Rocznik Polityczny Gospodarczy 1981–3 (1984), Warsaw.

Rocznik Statystyczny Rolnictwa i Gospodarki Żywnościowej (1982), Warsaw.

Spożycie Napojów Alkoholowych w Latach 1970–1982 (1984), Warsaw.

Struktura Gospodarki Narokowej (1969), Warsaw.

Warunki Życia Ludności w Latach 1980–1983 (1984), Warsaw.

Zatrudnienie w Gospodarczy Narodowej 1980 (1980), Warsaw.

Zróżnicowanie Dochodów, Kosztów Utrzymania i Spożycia Gospodarstw Domowych w 1982r (1983), Warsaw.

NAME INDEX

The index does not include names of authors from the bibliographical references.

SUBJECT INDEX